Criminality, Public Security, and the Challenge

to Democracy in Latin America

Criminality, Public Security, and the Challenge to Democracy in Latin America

Edited by

Marcelo Bergman

and

Laurence Whitehead

University of Notre Dame Press
Notre Dame, Indiana

Copyright © 2009 by University of Notre Dame
Notre Dame, Indiana 46556
www.undpress.nd.edu
All Rights Reserved

Manufactured in the United States of America

Library of Congress Cataloging-in-Publication Data

Criminality, public security, and the challenge to democracy in Latin
America / edited by Marcelo Bergman and Laurence Whitehead.
    p. cm. — (From the Helen Kellogg Institute for International Studies)
Includes bibliographical references and index.
ISBN-13: 978-0-268-02213-6 (pbk. : alk. paper)
ISBN-10: 0-268-02213-5 (pbk. : alk. paper)
1. Criminal statistics—Latin America. 2. Democracy—Latin America.
I. Bergman, Marcelo.   II. Whitehead, Laurence.
HV6018.C727   2009
364.98—dc22

                        2009027701

∞ *The paper in this book meets the guidelines for permanence and
durability of the Committee on Production Guidelines for Book Longevity
of the Council on Library Resources.*

CONTENTS

Acronyms   vii

Introduction: Criminality and Citizen Security in Latin America   1
Marcelo Bergman and Laurence Whitehead

PART ONE   **Trends in Criminality**

CHAPTER ONE
Regional Homicide Patterns in Brazil   27
Claudio Chaves Beato and Frederico Couto Marinho

CHAPTER TWO
Citizen (In)Security in Chile, 1980–2007: Issues,
Trends, and Challenges   47
Lucía Dammert

CHAPTER THREE
Rising Crime in Mexico and Buenos Aires: The Effects of Changes
in Labor Markets and Community Breakdown   62
Marcelo Bergman

PART TWO   **Police and Criminal Justice System Reform**

CHAPTER FOUR
La Mano Dura: Current Dilemmas in Latin American Police Reform   93
Mark Ungar

CHAPTER FIVE
Public Opinion and the Police in Chile   119
Hugo Frühling

CHAPTER SIX
The Weaknesses of Public Security Forces in Mexico City   147
Elena Azaola

CHAPTER SEVEN
The Pursuit of Efficiency and the Colombian Criminal
Justice System   173
Elvira María Restrepo

CHAPTER EIGHT
Criminal Process Reform and Citizen Security   203
Luis Pásara

CHAPTER NINE
Latin America's Prisons: A Crisis of Criminal Policy and
Democratic Rule   223
Mark Ungar and Ana Laura Magaloni

PART THREE   Citizen Security, Democratization, and the Rule of Law

CHAPTER TEN
"Security Traps" and Democratic Governability in Latin America:
Dynamics of Crime, Violence, Corruption, Regime, and State   251
John Bailey

CHAPTER ELEVEN
Citizen Insecurity and Democracy: Reflections on a Paradoxical
Configuration   277
Laurence Whitehead

Bibliography   315
Contributors   335
Index   339

ACRONYMS

AD	Acción Democrática (Democratic Action)–Venezuela
ANAPOL	Academia Nacional de Policía (National Police Academy)–Bolivia
BCS	British Crime Surveys
CC	Carabineros de Chile
CCCP	Consejos de Cooperación y Control Penitenciario (Penitentiary Cooperation and Control Councils)–Honduras
CDHDF	Comisión de Derechos Humanos del Distrito Federal–México
CEDHU	Comisión Ecuménica de Derechos Humanos
CEJA	Justice Studies Center of the Americas
CEP	Centro de Estudios Políticos (Centre of Political Studies)–Chile
CEDE	Centro de Estudios sobre Desarrollo Económico
CEPAL	Comisión Económica para America Latina y el Caribe
CEPES	Centro de Estudios Penales de El Salvador (Centre of Penal Studies of El Salvador)
CESC	Centro de Estudios en Seguridad Ciudadana
CICAD	Inter-American Drug Abuse Control Commission
CICIG	International Commission Against Impunity in Guatemala

CICPC   Cuerpo de Investigaciones Científicas, Penales y
               Criminalísticas (Scientific, Penal, and Criminal
               Investigations Body)–Venezuela

CID   Classificação Internacional de Doenças (International
               Classification of Diseases)

CIDE   Centro de Investigación y Docencia Económicas

CNPCP   Conselho Nacional para a Política Criminal e
               Penitenciária (National Council for Criminal and
               Penitentiary Policy)–Brazil

COA   Unidad de Control Operativo Aduanero (Customs
               Operative Control Unit)–Bolivia

CONAMAJ   Comisión Nacional para el Mejoramiento de la
               Administración de Justicia (National Commission for
               the Improvement of the Administration of Justice)–
               Costa Rica

CONASIN   Consejo Nacional de Seguridad Interior (National
               Council of Internal Security)–Honduras

COPEI   Partido Social Cristiano de Venezuela (Social Christian
               Party of Venezuela)

COPP   Código Orgánico Procesal Penal (Organic Penal Process
               Code)–Venezuela

CPP   Código Procesal Penal (Penal Process Code)–Colombia

CRISP/UFMG   Crime Recording Information System for Police/
               Universidade Federal de Minas Gerais–Brazil

CSJ   Consejo Superior de la Judicatura (Superior Council of
               the Judiciary)–Colombia

CTSP   Comisión Nacional para la Transformación del Sistema
               Penitenciario (Commission for the Transportation of
               the Penitentiary System)–Guatemala

DANE   Departamento Administrativo Nacional de Estadísticas
               (National Administrative Department of Statistics)–
               Colombia

DAS   Dirección General de Adaptación Social–Costa Rica

DATASUS   Banco de Dados do Sistema Único de Saúde (Database
               of the Unified Health System)–Brazil

DCP	Dirección de Carceles y Prisiones–Cuba
DF	Distrito Federal (Federal District)–Mexico and Venezuela
DCPCR	Dirección de Cárceles, Penitenciaría, y Centros de Recuperación (Directorate of Prisons, Penitentiary, and Recovery Centers)–Uruguay
DGIC	Dirección General de Investigación Criminal (General Directorate of Criminal Investigations)–Honduras
DGIP	Dirección General de Institutos Penales–Paraguay
DGP	Dirección General de Prisiones–Dominican Republic
DGPRS	Dirección General de Prevención y Readaptación Social–Mexico
DGRP	Dirección General de Régimen Penitenciario (General Directorate of the Penitentiary Regime)–Bolivia
DGSP	Dirección General del Sistema Penitenciario–Guatemala
DIE	Dirección de Inteligencia del Ejército (Army Intelligence Directorate)–Venezuela
DIM	Dirección de Inteligencia Militar (Directorate of Military Intelligence)–Venezuela
DISIP	Dirección Sectoral de los Servicios de Inteligencia y Prevención (Sectoral Directorate of the Intelligence and Prevention Services)–Venezuela
DMCS	*delitos de mayor connotación social* (crimes of greater social significance)
DNIP	Dirección Nacional de Identificación Personal (National Directorate of Personal Identification)–Bolivia
DNP	Departamento Nacional de Planificación (National Planning Department)–Colombia
DNRP	Dirección Nacional de Responsabilidad Profesional (Office of Professional Responsibility)–Bolivia
DP	Defensoría del Pueblo (Ombudsman)–Honduras and Bolivia
DPN	Departmento Penitenciário Nacional (National Penitentiary Department)–Brazil

DRS	Dirección de Rehabilitación Social–Ecuador
EAP	Economically Active Population
ECLAC	Economic Commission for Latin America and the Caribbean
EME	Mafia Mexicana (criminal gang)
ENH	Encuesta Nacional de Hogares (National Household Survey)–Colombia
ENUSC	Encuesta Nacional Urbana de Seguridad Ciudadana
FBI	Federal Bureau of Investigation–USA
FELCN	Fuerza Especial de Lucha Contra el Narcotráfico (Special Force to Combat Drug Trafficking)–Bolivia
FENAVIST	National Federation of Security and Valuables Transport Businesses
FESCOL	Friedrich Ebert Stiftung in Colombia
FESPAD	Fundación de Estudios para la Aplicación del Derecho (Study Foundation for the Application of Law)– El Salvador
FGN	Fiscalía General de la Nación
FIEL	Fundación de Investigaciones Económicas Latinoamericanas (Foundation of Latin American Economic Research)–Argentina
FLACSO	Facultad Latinoamericana de Ciencias Sociales
FMLN	Farabundo Marti Liberación Nacional
FPC	Fundación Paz Ciudadana (Citizen Peace Foundation)– Chile
FTC	Fuerza de Tarea Conjunta (Joint Task Force)–Bolivia
FTE	Fuerza de Tarea Expedicionaria (Expeditionary Task Force)–Bolivia
FULIDED	Fundación Libertad, Democracia y Desarollo
FUNDAPPAC	Fundación de Apoyo al Parlamento y a la Participación Ciudadana (Foundation to Support the Parliament and Citizen Participation)–Bolivia
GDP	Gross Domestic Product

GN	Guardia Nacional (National Guard)–Venezuela
ICESI	Instituto Ciudadano de Estudio Sobre la Inseguridad
ICMP	Illicit Crop Monitoring Program (of the UNODC)
IDB/BID	Inter-American Development Bank (Banco Interamericano de Desarrollo)
IGP	Inspectoría General de la Policía (National Police Inspectorate)–El Salvador
IGS	Inspección General de Seguridad (General Security Inspectorate)–Argentina
ILANUD	Instituto Latinoamericana de las Naciones Unidas para la Prevención del Delito y la Tratamiento del Delincuente
ILO	International Labor Organization
IMF	International Monetary Fund
INDEC	Instituto Nacional de Estadísticas y Censos (National Institute of Statistics and Censuses)–Argentina
INE	Instituto Nacional de Estadísticas (National Statistics Institute)–Chile
INEGI	Instituto Nacional de Estadística Geografíca e Informática (National Institute of Geographical Statistics and Computing)–Mexico
INPC	Insituto Nacional Penitenciario y Carcelario–Chile
INPE	Instituto Nacional Penitenciario (National Penitentiary Institute)–Peru
INPEC	Instituto Nacional Penitenciario y Carcelario (National Prison and Penitentiary Institute)–Colombia
INPP	Instituto Nacional Penitenciario y de Prisones (National Penitentiary and Prison Institute)–Colombia
IPCS	Instituto de Política Criminal y de Seguridad (Institute of Criminal and Security Policy)–Argentina
IPEA	Instituto de Pesquisa Economica Aplicado (Institute of Applied Economic Research)–Brazil
ISI	Import Substitution Industrialization

ITESO	Instituto Tecnológico y de Estudios Superiores Occidente
IUDOP	Instituto Universitaro de Opinion Publica
IUSP	Instituto Universitario de Seguridad Pública (University Institute of Public Safety)–Argentina
LPP	Ley de Participación Popular–Bolivia
MG	Ministerio de Gobierno
MGJ	Ministerio de Gobierno y Justicia–Panama
MI	Ministerio del Interior
MIJ	Ministerio del Interior y Justicia
MIMIC	Multiple Indicators Multiple Causes Model
MINIGUA	United Nations Mission to Guatemala
MIS/DATASUS	Mortality Information System/Database of the Unified Health System
MJ	Ministerio de Justicia
MP	Ministerio Público (Attorney General)–various countries
MQR	Movimiento Quinta República (Fifth Republic Movement)–Venezuela
MRS	Metropolitan Region of Santiago
MUCOPOL	Mutual y Cooperativa Policial (Police Cooperative and Mutual Society)–Bolivia
MVR	Movimiento Quinta República–Venezuela
NGO	Nongovernmental Organization
NUVS	National Urban Victimization Survey
OCEI	Oficina Central de Estadística e Información–Venezuela
ODCCP	United Nations Office of Drug Control and Crime Prevention
OECD	Organization for Economic Cooperation and Development
PAHO	Pan American Health Organization
PAP	Plataforma de Atención al Público (Platform to Attend the Public)–Bolivia

PCC	Primeiro Comando de Capital (First Capital Command, a criminal organization)
PFA	Policía Federal Argentina (Argentine Federal Police)
PFI	Federal Invesitigations Police–Mexico
PFP	Federal Preventive Police–Mexico
PI	Policía de Investigaciones de Chile (Investigations Police of Chile)
PJT	Cuerpo Técnico de la Policía Judicial (Technical Body of the Judicial Police)–Bolivia and Venezuela
PM	Policía Metropolitana (Metropolitan Police)–Venezuela
PM	Policía Militar (Military Police)–Brazil
PN	Policía Nacional (National Police)–El Salvador
PNC	National Civilian Police–various countries
PNC	Policía Nacional de Colombia (Colombian National Police)
PNUD/UNDP	Programa de Naciones Unidas para el Desarrollo (United Nations Development Program)
PP	Policía Preventiva–Honduras
PPP	Purchasing Power Parity
PROVEA	Programa de Educación y Acción en Derechos Humanos–Venezuela
PTJ	Policía Técnica Judicial
RM	Región Metropolitana (Metropolitan Region)–Chile
RPP	Reforma Procesal Penal (penal reform process)
SENAME	Servicio Nacional de Menores (National Minors' Service)–Chile
SENASP	Secretaria Nacional de Segurança Pública
SERNAM	Servicio Nacional de la Mujer (National Women's Service)–Chile
SERPAJ	Servicio, Paz y Justicia–various countries
SES	Socio-economic status
SIM	Sistema de Informações sobre Mortalidade (Mortality Information System)–Brazil

SISIPC	Servicio de Investigaciones y el Servicio de Identificación y Pasaportes (Investigations Service and Service of Identification and Passports)–Chile
SL	Sendero Luminoso
SNSP	National System of Public Security–Mexico
SPF	Servicio Penitenciario Federal–Argentina
SPP	Secretaría de Programación y Presupuesto–Mexico
SSP	Secretaría de Seguridad Pública (Secretariat of Public Security)–Mexico
TDS	Tribunal Disciplinar Superior (Superior Disciplinary Tribunal)–Bolivia
UAI	Unidad de Asuntos Internos (Internal Affairs Unit)–Honduras
UNICRI	United Nations Interregional Crime and Justice Research Institute
UMOPAR	Unidad Móvil de Patrullaje Rural (Rural Patrol Mobile Unit)–Bolivia
UNDP/PNUD	United Nations Development Program (Programa de Naciones Unidas para el Desarrollo)
UNODC	United Nations Office on Drugs and Crime
USAID	U.S. Agency for International Development
WB	World Bank
WHO	World Health Organization

Introduction

Criminality and Citizen Security
in Latin America

MARCELO BERGMAN

& LAURENCE WHITEHEAD

Among the most striking developments in Latin America in recent years have been the dramatic rise in reported criminality and changing perceptions of crime, even as new democratic regimes have taken root. It seems that over the last fifteen years, homicides have more than doubled in some places, and property crime has (at times) tripled. There are major differences within and between Latin American countries, but this crime surge is a regional phenomenon. Juvenile gangs have become much more visible and threatening, and drug-related crime has captured the headlines as never before. Shocking forms of violence have generated widespread public alarm and insecurity, prompting citizen demands for state intervention. Indeed, voters in most of these recently democratized countries are coming to view crime and citizen insecurity as central issues of political concern, and are beginning to evaluate their political leaders accordingly. This can lower public confidence in state institutions (especially the justice system) and can weaken support for the

1

human rights standards that emerged in the course of the struggle for democratization. It may even allow authoritarian practices to return under the guise of *mano dura* policies purporting to correct weaknesses in the democratic approach to crime control.

Why has the increase in crime become such a salient political issue in the region? Why are police and courts so ineffectual in most Latin American countries? What can we expect from the judicial and penal reforms currently underway? How have the failings of crime fighting institutions affected the quality of incipient democracy in the region? Can the rule of law work with such constraints in place? Despite these important social and political questions, there is a surprising scarcity of academic research on the subject. There are few studies that engage in an in-depth analysis of the rise in criminal activity and thus often drastic deterioration in perceptions of public security. More importantly, scholars have not yet produced sound research to support proposals on how state authorities—which lack the necessary credibility among citizens—can forge a set of institutional responses to rising crime.

The chapters in this book examine the perceived and actual rise in criminality from an empirical perspective. The contributors also address the impact of rising crime rates on the quality of institutional performance in Latin America, and the challenges that crime fighting pose to the consolidation of democracy and the rule of law in the region. The book addresses three critical aspects of the problem: it documents empirically new trends in criminality; it analyzes major components of the criminal justice system in the region; and it exposes the strengths and weaknesses of Latin American democracies in their attempts to combat the surge in crime.

CRIMINALITY AND CITIZEN SECURITY: ALTERNATIVE SCHOLARSHIP

Most of the literature on crime and institutional responses to it in Latin America has emerged from the legal area, so the focus tends to be normative, lacks rigorous empirical backing, and does not often study how new laws work in practice. The collection of data on crime and crime-related statistics in most countries is recent. The aim of this book, a result of a project initiated in 2002, is twofold: to examine crime using the new empirical data that is available, and to examine the impact of crime on democratization and the rule of law in Latin America. Prominent scholars from different Latin American countries experiencing similar patterns of criminality and erratic state responses, analyze the issue from a strongly empirical comparative perspective, offering the "state of the art" in what is an incipient field of study in the region. The contributors describe the trends and scope of crime in Latin America empirically, taking into account recent, rigorous social science analyses of the problem. Chapters are based on the most up-to-date data and literature to explain criminal trends in specific geographical areas and contribute substantially to current debates. The empirical and regional comparative focus bypasses the lack of perspective and sensationalism typical of a more parochial coverage of the topic (the kind that leads people in various Latin American countries to claim that "we have the highest homicide rate in the world").

Some chapters refer to alternative explanations given for the crime wave in the region, such as the breakdown of social networks and of the extended family, which have traditionally served to contain criminality and weak states.[1] The goal here, however, is to explore state institutional responses and the limits of "getting tough on crime" policies as the cornerstone to combat public insecurity and criminality, especially when not accompanied by a concerted effort to deal with the structural causes of crime, brought about by the deep social transformations of the 1980s and 1990s. We hope that the book will show that focusing only on repressive responses to crime is inadequate. In addition to providing proper empirical analyses of the crime problem, the goal of this volume is to examine the challenge that crime poses to the consolidation of democracy and the rule of law in the region.

ON DATA AND METHODS

The failure to make significant progress in the study and evaluation of crime, and to recommend policies to combat crime and promote public security in Latin America, is partly a result of the dearth of data. Sources are scant, organization is poor, and the quality of data substandard. This is a field in dire need of systematization and diversification of data and sources, and investment in the collection of strong data. The reasons for the poor quality of information range from a lack of tradition in a field of study dominated by scholars averse to quantitative approaches, to the unwillingness of state officials to invest in data collection. However, as the data used in this volume shows, new sources of information have become available over the last two decades. The quality of information for the preceding period, between the 1950s and 1980s, is very bad, so there are few references to the populist and authoritarian periods. There are some good historical accounts that tend to suggest that "nothing new" is going on, but the fact is that there have been changes, which this book attempts to describe.[2]

There are typically three sources of data for crime and citizen security: official data collected by state agencies like the police, courts, or morgues, among other institutions;[3] self-reports such as victimization or inmate surveys; and qualitative data in the form of personal observations and interviews. Official data on crime in Latin America is for the most part unreliable and raises serious validity questions. The (correct) assumption is that the general public vastly underreports crime to authorities. But this is not the main problem—the major concerns are the complete collapse of the auditing process and the lack of a systematization of records. There are serious biases in the way officials record crimes reported by members of the public, there are no clear guidelines about how to code information, and there are no proper standards to judge the quality of information. All this poses various questions regarding validity, not least since the number of homicides reported do not necessarily account for all the bodies presumed to result from intentional murders, the number of violent aggressions are not good proxies of levels of violence, and the number of thefts is not a good measure of property crimes. What Gottfredson says about the U.S. is perhaps even more valid for Latin America: "Crime statistics might be measuring the conduct of officials rather than real crime."[4]

The chapters in this book rely on the best data available in the context of these shortcomings, and they are the product of a lively debate throughout the duration of the project about different qualitative and quantitative studies and on different methodological approaches. The authors are careful to indicate when interpretations are tentative. Most chapters are descriptive because causal models cannot be seriously tested in light of the nature and quality of information and the reliability of sources.

THE SCOPE OF THE PROBLEM

As illustrated by tables I.1 and I.2, although the dates are rough, it is probable that there is an objective basis for the widespread perception of a strong rise in crime over the past two decades in most of Latin America.

Not only has recorded crime risen sharply over more than a decade, but the rate of increase is higher than the sharp rise in crime in the U.S. during the "bad" decade of the 1980s. In some cases, the trend may have been distorted by improvements in reporting the data, but the extent and consistency of these increases confirm what the public believes is true and what victimization surveys also show: that Latin America and the Caribbean are experiencing a massive crime wave. Since this has occurred in the context of regional democratization and a freer and more competitive mass media, it has generated massive public outcry. Citizens are demanding that governments should fulfill their primary task: the

Table I.1 Changes in the Homicide Rate for Selected Countries between 2000 and 1985

	Total male (%)	*Male 15–24 yrs old (%)*
Argentina[a]	46	48
Brazil	84	121
Chile[b]	72	178
Colombia[c]	50	101
Costa Rica	28	19
Ecuador	101	102
El Salvador[d]	6	62
Guatemala[e]	506	1066
Mexico	-43	-46
Panama	86	139
Paraguay	118	287
Uruguay	76	495
Venezuela	187	272

Source: WHO Mortality Database, World Health Organization, 2005.

[a] 2001 data. [b] 2001 data. [c] 1999 data. [d] 1984 and 1999 data. [e] 1984 and 1999 data.

Table I.2 Increase in Property Crime in Selected Cities

	Rate of Change (%)[a]
Buenos Aires	165
Caracas	46
Mexico City	141
Quito[b]	71
Rio de Janeiro	122
Santiago	49

[a] Rates of change: Buenos Aires 1999/1990; Caracas 1994/1987; Mexico 1997/1985; Quito 1999/1995, Rio de Janeiro 2003/1995; Santiago 2001/1999.
[b] Data for the whole province of Pichincha where Quito is located

Sources: Buenos Aires: Ministério de Justiça, Encuesta de Victimización para la Ciuda de Buenos Aires; Caracas: Briceño-León and Pérez Perdono, "Morir en Caracas," page 17; Mexico City: reported in Ramirez et al., "Tendencias y Causas del Delito Violento"; Quito: Reported in Arcos et al., *Informe Ecuador, Seguridad Ciudadana y Violencia,* page 91; Rio de Janeiro: Ministério de Justiça do Brasil, http://www.mj.gov.br/data/Pages /MJCF2BAE971TEMIDC5C3828943404A54BF47608963F43DA7PTBRIE.htm;Santiago:Min isterio del Interior, http://www.seguridadpublica.gov.cl/filesapp/1.2_Anx_conn_VIF_NAC _REG_00_v_corr.pdf.

provision of domestic security. They want the police to catch delinquents, the courts to deal with them expeditiously, and prisons to lock them up so that delinquents are taken off the streets. Public opinion polls also indicate that there is a great level of dissatisfaction with the performance of institutions and justice systems in Latin America. As table I.3 shows, in only a few countries are citizens moderately satisfied with the ability of authorities to provide a modicum of security.

Perceptions of lack of public security have an obvious impact on the quality of life and on institutional trust. Large areas of major Latin American cities have become "security free" zones or "law and order free" areas, where the only recognized authorities may be drug lords or gangs. In many poor areas, and even in city centers, streets have become less safe, and the middle classes in many countries now avoid them. Gated communities have sprung up everywhere, while private security is in high demand and available only to those who can afford it. In smaller towns and rural areas there may be no such escape. Although the real danger is concentrated in a limited part of Latin America's hinterland, the fear of crime is widely diffused. Hence, the feeling of "danger" is greater today than twenty years ago.[5]

Table I.3 Trust in Institutions in Latin America

Country	Police Mistrust (%)[a]	Lack of trust in the Penal System(%)[b]	Trust in Government(%)[c]
Argentina	77	84	10
Bolivia	84	69	11
Brazil	63	49	21
Colombia	64	68	14
Costa Rica	64	63	7
Chile	51	69	17
Ecuador	82	71	4
El Salvador	64	63	8
Guatemala	78	64	5
Honduras	67	53	23
Mexico	83	69	4
Nicaragua	72	51	9
Panama	63	66	5
Paraguay	76	85	5
Peru	77	63	5
Uruguay	49	49	5
Venezuela	73	56	12

[a] Percentage of valid responses from those who responded "little or no trust" to the question "How much do you trust the police? Would you say that you trust the police a lot, a little, or not at all?"
[b] Percentage of valid responses from those who disagree or strongly disagree with the statement "the judicial system punishes delinquents."
[c] Percentage of respondents who responded spontaneously to the question "Who do you trust in this country? (Multiple responses allowed).

Source: Latinobarómetro 2003.

There have been different responses to this perception of insecurity. The rich have been able to "buy" private security, but the poor remain largely unprotected. This weakens the social fabric, widening the gap between social classes and deepening ethnic cleavages in some countries. It elicits a range of different self-defense strategies, from gated communities among the wealthy to *justiçieros,* community patrols, and even lynching among the poor.[6] Explanations also differ: whereas some blame a new underclass or family disruption, others point the finger at corrupt policing and other institutions. Scholarly accounts tend to report multiple overlapping factors and cumulative causation.

Political responses have also varied. Those calling for a *mano dura* approach often win at the polls, because the public mood has become less tolerant, particularly among those who cannot afford private security arrangements and can no longer rely on neighbors' solidarity. Institutional responses have varied as well, but the main tendency has been to embrace "tough on crime" postures. Legislative reforms are frequent, but effective implementation of well-judged reform measures is rare, and, when elected politicians have failed to deliver real security improvements, public disenchantment has followed.

INSTITUTIONAL RESPONSES

This book examines reform measures, and the conditions under which some have succeeded and others failed. The causes of crime are many, of course: social, demographic, economic, technological,[7] and other variables come into play. The rise in crime has structural causes that outstrip governmental capacities. As some of the chapters in this volume show, major social and economic transformations of the 1980s and 1990s— including rising unemployment, community breakdown, widening income gaps, and growing poverty—correlate with the recent rise in crime. In this volume, the focus is on the political response of the state, how political actors have reacted to the new challenges, on institutional responses to the crime epidemic, and on the limits on the ability of institutions to fight and reduce crime in the region.

Institutional performance varies a great deal across the region, of course: some countries have managed to establish credible law enforcement institutions that operate according to the rule of law. But most are struggling to achieve even limited levels of deterrence. The contributors to this volume show that, in light of the available literature and various methodological instruments, legal changes have not produced great results. Since the state is the key for the development of credible, rule of law–based crime fighting institutions, countries with strong state traditions have tended to address the challenge much better than weak states, which have grappled unsuccessfully with the problem. Weak states have also been less successful (or more unwilling) to address some of the structural correlates of crime such as unemployment, declining health and education, and community breakdown.

All of the above intertwines with the quality of democracy. Citizen demands for tougher anticrime policies may be at odds with democratic values. There have been many calls to bring back tough law and order governments, even at the expense of civil and political rights, in a context of regional redemocratization. Although there have not been any direct challenges to free elections, democracy may be at risk when citizens consent to the abrogation of basic rights.

DEMOCRACY, ACCOUNTABILITY, AND CRIME

One of the most flourishing subthemes in the comparative study of new democracies has been "accountability" (an English language term with no direct Spanish equivalent, although the usual translation is *rendición de cuentas*). The key assumption is that subjects of authoritarian regimes cannot hold those regimes accountable, whereas in a high quality democracy citizens do indeed possess the means to exercise such vigilance over their elected representatives and the public institutions for which they are responsible. In new democracies, where the institutions and the expectations required for effective accountability are either absent or incipient, it is conventional to assume or assert that one of the key reforms required to stabilize and deepen a new regime is to build up appropriate mechanisms of accountability. This line of argument requires more careful examination and disaggregation at the comparative and conceptual levels; it is particularly in need of scrutiny as it applies to crime control, the reform of justice systems, and the reinforcement of citizen security.

Taking the broader comparative issues first, there are indeed some key areas where this approach is convincing. Among other things, electoral processes have to be insulated from manipulation by the contending parties; candidates for public office need to learn that they will be held to account for the fulfillment (or otherwise) of their election provinces; those in control of taxpayer funds need to disburse them in accordance with the public purposes for which they are legally authorized. A broad conception of "accountability" may encompass all these aspects, and all constitute signature issues differentiating democratic and constitutional principles from those said to characterize authoritarian rule. However, it would be a mistake to overgeneralize from these important yet restricted spheres of governmental activity. Under stable forms of authoritarian rule it may well be that quite effective systems of vertical governmental accountability are developed—after all, the ruling elite may wish to monitor and control the activities of its subordinates quite as much as (or perhaps even more than) a typical democratic electorate does. The Chilean Controlaría exercised considerable powers of investigation and control under the Pinochet dictatorship (although not over the authoritarian ruler himself), and the Mexican Secretaría de Programación y Presupuesto (SPP) was arguably more successful in holding other sectors of the federal bureaucracy to account for its spending than its democratic successor institution (Secodam). On the other side of the ledger, we need to question just how much real accountability there is, even in the most well-regarded and long-established democracies. This question is particularly pertinent when national security, some political areas of criminal justice, or immigration controls are at stake. It could be a mistake to jettison established structures of vertical accountability just because of their authoritarian antecedents (reshaping authoritarian institutions to make them more subject to democratic accountability is another matter); and it would perhaps be inappropriate—even naive—to insist that fragile new democracies must embrace overgeneralized and impractical forms of public policy accountability that are not the norm even in advanced democracies.

If these caveats are applicable to the accountability debate in general, they may be of greater significance when we turn to the specific policy area of crime control and justice system reform in most new democracies, since the obstacles to improvement are so interlocking and the scope for dislocation is so great. Let us start with the criminal justice system in a typical Latin American new democracy. There is a huge backlog of cases; a high level of impunity; the police are not held in high public esteem, nor are they trained or equipped to inspire collective trust and respect; prisons house many social failures and petty villains but few major criminals; with scant access to justice it may be the ombudsman or the human rights community who articulates legal grievances rather than the (often hugely politicized) public prosecutors; the best lawyers are rewarded for delaying and obstructing the prosecution of their well-heeled clients; judges often owe their appointment to political patrons, and may risk serious personal liability if they step outside the status quo. Democratization has opened the way to more competitive elections and the emergence of new political demands, but this only adds to the uncertainties and anxieties surrounding the activities of this inflexible, unwieldy, and low quality system of justice. What happens if one injects the fashionable nostrum "reforms to promote democratic accountability" into this system?

In such a context, it must be apparent that, for a considerable period of time, the inherited institutions will not be capable of delivering the full panoply of crime control and citizen security services that citizens in a modern democracy are entitled to expect. Democratic theory offers at least two channels connecting justice systems to regime types. To ensure free expression and peaceful dialogue over political alternatives, a democratic regime will undertake to provide some minimum standards of public order and security. And if citizens and voters come to the conclusion that this feature of a democratic system is seriously underprovided, they can exert strong pressure on their rulers to reform the justice system and provide better crime control by making this demand a central criterion for electoral success. So here we find both a linkage between a democratic political system and the provision of citizen security and an accountability mechanism to underpin the linkage. However, our concern here is with the transitional democracies that face an interregnum—perhaps indefinitely extended—where minimum standards of public order and security cannot be reliably provided to the satisfaction of the electorate (because of the institutional inertia and decisional disorders of the democratization process), and where the relevant accountability mechanisms are either too weak or too erratic to remove this issue from the forefront of citizen concerns.

In this context, we need a closer examination of the principles and practices of democratic accountability as they apply in the specific policy realm of policing and criminal justice provision. A core feature of democracy is that political officeholders (presidents, governors, and congressmen, among others) are subject to electoral accountability. But in Latin America, judges, public prosecutors, police chiefs, and prison directors (all the key figures in the justice system) are appointed, not elected. In principle, they should be appointed for their professional skills and left free to serve so long as they act legally and competently. But this is not what much of public opinion has come to believe. Under authoritarian conditions, it was standard for these post-holders to owe their tenure to their acceptability to the ruling clique, but under democratic conditions they should be entitled to more professional autonomy and security of appointment (so that politicians can only dismiss them for a publicly justified "cause," rather than "at will"). Professional standing may indeed be more likely to influence promotions, with organizations like the Consejo de la Judicatura or the Ordem dos Advogados better placed to resist political or interest based placements, if necessary by appealing to public opinion.

However, these are only tendency statements, and the actual patterns observable are quite diverse. There have been "pacted" democratizations in which the protégés of the outgoing authoritarian regime benefited from a high degree of continuity and impunity for past acts of undemocratic complicity. There are "democratic ruptures," in which most of the old guard is abruptly replaced by a new cohort strongly associated with the opposition and the human rights community. There are highly politicized arrangements where party quotas determine the allocation of public posts. And there are cases of insulated institution-building where professionalism trumps other considerations in the running of the justice system. All these variants share a high degree of contestability. The post-transition status of the justice system is likely to be a focus of disagreement and dissatisfaction, not least if questions of transitional justice are unresolved or if citizen security fails to improve under the new regime.

Different components of the justice system need to be distinguished here. The Supreme Court is likely to experience substantial new demands, not necessarily because of its role in controlling crime and insecurity but more because of its enhanced constitutional autonomy in a "separation of powers" system. These new demands may even deflect its energies away from the core functions of the criminal justice system. Public prosecutors are likely to find themselves at the heart of controversies over the handling of transitional justice issues. This important additional function may divert energies from the good functioning of the current justice system. Such problems are not insurmountable, but they add to the obstacles impeding constructive reform. Typically, public security agencies are divided into rival corporations, each of which may be aligned with a different ministry or level of government. Under authoritarian rule, these divisions may perhaps have been contained by "top down" methods of control (often through the command structure of the armed forces or the secret police); but under more democratic conditions the military and the intelligence services are likely to be curbed, and the regular police forces will assume a more independent role. While this shift could permit more democratic and accountable policing, it can also entrench dysfunctional practices. Bureaucratic and budgetary rivalries and the plurality of political interests involved often impede coordination between these corporations. Again, therefore, a democratic transition can add to problems impeding unified and effective crime control. Finally, in nearly all of Latin America prisons are the poor relations of the justice system. This is true both of authoritarian and democratic regimes. It is hard to judge whether the manifold deficiencies of the region's penitentiary systems, which become visible under the scrutiny of democratic publicity, have in fact worsened because of regime change, or have merely seen the light of day for the first time.

The cumulative effect of these changes to the justice system, which can all be associated with a democratic transition, is to unsettle public opinion about its stability. This can be costly for democracy, especially when it is associated with the perception that crime is out of control and citizens are not secure. Press freedom tends to facilitate the emergence of sensationalist reporting of these issues; and in a more open climate, there is also more "inside" information about key institutions. Thus, it is not uncommon to be told that a high proportion of congressmen are themselves guilty of felonies; that many judges and prosecutors are either bribed or intimidated to pervert their functions; that ministers use the justice system to persecute their political rivals and cover up their own financial misdeeds; that police forces collude with both petty criminals and organized crime; and that prisons are controlled not by their directors but by their most powerful inmates. In this kind of environment, voters may seek shortcuts to bring so much disorder back under control. It becomes possible for candidates with a reputation for advocating harsh discipline and with few "rule of law inhibitions" to secure strong electoral support. Their *mano dura* policies are likely to accentuate the climate of violence and distrust, separating suspect sectors of the community from those that are better off. There have even been decisions to sacrifice national sovereignty on the grounds that it is only through extradition that the worst offenders can be punished.

Such dysfunctional features of the criminal justice system have the potential to feed back to undermine the "quality" of these new democracies and even eventually to jeopardize their legitimacy. This is possible simply because of public fears about common crime and the insecurities that can accompany a democratic transition. If, in addition, there are larger forces at work—drug-trafficking, political insurgency, and even terrorism—it is not difficult to see how such negative feedback loops can become entrenched and self-reinforcing. Our comparative evidence so far suggests that there is no simple democratic accountability method that can be relied on to block such possibilities. And yet, in the long-run, a well-ordered democracy should enable the electorate to reward and sanction rulers according to their performance in crime control and the provisions of justice.

THE STRUCTURE OF THE BOOK

The overall theme of this book is the problem of criminality and institutional responses to it in the context of democratization processes and in the light of rule of law requirements. Authors were asked to identify how the specific problems or issues they assess might undermine or strengthen the region's democratic institutions and the successful implantation of the rule of law, as well as how far state capacities have developed to cope with crime. Furthermore, the contributors to this volume were encouraged to address two basic issues: the impact of rising crime on the quality of institutional performance in Latin America, and the challenge that rising crime poses to the quality of democracy and to the rule of law in the region.

The book is divided into three parts. In the first two, each chapter presents a case study, usually about a single country. Some of the chapters are comparative, typically focusing on two cases. One of the major tasks for the authors was to identify general trends and problems within each country. They sought to answer questions such as whether the available evidence allowed them to reach reliable conclusions, what they were unable to determine based on available information, what was singular about their case study, and what could be identified as part of a general trend. The third and final part includes two chapters that address this comparative aspect from a theoretical perspective.

Crimes and Criminals

The "story" told in this book starts with analyses of crime in Mexico City and Argentina, in Chile and in Brazil. On Brazil, Claudio Beato and Federico Marinho look at the incidence of homicides committed with firearms and the differences between regions as an explanation of homicide rate variations. They record important changes in the evolution of violence and in the homicide dynamic over the past two decades, and argue that variations in crime are the result of varying cultural traits and patterns of conflict and control specific to each region. They reject the "subcultures of violence" argument, and focus instead on theories of social disorganization and traditional control mechanisms that come into play when formal ones are absent. The authors call for more research on various social and institutional issues to understand the cause of crime, including informal control networks operating alongside formal external control institutions to understand how social life has become governed by a private logic that rules the lives of the young inhabitants of urban centers.

Lucia Dammert then analyzes new trends in criminality in Chile and problems of data collection in that country. Although Chile has a solid police force and an adequate judicial system, and has had a successful economic record, crime has risen sharply, leading to a public outcry. Levels of victimization in violent crimes are much lower than those in neighboring countries, but property crimes (particularly "minor" ones) claim many victims. She examines reported crime rates and "fear" of crime using the first national urban victimization survey (NUVS) undertaken at the beginning of 2004 and the "fear index" developed by the Fundación Paz Ciudadana. She argues that it is necessary to develop more accurate data collection tools, notably an integrated information system to allow cross-referencing of data on reported crimes, detentions, penal population, and judicial process, and victimization surveys. She concludes that reported crimes have tended to rise, signaling a worsening crime situation nationally from the mid-1990s onwards, coinciding with a bad economic crisis, and only improving from 2005 onwards, and that a high proportion of the population is fearful, so that policies to address fear are necessary since lowering the crime rate does not necessarily improve citizens' sense of security.

Marcelo Bergman then compares crime in Buenos Aires and Mexico City. The author notes that there are no comprehensive explanations about the steep rise in crime in both cities. After reviewing a number of theories that attempt to explain rising crime the author notes that there are major sociostructural transformations in Argentina and Mexico that have an impact on crime, such as the abrupt transformation of the labor market as well as the institutional eclipse of the state. The widespread incorporation of women into the work force, the scarcity of jobs for youths and males, changing patterns of control and child rearing practices, family disruption, and dramatic shifts in the labor market have all contributed to higher crime rates. He calls for more research on the profound change in social institutions and on the link between "marginality," the "underclass," unemployment, drugs, and crime. Unregulated and unprotected economic growth, and the poor performance of institutions that are meant to detect, prevent, and punish crime are also major elements explaining rising crime rates.

Fighting Crime and Police Reform

The story continues with a look at police forces of the region. Mark Ungar shows in his comparative study how governments throughout Latin America have enacted various reforms to make the police more effective and accountable, curb a sharp rise in violent crime, and boost public faith in police probity. He looks at structural reorganization, criminal justice reform, and community policing. He claims that while many of these reforms are too new to have produced substantial results, most of them have already been weakened and undermined—even those that have been carefully designed and that gained broad support—because of three interrelated obstacles: political pressures to crack down on record crime rates; police force resistance to reform, or an inability to take on new regulations and implement oversight instrument; and "zero tolerance" laws based on preventative detention, which discourage officers from respecting due process and civil rights. He also claims that even when governments are able to enact legislation, better strategies are necessary to ensure that penal codes, oversight agencies, restructuring, and other changes survive long enough to overcome political and institutional obstruction.

Hugo Frühling looks at Chile, using various surveys to explain high public support for the police. Like Dammert, he notes that crime rates, particularly of property crimes, have risen significantly since the reestablishment of democracy in 1990, but shows that Chileans still trust the Carabineros de Chile (CC), which is responsible for preventative public safety, because of their high levels of institutionalization and professionalization, their successful adjustment to democratic rule, the quality of public service they offer, and the polite and disciplined way they deal with the public and with crime. The author points out that levels of support vary according to socioeconomic status, with lower income sectors more critical and less trusting of the Carabineros, which they view as offering them less protection. Despite public backing, the Carabineros face significant challenges in large part as a result from a distance between the force and the population. Further, the police would benefit from decentralization, since the problems vary according to social class or sector.

Elena Azaola examines the state of the preventative police in Mexico City. The contrast with Chile could not be greater: the seventy-six thousand strong police force is underfunded, underequipped, and rife with corruption; officers are mistreated by superiors and by civilians alike, and self-image and morale is very low; and various problems emerge as a result of constant changes in police leadership, lack of expertise in police reform, and the absence of a strategic plan to combat the culture of corruption and the predominance of a paralegal regime. According to one testimony, "we [the police] are the scum of the earth for society because they say we are evil and corrupt and it does not occur to them that we are part of that same society and we are as corrupt as it is. The whole of society has lost its values . . . It is not worth talking to a society that is more corrupt than we are." The author argues that while there have been improvements over the last quarter century, rising crime has made the deficiencies of the police more obvious, "human rights" is only just making an appearance on the institutional police agenda, and the required organizational changes have yet to be implemented and to bear fruit.

Punishing Crime: The Criminal Justice System

The story then continues with a look at criminal justice and police reforms. Elvira Restrepo looks at the case of Colombia, which has a striking record in terms of the number of substantial reforms to the system of criminal justice. She compares the old inquisitorial criminal justice system with the new "semi-accusatorial" system headed by an Attorney General (Fiscalía General de la Nación; or FGN). The author argues that the enormous powers of the FGN and the semi-accusatorial system may leave the way open for greater efficiency (compared to the old system) but also for greater arbitrariness. The new system performs better (more cases are terminated in shorter periods of time), but this has not translated into trust among the general public, nor is it having an impact on deterrence or impunity. She concludes that society may have to choose between quantity and quality, as it seems doubtful that the new system will achieve both.

The chapter by Luis Pásara offers a regional overview, focusing on the question of whether the reform of criminal trial systems has improved citizen security. The author says that in some cases (albeit a minority) crimes are dealt with faster and are in fact solved by the new system, and that legal rights are more effectively guaranteed as a result of better provisions for the rights of defendants, but he notes that these achievements are not causally related with how successfully criminality is combated nor do they contribute to improved citizen security, either objectively or subjectively. Thus, while reforms increase and expedite the process of punishment, thus raising the cost of crime and reducing criminality, it is nonetheless the case that penal reforms cannot resolve the social problems that transcend the criminal justice system. In his view, there are social variables at play so that criminal justice reform cannot be expected to resolve criminality on its own. Thus, it is necessary to understand the limited sphere of action of the criminal justice system and the scope of improvements that can arise from reform. This raises the issue of how to measure "success" given the dearth of qualitative evaluations of judicial decisions. The author concludes that it is necessary to distinguish between security and prevention on the one hand, and the punishment of crimes on the other. This involves looking at public policies on growth and employment and social investment as generators of security or insecurity. It also involves increasing crime prevention programs. He suggests that it is necessary to develop a crime fighting policy that focuses on organized crime and crimes with a high social cost or impact, among them economic crimes. In addition, it is important to address crimes in such a way as to address the legitimate demands for justice of the victims.

This would go far beyond the changes wrought by the criminal justice reform thus far.

Containing the Criminals: The Prison System

The story ends in a "Mexican jail," so to speak, with a chapter by Mark Ungar and Ana Laura Magaloni on Latin America's prison system. They argue that patterns of discrimination are entrenched, criminal justice systems are in disarray, and tolerance of human rights abuse is an ongoing reality. As they add, "Killings, overcrowding, disease, torture, hunger, corruption, and the abuse of due process that occurs under the twenty-four-hour watch of the state belie the principles underlying contemporary Latin American democracy." The authors focus on three possible justifications for the penitentiary system, and show that none appears to work in Latin America. One goal is deterrence (which is apparently a still distant one); another is to prevent crimes by simply keeping criminals locked up. As most prisons systems house a large percentage of petty offenders, the incapacitating argument is weak. Indeed, minor offenders often are so brutalized by imprisonment that they are more likely to become hardened offenders once they are released. A third justification for penitentiary systems is rehabilitation. As their chapter documents, however, conditions in Latin American prisons are not likely to rehabilitate anyone. A final justification is just punishment, social vengeance, or retribution. The authors say that Latin American prisons may be fulfilling this objective to some extent, but as long as penal institutions remain open to corruption, and as long as only a small percentage of real offenders are actually incarcerated, punishment remains selective and biased against the weakest and least protected segments of society. Consequently, punishment as just desserts is undermined. The authors conclude that, to the extent that penitentiary systems in Latin America are filled overwhelmingly by minor offenders, overcrowded, and allow torture, corruption and abuse, it is hard to find any social justification for them.

What Crime Does: Security Traps

The book concludes with two analytical and comparative perspectives. The chapter by John Bailey describes the "security trap" that Latin

America finds itself in. The author asks why only some political units (cities, regions, countries)—and not others—fall into security traps in which crime, violence, and corruption become mutually reinforcing, thereby affecting civil society, state, and regime, and contributing to low-quality democracy. He adopts two models, one depicting a "positive equilibrium" set of relationships between public security and democratic governability, and another that depicts a "negative equilibrium," or a security trap. A "negative equilibrium" exists when the components of public security, its linkages and feedback, remain unreformed and the overall legitimacy of the political unit is weak or absent. In it, the essential public-private differentiation is blurred or absent. In the worst cases, corruption filters down from the top, permeates regime and state institutions, and penetrates deep into the economy and society. In this negative equilibrium, regime and civil society are unable to correct themselves and therefore are also unable to correct problems of public security. The major feedback loop emanates from civil society in corrupt collusion with state and regime; the "corrective" feedback loop is relatively weaker. Civil society views the state bureaucracy and judicial apparatus as inefficient and ineffective. The negative equilibrium model, however, does not describe a "failed state" as it is more ordered and coherent; indeed, it is likely that "we shall find a range of positive and negative equilibriums, and it is more useful to think in terms of a unit's falling into *a* (rather than *the*) security trap." Bailey then goes on to explore the relationships between public security and democratic governability, and argues that the Schumpeter-Dahl model of democracy focused on access to power and accountability cannot account for the impact of public insecurity, widespread poverty, extreme inequality, and slow growth on socioeconomic development and public safety, which have a key impact on democracy. It is necessary to consider whether governments can effectively enforce laws that are accepted and shared by the community it rules. As the author concludes, "democratic governability encompasses not only how power is achieved and the rules of the game (democratic regime) but also the exercise of power within a legal framework (governability)."

Finally, in the concluding chapter, Laurence Whitehead addresses the broad underlying issue of the relationship between Latin America's experience of democratization at the political level, and citizen experiences of insecurity and ineffective justice systems at the societal level. He sees this as a "paradoxical configuration" with lasting implications for both the "quality" of the region's new democracies and the volatility of its citizenship rights. Enough time has already elapsed since the major democratic transitions of the region to dispel the illusion that these are merely temporary or fictional inconsistencies. The new democracies are mostly reasonably durable, if of doubtful quality. The deficiencies of the justice systems also seem highly embedded and unlikely to change drastically (at least not for the better) in the near future. The coexistence of these two parallel realities is therefore not transitional. Yet they do not operate in self-contained compartments, and the interactions between them are likely to produce powerful effects on both. This "paradoxical configuration" is systematically at variance with the standard templates of mainstream democratic theory (although not necessarily with the actual practice of democracy in some longstanding instances, such as Sicily). The author reflects on the main distinctive features of this configuration and on the question of its ultimate stability. Distinguishing between macro and micro levels of analysis may help to explain both how it can persist and where to look for evidence of change. The potential clearly exists for an accumulation of reforms and adjustments, which could progressively diminish citizen insecurity and improve the quality of democracy (probably to the initial benefit of only some social sectors and communities, with others left behind). But, as Bailey's account of vicious and virtuous circles also indicates, a darker alternative pattern is also possible. It is only through careful comparative and empirical analysis and in-depth contextual study that these emerging trends can be calibrated accurately.

A FINAL WORD

It is assumed throughout this volume that for democracy and the rule of law to flourish they must "deliver" some minimal "goods." So when the institutionalized battle to contain crime shows such poor results, it is assumed that the quality of democracy and the rule of law are endangered. Does this failure contribute to public *desencanto* with democracy? To what extent does a "tough on crime" approach undermine the values of democracy and rule of law in Latin America? These are central issues for this book. While the authors address a broad gamut of questions, many others are left unanswered and should be the subject of future study. Topics such as race, ethnicity, and gender have not merited sufficient attention although they are related to crime and violence. It is also important to gain a more international comparative view of crime and crime fighting. There is no more than passing reference to the active role of the United States in developing policies to combat crime, particularly related to drug trading, as well as issues such as deportation, extradition, and arms and people trafficking. Future research should do justice to these and other important topics that require special treatment. This book is the product of studies by scholars who are interested in the current Latin American debates, and who are seeking to define the role that academic research should play in policy making in this field. Their hope is that they can participate in the building of epistemic communities that can contribute intelligently and responsively to the challenges of crime. These are scholars who hope to get beyond an *amarillista* or purely denunciative approach, and to develop a more consensual understanding of the problems of crime and crime fighting. There is a need to bridge the "pro rights" and "tough on crime" approaches so that the quality of democracy and the rule of law in the region are ultimately strengthened. We hope this volume makes a modest contribution to that goal, or represents a step in that direction.

NOTES

1. We would like to thank the anonymous reviewer for the University of Notre Dame Press for this insightful comment.

2. Several works discuss crime historically. See, for instance, R. Salvatore, C. Aguirre, and G. Joseph, *Crime and Punishment in Latin America: Law and Society since Late Colonial Times* (Durham, NC: Duke University Press, 2001); Lila M. Caimari, *Apenas un delincuente: Crimen, castigo y cultura en la Argentina, 1880–1955* (Buenos Aires: Siglo Veintiuno Editores Argentina, 2004); P. Piccato (2001). *City of Suspects: Crime in Mexico, 1900–1931* (Durham, NC: Duke University Press).

3. Because El Salvador is small and has compact communications and a well-developed administrative structure, it is easier to collate homicide statistics there than in most other places in Latin America. In 2000, however, three different agencies produced three quite different sets of figures. According to the Attorney General, the rate was 56.6 per 100,000, the Institute for Legal

Medicine put the number at 42.9, and the National Civilian Police at 37.3. The data comes from Fundación de Estudios para La Aplicación del Derecho Metodología para la Cuantificación del Delito (FESPAD), San Salvador, 2002; see http://felpad.org.sv/wordpress.

4. Michael R. Gottfredson, "Substantive Contributions of Victimization Surveys" in *Crime and Justice,* ed. Michael Tonry and Norval Morris (Chicago: The University of Chicago Press, 1986), 7:251–87.

5. Civil war zones where violence was much higher, like Central America in the 1980s, are probably exceptions.

6. There are numerous accounts of lynching and "private justice." See C. Vilas "Linchamiento: Venganza, castigo e injusticia en escenarios de inseguridad," for a study of social transformation, rising crime, and lynching in Mexico.

7. New firearm technology has a significant impact on criminal activity, as do new channels for the distribution of illegal drugs, among other factors.

PART 1

Trends in Criminality

CHAPTER ONE

Regional Homicide Patterns in Brazil

CLAUDIO CHAVES BEATO

& FREDERICO COUTO MARINHO

Brazil is one of the most violent countries in all of Latin America; indeed, it is one of the most violent countries in one of the most violent regions in the world. This is undoubtedly a key challenge for Brazilian development because it has a direct impact on economic and political life, contributes to the deterioration of and limits access to public health and education services, and greatly reduces employment opportunities for those living in high-risk areas. One of the most noxious effects of violence is that the climate of fear and distrust it generates limits people's freedom, restricting mobility in certain urban areas, rendering ineffective self and external policing mechanisms. And the effect on family life is devastating: violence has led to the breakdown of thousands of homes.

This chapter looks at homicide in Brazil, using accumulated data covering large areas and population. Various studies have attempted to explain why rates of violent crime vary between cities, metropolitan areas, or states, and have correlated such variations with social, demographic, and economic variables.[1] A study of homicide in the U.S., for instance, lists the following factors, starting with the most important: high economic disparities or inequality, population structures and density (the larger areas with the densest population have the highest homicide rates), and high unemployment rates.[2] Various authors have tested the idea that socioeconomic inequality in specific areas, regions, and cities helps to explain the distribution of homicide rates in Brazil. They have pointed to the relevance of economic cycles,[3] poverty,[4] and income and other economic variables related to inequality or investment in public safety at the city level.[5]

The central role of firearms in violence in Brazil is alarming. According to international comparisons of firearm deaths undertaken by the World Health Organization, which take total population into account,[6] out of twenty-two ranked countries Brazil comes second in the number of homicides caused by firearms and first in juvenile firearm deaths. International data indicate not only the extremely high level of lethal violence in Brazil (over 70 percent of homicides were committed with firearms, as compared with around 10 percent for the other countries in the group), but also the predominance of the use of firearms in the resolution of conflicts. Research and studies about the regional determinants of firearm deaths allow us to understand better the demand for and potential benefits of national and regional policies to control firearms and ammunition effectively, and to reduce legal and black market supply and demand.

Thus, the aim of this chapter is to look at the incidence of homicides committed with firearms and to examine the extent to which regional variations can explain variations in the homicide rate. For the period 1980–2000, the relevant regional variations include cultural traits and patterns of conflict and control specific to each region. However, rather than using the "subcultures of violence" argument,[7] the chapter looks at theories of social disorganization and control.[8] One can analyze regions with historically high rates of firearm homicides in light of social disorganization resulting from land disputes where there are no formal control mechanisms. In such contexts, the resolution of conflicts through honor and traditional social behavior patterns replace formal and informal control mechanisms.[9] Curiously, these patterns emerge also in metropolitan areas, particularly those dominated by armed groups that are fighting for territorial control of urban centers. Looking at rates of homicide is, then, a way of understanding the diversity of experiences in Brazil. We have yet to take into account the level of diversity of experiences within large urban centers.

The phenomenon most closely associated with the rise of homicides in Brazil is urbanization. Strictly speaking, it can be said that, as in other countries, violent crime is an urban phenomenon associated with processes of disorganization and the deterioration of control mechanisms in Brazilian urban centers.[10] There are various competing theories about the links between homicide and urban dynamics. One pioneering theory proposed by the Chicago School is the so-called *social disorganization* theory. It analyses different territories within cities and the association between social disorganization and violence, transition zones and criminality, and urban violence and youth.[11] This disorganization was observed in some areas of cities in the U.S., where the absence or decadence of traditional values was a cause of moral and family crisis, which in turn led to criminality. Such territories became *sui generis* regions of sorts, in which social order was not clearly defined. Conflicts emerge, then, in deteriorated communities, characterized by constant changes in the population and intense mobility. In other words, these are areas lacking any kind of infrastructure. Together, these facts led to a transition process culminating in criminal activities by adolescent gangs. These gangs are part of the *poverty belt* of communities constituted by people who live in a socioeconomic "transition zone." The theory of social disorganization, for instance, assumes that delinquency is a group rather than an individual phenomenon, and that community social disorganization makes it hard to control youth groups.

Another interpretation is proposed by strain theory, which assumes that deviance is the result of pressures caused by social structure. It is classified as a "systematic approach of social and cultural sources of a nonconformist behavior."[12] The emphasis that society places on cultural objectives can, and frequently is, much greater than the attention focused on means that the cultural targets recognize as socially valid. We have then a polarizing system, which varies the emphases on these two moments; balance would correspond to a situation in which the social satisfactions provided adjust to both pressures. Merton, for instance, argues that delinquency emerges when it is impossible to attain socially expected levels of consumption. The gap between aspirations, inflated in a consumer society, and achievements, limited by inequality and poverty, are the main explanation for crime.

Subcultural[13] and learning theories,[14] on the other hand, argue that deviance and crime are social or cultural products that do not necessarily emerge as a result of disorganized social structures, but rather as a result of the division of society into different groups which pursue their own goals—goals that are set independently of the mainstream or dominant culture. Once the use of violence has been normatively indicated, the counter-norm will be nonviolence. The individual that belongs to a community where violence is the established means to resolve conflicts will be ostracized or treated with indifference if they do not use violence "appropriately." This kind of social pressure foments adherence to subcultural values in which aggression is considered the usual means to deal with conflict. The hypothesis is that the open use of violence is part of a normative subcultural system which has ramifications on the individual psyche. Thus, the individual is forced to behave according to the norms of the social group to which they belong. Further, in addition to being socialized according to established standards, behavior is submitted to various types of control. On the one hand, the group makes a certain kind of behavior possible, promoting the acquisition of abilities, values, expectations, and objectives; and on the other hand, the group makes the individual behave in a suitable manner. Criminal or delinquent behavior is the result of belonging to a social group in both senses.

In contrast with theories in which crime is seen as a consequence of poorly integrated or collapsed systems, in social control theory, crime is a consequence of failed mechanisms of social control, in turn the result of conjunctural crisis or imperative tendencies in modern society.[15] Theories of social control emphasize the role of the family, school, religion, and other institutions in the prevention of crime in general and in juvenile delinquency in particular. Crime and delinquency are linked to the failure of the institutions responsible for the social control, so that researchers focus on incomplete families, the absence of parental orientation, or school truancy, among other such factors. These factors should be studied together with learning and socialization theories on the basis of the notion, crudely put, that "family, school, and church" teach citizenship, while "the streets" teach crime and delinquency. These theories are not mutually exclusive; on the contrary, socioeconomic factors are a feature they all share.

The empirical data used to confirm this hypothesis covers Brazil as a whole, five regions, twenty-six states and their respective capitals, and the Federal District. The population data used here is gathered from the official site of the Brazilian Health Ministry.[16] Data on homicides are from the Health Ministry's Mortality Information System. These data cover the period between 1980 and 2002. The information is coded according to the International Disease Classification (IDC), Revision IX (for 1980–1995), and Revision X (for 1996–2002).

THE EMPIRICAL DATA: SOME OBSERVATIONS

There have been important changes in the evolution of violence and homicide since the 1980s. In absolute terms, Brazil is the country where the most people die as victims of aggression. In 2000, there were 45,311 such deaths in Brazil, followed by Russia with 44,252, and Colombia with 25,832 deaths in the same year. In absolute terms, other countries are at a very different level: the U.S. has 16,590 such deaths, and the Philippines have 11,240, for instance.[17]

Research done for the Human Safety Commission shows that Brazilians say they have suffered twenty times more attacks over the last five years than Japanese and Indians say they have.[18] Brazil has the highest percentage of declared victims than any other countries known for violence, such as South Africa, Russia, or the U.S. Further, 75 percent of Brazilians believe that they will be victims of violence in the near future. For the segment under consideration, Brazil has the highest victimization rates: 20 percent of the population declared having been victims of aggression or the threat of violence over the last five years (the rate for South Africa is 15 percent, for Thailand it is 7 percent, and for Russia it is 15 percent). It is important to note that there is no clear connection between feelings of insecurity and actual victimization.

There is a need for national level surveys on crimes other than homicides to enable us to study criminality in Brazil more fully. There has been systematic and standardized data collection since the late 1970s by the health system. Although there may be some bias in the collection of data[19] and its classification,[20] the Mortality Information System has become the most frequent source for criminological studies when it comes to making national comparisons. This has led to the construction of an incomplete picture of violence, as we know that the determinants of criminality against a person are different in various types of property crimes.[21] In addition, there are different expressive or instrumental motivations for homicide. When we talk about homicide, we are talking about many distinct phenomena in terms of motivation and the manifestation of motivation.[22]

More recently, together with states' civil police agencies, the Ministry of Justice has collected data on other types of crime for cities with over 100,000 inhabitants.[23] Although still incomplete, this gives us new information about the distribution of different types of crime for these cities. This data considers "nonlethal violent crimes" against individuals, such as attempted homicide, rape, violent sexual assault, and torture. In 2004 and 2005, 60,931 such occurrences were registered. Attempted homicide accounts for 55 percent of all nonlethal violent crime. The dynamics of this kind of crime is important because it follows the same logic of homicide (failed homicide). The highest concentration of such crimes occurs in the southeast, which accounts for 40 percent of the total. São Paulo and Minas Gerais alone account for 30 percent of crimes in Brazil.

Although homicide and lethal crimes against people are obviously central, property offenses are much more common occurrences in everyday life, particularly for residents of large urban centers. According to SENASP, in 2005 the chance of being robbed was 23 times higher than being the victim of homicide if one lived in a city with over 100,000 inhabitants.[24] Intentional lethal crimes account for only 0.8 percent of crimes recorded by civil police agencies, while theft, for example, accounts for 40 percent of all recorded offenses in Brazil's major cities.

The bulk of crimes registered by civil police agencies is taken up by property crimes (17.7 percent, or 942,687 of over 5 million recorded crimes in cities with over 100,000 inhabitants). The most common property crimes in urban centers is theft from pedestrians (particularly in commercial areas where many people walk around), which account for 73.6 percent of all crimes registered by the police. This is followed by car theft (15.6 percent) and theft from commercial establishments. In 2005, there were 942,687 registered violent property crimes, of which 55 percent were in the southeast and 20 percent in the northeast. São Paulo accounted for 30 percent of all crimes in the country as a whole, and 46 percent of the 2,152,681 registered thefts nationwide occurred in the south. In addition to these crimes, the police registered 722,202 instances of assault and injury (48 percent in the southeast and 20 percent in the south). Again, São Paulo accounted for approximately 28 percent of the total. Also recorded were 15,268 rapes and 10,806 cases of violent sexual assault.

Some of the data collected by SENASP refer to "Offenses Involving Drugs," an aggregation of data on the possession, use, and trafficking of drugs. In 2005, 70 percent of a total of 89,261 recorded offenses involved drug use and possession. This data aggregation is an orthodox approach that contravenes legislation, which calls for a separation between drug use and drug trafficking (to permit a focus on the latter). However, in addition to reflecting what goes on in large cities, these figures are not accurate since these crimes are underreported. Studies show that for each youth that is murdered, there are between twenty and forty aggressions and other nonlethal violent aggressions requiring hospital treatment.[25]

At the start of that decade, homicides were overwhelmingly concentrated in the midwestern, western, and northern regions of the country, particularly in southern Pará, Roraima, and Mato Grosso. Further, from the 1970s onward, there were high homicide rates in the countryside in the state of Pernambuco and in some areas of Espírito Santo. However, the Rio de Janeiro metropolitan area has the highest rates. In the 1980s, homicide rates increased in the largest metropolitan regions such as Rio de Janeiro (mid-decade) and in the city of São Paulo (late in the decade and in the early 1990s). From the 1990s onwards, homicide rates spread to other metropolitan regions such as Belo Horizonte and Curitiba, to larger cities in the countryside of São Paulo, and to cities in south and southeastern Brazil.

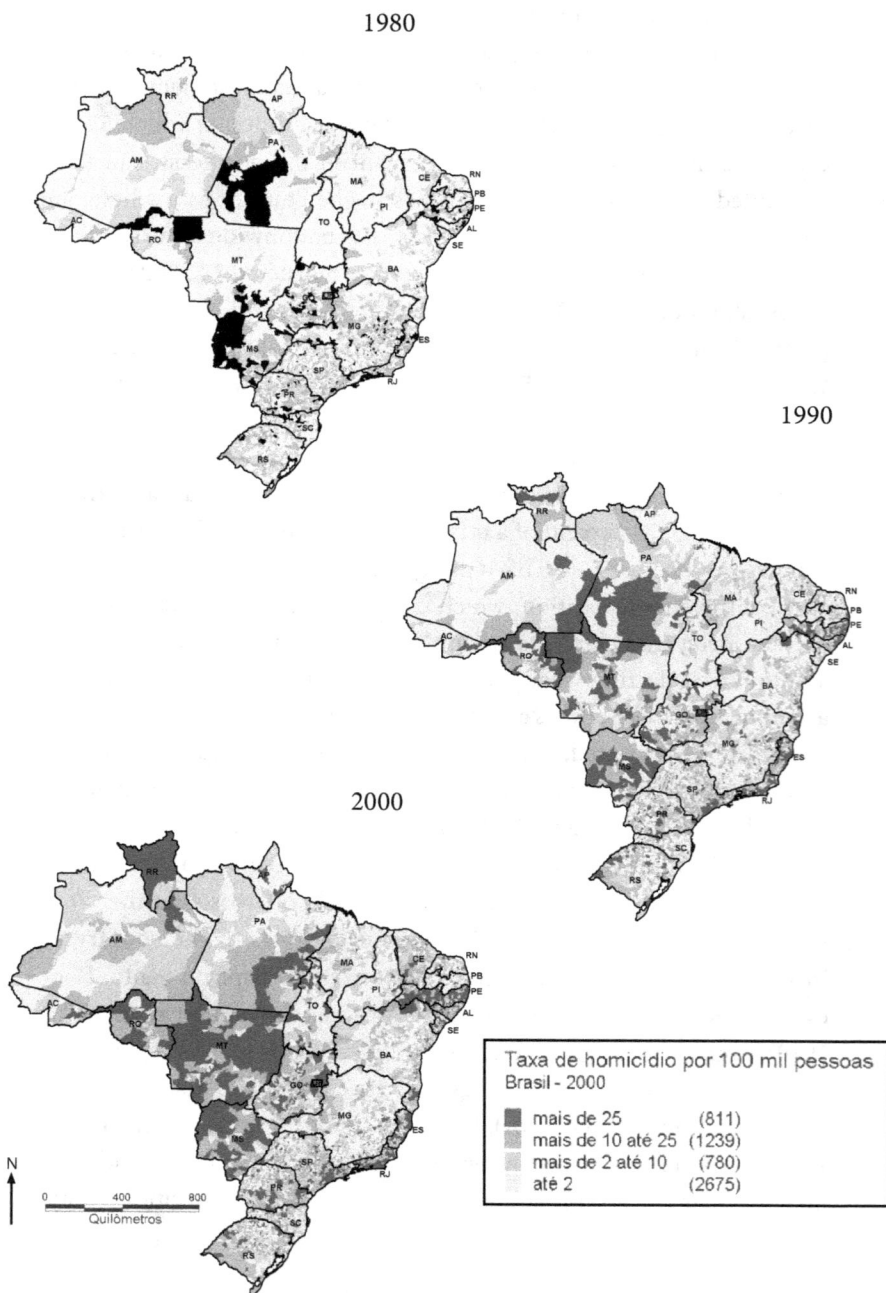

Graph 1.1 Regional Homicide Tendencies, 1980–2000

1980

1990

2000

N

0   400   800
Quilômetros

Taxa de homicídio por 100 mil pessoas
Brasil - 2000

mais de 25   (811)
mais de 10 até 25 (1239)
mais de 2 até 10   (780)
até 2   (2675)

Table 1.1 Registered National and Regional Homicides, 2002

Area	Number of Homicides	Percentage	Rate	Rate with Firearms
Brazil	53,325		30.6	20.8
Southeast	29,530	55	39.8	27.14
Northeast	12,183	23	25.1	17.7
South	4,947	9	19.3	12.8
Midwest	3,681	7	30.6	20.1
North	2,984	6	22.1	11.4

Source: Ministério da Saúde, CRISP/UFMG.

COMPARING REGIONS

In 2002, the most recent year for which there is recorded data, there were 53,325 people murdered in Brazil, of which 36,203 were killed with firearms. Homicide is the third highest cause of death in Brazil, and the highest cause of death for youths between the ages of 15 and 24.[26]

The national homicide rate rose by two and a half times between 1980 and 2002, increasing from 12.2 homicides in 1980, to 30.6 homicides per 100,000 inhabitants in 2002. In other words, there were 14,435 people murdered in the country in 1980, and in little more than two decades, 53,325 people began to die for the same reason in a single year. This increase was broken up by a period of stability and even decreasing rates until 1995, but in that year the rate doubled, shooting up from 12.2 to 24.3 homicides for every 100,000 inhabitants.

In 2002, the southeast accounted for more than half of the homicides registered by MIS/DATASUS; it also had the highest and fastest growing rates in that period. The homicide rate in the southeast (39.8 per 100,000 inhabitants) is two times higher than the rate for the south, and 1.8 times higher than that for the north. The pattern is similar for firearm homicides in the region, which is the highest of all the regions (27.4 homicides per 100,000 inhabitants, or nearly two times the rate for the south and north).

Regional homicide rates have not increased homogenously: in the northeast, the rate increased by 2.74 times, leaping from 9.1 to 25 per 100,000 inhabitants; in the southeast, it rose by 2.6 times, from 15.3 to 39.8; and in the midwest, it rose by 2.2 times over the same period. The south and north experienced a similar rise, with rates doubling over the period, from 11.3 to 22.1 murders and from 9.2 to 19.3 per 100,000 inhabitants, respectively.

COMPARING REGIONS AND STATES

Table 1.2 compares national and regional (comparing states) homicide rates in 1998–2002 and oscillations thereof. There were 737,697 homicides during that period, of which 413,215 involved firearms. In 2002, 78 percent of registered homicides were concentrated in two regions: the southeast (29,530 homicides) and the northeast (with 12,183). The states of Rio de Janeiro and São Paulo accounted for 47 percent of all homicides even though they only hold 30 percent of the total population. The increase in the homicide rates varied regionally in the 1990s (as compared with the 1980s): throughout the decade, the rise in the national rate was very high (60.6 percent), and surpassed that of all regions with the exception of the southeast (where the rate increased by almost 80 percent). The lowest increase occurred in the north and midwest (which had a similar rate of increase of around 37 percent in the same period). In the south and northwest, the average growth rate was 42 percent. Overall, there was a clear tendency toward the urbanization of homicide during the period.

Firearms and Homicide

The most devastating expression of violence is the growing rate of firearm homicides: between 1980 and 2004, there were 835,418 homicides, of which 488,629 were committed with a firearm.

The proliferation of firearms in the 1980s is central to this explosive rise in firearm homicide. At the beginning of the decade, half of reported homicides involved firearms and accounted for nearly 45 percent of

Table 1.2 Homicide Regional Distribution, 2002

Region and State	Homicides			Homicides Committed with Firearms			
	Number of homicides 2002	2002 homicide rate	Increase in homicides, 1990s–1980s	Number of firearm homicides	% of firearm homicides	2002 firearm homicide rate	Increase in firearm homicides, 1990s–1980s
North	2,984	22.1	36.4	1,545	51.8	11.4	43.1
RO	625	43.7	12.9	395	63.2	27.6	26.0
AC	151	25.7	-7.1	67	44.4	11.4	-24.2
AM	511	17.3	4.8	199	38.9	6.7	-7.4
RR	128	36.9	20.3	49	38.3	14.1	-13.7
PA	1,198	18.6	15.2	694	57.9	10.8	16.9
AP	185	35.8	4.9	50	27.0	9.7	-35.9
TO	186	15.4	42.7	91	48.9	7.5	84.3
Northeast	12,183	25.0	43.0	8,640	70.9	17.7	75.4
MA	596	10.3	7.7	253	42.5	4.4	1.8
PI	321	11.1	66.6	123	38.3	4.3	74.3
CE	1,458	19.1	32.2	747	51.2	9.8	58.7
RN	425	14.9	12.1	278	65.4	9.8	6.0
PB	610	17.5	5.0	428	70.2	12.3	36.7
PE	4,540	56.2	41.4	3,696	81.4	45.7	54.1
AL	982	34.2	4.1	718	73.1	25.0	11.5
SE	538	29.1	7.7	395	73.4	21.4	22.9
BA	2,713	20.4	12.2	2,002	73.8	15.1	15.1
Southeast	29,530	39.8	78.4	20,322	68.8	27.4	159.3
MG	3,046	16.6	43.1	2,054	67.4	11.2	70.6
ES	1,644	51.5	15.9	1,224	74.5	38.3	46.3
RJ	8,746	60.1	3.1	7,091	81.1	48.7	4.3
SP	16,094	42.2	27.5	9,953	61.8	26.1	65.6
South	4,947	19.3	41.2	3,288	66.5	12.8	88.3
PR	2,332	23.8	25.4	1,534	65.8	15.7	34.2
SC	594	10.8	8.6	333	56.1	6.0	13.5
RS	2,021	19.6	14.4	1,421	70.3	13.8	23.5
Midwest	3,681	30.6	38.1	2,408	65.4	20.0	65.1
MS	691	32.3	-5.0	435	63.0	20.3	-4.7
MT	959	37.4	39.6	591	61.6	23.1	55.3
GO	1,287	24.8	18.4	838	65.1	16.1	28.5
DF	744	34.7	0.0	544	73.1	25.4	3.5
Brazil	53,325	30.6	60.6	36,203	67.9	20.8	111.7

Source: MIS/DATASUS, CRISP/UFMG.

Graph 1.2 Evolution of National Firearm Homicides, 1980–2000

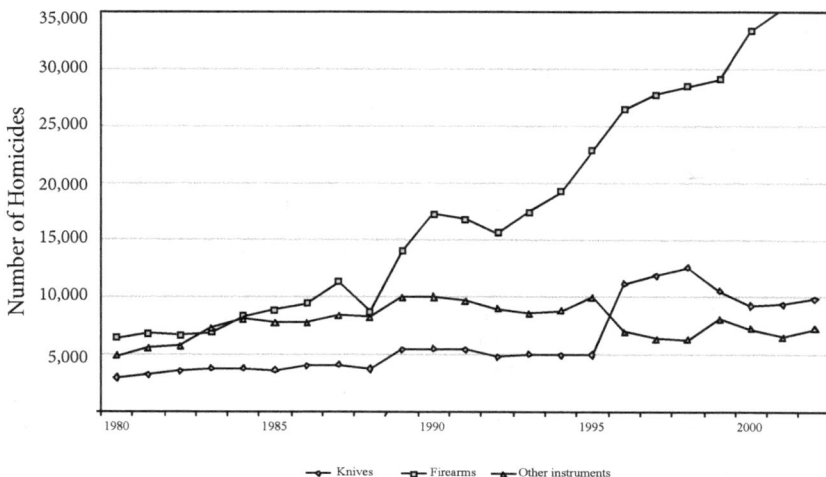

deaths; by 2004, 77 percent of all homicides involved the use of firearms. In larger capitals such as Rio de Janeiro, Recife, Belo Horizonte, Vitória, or Salvador, firearms accounted for 80–85 percent of deaths. It is not a coincidence that gun death rates increased significantly during the 1980s. In this period, there was a mass influx of firearms available at ever lower costs into larger urban centers. Today, Brazilians can acquire firearms legally as well as through various illegal outlets. The southeast began to register the highest rates from the first half of the 1990s onwards, well above the national rate and above that of all the other regions; by contrast, the south registered the lowest firearm homicide rates throughout the period under analysis. The evolution of firearm homicides follows the same general and spatial distribution pattern as that for homicides in general.

The increase in homicides nationally was very high (111.7 percent): only the southeast surpassed the national rate (with 159.3 percent). The north and midwest experienced the lowest increase (43.1 and 65.1 percent, respectively), while the south and northeast registered increases of 88.3 and 75.4 percent, respectively. The use of firearms in homicides

Graph 1.3 Tendencies in Firearm Homicides, 1980–2000

1980

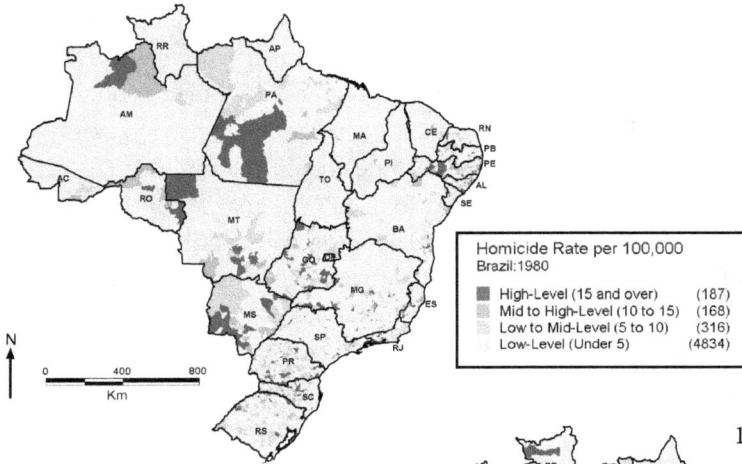

1990

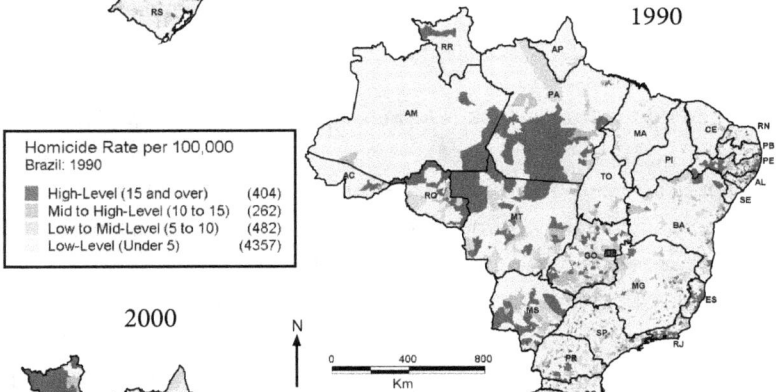

2000

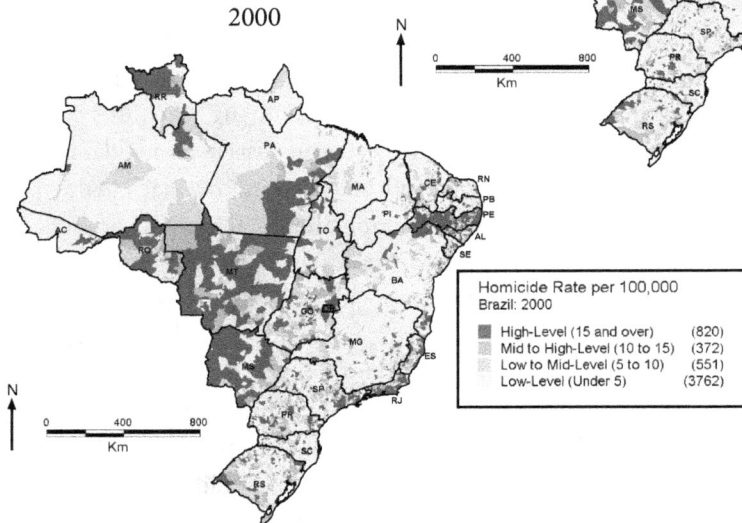

varies significantly from region to region. The use of firearms increased systematically in four of the five regions from 1980 to 2002, and was particularly pronounced in the south and northeast (a 12 percent increase between 1980 and 2002). In the south, the rate of firearm homicides rose from 61 percent in the 1980s to 73 percent by the end of the period; the northeast and southeast, which have the highest rates, registered an increase of 79 to 85 percent. The lowest rate was in the midwest (from 66 percent in the 1980s to 70 percent in 2002). An analysis of the data shows that the increase in firearm homicides was particularly significant in the northeastern states, particularly Pernambuco, Bahia, Sergipe, and Alagoas. Other states that contributed to the higher rate were Rio de Janeiro, Espírito Santo, the Federal District, and Rio Grande do Sul. The southeast region registered a higher rate of homicides (per 100,000 inhabitants) than the northeast, but a lower percentage rate of firearm homicides.

The Population at Risk: The Sex, Age and Population Victim Profile

Homicides can be broken according to the profile of victims.[27] Youths are among the most vulnerable (in terms of both aggressors and victims). In Brazil, violence is the main cause of death for young people between the ages of 15 and 25. In the 1980s, 33 out of every 100,000 youths died from gunshots; today, the number is 55 in every 100,000. A breakdown of the data shows that there is a strong concentration within specific groups: the mortality rate for young black males living in cities with populations over 250,000 is extremely high. The analysis of homicides by region reinforces the disproportionate mortality rate among black males. Black males make up 36.3 percent of the population in the southeast, but account for 51.6 percent of homicide victims. In the northeast, the difference is even greater: while black males make up 66.28 percent of the population, they are the victims of 86.6 percent of all homicides. Teenagers and young adults are the most effected by violence involving the use of firearms. About 60 percent of this group is a victim of firearm homicides. In 1995, the firearm homicide rate among youths aged 15 to 24 was 8.6 times higher than the rate for people over 65 years old. Young men are by far the most frequent victims of firearm homicides.

In metropolitan centers, the increase in homicides is connected to an as yet understudied phenomenon that is often confused or conflated with drug trafficking, namely the existence of gangs and youth groups. These groups—*barras* in Argentina, *galeras* and *quadrilhas* in Brazil, *pandillas* in Chile and Nicaragua, *sicários* and *gamines* in Colombia, *chapulines* in Costa Rica, *maras* in El Salvador, *posses* in Jamaica, *clikas* in Mexico, *bandas* in Peru—are a recurrent feature of contemporary violence in Latin America as a whole.[28] These names designate groups that are involved in illegal activities to varying degrees.[29] Their structure varies according to their activities, rituals of initiation, and the predominant ages of group members.

CONCLUSION

One of the most remarkable recurring aspects of public debate in Brazil about the causes of violence is the tendency to focus on one or another

Graph 1.4 Evolution of National Firearm Homicide Rates by Race, 1980–2000

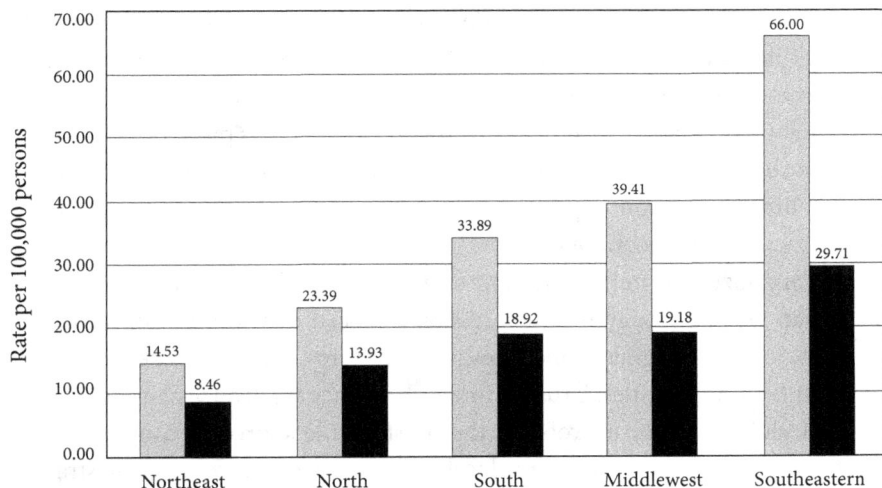

Table 1.3 Brazil Homicide Victim Rates According to Risk Factors, 2002

Year	Homicide Rate, Total Population	Homicide Rate, 15–24 year olds	Homicide Rate, 15–24 year olds in cities over 250,000	Risk of homicide, Black to White population
2002	30.1	58.16	100.36	2.1

Source: MIS/DATASUS, CRISP/UFMG.

cause of crime to the exclusion of others. Thus, the focus was initially on impunity of all levels of the legislative system, which made justice slow to act. Later, drug trafficking and firearms became the focus of debate. The control of violence and corruption through police reform was the proposed solution. Organized crime has been and remains central in public debates. The latest trend has been to focus on drug users, particularly recreational users, as those responsible for sustaining the cycle of crime. In some cases, albeit with less zeal, the consumption of alcohol has also been associated with rising violence. But none of these factors alone suffices to explain the extreme deterioration experienced in the greater metropolitan areas of Brazil. A close analysis of the evidence shows that there are countries with higher indices of firearms that have not experienced a similarly dramatic rise in rates of violence, and there is more drug use in some of the most peaceful countries of the First World. In addition, while the Brazilian prison population has increased, this has had little or no impact on current crime rates.

Organized crime theories fail to account for the fact that much of urban violence today is an expression of social disorganization, which translates into higher crime rates in the poverty stricken pockets of the country's largest cities. Urban crime and violence are diverse phenomena, and violence is most probably the most visible source of concern for Brazilians. Although both are closely related, each calls for specific strategies and policies.

Although all the publicly debated factors contributing to crime play a role in the various regional and urban contexts, there is no single solution to the problem. The academic debate about the causes of violence is not consensual, so that the identification of "causes" may not produce sound public safety policy making. It is necessary to identify the factors that may be influential and that may serve to establish tangible objectives. It is necessary to have clear, well-defined goals, reliable instruments to measure progress, and to make use of all available means to ensure that means and ends comply with democratic standards.

It is not difficult to deduce that the causes of homicides are distinct for every region. Border conflicts and disputes over land such as those in the south of Pará are historical expressions of violence associated with rural conflict. They are also manifestations of a culture of violence and conflict resolution originating with local *mandonismo* and *coronelismo*. From the mid-1980s onward, homicide rates began to increase in the greater metropolitan areas of Rio and São Paulo, and from the mid-1990s onward in state capitals and the country's largest cities. Brazil has also been experiencing the spread of violence to the countryside in states such as São Paulo and Pernambuco, and even to metropolitan centers that were once relatively calm, such as Horizonte, Curitiba, Florianópolis, Natal, João Pessoa, and Salvador. Social disorganization in large parts of the country's metropolitan centers needs closer examination. The regulatory and supervisory capacity of the state has diminished in some high violence areas as a result of rapid population changes, and this needs further research covering more extended periods of time. It is necessary to look at the informal control networks operating alongside formal external control institutions to understand how the private logic of organizing social life has begun to rule the lives of the young inhabitants of urban centers. This is a rich and as yet unexplored area of research in the Brazilian context.

NOTES

1. See William C. Bailey, "Poverty, Inequality and City Homicide Rates: Some Not So Unexpected Findings," *Criminology* 22 (1984): 531–50; Judith R. Blau and Peter M. Blau, "The Cost of Inequality: Metropolitan Structure and

Violent Crime," *American Sociological Review* 47 (1982): 114–29; Kenneth C. Land, Patricia L. McCall, and Lawrence E. Cohen, "Structural Covariates of Homicide Rates: Are there Any Invariances across Time and Social Space?" *American Sociological Review* 95, no. 4 (1990): 922–63; Leo Schuerman and Solomon Kobrin, "Community Careers in Crime," in *Crime and Justice,* vol. 8, ed. Michael Tonry and Norval Morris (Chicago: The University of Chicago Press, 1986).

2. See Land, McCall, and Cohen, "Structural Covariates of Homicide Rates."

3. See M. V. Andrade and M. B. Lisboa, "Desesperança de vida: homicídios em Minas Gerais, Rio de Janeiro e São Paulo no período 1981–97" in *Desigualdade e pobreza no Brasil,* ed. R. Henriques, 347–84 (Rio de Janeiro: IPEA, 2000).

4. M. Drumond Jr., *Vida e morte em São Paulo* (São Paulo: Brasiliense, 2002).

5. See Cláudio Chaves Beato Filho and Ilka Afonso Reis. "Desigualdade, desenvolvimento sócio-econômico e crime," in *Desigualdade, desenvolvimento socio-êconomico e crime: Anais do Seminário Desiguladadde e pobreza no Brazil-IPEA,* ed. IPEA, 385–405 (Rio de Janeiro: IPEA, 2000); M. J. C. Mendonça, P. R. A. Loureiro, and A. Sachsida, "Criminalidade e desigualdade social no Brasil," IPEA discussion Paper no. 967, Rio de Janeiro, 2003; Daniel Cerqueira and Waldir Lobão, "Condicionantes sociais, poder de polícia e o setor de produção criminal," IPEA discussion Paper no. 957, Rio de Janeiro, 2003.

6. World Health Organization, *Informe mundial sobre violência e saúde* (Geneva: World Health Organization, 2002).

7. See Marvin Eugene Wolfgang and Franco Ferracuti, *The Subculture of Violence* (London: Tavistock, 1967).

8. See Robert J. Bursik Jr, "Social Disorganization and Theories of Crime and Delinquency: Problems and Prospects." *Criminology* 26, no. 4 (1988): 511–51; Robert J. Sampson, "Communities and Crime," in *Positive Criminology,* ed. Gottfredson and Travis Hirschi, 519–51 (Beverly Hills, CA: Sage Publications, 1987).

9. See Cláudio Chaves Beato Filho, et al., "Conglomerados de homicídios e o tráfico de drogas em Belo Horizonte, Minas Gerais, Brasil, de 1995 a 1999" *Cadernos de Saúde Pública* (Rio de Janeiro) 17, no. 5 (2001): 1163–71.

10. See Cláudio Chaves Beato Filho, "Determining Factors of Criminality in Minas Gerais," *Brazilian Review of Social Sciences* (São Paulo) no. 1 (2000): 159–73.

11. Robert J. Sampson, Stephen W. Raudenbush, and Felton Earls, "Neighborhoods and Violent Crime: A Multilevel Study of Collective Efficacy," *Science Magazine* 277 (15 August, 1997): 918–24.

12. R. K. Merton, *Social Theory and Social Structure* (New York: Free Press, 1968), 186.

13. R. Cloward and L. Ohlin, "Differential Opportunity Structure," in *The Sociology of Crime and Delinquency*, ed. M. Wolfgang and F. Ferracuti, 300–318 (New York: John Wiley and Sons, 1970).

14. See Mark Warr, "The Social Origins of Crime: Edwin Sutherland and Theory of Differential Association," in *Explaining Criminals and Crime*, ed. Raymond Paternoster and Ronet Bachman, 182–91 (Los Angeles: Roxbury, 2001).

15. Albert J. Reiss, "Delinquency as the Failure of Personal and Social Controls," *American Sociological Review* 16 (1951): 196–207; Travis Hirschi, *Causes of Delinquency* (Berkeley: University of California Press, 1969).

16. See the website of the Brazilian Health Ministry: http:///www.dataus.gov.br.

17. World Health Organization, *Informe mundial*.

18. Human Security Center, *Human Security Report 2005* (The University of British Columbia: Oxford University Press, 2005).

19. See M. Castro, et al., "Regionalização como estratégia para a definição de políticas públicas de controle de homicídios," *Cadernos de Saúde Pública* 20 (2004): 1269–80.

20. See Cláudio Chaves Beato Filho, "Fontes de dados policiais em estudos criminológicos: limites e potenciais," in *Criminalidade, violência e segurança pública no Brasil: uma discussão sobre as bases de dados e questões metodológicas*, Fórum de Debates, ed. Daniel Cerqueira, vol. 1, no. 1, 88–110 (Rio de Janeiro: IPEA, 2000).

21. Ibid.

22. Jack Katz, *Seductions of Crime: Moral and Sensual Attractions in Doing Evil* (New York: Basic Books, 1988).

23. See Ministry of Justice's website: www.mj.gov.br/senasp.

24. See the website for SENASP at the National Department of Public Security website: www.mj.gov.br/senasp.

25. Maria Cecília de Souza Minayo et al., "Perfil de mortalidade por causas externas no Brasil: uma análise temporal das décadas de 80 e 90; Relatório de pesquisa," in *Violência sob o olhar da saúde: a infrapolítica da contemporaneidade brasileira*, ed. Maria Cecília de Souza Minayo and Edinilsa Ramos Souza, 83–108 (Rio de Janeiro: Editora Fiocruz, 2003).

26. See Edinilsa Ramos Souza, et al., "Análise temporal da mortalidade por causas externas no Brasil: décadas de 80 e 90," in *Violência sob o olhar da saúde*, ed. Souza Minayo and Ramos Souza.

27. See Jorge Mello, et al., "Análise dos dados de mortalidade," *Revista de Saúde Pública* 31, no. 4 (1997): 5–25.

28. See Cláudio Chaves Beato Filho, "Toward a Society under Law: Citizens and their Police in Latin America" (working paper, Woodrow Wilson Center, Washington DC, 2005); Alba Zaluar. "Gangues, galeras e quadrilhas: globalização, juventude e violência" in *Galeras cariocas: territórios de conflitos e encontros*

culturais, ed. H. Viana, 180–215 (Rio de Janeiro: Editora UFRJ, 1997); Caroline Moser and Bernice van Bronkhorst, "Youth Violence in Latin America and the Caribbean: Costs, Causes, and Interventions" (LCR Sustainable Development working paper, no. 3, Urban Peace Program Series, Washington DC, The World Bank, 1999).

29. See Cláudio Chaves Beato Filho. "Determining Factors of Criminality."

CHAPTER TWO

Citizen (In)Security in Chile, 1980–2007

Issues, Trends, and Challenges

LUCÍA DAMMERT

Chile has often been regarded as an anomaly in Latin America due to its relatively low levels of violence and crime. However, rates of reported crimes and victimization have tended to rise over the past few years, and Chileans have also begun to feel an intense sense of insecurity. Although the causes are hard to pinpoint, socioeconomic factors (residential segregation, income concentration, and precariousness) as well as constant coverage of crime by the media have played a role in fueling this perception.

Chile continues to differ from the rest of the countries in the region in two ways. First, levels of public trust in the police are high. The national police force is seen as a professional, noncorrupt institution that effectively addresses safety issues as well as other daily concerns of the population. Second, the government has undertaken crime prevention and control initiatives that seek to curb increasing crime rates. This chapter presents a diagnosis of citizen security in Chile over the past decade. It aims to establish a frame of reference to interpret the phenomenon and enable us to identify the most pressing problems and needs—particularly as related to improved public policy responses. It also aims to develop a comparative analytical perspective on a highly relevant issue in Latin America and other parts of the world.

Although there have been no effective interinstitutional coordination mechanisms or established evaluation systems, measures are being taken to diversify data collection. Concrete information on crime has improved substantially over the past few years, increasing our capacity to analyze the problem in Chile. Since 1999, the Ministry of the Interior has been standardizing the information provided by police forces on the crimes considered to have the greatest impact on society (*delitos de mayor connotación social*, DMCS).[1] The information reveals that longitudinal analyses of crime rates cannot be based on one source of information alone, which complicates efforts to analyze trends over time. DMCS constitute less than half of crimes reported to the police, highlighting the need to analyze further other types of crime, such as economic crimes. On the other hand, the Interior Ministry has gathered information about victimization for the metropolitan region of Santiago (MRS) on several occasions.[2] Unfortunately, however, it has not been easy to undertake longitudinal analysis because of variations in the questionnaires and in information sampling methodologies. The first national urban victimization survey (ENUSC in Spanish) dates from early 2004, and while the results are not comparable to those obtained in previous years, they constitute a very significant analytical tool to deepen understanding of violence in the country. The methodological strategy designed by the government was to administer the ENUSC every other year. Thus, the survey was undertaken a second time in 2005. However, the government came under pressure to collect victimization information more frequently because of the increasing perception of public insecurity, which is the genesis of the annual surveys.

Results are difficult to assess given the complexity of the indicators involved, but now there are various opinion polls used to measure public insecurity. The main tool designed to understand this phenomenon is the "fear index" developed by the Citizen Peace Foundation (*Fundación Paz Ciudadana*), which has been used for over a decade. This politically influential institution publishes reports every semester detailing variations of the index. The ENUSC provides information that is more detailed, but, given that it is very recent, it can shed no light on long-term tendencies.

The chapter is divided into five sections. The first analyzes crime reporting rates over the past decades, highlighting the importance of the regional distribution of crimes and of using homicide rates in such a way as to enable international comparisons. The second presents the main results of victimization surveys, allowing for the identification of crimes not reported to the police, which give one a better sense of the true magnitude of the phenomenon. The third section addresses fear of crime from different perspectives to show its impact on citizens. The fourth section consists of a brief comparative analysis of the Chilean case in light of the situation in other Latin American countries based on the United Nations Victimization Survey.[3] Finally, I tentatively interpret the phenomenon at the national level and examine the mid- and long-term challenges that must be addressed to tackle this problem, one of the main ones currently affecting Chileans.

REPORTED CRIMES

Despite the limitations presented by changes in the definition of crimes and in data collection systems, it is possible to analyze trends in reported crime over the past few years. Graph 2.1 shows the increasing reported crime rates for every 100,000 inhabitants. It shows that the rates of property crimes[4] and personal crimes[5] have both increased; the trend accelerated in the late 1990s.

Although it is likely that the increase in reported crimes is influenced both by the improvement of the recording systems and by greater citizen trust in institutions, it is clear that citizen security is worsening. In the period between 1973 and 2006, reported rates of property crimes tripled, and crimes against individuals increased by 100 percent. An interesting change occurred in 2004 when the increase slowed down, but there is insufficient evidence to state that there is an ongoing decrease in crime rates in Chile.

A disaggregated analysis reveals that the most common crime against people is assault and that the most common property crime is theft with

Graph 2.1 Chile: Reported Crimes, 1977–2006

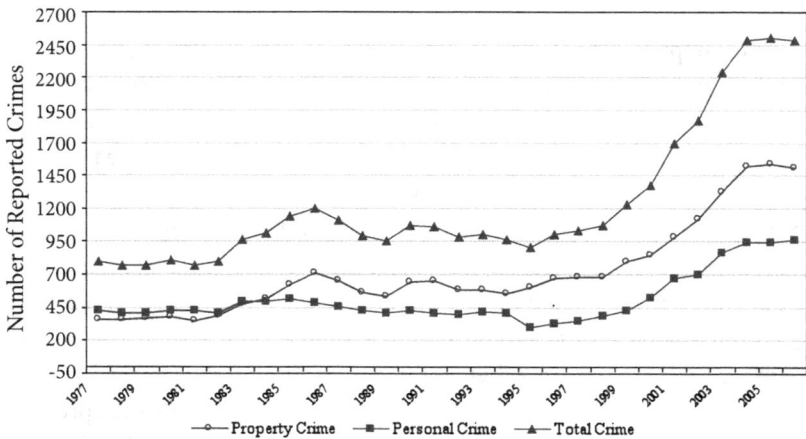

Source: Elaboration based on Ministry of the Interior, Forum of Experts on Citizen Security, "Diagnóstico de la Seguridad Ciudadana en Chile" (working paper 1, Ministerio del Interior, Santiago, Chile, 2004).

the threat of violence. However, there have also been significant increases in theft: theft rates rose by more than 8 times over the period analyzed. In 2006, as in the preceding years, the most-reported crimes included the following: theft with the use of force (38.6 percent), followed by theft (22.1 percent), and injury (21.7 percent). Regarding the geographical distribution of crime, official sources reveal that the rate of DMSC increased in all regions between 1999 and 2006. Although the magnitude and impact of this tendency varies, it is important to note that in regions I, V, and VI, and in the MRS, personal crimes increased much more, while property crimes increased most in regions III and IV.[6] Overall, the rates of both indexes (crimes against people and property crime) increased by more than 50 percent in nine of the thirteen national regions over the period. Furthermore, the geographical distribution of crimes has ceased to be concentrated in the MRS (which until the mid-1990s experienced much higher crime rates than all other regions) and has become decentralized. The data for 2006 shows that several regions have rates of both personal and property crimes higher than the MRS.

VICTIMIZATION

An analysis of crimes reported to the police provides initial information on crime, but such statistics say nothing about the "black figure" (the unreported number of crimes). For this reason, victimization surveys have become an essential tool to shed light on the "black figure" as well as on significant variations in types of crime and their geographic distribution. It also allows for a more precise analysis of tendencies over time, as well as the percentage of crimes reported and the reasons why some events go unreported. Victimization surveys therefore improve the quality of crime analysis, and their proper use allows for the ongoing improvement of official data. In turn, this establishes a virtuous cycle that deepens knowledge about the issue and results in more effective public safety proposals.

Despite their positive attributes, victimization surveys have limitations, of which the most significant is their high cost. The majority of developed countries have vast experience with national and even regional and local victimization surveys. In Latin America, by contrast, there are only a few countries that undertake organized and systematic surveys with national coverage. In many cases, only the main cities are surveyed, and the data cannot be used to understand effectively crime nationwide.

Until 2003 in Chile, the experience with these surveys had been limited. Several surveys of the MRS were undertaken beginning in the 1990s, but unfortunately, given changes in methodology, including question format and territorial focus, it has been virtually impossible to assess trends. The Forum of Experts on Citizen Security undertook a first effort to compare preliminary results of these surveys.[7]

From 1998 onwards, the Citizen Peace Foundation has also carried out a semiannual crime survey that includes information about victimization.[8] Methodological considerations aside,[9] these surveys are clearly one of the few trustworthy sources for longitudinal analysis. The aforementioned sources, however, are insufficient to offer an overall picture of crime in Chile. Therefore, the Ministry of the Interior, together with the National Statistics Institute (*Instituto Nacional de Estadística*, INE) undertook the first-ever ENUSC in 2003, covering the most densely populated communities throughout the thirteen regions of the country.

The following section presents the main results of all three rounds of the ENUSC (2003, 2005, and 2006).

Personal and Property Crimes

The ENUSC shows that in the twelve months prior to the survey, 43 percent of Chilean homes registered at least one crime victim in 2003; with a decline to 38.3 and 38.4 percent in 2005 and 2006, respectively. The results reveal the importance of crime in general, affecting around one third of the national population over fifteen years of age. A more detailed analysis shows key elements that require full consideration to permit a proper understanding of the phenomenon of crime in Chile. On one hand, victimization by socioeconomic groups shows a concentration in upper levels (more than 45 percent of victims in all years surveyed). On the other hand, all surveys show that the young are more frequently victims than any other group in the country. Furthermore, a regional analysis shows a vast disparity in victimization. For instance, victimization in 2005–2006 surveys showed high crime incidence in the northern part (regions I and II) but also in the capital (MRS). Also, there are no clear national trends; there are regions where victimization rates have decreased while others have followed an opposite pattern.

The analysis of victimization rates by type of crime shows that almost one out of every three car owners has been a victim of car theft or theft of car parts. In this sense, car-related crimes have the highest frequency, most of which does not include the use of violence. Also, less than 10 percent of the population reports the more violent crimes (robberies and injuries). It is possible to pinpoint a general problem of opportunistic crimes that do not use force or violence, but impact general perceptions of insecurity.

The "Black Figure"

In order to understand crime, it is necessary to estimate the number of unreported crimes—the so-called "black figure." Clearly, crimes are more likely to be reported when the recovery of property is possible or when property has been insured. According to the ENUSC of 2006, the analysis by type of crime shows variations similar to those observed in other

Graph 2.2 Chile: Victimization by Type of Crime, 2005–2006

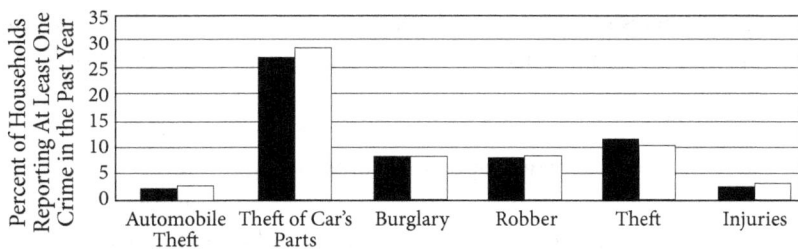

Source: Ministry of the Interior, 2007.

countries in that reporting rates are higher for property crimes (around 67 percent of those reported) compared to petty theft (only 27 percent reported).[10] This is mainly because many victims do not value the stolen objects or believe that the police and the courts will not be able to solve the case.

THE PERMANENT SENSE OF CITIZEN INSECURITY

This book argues that fear of crime has become a top public policy problem in the region. As shown, Chile is no exception. Although there is still debate about the causes and nature of public fear, it is clear that a significant percentage of the population shows high levels of anxiety about crime. A qualitative United Nations Development Program (UNDP) study states that "Chileans tend to associate spontaneous insecurity with criminality."[11] It shows that fear of the "other" has become a central element of daily life in Chile. The study also emphasizes, however, that this feeling of insecurity is a product of modernity and the subjective consequences of political and cultural upheaval, rather than lack of confidence in public security institutions.[12] The UNDP study concludes that the source of insecurity of Chileans is threefold: first, the gap between individuals' expectations and actual economic and institutional performance (health and social security privatization, for example); second, the insufficiency of public security policies and of education and health policies to fully address the causes of insecurity; and third, shifting subjectivities resulting from weakened social capital, as evidenced by decreasing levels of interpersonal trust and the fragmentation of collective identities.[13] Empirical analysis confirms this hypothesis, showing that other kinds of insecurities play an important role in fomenting a general sense of insecurity among citizens.[14]

The Importance of Security

It is not surprising that security became a central citizen concern in the 1990s in Chile, competing for first place with unemployment and even poverty in some cases (the trends are the same in Argentina and Mexico, as shown by Bergman in chapter 3). It is noteworthy that during this decade surveys by the Center for Public Studies (*Centro de Estudios Públicos,* CEP) show that citizens are more concerned about public insecurity than about issues such as health and education. This is confirmed by the ENUSC of 2006, which shows that crime is the most cited concern (20.7 percent), while other problems closely linked with crime such as drug-trafficking (10.8 percent) and drug use (7.4 percent) are also important concerns. The level of concern may be influenced by the perception that the situation is worsening (around 78 percent of those interviewed believed that crime had increased relative to the previous year).

Feelings of Insecurity

There is still much debate about indicators to measure levels of fear. On the one hand, there is "environmental" fear of insecurity, or fear caused by criminal or dangerous activities. This kind of fear is measured by questions about the level of security that people feel when they walk at night in their neighborhood. This is the type of fear that leads populations towards self-enclosure or retirement from public spaces in everyday life. In Chile, the 2006 ENUSC shows that 23.2 percent felt very unsafe in such situations and, even more disturbingly, 5.0 percent said they never leave the house after sunset. There is more "self-enclosure" among women (6.9 percent), and among those over the age of 60 (15.4 percent). On the other hand, there is "objective" fear of crime, which arises when an individual takes various personal and contextual variables into account to determine the likelihood of becoming a victim of a crime: according to the ENUSC survey, 52.3 percent believed that they would be a victim of a crime in the following twelve months, and 44.8 percent felt that it was likely that someone would try to break into and burglarize their home. These results confirm previous studies that emphasize the high levels of insecurity experienced by the Chilean population.[15] There are gaps in our knowledge, however. The nature of and reasons for the extent to which people feel insecure (particularly among women and the elderly) remain unclear.

Citizen Reponses to Insecurity

Citizens respond in many ways to feelings of insecurity. On the one hand, people call for greater police presence, faster judicial procedures, and effective punishment of criminals; on the other hand, people choose strategies of individual "prevention" and "protection" (37.6 percent of those interviewed in the ENUSC of 2006 said they had adopted measures to protect themselves from crime over the preceding year). The most common protection measures were the use of home alarm systems, fences, and guard dogs, and, for the most part, it was the upper socioeconomic class that took such measures. In addition, 6.8 percent of those interviewed said they kept a firearm at home (a number well below the Latin American average), which suggests a predisposition to resolve problems "proactively." It is interesting to note that 43.2 percent of those who admitted to the possession of a firearm claimed that they got one to protect themselves from crime. It should be noted in this context that private security firms have multiplied as citizens emphasize the insufficiency of state responses and the need to resort to alternative security.

From the above, one can conclude that levels of citizen fear are higher than the actual levels of victimization or the magnitude of criminal activity. But fear and feelings of vulnerability may arise as a result of petty rather than major crime, so that crimes such as petty theft may trigger more fear in the population than violent crimes.

CHILE IN THE LATIN AMERICAN CONTEXT

The increase of crime and insecurity has become one of the main problems facing Latin American citizens, and it occupies a central place on the political agenda. Thus, crime was central in all presidential election debates (thirteen in Latin America as a whole) held over the last two years. The reason why people pay so much attention to the crime problem is the persistence of increased crime rates in all the countries of the region over the last two decades, as well as rising media coverage of and attention to that phenomenon. Although crime data is limited and precarious, cross-temporal analysis shows a clear intensification of the problem, particularly where violent crime is concerned. Indeed, the problem has spiraled out of control, so that Latin America is becoming the second most violent region of the world.[16]

Homicide rates reflect the critical situation: there is a regional average of 29 homicides per 100,000 inhabitants, roughly double the world average.[17] The regional average obscures the enormous difference between countries, which ranges from those with the highest rates in the world such as Colombia and El Salvador (89 and 150 respectively) to those with the lowest rates such as Chile and Argentina (4.8 and 3.0 respectively).[18] Nevertheless, some countries where there are few homicides experienced a significant increase in other reported crimes,showing that insecurity is not related solely to rising homicide rates.[19] As graph 2.3 shows, using the most recent information available, in some countries there is a gap between the rate of homicide in the countryside and in the main urban centers, as well as great variations in the magnitude of the problem throughout Latin America. For this reason, any analysis based on homicide rates should avoid generalizations and oversimplification of what is a complex phenomenon of crime and insecurity.

There are three main problems with the information gathered from reported crimes: limited rigor, political or corporative use, and lack of transparency. First, in many countries crime reporting depends on police institutions whose main indicators of success are still arrest numbers and reported crimes. Paradoxically, there is no incentive for police officials to increase reporting since it could damage their institutional image. On the contrary, data can be used to suggest artificial changes of crime rates or alleged police effectiveness in crime control. This situation further limits the possibility of long-term analysis, since annual crime rates are changed constantly in official documents without technical explanations. Furthermore, in some countries, crime data is presented to tackle specific police or political crises, but there is no regular publication or crime review schedule. All the above stands in the way of any long-term

Graph 2.3 Chile: Homicide rate, 2005

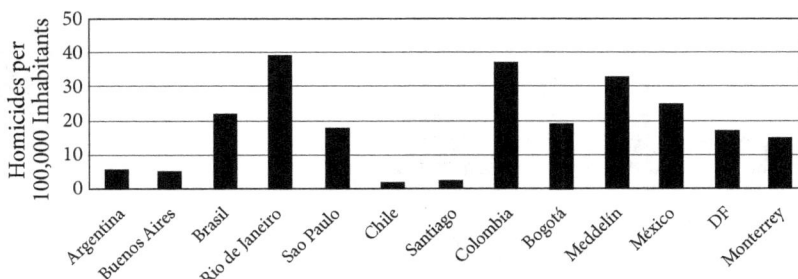

Source: Lucía Dammert, Felipe Slazar, and Felipe Ruiz, *¿Policias de sequridad a ciegas? Desafíos para la construcción de sistemas de información en América Latina* (Chile: FLASCO, 2008). Colombian rates are for 2006.

comparative analysis of crime rates and even country-based studies, because many statistical systems are still precarious.

Although it is difficult to use crime rate data for cross-national comparative analysis, there are other tools that can be useful. Victimization surveys have become the most appropriate tool to compare crime, insecurity, and other related issues at the regional level. Nonetheless, one must be careful with possible methodological differences (differences in data collection strategies as well as in the wording of victimization questions).[20] Despite methodological differences, several comparative analyses show that Chilean victimization rates are lower than those found in other Latin American countries, particularly for violent and personal crimes.[21] A recent analysis based on the Barometer of the Americas (2006) showed a different picture when this survey asked for any type of victimization, and Chile ranked among the worst in the region (see graph 2.4). This data has not been analyzed any further, but much of the victimization concerns minor crimes rather than violent ones.

An analysis of levels of victimization of property crimes tells a very different story, however. The reversal of the regional pattern is especially evident when it comes to theft of objects from cars (one in every three car owners in Chile was the victim of such a crime over the preceding year).[22] But is Chile truly an exceptional case in the region? Before analyzing the

Graph 2.4 Victimization of Any Crime over the Last Year

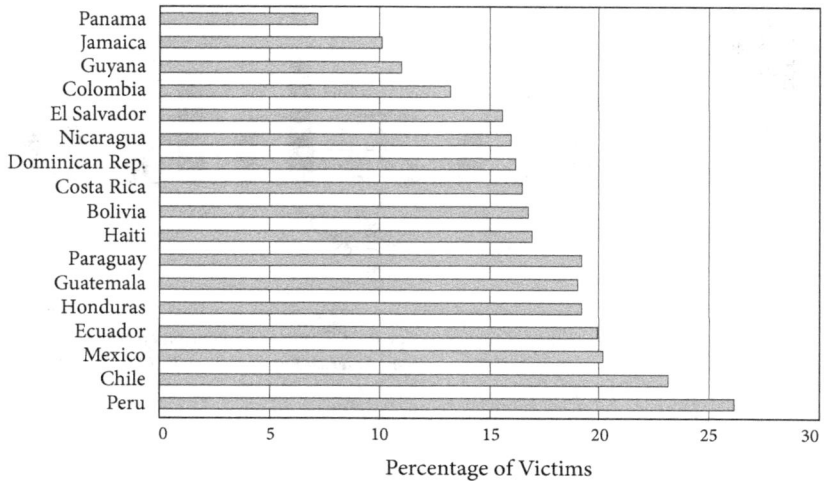

Panama		
Jamaica		
Guyana		
Colombia		
El Salvador		
Nicaragua		
Dominican Rep.		
Costa Rica		
Bolivia		
Haiti		
Paraguay		
Guatemala		
Honduras		
Ecuador		
Mexico		
Chile		
Peru		

Percentage of Victims

Source: Barómetro de las Américas, 2006.

national data, it is important to consider its subregional context. Most southern cone countries (Argentina, Uruguay, Paraguay, and Chile) are experiencing a similar crime situation: increasing property crimes but lower interpersonal violence. In fact, with the exception of Brazil, the subregion is considered to be the safest in Latin America in terms of homicide rates. Chile is different for several reasons, but perhaps the most notable one is the prominent level of civic trust in the police. A recent survey showed that the police are the second most trusted institution in the country, surpassed only by the Catholic Church.[23] However, this perception that the police are professional is accompanied by a negative view of the government and justice system. Interestingly, increasing crime rates have not undermined public confidence in the police but have increased levels of fear throughout the country. Chile's crime situation is also unique for a second reason: it is geographically distant from major organized crime routes. In fact, most crime problems faced by Chileans are caused by criminal organizations whose ties to international crime are still weak.

Another key to understanding the crime situation are the good economic results of the 1980s and 1990s, and important reductions in the percentage of Chileans living under the poverty line. The Chilean economic success story expanded the internal market and increased consumption for an important group of the population.[24] But not all is positive: high levels of economic and social inequality have left a great many people "out of the system." In sum, while there are clear differences between Chile and most other Latin American countries, there is still a need for effective policies to assist the most vulnerable groups and to prevent people from taking up careers in crime. It is also true that crime conditions are worsening. There is no doubt that being the "safest country in the neighborhood" is not a great source of relief for Chileans, who feel insecure and believe that crime is increasing.

CONCLUSION

Citizen security must be dealt with comprehensively, addressing the various issues and institutions at stake. This chapter has emphasized the importance of developing accurate tools for data collection. But an effective policy response to public insecurity also requires a thorough analysis of the legal and sociological context of the observed trends. The efficacy of the system as a whole should also be examined to understand the impact of low levels of public confidence in public institutions, and public beliefs about the inability of the criminal justice system to bring criminals to justice. Over the past decade, these issues have received greater attention, as people have become more concerned about rising crime, both locally and nationally.

There is much work to do to consolidate crime information systems in Chile, but some concluding observations are possible. First, more people are reporting crimes, which suggests there is more crime nationally. The situation worsened from the mid-1990s onward (coinciding with one of the worst economic crises in Chile), and it was only in 2005 that there was some improvement. Second, many Chileans are fearful, but the link between crime rates and an improved sense of security for citizens remains unclear. Third, levels of victimization for violent crimes in Chile are much lower than in neighboring countries. Nonetheless, it is worrying that the number of victims of property crimes (particularly "minor" ones) is increasing.

As outlined above, there are various challenges to face over the short to medium term if we are to increase our understanding of the problem and to design and implement effective crime prevention and control policies. One key element is an integrated information system that permits cross-referencing of data on reported crimes, detentions, penal population, and legal proceedings. Another is the development of victimization surveys to allow for longitudinal analysis. Furthermore, there are two interesting avenues for future research and analysis that should be considered. On the one hand, it is worth thinking about the validity of claims that economic success is not the sole remedy against crime. The Chilean case is an excellent example of the problem of the "trickle down" economic theory and the need for stronger public intervention for those left out of the system. On the other hand, the important gap between victimization and fear of crime requires further analysis and specific policies that could enhance Chileans' quality of life.

NOTES

1. The government defined each crime category in order to concentrate efforts on crimes that cause the highest level of public alarm, namely, homicide, rape, injury, violent robbery, robbery with intimidation, surprise robbery, and theft with the use of force.

2. For complete information see www.seguridadpublica.gob.cl.

3. The varying typologies of crime used in each country make it virtually impossible to compare reported crime rates.

4. Property crimes include robbery and theft.

5. Personal crimes include burglary, robbery involving violence, injuries, homicide, and rape.

6. Chile is divided into thirteen regions. Numbered from north to south, each region has different characteristics. The Metropolitan Region of Santiago concentrates almost 50 percent of the country's total population.

7. The Interior Ministry established the Forum of Experts to diagnose the situation, its main product is available at www.seguridadpublica.gob.cl/PNSCdoc.html.

8. For more information see www.pazciudadana.cl.

9. The main limitations of the survey are that it is a telephone-based survey; in addition, some cities are not represented.

10. Lucía Dammert and Alejandra Lunecke, *Violencia y temor: Análisis teórico y empírico en doce comunas del pais* (Santiago: Centro de Estudios en Seguridad Ciudadana, 2002).

11. UNDP, *Desarrollo humano en Chile 1998: Las paradojas de la modernización* (Santiago de Chile: UNDP, 1998).

12. Pedro Guell, "Una construcción social sobre un mapa de disyuntivas," En Foco 40 (Santiago: Expansiva, 2004).

13. UNDP, *Desarrollo humano en Chile 1998.*

14. Lucía Dammert and Mary F. T. Malone, "Inseguridad y temor en Argentina: El impacto de la confianza en la policía y la corrupción sobre la percepción ciudadana del crimen." *Desarrollo Económico: Revista de Ciencias Sociales* 42, no. 166 (2002): 285–301.

15. Dammert and Lunecke, "Inseguridad y temor en Argentina."

16. See Mayra Buvinic, Andrew Morrison, and Michael Shifter, "Violence in Latin America and the Caribbean: A Framework for Action" (technical study, Inter-American Development Bank Washington, DC, 1999).

17. World Health Organization, *Informe mundial sobre violencia y salud* (Washington, DC: WHO, 2002).

18. World Health Organization, *Informe mundial sobre violencia y salud.*

19. This is the same as Argentina, with an increase of more than 200 percent during the 1990s. See Dammert and Malone, "Inseguridad y temor en Argentina."

20. The variations are linked to the subject of the crime (interviewee, family, or friends), the time period of the crime (twelve or six months), and the type of crime (general or specific).

21. Lucía Dammert and John Bailey, eds., *Seguridad y Reforma Policial en las Américas* (Mexico: Siglo XXI, 2005); Hugo Frühling and Joseph S. Tulchin, eds., *Crime and Violence in Latin America: Citizen Security, Democracy, and the State* (Washington, DC: Woodrow Wilson Center, 2003); P. Fajnzylber, Daniel Lederman, and Norman Loayza, eds., *Crímen y violencia en América Latina* (Washington, DC: Alfaomega and World Bank, 2001).

22. For complete information see www.seguridadpublica.gob.cl.

23. For more information see www.cep.cl.

24. The percentage of population under the poverty line has systematically decreased since the beginning of the 1990s.

CHAPTER THREE

Rising Crime in Mexico and Buenos Aires

The Effects of Changes in Labor Markets and Community Breakdown

MARCELO BERGMAN

By the late 1990s crime rates in Buenos Aires and Mexico City had more than doubled compared to the early part of the decade. For the first time in recent history, crime became a major public concern, and citizens began to rank feelings of insecurity as one of two top concerns. Both cities, particularly Buenos Aires, which has been one of the less crime-ridden cities in the region, changed abruptly.

There are no comprehensive explanations of why crime has risen so sharply in these cities and throughout the region. Several theories on criminality have been advanced to account partially for these new trends. Economic recession, rising poverty, debilitated state institutions, inadequate judicial organizations, and outdated legal statutes as well as poor police performance have been proposed to explain—at least partially— these changes in the social and political landscape. In this context, the goal of this chapter is twofold. First, I will document with available data the recent trends in criminality. This may seem trivial but is in fact an important milestone because most studies about the region rely on "snapshot information," and there are only time series data for homicides (Fajnzylber, Lederman, and Loayza 2001). So the goal here is to describe a similar process for two very different cities experiencing a remarkably similar trend: the slow but steady rise in crime rates, which is compounded by a spike in levels of crime over a two year period. Second, I attempt to make sense of these overlapping trends by identifying the "usual suspects" that explain criminal activity. The type and quality of data does not allow theories to be adequately tested, so I provide crime correlates associated with major changes in the urban landscape and the economic and social changes of the 1990s. Despite the absence of a sound data collection system, different available measures show that the total number of offenses increased significantly over the 1990s. Because of severe problems with the validity and reliability of data collection, it is best to use longitudinal data, as "snapshots" of cross sectional information cannot be trusted, particularly for comparative analysis. Conversely, time series of same measures allow one to identify and track changes, as the same method of collection is usually applied over years, even if this is far from accurate. In other words, it is best to identify trends rather than determine crime rates.

An analysis of this data suggests that the surge in delinquency does not follow a stable pattern. In addition to a moderate upward trend in criminal activity, there was a sharp increase in both cities in 1994–1996. According to different measures, criminal activity in 1997 was at least double that of 1994. In other words, this study identifies two clearly distinctive processes: a modest upsurge over the last fifteen years, on the one hand, and a significant leap in a short two year span, on the other. In short, this paper focuses on the 1990s because it was during that decade that the drastic increase in criminality was observed. Although crime fell slightly between 2003 and 2007, it has never returned to the relatively low levels of criminality that existed before the 1990s.

The argument here is that the sharp rise in criminality in both cities is strongly correlated with major social transformations in the 1990s such as unemployment, the composition of relative size cohorts, and the structure of the labor market. This macrolevel transformation and new social contexts gave rise to very explosive social conditions. In short, the slow increase in criminality documented from the 1980s onwards (and perhaps even before) was compounded by a more explosive surge in the mid-1990s as social conditions facilitated a rapid rise in criminal activity. It appears that the slow increase produced by changing labor market conditions and marginality exploded with the severe economic crisis in Mexico and Argentina, increasing the number of potential delinquents to unprecedented new levels.

NEW TRENDS IN CRIMINALITY: HOMICIDE RATES

Due to the different nature and the coding of the information on criminality in both metropolitan areas, it is necessary to provide separate trends for each city. Given standard concerns about the collection of information, the data on homicides is the most reliable measure of criminal activity, and can be regarded as a good barometer of crime trends.[1]

Buenos Aires

According to a 1999 court report (Ministry of Justice 2000), in 1998 there were 2,700 homicides in the whole of Argentina, or 7.5 per 100,000 (see graph 3.1). This is the highest homicide rate registered in the nation's history. The reason for the rising trend in homicides is a result of its increasingly random nature. In 1992, 48 percent of offenders previously knew their victims; four years later only 32 percent did. In other words, the number of homicides in which the victim was known to the offender remained constant as homicides doubled between 1992 and 1996, so that the increase resulted from a rise in the "unknown victims" category.

In 1991, 79 percent of offenders who were thirty-five years old or older knew their victims (Ministry of Justice 1998), while in 1996 70 percent of homicides were committed by offenders who were 30 years old and younger.

In addition, while in 1991 firearms were the direct cause of one out of two homicides, in 1997 they accounted for more than three out of four

Graph 3.1 Homicide Rate and Violent Crime in the City of Buenos Aires

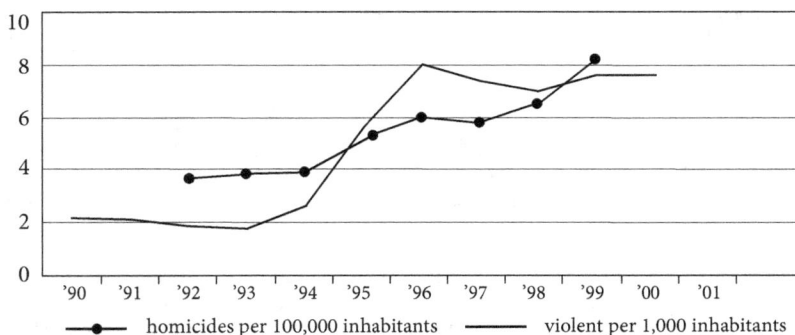

Source: Registro Nacional de Reincidencia y Estadística Criminal, Dirreción Nacional de Política Criminal, Ministerio de Justicia, Buenos Aries.

homicides. Ninety-one percent of homicides were perpetrated after a felony. Guns were also increasingly used by adolescents. Killers got younger and, as chapter 1 on Brazil shows, access to weapons became easier (which was true in both Buenos Aires and Mexico). In other words, the increase in homicides results from greater use of guns in assaults, burglaries, and robberies.

Total crime has also risen sharply over the last two decades. From the fragmented data available, it can be inferred that total crime in Buenos Aires rose from an average of approximately 1,500 crimes per 100,000 inhabitants during the 1980s, to 5,700 per 100,000 during the second half of the 1990s. This information is presented in graph 3.2.

The drastic spike of the mid 1990s is captured by the first series of victim surveys. Over a period of two years people reported higher rates of random crimes. Most victims are clearly from the low-income segments. However, once controlled for the high proportion of low-income groups in the population, the level of victimization is uniform across class, so that vulnerability to crime is not apparently associated with income level. According to a survey by Catterberg and Associates (2000), of the families that suffered victimization during the previous year, 34 percent were within the higher income bracket, 33 percent within the middle income bracket, and 28 percent among the lower income bracket.

Graph 3.2 Buenos Aires Crime Rates

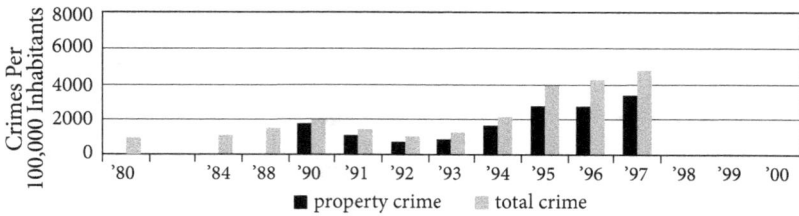

Source: Own elaboration based on Ministry de Justice (2000) and *Instituto Nacional de Estadísticas y Censos* (National Institute of Statistics and Censuses, 1999a data. For property crimes only the years shown above are available. Some property crimes may be included in other categories Sistema Nacional de Información Criminal, *Informe anual, 1999*).

To summarize, the data shows that Buenos Aires experienced two across-time and overlapping trends in criminal activity: first, there was a moderate increase in the crime rate from the mid-1980s onwards, and despite some fluctuations and moderation over a two-year period (1991–1992) there has been an overall upward trend; second, there was a remarkably steep rise in criminal activity starting in 1994, increasing the crime rate in general and homicides in particular to new highs. Thus, in addition to a steadily evolving upward trend, the data indicates that criminal activity has reached unprecedented levels.

Mexico

The time series for Mexico City are even more fragmented than those for Buenos Aires. It was only after 1997 that the authorities began to collect data according to uniform criteria (the residents of Mexico City elected their own authorities, and the district attorney's office, in charge of crime reporting, began to assemble information more systematically). Nonetheless, there are still many questions regarding validity and reliability. Court data on processed homicide felons allow some general inferences to be made about the homicide rate as a whole.

Like Buenos Aires, the Federal District is fully integrated with the outskirts of another state. Half of the population of the state of Mexico live

Table 3.1 Percentage of Victims in the City of Buenos Aires

Type of Crime	1995	1997
Violent Theft	4.2%	8.6%
Property Crimes	23.6%	37.3%
% of victims who knew thieving offender (with violence)	11.3%	5.9%
Victim of violent theft more than once	N /A	31%

Source: Victimization Surveys 1995, 1997.

Graph 3.3 Actual Homicide Rate Compared with Processed Felons in Mexico City

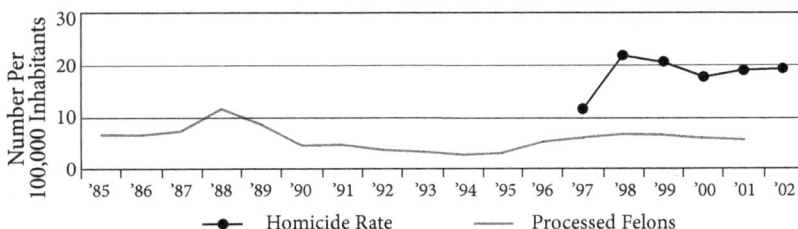

Source: Own elaboration based on reported homicides. See ICESI Delitos 1997–2004 y serie historica.

in the outskirts of the Federal District and most inhabitants live in very adverse economic and social conditions. Unfortunately, the official data for the state of Mexico does not disaggregate crimes for the suburban areas and other (mostly) rural areas, but most criminal activity can be safely assumed to be metropolitan. The graphs 3.4–3.6 show a somewhat inconsistent trend: while the homicide rate for Edomex (state of Mexico) was more than double the Federal District (DF) rate, other violent crimes did not follow the same pattern (if we control for the interior of the state of Mexico, the rate is even higher in the communities that surround the Federal District). In addition, it is quite remarkable that more than a quarter of total reported crimes nationwide took place in the metropolitan area, even though only 18 percent of the Mexican population lives there.

Graph 3.4 Comparison of Homicide Rates

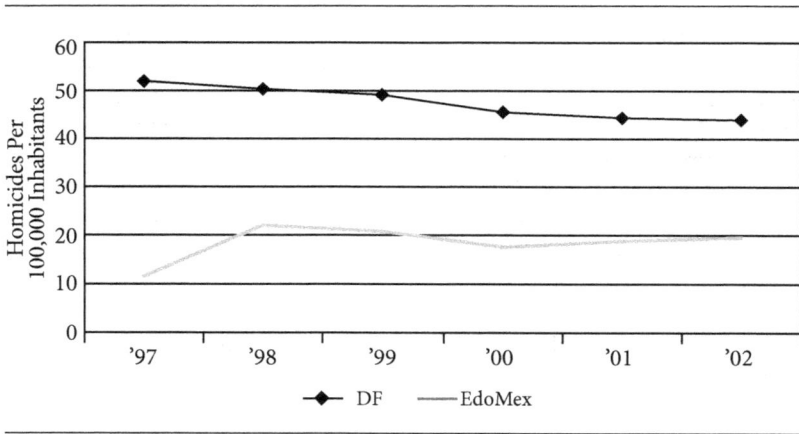

Source: Own elaboration based on official data. See ICESI Delitos Denunciados 1997–2004 in http://www.icesi.org.mx/estadisticas/estadisticas.asp.

Although there are no reliable data on trends in nonviolent crime in the 1980s, it is possible to construct quite a revealing series for the Federal District in 1993.[2] It is notable (notwithstanding the impossiblity of proving a trend) that crime was rising even before the 1995 economic crisis, and as in Buenos Aires there was a sharp rise between 1995 and 1997, followed by a slower decrease thereafter. However, even after this fall in reported crime, rates did not return to 1993 levels.

CRIME RISE AND PUBLIC PERCEPTIONS

In contrast to the asymmetry between rising public awareness of crime levels and diminishing crime rates in the U.S. in the 1990s (Roberts and Stalans 1998), the data for Argentina and Mexico suggest that public concern reflects a real increase in violent crime. This challenges the idea that public anxiety is a reflection of media influence, as it can be argued that this is not a false anxiety, a media generated issue, or a moral panic, but a reflection of actually increasing crime. The data below also reveal that even after reported crime began to decrease moderately in both

Graph 3.5 Comparison of Injuries and Kidnapping

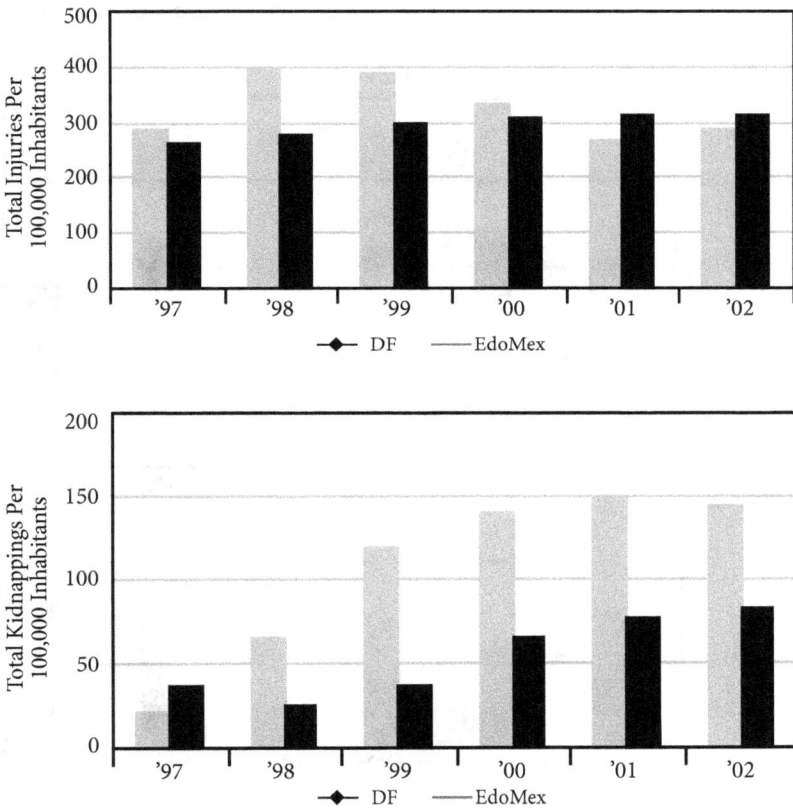

Source: Own elaboration based on official data. See ICESI Delitos Denunciados 1997–2004 in http://www.icesi.org.mx/estadisticas/estadisticas.asp

cities, public perceptions did not follow suit. This could be so for three different reasons: first, because once crime rises, fear of crime follows an uncorrelated path, or that wshen a certain "crime threshold" has been reached fear of crime remains stable or even increases; second, public anxiety lags behind actual crime rates; and, third, rates of crime as reported to authorities obscure the real crime rate, so that crimes reported to the authorities drop but the real crime rate does not.

Graph 3.6 Comparison of Thefts and Reported Crimes

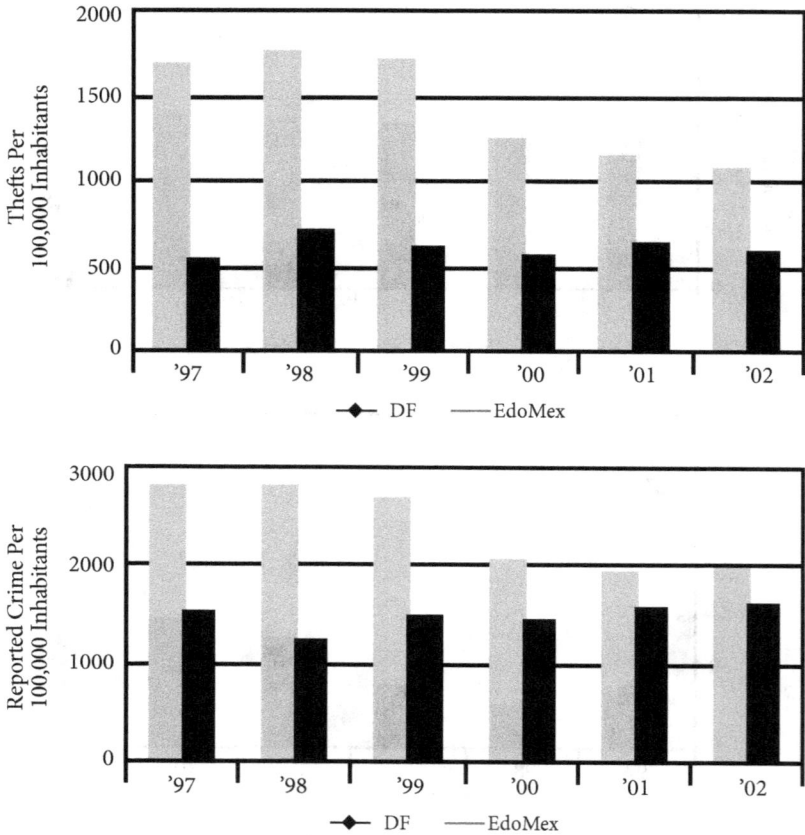

Source: Own elaboration based on official data. See ICESI Delitos Denunciados 1997-2004 in http://www.icesi.org.mx/estadisticas/estadisticas.asp

Buenos Aires

Despite several attempts, it was unfortunately impossible to assemble a time series on public perceptions in Buenos Aires. However, based on national series,[3] it is possible to extrapolate the Buenos Aires response to

Table 3.2 Mexico City and State of Mexico Share of Total National
Crime, 1997–2002

Crime	DF	EdoMex	Total
Homicide	4.9%	18.9%	23.8%
Injuries	11.5%	13.5%	25.0%
Property crime	10.8%	7.5%	18.3%
Theft	22.6%	14.1%	36.7%
Reported kidnappings	23.4%	10.8%	34.2%
All crime	14.5%	13.5%	28.0%

Source: Own elaboration based on official data. See ICESI Delitos Denunciados 1997–2004
in http://www.icesi.org.mx/index.cfm?artID=1353

Graph 3.7 Reported Crime in Mexico City

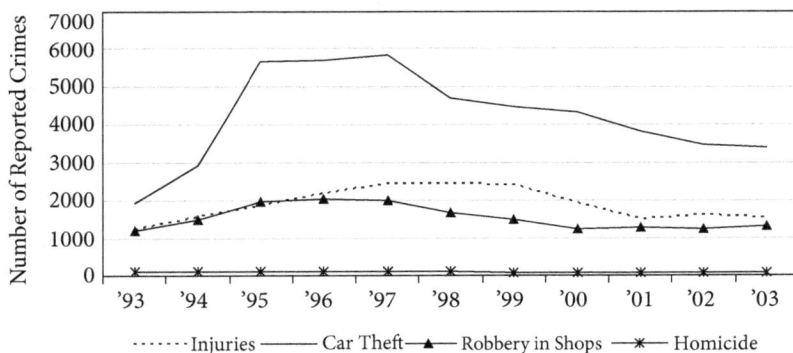

Source: Own elaboration based on official data. See ICESI Delitos Denunciados 1997–2004 in
http://www.icesi.org.mx/estadisticas/estadisticas.asp

the question, "What is the most important problem of the country?"
Crime rose from the bottom to the top of a list of more than fifteen items
(including unemployment or jobs, which are consistently the most urgent concern for an average of 40 percent of respondents). Results are
shown in table 3.3.

Table 3.3 Ranking of Crime as a Key Problem in Argentina

'95	'96	'97	'98	'00	'01	'02	'03
9	7	4	4	4	3	3	3

Source: Latinobarómetro 2005.
Note: There is no information for 1999. The ranking is based on a valid response of the percentage of respondents who graded crime as the main problem in the country.

Mexico

The data for Mexico is much richer than for Buenos Aires. Pollsters working for the presidency have been tracking trends since the early 1990s
and generously provided the information used here. The spike in criminal
activity was reflected in public perceptions. In 1990, to the question "Do
you believe that crime has increased, decreased, or remained stable
lately?" 38 percent said that it had increased, compared with 60 percent
in 1994 and 86 percent in 1996. Table 3.4 and graph 3.8 provide additional proof to such an assertion.

Table 3.4 Survey of Public Safety in Mexico City

	% of 800 respondents who reported affirmatively	
Select Questions on Survey	*1995*	*1997*
Public safety is the main problem	21.3	36.5
Public safety is the main problem barring the economy	36.1	40
Public safety is bad or very bad	75.8	76.5
Feel personally threatened	64	69

Source: Own elaboration based on *Encuestas cara a cara en viviendas sobre seguridad publica
y seguridad en el D.F.,* provided by the Office of the Presidency of Mexico.

Graph 3.8 Percentage of Respondents Who See Public Safety as the Main Problem

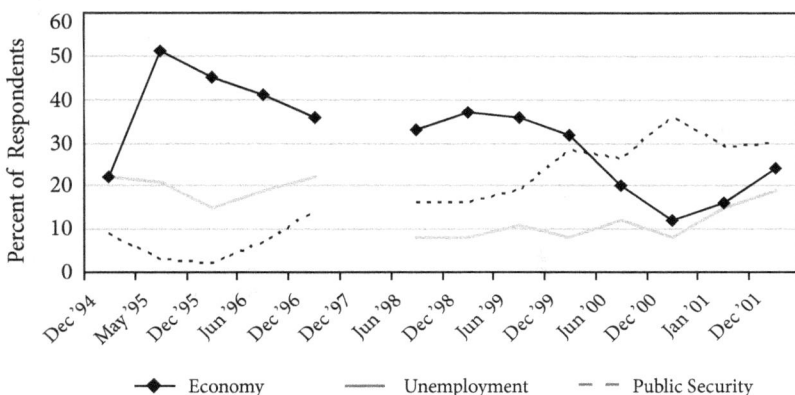

Source: Own elaboration based on *Encuesta cara a cara en viviendas sobre seguridad publica y seguridad en el D.F.*, provided by the Office of the Presidency of Mexico.
Note: Rates in the 1990s correlated with perceptions that crime levels were higher. The number of people in the mid-1990s who reported a perception of increased crime is unusually high. To the question "Do you believe that crime has increased, decreased, or stayed the same since Zedillo became President?" 82 percent answered that crime has increased in 1995, compared with 86 percent in 1996, and 85 percent in 1998.

VULNERABILITY TO CRIME

This section examines patterns of vulnerability to crime in Mexico City and Buenos Aires. The findings are based on similar victim surveys conducted in each city. For Buenos Aires the survey was undertaken in early 2004 (covering 2,427 respondents) and asked questions about victimization in 2003. For Mexico, the findings are based on the July 2005 responses of 1,924 people interviewed about victimization in the metropolitan area over the preceding six months (the first half of 2005). It should be underlined that rates must be compared with caution because there are some differences in wording, administration, and particularly on bounding. The Buenos Aires survey covers a twelve-month period while the Mexican covers only half that time. The results are presented in table 3.5.

Table 3.5 Victimization in Buenos Aires and Mexico City

Crime	*People Reporting Victimization (%)*	
	Buenos Aires	*Mexico City*
Burglary	3.2	2.2
Car theft	1.9	3.1
Theft	14.5	16.5
Aggression and Violence	3.8	3.2
Total	37.5	29.2

Source: Victimization Survey in Buenos Aires (2003) and Victimization Survey in Mexico (2005).

I estimate one *logit* model for each city to analyze vulnerability to crime. The dependent variable is the person victimized either by theft (violent or not), aggression, or burglary. The dependent variables are gender (dummy for male=1), age, education, a dummy for arm possession (P-weapons), the number of household members (members), a dummy for working outside the house (Dfuera), and dummies for type of residence (Du_re1, 2, 3). The specification of this model follows the standard variables identified in the literature as the best predictors of personal vulnerability to being a crime victim.[4]

Buenos Aires

Thus far, research shows that the people who are more vulnerable to crime are those who spend more time outside the home, use public transportation, and have higher education (the more education the higher the income and therefore the more likely that predators will try to rob them). Women are less likely to be victims, and younger people are more prone to be victims than older people. An intriguing variable (measured in one case, as the question was available) is whether victims possess a firearm. For Buenos Aires, the dummy variable (*d_outside*) was recoded according to occupation, so as to differentiate people who spent more time outside the home (work, study, =1) from those who stay home most of the time (such as housewives, pensioners, or people who do not work). The type of residence, originally a three-value variable to signal the type of residence (1=poor, 3=rich), was transformed into three dummies. The model excludes 1 (the poor) to be the base of comparison. Results are contained in table 3.6.

The result is consistent with the general trend of other major urban areas in the region although the tendencies are milder. The classical reservation with Pseudo R2 and the goodness of fit are in place in this case. This model predicts 65 percent of cases. Only two variables are statistically insignificant, although household members is marginally significant. Males are prone to be victimized, and young people are also more likely to be victimized. Those who have arms are more likely to be victims compared to those who do not. Unsurprisingly, the most insecure place is outside the home, and the poorer the neighborhood the higher the vulnerability (notice the negative coefficients for du_2 and du_3, which represent higher income residences). On the basis of this model, the probabilities of being a victim are as follows: holding constant the rest of the variable, being male increases the chances of being a victim by

Table 3.6 Logit Model of Vulnerability to Crime in Buenos Aires

	Coefficient	Error	Z	P > 1=1
Gender	.0978	.0902	1.08	0.279
Age	-.0146	.0028	-5.17	0.000
Education	.1155	.0426	2.71	0.007
P-weapons	.3450	.1431	2.41	0.016
Members	.0507	.0270	1.88	0.060
D_outside	.4299	.1196	3.59	0.000
Du_re2	-.3645	.1919	-1.90	0.058
Du_re3	-.4645	.2108	-2.20	0.028
-Cons	-.5208	.3238	-1.61	0.108

Number of obs.: 2462
Prob. of chi2 =.000
Pseudo R2= .05
Log likelihood= -1557.8844
Source: Victimization Survey of the city of Buenos Aires (2003).

45 percent (it should be reiterated that this coefficient was not significant). The most significant "modifiers" of vulnerability in Buenos Aires are the possession of arms (the risk of victimization is 8 percent higher), having a permanent occupation outside the home (probability of crime increases by 10 percent), and living in a better off neighborhood (chances decrease by 11 percent). These probabilities are lower compared to Rio de Janeiro, Bogotá, Caracas, and many other cities, so the impact of crime on personal vulnerability in Buenos Aires is apparently more evenly divided among the population.

Mexico

The model for Mexico renders similar results with some differences from Buenos Aires. It should be reiterated that surveys are not identical, so there are differences in variables and measurements. Still, trends in both models remain similar for a number of variables. There are no measures for firearms possession or type of neighborhood. In Mexico, however, there is a dummy variable for having a home security system of some kind (0=having security, 1=no security).

Table 3.7 Logit Model of Vulnerability to Crime in Mexico

	Coefficient	*Error*	*Z*	*P > |z|*
Gender	-.001	.124	-0.01	0.994
Age	-.0199	.0037	-5.39	0.000
Education	.2751	.0481	5.72	0.000
Household (n)	.0937	.0285	3.28	0.001
D_outside	.1545	.1308	1.18	0.237
Income	.3023	.1037	2.91	0.004
Security	-.4905	.1976	-2.48	0.013
-Cons	-1.7983	.2970	-6.05	0.000

Number of obs: 1993
Prob. of chi2 =.000
Pseudo R2= .06
Log likelihood= -1094.9124
Source: Victimization Survey in Mexico (2005)

Surprisingly, gender does not appear to be a predictor of crime in Mexico City. Conversely, age, education, income, and number of household members have similar effects to those found for Buenos Aires, while spending more time outside the home increases the likelihood of victimization, although the coefficient is not statistically significant in this case (there are some measurement problems that bias the estimator, but the trend is similar to that in Buenos Aires). Predictably, having a home security system considerably reduces vulnerability to crime. Overall, the model successfully predicts 62 percent of the cases. Being older, more educated, and having access to home security reduced the probability of being victimized by more than 20 percent.

EXPLAINING THE RISE IN CRIME

The findings presented here raise two questions: first, what explains the moderate upward trend in criminality; and second, what process or factors might account for the dramatic increase of the mid-1990s? In this section, the available information is used to analyze the effects of some correlates with crime in each city.

The Rise in Crime in Argentina

Demographics

The high crime rate in the U.S. in the 1960s and 1970s was related to the coming of age of the baby boom generation, the size of which explains the significant impact on the fluctuation of crime rates. Different theories of demographic trends have emerged from the assumption that the increasing numbers of "at-risk" youngsters produced a larger cohort of delinquents, and consequently a higher crime rate.

The relative size of cohorts has proved to be a good predictor of fluctuations in homicide rates (O'Brien, Stockard, and Isaacson 1999). The more disadvantaged the cohort (or the larger its relative size, and the greater competition for jobs and resources within it), the higher the rates of homicides. Crime is associated with the relative size of the at-risk cohort. Given that age and gender are also known to be good predictors of crime, it is crucial to trace the changes in the number of 15–24-year-old males throughout the period. Graph 3.9 plots the size of two cohorts in Buenos Aires for every five years and offers some information about the 20–24-year-old cohort in Mexico.

As shown, the fluctuation of male cohort size is partially correlated with the crime trend. There was a higher proportion of 15–24-year-old males in both countries during the second half of the 1990s compared to other years. In Buenos Aires, the apparent low incidence of crime occurred in the first half of the 1980s, which coincides with a smaller share of young males in the population. No information about the 1980s could be obtained for Mexico, but information about 1970 suggests a similar trend to that of Buenos Aires (that by the mid-1990s the relative size of the young male cohort peaked). In Buenos Aires, for instance, the difference between 1985 and 2000 is not merely 1.2 percent: in 2000, this age group was 15 percent larger than in 1985. Ceteris paribus, had all crimes been committed by males between the ages of 15 and 24, it would be expected that in 2000 the incidence of crime would have been 15 percent

Graph 3.9 Male Cohort Size

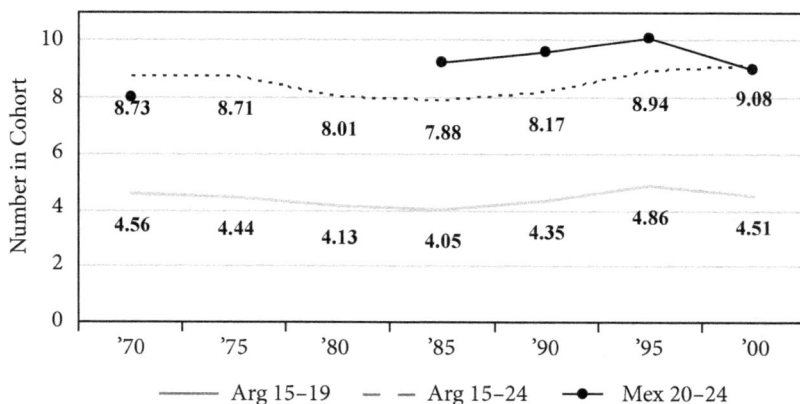

Source: Own elaboration based on INDEC (1995).
Note: This data covers the two countries as a whole. The information for the province of Buenos Aires and Mexico City (the metropolitan area) is incomplete but follows the same trend. See INDEC (1996) and *Instituto Nacional de Estadística Geográfica e Informática* (National Institute of Geographical Statistics and Computing, INEGI) (2005) at http://www.inegi.gob.mx.

higher than in 1985. This is not the claim here, but the size of these co-horts does correlate positively with crime rates, and suggests a causal effect that has yet to be estimated with precision.

This data indicates that, other variables being constant, the demographic trend partly accounts for crime rate fluctuations in Mexico and Buenos Aires. In fact, changes in cohort size have an indirect marginal effect on unemployment, as competition to enter the job market becomes tougher and punishes less competitive individuals, thus alienating and frustrating a growing proportion of youths. The association between demographic trends and increased crime in the 1990s partly explains the first moderate surge in criminality. The abrupt increase of the mid-1990s, however, must be explored in terms of the dramatic changes affecting job markets and the demise of the welfare state in Mexico and in Argentina alike.

Unemployment

Several studies indicate that labor market conditions are related to crime. Unemployment has been found to have a modest positive effect on criminality both in longitudinal (Chiricos 1987; Freeman 1995, "Disadvantaged" 2000), and cross-sectional (Butcher and Piehl 1999) studies. A persuasive qualitative study (Kessler 2004) has shown how the changes in the labor market and unemployment among youngsters triggered amateur delinquency in the poverty-stricken outskirts of Buenos Aires. Furthermore, the data supports the claim that crime and unemployment are positively associated. The number of unemployed in greater Buenos Aires tripled over the last decade (the average rate in 1983–1987 was 5.1 percent, while a decade later, in 1993–1997, it was as high as 15.4 percent). However, the association of unemployment and crime needs to be specified, and we need to study the particular impact of the rate of unemployment among young males. Table 3.8 presents the age-range category (not stratified by gender) as reported in official statistics.

The steep increase in unemployment in the late 1990s affected young cohorts, particularly new active job seekers. The 20–34-age category had similar coefficients to the overall rate (endogenous); however, in absolute terms, the tightening of the job market reduced the likelihood that a youngster would find a job. Although the official data provides no

Table 3.8 Average Unemployment Rate for Greater Buenos Aires

Age	'80–'84	'85–'89	'90–'94	'95–'99
15–19	13.5%	19.3%	22.1%	41.4%
20–34	4.6%	6.8%	8.9%	17.3%
Total Rate	4.2%	6.1%	8.7%	17.1%

Source: Own elaboration based on INDEC (1999).

breakdown for the 20–34-year-old category, it is assumed that the younger the person the more likely they are to face difficulties finding stable employment. Adverse market conditions affect not only active job seekers but also alienate youths who have never been employed. Unemployment rates do not take into account people who are not seeking employment, and whose numbers presumably increase during periods of labor market tightening. In sum, the total number of young males who find it difficult to enter the labor market grew substantially over this period. A high rate of idleness does correlate with criminal activity.[5] Graph 3.10 summarizes the association between crime and measures of unemployment for the greater Buenos Aires area in 1986–1999.

Homicides and the total number of crimes in particular (overwhelmingly property crimes), were strongly correlated to unemployment rates among adolescents and young adults. Because the data for the 1980s is incomplete, it is not possible to plot the entire period; however, available information shows that low levels of unemployment during the 1980s also correlate with low levels of criminality. Graph 3.10 clearly shows that unemployment, homicides, and property crimes at least doubled in the mid-1990s. It also suggests that unemployment had a lagged effect on crime in the mid-1990s.

The Labor Market

Like many other countries in the region, Argentina and Mexico underwent wide-ranging economic transformations in the 1990s, as liberalization transformed the structure of the labor market. In addition to growing unemployment, the composition of the active labor force changed, which

Graph 3.10 Homicide, Crime, and Unemployment

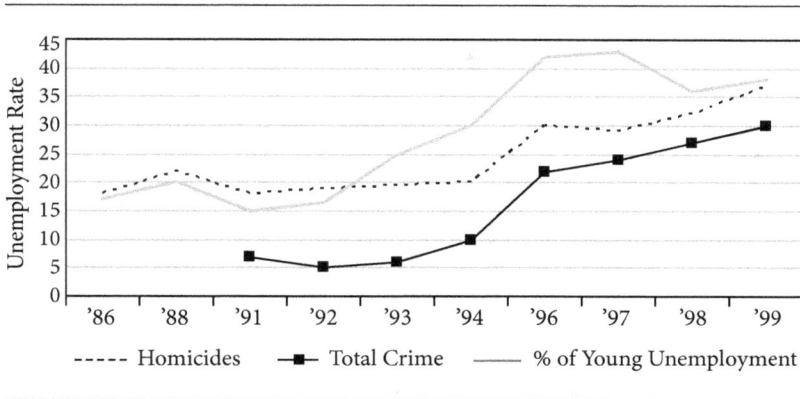

Source: Own elaboration based on INDEC (1999b) and Ministry of Justice (2000).
Note: The total number of crimes per 1,000 inhabitants was divided by 10, and homicides per 100,000 was multiplied by 5 for presentation purposes

indirectly and significantly affected crime. Graph 3.11 plots the drastic transformations in the labor market for age and gender in greater Buenos Aires.

These trends indicate a subtle but long-term effect. The percentage of females in employment increased, particularly the 35–49-year-old female cohort, from 37 percent in the early 1980s to 54 percent in the late 1990s. This is particularly striking given that there was a very tight labor market. In fact, except for 20–49-year-old females, all other groups saw their participation in the labor market decrease.

The percentage of single-head households increased by 75 percent between 1985 and 1998.[6] Moreover, in 1998, 20 percent of females over the age of fifteen headed a household (Geldstein 2000). According to INDEC (1999C), for 29 percent of two-head households, the main income was earned by females, while in 1980 the figure was less than 18 percent. Patterns of child rearing practices changed, as there were more working mothers entering the job market and more children probably left unattended. Communities collapsed due to the breakdown of traditional patterns of social control, the bankruptcy of the state, the lack of social services, lawlessness in poor neighborhoods ineffectively controlled by a corrupt police force,[7] and the explosion of the drug trade.[8]

Graph 3.11 Employment Rate in Buenos Aires

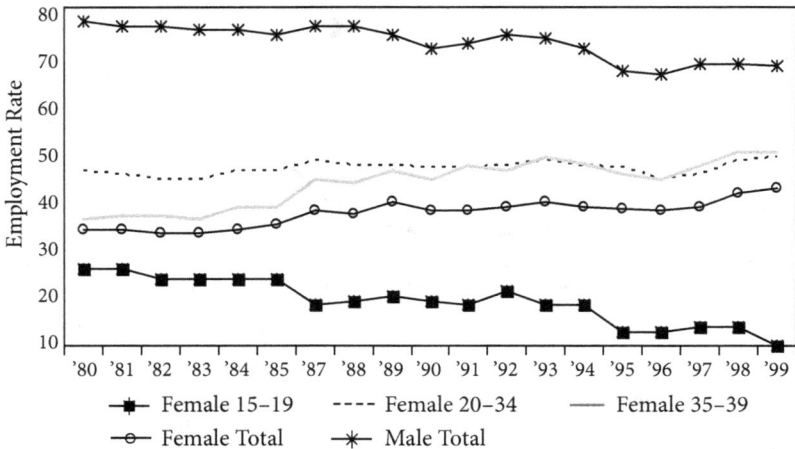

Source: INDEL (1999c).

In other words, the transformations of the labor market introduced dramatic changes in the social organization of communities and in child rearing practices. Mothers (particularly in poor neighborhoods) left home to work for extended hours, the percentage of single mothers increased, extended families as facilitators of child rearing were weakened, and state institutions such as schools and trade union resources were unable to adjust and create alternative support and assistance programs.[9]

Growing Poverty and the Demise of Safety Nets

The major economic transformation of Argentina in the 1990s generated a wider gap in income distribution. In 1997, the Gini coefficient was .605, compared to .54 in 1992. The first and second quintile reduced its share of national income by 25 percent during the same years (Fiel 1999). At the same time, in the late 1990s school dropout rates reached record highs. A World Bank study estimates that 37 percent of low income adolescents aged 14–18 nationwide did not attend school in 1999. Only 23 percent of this cohort is expected to finish high school (among high income families, only 8 percent do not attend high school and 78 percent of upper income high school students are expected to graduate).[10] Thus, several indicators show that there is a variable that has been largely over-looked, that may account for increased crime rates: a growing level of low-paid, female participation in the job market with adverse effect on child rearing practices, as well as the breakdown of communities, accentuated as fiscal crisis and debilitated public safety nets. These trends may breed more youths who are prone to delinquency. A clarification is in order here: I am emphatically not claiming that women should not be active participants in the job market. On the contrary: the situation is an indictment of the dwindling role of fatherhood in marginal communities, of the demise of the state as a public service facilitator, of the shifting precariousness of the job market in which women of all ages take very low paid jobs that more established workers would refuse. In short, I claim that the hardships imposed by changes in the labor market were not accompanied by the kinds of changes in family and community structures in poor neighborhoods that might have eased the transition. This may have a devastating effect, increasing the number of at-risk youths with inferior work skills and who are more prone to delinquency and drug consumption.

The Rise in Crime in Mexico

The data for Mexico does not exactly replicate that for Buenos Aires, but similar patterns are apparent.

Unemployment

Male youth unemployment rates in Mexico City rose sharply in the mid-1990s from relatively low rates at the beginning of the decade. As shown in Graph 3.12, this correlates strongly with two measures of property crime. As in Buenos Aires, it appears to have a one or two year lag effect, suggesting that youths who fail to find jobs do not opt for delinquency immediately.

Labor Market

In terms of the composition of the labor market and family structure Mexico differs from Argentina. In Mexico, lower class women have historically participated more actively in the labor market, and family

Graph 3.12 Property Crimes and Young Male Unemployment in Mexico City

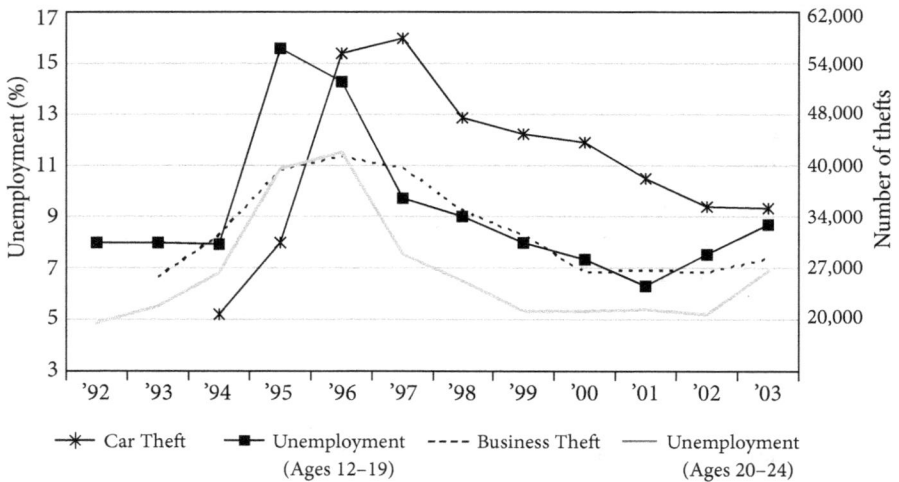

Source: Own elaboration based on INEGI (2005) and ICESI serie histórica at http://www.icesi.org.mx.

structure is "looser" (poor women have a longer history of being the heads of households and bearing responsibility for child rearing). There is, however, a remarkably similar trend when it comes to the incorporation of relatively mature women into the labor market (as compared to younger women). Graph 3.13 presents data for women in different age categories. The lines represent the share of working women in Mexico City who work out of the total of women in that age category. As in Buenos Aires, the percentage of younger women decreased their participation in the labor force, middle aged women remained steady with a slight upward trend, and mature women increased their share in the labor market.

Although the series starts in 1998 the differences for younger and mature women between that year and 2003 are statistically significant. It is likely that this is a continuous trend that started in the 1980s or in the early 1990s. The large proportion of mature women entering the labor force implies that there is less supervision of children in the household

Graph 3.13 Participation of Women in the Labor Market in Mexico City

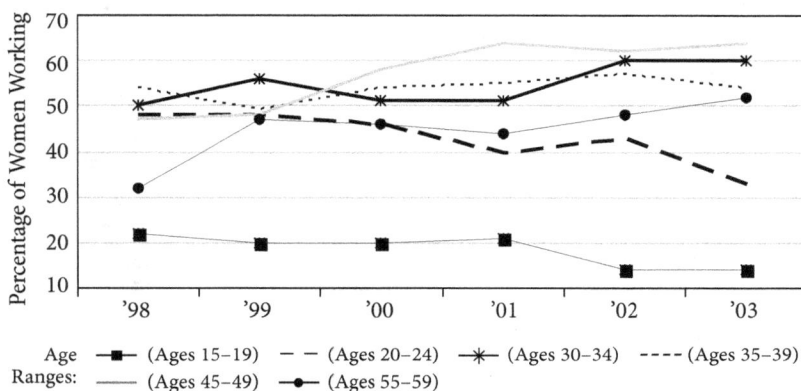

Source: Own elaboration based on the economically active population (EAP). See: http://www .incgi.gob.mx.

(a large portion of working class mothers are single and are helped with child rearing by older female family members). A second drastic change in labor market structure is the share of women who enter the labor market. As table 3.9 shows, over a ten-year period more mothers with children are entering the labor force.

These transformations correlate with an increase in criminality. The implications are similar to those found in Argentina. There is likely to be a higher number of unsupervised children, given depleted social services (poor schooling and after school programs, among others), lower investment in community structures, and the fact that more mothers are entering the labor force and fewer grandmothers or other family members are available to help rear children. Some of these children have ultimately taken the path of delinquency.

CONCLUSION

Why has crime risen so rapidly in Buenos Aires and Mexico? What factors account for rising crime and for the significant changes that occurred over a very brief period of time? Demographic trends are usually

Table 3.9 Percentage of Mothers Who Are Part of the Economically Active Population

	1–2 children	*3–5 children*
1995	24.2	23.0
1996	26.0	23.5
1997	24.9	24.1
1998	26.2	24.5
1999	27.3	24.7
2000	28.3	25.1
2001	28.8	25.5
2002	29.4	25.9
2003	29.3	27.0
2004	30.9	27.1

Source: Own elaboration based on labor data from INEGI at http://dgcnesyp.inegi.gob.mx.

incremental and partially explain the trend, but slow changes in population composition (relative size cohorts, changes in family structure) cannot explain sharp rises. It is argued here that transformations of the labor market and a rapid deterioration of social services have had a direct and indirect effect upon the rapid rise in criminal activity. Graphs 3.10 and 3.12 clearly suggest that major changes in employment structures are strongly associated with criminality. The two-fold rise in unemployment among young males parallels the two-fold increase in reported crime. This robust evidence suggests that adverse labor market conditions have a significant causal effect on crime.

At the macrolevel, the institutional demise of the state, economic transformation without safety nets, and the acute impact of high unemployment among youths explain rising crime. These changes had a devastating effect on lower income populations. However, as accumulated research has demonstrated, unemployment and socioeconomic status have an indirect effect on delinquency. Family structure also correlates powerfully with future delinquent behavior (Farrington 1998; Nagin and Patternoster 1993; Sampson and Laub 1993). Growing up in poverty among larger cohorts with diminished social resources and in a context of dwindling guardianship and other social control mechanisms has increased the likelihood of youths engaging in delinquent behavior. Although no data at the individual level are available to measure the exact magnitude of such effects, the impact of these social changes on the coming of age of new economically deprived cohorts is noticeable. The aggregate data presented here suggest that such deep and sudden changes in the social fabric have a profound impact on traditional patterns of control and result in the eruption of crime. The findings in this chapter also support Sampson's argument (leaving aside the racial aspect of his study) about the indirect effect of significant changes in female occupational status (Sampson 1987b). These major transformations in the structure of labor markets directly affect family and community by changing macro-level patterns of guardianship. The decreasing age of criminals in Buenos Aires and Mexico suggests that juvenile delinquency and the unprecedented levels of violence are related to family disruption and the breakdown of the community.

This chapter suggests that Argentina and Mexico are in the midst of major ongoing structural social transformations. The widespread incorporation of women into the work force and the scarcity of jobs for youths and males are changing traditional family organization and communities, transforming patterns of control, and changing child rearing practices. Family disruption has been a good predictor of juvenile violence and delinquency (Sampson and Grove 1989; Gottfredson and Hirschi 1990), and the data indicate that such disruption is increasingly due to dramatic shifts in the labor market. These major social and cultural transformations have generated the conditions associated with higher criminality. Moreover, when institutions that work to detect and punish or prevent and contain crime perform poorly (as is the case in Argentina), or very badly indeed (as they do in Mexico), there is a further lowering of the already subjectively perceived low costs of crime among offenders.

This chapter has presented initial evidence of the dramatic rise in crime in the cities of Buenos Aires and Mexico City, and shown that there was a sharp increase in the mid-1990s. It presents a set of plausible variables closely associated with the availability of firearms, increased unemployment, greater consumption of drugs, and rising dropout rates, among other factors. However, it has also argued that it is necessary to study the profound changes in social institutions over the last fifteen years in order to increase our understanding of why there was substantially more crime in the late 1990s than during the preceding decade. The precise connection between "marginality," the "underclass," unemployment, drugs, and crime needs to be researched on the basis of how crime has affected new generations, among which a greater proportion of youths reaching adolescence and maturity are prone to delinquency than was the case in the past.

NOTES

1. Particularly in cities where statistics are not collected systematically, homicides are the most reliably registered criminal offenses.

2. Ministry of Justice 1998. It should be noted that there are many doubts as to the quality of data. For instance, the "robbing passersby" crime in DF was 4,600 per 100,000 inhabitants in 1994, and increased steadily by approximately 20 percent a year until it peaked at 13,500 in 1999. In 2000 it dropped by half to 6,600 and remained constant until 2003 (6,100). There is no reasonable or sensible explanation for the 48 percent reduction between 1999 and 2000.

3. Latinobarómetro 2005.

4. For various studies of several Latin American cities see Fajnzylber, Lederman, and Loayza 2001. Other standard variables tested such as alcohol and drugs, lifestyle, among other factors, were unfortunately unavailable.

5. In 2000, in greater Buenos Aires there were 320,000 adolescents and young adults who did not work or attend school. In the first quintile (under the poverty line) 116,000 (85 percent males) and in the second quintile an additional 90,000 youngsters are idle. In poor households, one out of four adolescents faces everyday idleness. This "marginality" or "underclass" condition increased after 1992 by 62 percent (*Clarín*, March 24, 2000).

6. In 1980, 12 percent of households in greater Buenos Aires (the outskirts of the Federal District) were headed by females, compared to 21 percent in 1998 and 29 percent in 2000.

7. The police departments in the Federal District, and in the suburban Buenos Aires area in particular, faced major institutional reforms that led, paradoxically, to higher crime rates during those years. Accounts of police corruption have mushroomed in the last ten years. Suspicions of police-force links to the bombing of the Jewish community headquarters in 1994 triggered several investigations that yielded detailed accounts of corruption networks permeating all levels of the police. In 1997 and in 1999 two major overhauls of the police department failed to create a more efficient force. Police officers have been known to act as behind-the-scenes coordinators of drug trafficking, ransom

schemes, and protection rackets. In some cases, they even temporarily released inmates for a few days in exchange for a fixed percentage of inmates' criminal revenues.

8. Unfortunately, there are no reliable historical data on drug consumption. However, the explosion of crime is closely related to the large-scale commercialization and consumption of drugs in greater Buenos Aires. Since the majority of homicides were robbery related, one cannot really compare rising crime in greater Buenos Aires with the U.S. crack-induced eruption in crime in the late 1980s. Nonetheless, there is evidence that suggests that many offenders consume drugs regularly, a qualitative difference between the late 1980s and early 1990s (Ministry of Justice 1998).

9. See Kessler 2004 (chapter 7) for a description of the inability of schools to deter youths from becoming delinquents.

10. Reported in *Clarín*, March 24, 2000.

PART 2

Police and Criminal Justice Reform

CHAPTER FOUR

La Mano Dura

Current Dilemmas in Latin American Police Reform

MARK UNGAR

Amid mounting crime in Latin America over the past ten years—including a 41 percent rise in homicides that has made it the world's most crime-ridden region[1]—governments throughout the region have enacted a wide range of reforms to make the police more effective and accountable. While such changes extend over a broad range of proposals, most fall into three general areas. First is structural reorganization of police agencies through regional decentralization, simplified hierarchies, more professionalized security, oversight and disciplinary bodies, and other measures to improve efficiency, professionalism, and accountability. Second, since the early 1990s, fourteen countries have addressed their notoriously slow and biased criminal justice systems—most of which resolve fewer than 2 percent of homicides—with new penal process codes to strengthen defendant and due process rights, replace slow and biased written procedures with oral trials, transfer investigative authorities from the police to prosecutors (*fiscales*) in the Attorney General's Office (*Ministerio Público*, MP), create investigative and sentencing courts, and improve institutional cooperation. The third change is the introduction of community policing, which aims to empower citizens to respond directly to crime through neighborhood patrols, education programs, social services, and councils comprised of citizens, politicians, and police officials. Often, police restructuring measures to increase policy-citizen interaction, such as giving more autonomy to neighborhood police commissioners (*comisarios*), supplement community policing. In addition to reducing violence, community policing is also one of the most popular bases of police reform around the world because it bypasses dysfunctional criminal justice systems.

While many of these reforms are new and so have yet to show results, most of them have already been weakened and undermined—even those that have been carefully formulated and gained broad support. The range and complexity of obstacles to reform is as wide as the reforms themselves, of course, but this chapter identifies three interrelated levels of obstruction that begin to demonstrate the challenges facing attempts to reform Latin America's police. I describe these obstacles and show how they reinforce each other in four countries in each of the main subregions of Latin America with highly different political and socioeconomic conditions: Honduras, Venezuela, Bolivia, and Argentina. I explain how the interaction of political, legal, and functional obstacles in each case undermines promising police reforms and lead instead to a *mano dura* (iron fist) approach. In doing so, I also explain how community policing is helping overcome those obstacles. In fact, as is stressed in this volume, specifying impediments to change is one of the best ways to understand what kinds of reforms may be actually realistic and feasible.

OBSTACLES TO REFORM

The first type of obstacle to reform is political. On one level, changes to established practices usually clash with the interests of police forces and state officials—that is, with those responsible for implementing any police reform. Most alterations of police functioning are seen as meddling or as punitive means to reduce police power, so obstruction by police and criminal justice agencies is common. Even reform packages that balance such changes with rewards such as higher pay and better technology may still fall prey to such resistance. On a broader level, political pressures to crack down on crime—the first or second concern in national polls throughout Latin America since the mid-1990s—undermine police reforms.[2] Most governments have been unable to develop effective long-term policy responses due to financial limitations, sharpening political divisions, and the state's institutional incapacities. Far easier and more popular is a *mano dura* approach by presidents and governors, who, usually limited to one term, want immediate results. *Mano dura* is a toughened version of "zero tolerance," a policy based on the "broken windows" theory,[3] which argues that petty crimes, intimidation, and physical deterioration are the real causes of crime because they scare off law-abiding citizens and allow delinquency to take root in an area. Detentions for misdemeanors and antisocial behavior would therefore prevent the conditions in which crime grows, taking criminals off the street and catching those with illegal arms or wanted for outstanding crimes. This policy is said to have brought about the record-breaking drop in homicides of 71 percent in New York City between 1990 and 1998.[4] In Latin America, of course, zero tolerance is a newcomer, compared to *mano dura* policing, but the success of the former in New York serves to justify the latter. To be both effective and remain within the bounds of civil rights, though, zero tolerance requires solid training for police officers, consistent oversight over their practices, coordination with social services to resolve the problems that lead to public disorder, and more effective courts to process detainees. But in Latin America, zero tolerance is applied without such supports or outside controls, so that the *mano dura* is often just a continuation of predemocratic practices and a justification for the dividing line drawn by many officials between "public order," associated with a strong state, and "human rights," associated with delinquency.

The politicization of police reforms further damages their prospects. Political parties often reject plans enacted by their predecessors in office, while the frequent rotation of security ministers during one administration further impedes change. Moreover, many reforms that attempt to control or oversee the police are enacted as a reaction to specific abuse or in the midst of political change, which usually means that support for them dries up once those temporary political conditions pass. When they do not, attacks on reforms as "soft on crime"—often orchestrated by the police or opposition parties—effectively stop any change. Politicization also affects community policing. In many countries, police actively discourage the citizen participation needed for such programs, marginalize police in the program as "social workers," and often control or manipulate citizen-based security councils. Even international aid, particularly in the form of drug eradication and interdiction policing, may run contrary to reform. In both producer and transit countries—which include most of the Andean and Central American nations—the U.S. focus on antitrafficking efforts has let governments ignore abuses by police forces pulled into the drug war as well as deterioration of penal reforms that the U.S. supported.

The second type of obstruction to police reform is legal. The basis of police reform in Latin America is a set of new laws, particularly new penal process codes, fortified due process, and judicial restructuring. But several elements impede the implementation of these measures. First, as part of the zero tolerance approach, many countries are using police edicts from the past and introducing laws that further increase the police's unregulated control over citizens. Throughout the history of the region, the police have been greatly empowered by edicts and other misdemeanor regulations. Until the mid-1990s, for example, most police activity in Buenos Aires was taken under unregulated edicts, such as for disorderly conduct; and in Venezuela, the 1939 Law of Vagabonds and Crooks allowed detention of anyone deemed "suspicious" until it was finally declared unconstitutional in 1997. In nearly every country where such regulations have been struck down, governments try to reinstate them by stepping up use of other regulations or enacting new "social control" laws that erode the due process rights of new penal processes and the accountability mechanisms of restructuring reforms. What is more, many of those reforms have yet to be implemented and enforced. Above all, most new penal process codes lack the funding, training, and political support that is necessary for implementation. The new codes are subsequently criticized for being "ineffective," which only serves to undermine them further.

A third obstruction to reform is institutional: most police forces simply do not function well enough to absorb change. The quality of policing varies widely, of course, but similar problems afflict it all over the region. First, there is poor coordination among the preventative and investigative branches, as well as among geographic entities. Inadequate or nonexistent information sharing, institutional territoriality, and other limitations, all prevent the cooperation needed for effective and geographically uniform law enforcement. The extraordinary proliferation of police units, as discussed below, has greatly aggravated this lack of coordination. Second, the working conditions of most officers—characterized by inadequate training, low salaries, professional insecurity, archaic hierarchies, and exhausting work schedules—make officers reluctant to take on the extra work needed to implement new policies. Such institutional limitations even make it difficult for officers to carry out their most important tasks, from patrols to investigation. Throughout Latin America, basic criminal investigation steps such as crime scene protection and forensics are executed poorly, and there is little citizen cooperation to obtain the necessary evidence and witnesses. Without adequate funding or societal trust, frustrated police forces resort to blunt, abusive, and ineffective tactics like rounding up suspects, raiding neighborhoods, and intimidating witnesses. Finally, as the cases discussed below illustrate, the financial and professional accountability needed to keep agencies efficient and honest is absent.

HONDURAS

Honduras's extremely high rates of violent crime have undermined its promising police reforms, which were based on a 1996 constitutional reform that created a civilian police force, the 1997 Police Law and Organic Police Law, a new penal process code, and judicial reforms such as the establishment of a judicial council to select most judges. But as the limits of the *mano dura* become apparent, the country's popular community policing program provides a viable alternative.

Dismantling of most reforms began with the aggressive "zero tolerance" policy of the National Party government of President Ricardo Maduro. A businessman whose son was killed by criminals, Maduro was elected in 2002 on an anticrime campaign platform. The focus of his policy was the youth gangs (*maras*), which even the police acknowledge commit less than a third of all crimes but are nonetheless held responsible for the crime problem. Anti-*mara* rhetoric saturates the media and—with high levels of approval from the public, Congress, and the judiciary—dominates criminal legislation. The centerpiece of this legal change was Provision 332, an amendment to the penal code, which punishes gang membership with nine to twelve years' imprisonment. In two of the country's main prisons, over a third of gang members are incarcerated under Provision 332. The Law of Police and Social Coexistence (*Ley de Policía y de Convivencia Social*) also allows officers to "control" people in a certain area in order to fight crime and to detain arbitrarily "vagabonds"—people who have no honest means to earn a living or are suspected of intending to engage in criminal activities.

This approach rests on what officials consider a stark choice between fighting crime and protecting rights. As Maduro's Minister of Security asserted, the new penal code embodies the *garantista* approach of rights protection, is ineffective to combat crime, and should be scrapped.[5] Many gang members now shun tattoos and other overt marks of gang membership, for example, which often leads prosecutors and judges to declare insufficient proof to convict under the new penal process code. This reluctance to prosecute angers state officials, aggravating the split between the *garantista* and *mano dura* approaches. Along with the lack of training to implement the new penal process code, the new law has also encouraged increased use of mass raids, extended preventative detention, forced confessions, and extrajudicial killings of suspected *mareros* (gang members). Most state officials agree off the record with the estimate of 2,300 extrajudicial killings of youth and children from 1998 to 2005. Of the approximately 1,600 such killings between 1999 and 2003, 39 percent had evidence of police involvement.[6] Youths living on the street complain of continual harassment,[7] and residents of poor neighborhoods report that unmarked vans roam areas like basketball courts where youths congregate. Some human rights commission officials estimate that over 80 percent of detainees are beaten and that already overwhelmed judges and *fiscales* do not investigate these instances of abuses.[8]

Implementation of reform is also difficult because the police are poorly prepared, funded, and equipped. The six months of cadet training focuses on the use of firearms, and there is little legal or sociological education. Many police officers are functionally illiterate, their average monthly wage of US$225 is inadequate for a middle class existence, and their seventeen-hour shifts are taxing. There is a chronic lack of personnel—even in San Pedro's Choloma, a test case for community policing, there are only ten officers and one permanent vehicle to cover seventy thousand residents. Also hurting all three areas of reform is the poor investigative capacity of the police. About 90 percent of the force's budget goes to the Preventative Police (PP), while the Investigative Police (Dirección General de Investigación Criminal, DGIC) has only five hundred officials compared to the nine-thousand-strong PP. Although receiving practically no investigative training, PP officers intimidate witnesses, inadequately protect crime scenes, and pass themselves off as detectives to conduct their own parallel investigations. As a result, officials say, only crimes where the perpetrator is caught *in flagrante delicto* are likely to be resolved. State officials agree with this assessment, but their proposed solutions center on augmenting police power—such as by giving it more than twenty-four hours to investigate a detainee. The lack of a centralized information network also inhibits effective responses. As in many other countries, the drug war has further militarized the police and brought the military into regular policing. Since 2002, soldiers have been used in police sweeps and inundations of gang-controlled urban areas and to control prison riots. Such tactics are effective in the short-term, but they are abusive and inappropriate because soldiers are trained for war, not citizen security. Thus, many of the victims of prison massacres in April 2002 and June 2004 were killed by soldiers who had been sent to restore order. [9]

Exacerbating the situation, the accountability agencies that were a cornerstone of police structuring have been weakened. The main such agencies are the National Council of Interior Security (Consejo Nacional de Seguridad Interior, CONASIN), which advises the government on criminal policy, and the Internal Affairs Unit (Unidad de Asuntos Internos, UAI), which investigates police wrongdoing. CONASIN is rarely convened, removing an important check on state policy.[10] And many concur with the view that since it was established in 1997 and given control over nearly all police agencies, the Security Secretariat initiated a "process of counter-reform and deterioration of the police . . . characterized by halting the process of depuration of corrupt officers and those involved in right violations and in death squads."[11] In turn, the UAI is weak because of deficient resources, unclear regulations, and rivalry with the Security Secretariat's Office of Professional Responsibility, which the new police law was supposed to eliminate. The most controversial issue, however, is UAI investigation of youth killings. After an investigation in September 2002, UAI Chief María Luisa Borjas,[12] who implicated Security Ministry and Police officials in at least twenty extrajudicial executions of youths, immediately began to receive death threats, her staff was reduced, and two months later she was suspended for allegedly failing to present proof of her claims. Although continuing pressure and bad publicity led the government to create the Commission on Summary Executions, to date the commission has not published a report or initiated prosecutions. Honduran *fiscales* can also investigate police wrongdoing—but lack the institutional, political, and legal power to instigate real change. The country's Human Rights Prosecutor complains that any investigation of the police is constantly delayed and obstructed, and that there is a lack of will and personnel to follow up on cases.[13]

The national community policing program, Safer Community (*Comunidad Más Segura*), is based on a different approach. It started in 2002 and now operates in thirty of the country's most crime-ridden areas, and its preventative strategies, such as regular community meetings and fixing street lights, have led to a marked decline in homicides, robberies, and domestic violence. In the San Pedro Sula Valley city of Choloma, for instance, where regular community meetings are held,[14] both police and citizens reported a steep drop in homicides after the program began. There has been police and citizen violence associated with the program.[15] The head of community policing of one district was arrested in connection with police killing youths, for example, and a member of the citizen policing group in La Ceiba said that they used it to attack suspected delinquents.[16] But the drop in violence and popular support for community policing—with 89.9 percent of citizens in a survey expressing more confidence in the police[17]—led President Manuel Zelaya, Maduro's successor, to strengthen it. Some of the harmful effects of *mano dura* may lessen over time, but the government will under pressure use this approach if the security system remains unable to bring crime under control (homicides continue at the astonishing rate of 46.2 per 100,000).[18]

VENEZUELA

Although it is a far wealthier country than Honduras, and is led by a "leftist" government, Venezuela has likewise undermined both enacted and proposed police reform. As long-standing demands for a *mano dura* clash with the hands-off approach to police by the government of President Hugo Chávez, police reform has been effectively paralyzed. With the country's crime rate increasing nonstop over the past twenty years, security is a foremost public concern. In the 1990s, homicides rose by over 75 percent, and by another 67 percent between 1999 and 2006.[19] In the Federal District (*Distrito Federal,* DF), which encompasses Caracas and the surrounding areas, murder soared by 506 percent in the 1990s.[20] There is not only more crime, but more of it is violent. The proportion of property crimes that were violent increased from 16 percent in 1990 to 46.2 percent in 2002,[21] while violent crime as a whole increased by more than 150 percent between 2001 and 2002.[22] Only four other countries in the world—Russia, South Africa, El Salvador, and Colombia—are now more dangerous than Venezuela.

There have been various policy responses to address this problem, but they have had little impact. Even the proliferation of police forces has not solved the problem (105 new police forces have been set up since 1990, an increase of 363 percent). At the national level, the criminal justice police (Cuerpo de Investigaciones Científicas, Penales and Criminalísticas, CICPC) and the Office of Intelligence and Prevention Services (Dirección Sectoral de los Servicios de Inteligencia y Prevención, DISIP), which operate under the aegis of the Ministry of the Interior and Justice (Ministerio del Interior y Justicia, MIJ), investigate national security crimes. The military police have also become involved in policing, including the National Guard (Guardia National, GN), the Defense Ministry Office of Military Intelligence (Dirección de Inteligencia Militar, DIM), and the Office of Army Intelligence (Dirección of Inteligencia del Ejército, DIE). The country's twenty-three states have police forces that operate at the regional level, and there are hundreds of municipal forces at the local level, most created in accordance with the provisions of the 1989 Decentralization Law. Responsibility for policing of the Federal District lies with the Metropolitan Police (Policía Metropolitana, PM), which operates alongside nearly a dozen municipal forces, many hostile to one another because of mayoral political alliances.

A powerful and politicized police force is part of the modern Venezuelan state. After the 1958 democratic transition, the police became an instrument of a strong presidency and of the political parties. In this context, Congress rarely enacted legislation on police structure, training, or budget. Lack of oversight has led to widespread abuses and to the emergence of irregular forces, including death squads linked to the police.[23] After defeating the leftist guerrillas in the 1970s, the government addressed common crime with strategies such as mass round-ups in poor urban *barrios*. Attempts to reform the police in the 1980s foundered because of deteriorating economic and political conditions. After 1998, policing was politicized in the context of the confrontation between President Hugo Chávez and his opposition. Armed clashes have become routine in the Federal District. The opposition complains about repression by police forces controlled by Chávez allies and by the dozens of armed pro-Chávez Bolivarian Circles (*círculos bolivarianos*), while government allies criticize the PM and other opposition-controlled police agencies. One Congressman accused the PM of being "criminal and repressive," and claimed that anti-Chávez mayors allow police to kill progovernment figures.[24]

In this context of conflict, policing policy is formulated haphazardly, and often politicized. The 2001 Citizen Security Coordination Law, for example, formed councils to coordinate security agencies but did not specify how they would function in practice. In response to a 58 percent increase in firearm killings,[25] the 2002 Disarmament Law provided economic incentives to turn in privately owned firearms, but with little of the cooperation with community groups that would be necessary to actually collect the weapons. More seriously, the 2006 Police Reform Commission, which was established in 2006 and which made proposals to carry out extensive national surveys, is being undermined by politics and institutional instability. The Commission was the initiative of Jesse Chacón, the ninth Minister of Interior and Justice since Chávez was elected in 1998. Chávez declined to continue this work after firing Chacón in January 2007 and has since proposed sweeping constitutional changes that undermine the detailed recommendations of the commission.

As in other countries, Venezuela's 1998 penal process code has also been a casualty of political and institutional obstruction.[26] Detectives accuse prosecutors of continuing to protect the rights of detainees as under the old code and not prosecuting them as mandated by the new code (as they might say, "we speak different languages"). Although prosecutors reject such accusations,[27] delays and abuses continue. A September 2001 investigation at the CICPC discovered that there were fourteen thousand uninvestigated crime reports, while police agents continue to withhold information from judges, use false witnesses, tamper with evidence, and coerce confessions[28]—justifying such actions with their belief that judges want to stop preventative detention and that public defenders hide incriminating evidence.

As in Honduras and elsewhere, street policing gets far more resources than investigative work. Just about two percent of Venezuelan police work in the CICPC,[29] which had the same budget in 2003 as it did in 1999, and needs, its detectives claim, to triple its ten-thousand-officer body.[30] *Razzias* (mass roundups) are common in poor neighborhoods, as are "confrontations" with the police that end in the death of suspects. Indeed, law enforcement is particularly violent in Venezuela, with death resulting in over 40 percent of incidents of civilian resistance—one of Latin America's highest rates.[31] As in other countries, edicts and exceptions—from detentions for identification to illegal curfews—fortify the street powers of the police. The use of military forces for policing also increases tensions. Although deployment of the GN has lowered crime rates,[32] the use of tanks, machine guns, and other military equipment for policing has increased the rate of excessive force.

Meanwhile, internal police discipline is weak and only vaguely regulated by norms covering the use of arms and detainee mistreatment. About 90 percent of police rights violations go unpunished.[33] Most police forces still lack professional security, sufficient salaries, health benefits, and manageable schedules. According to police forces themselves, basic training is poor—particularly on social conditions, the use of firearms, and human rights. What is more, as in other countries, Venezuelan policing is balkanized: the wealthy eastern half of the city of Caracas, for instance, has ten times more police officers than the poor western half, where over 70 percent of the city's residents live. Most of the crimes—over two-thirds of the total and 43 percent of them violent—occur in the biggest Western municipality, Libertador.[34]

Given all of the above, citizens lack confidence in the police[35]—a view confirmed by the police, who recognize that society sees them "as an enemy."[36] The only solution both sides agree on is a *mano dura* approach. According to one poll, 60 percent favor more violence to combat crime, and 47 percent favor the killing of criminals by the police.[37] Some opt to do this themselves, getting involved in vigilantism, a phenomenon that first came to public attention in the early 1990s with calls for *barrio* residents to "declare war" against delinquency. Even in *barrios* with better physical conditions and community organization, meetings of "self defense" groups attract large attendance.[38] Lynching has become more open and brazen, with bodies often left in the middle of the street, and victims include not just criminals but also those accused of some form of "disrespect."[39] Para-police squads and criminal extermination groups have also stepped into the vacuum created by the lack of effective policing. These groups, many of which are comprised of police and funded by trafficking of contraband, have been responsible for hundreds of killings in at least seven states and the Federal District.[40]

BOLIVIA

Despite at least twelve security plans and an ever-increasing police budget, common crime in Bolivia has more than tripled since the transition to democracy in 1982.[41] The problem of maintaining public and political order, which is even more urgent, has compounded the country's security crisis. Two presidents fell after 2003 amid increasing levels of inequality, secessionist pressures, a destructive war on drugs, and growing public protest. By their own admission, the police, ranked in polls as the country's most (or second most) corrupt and untrustworthy institution, have responded to an "ungrateful" population,[42] with "brutality, authoritarianism, and violence."[43] The last two presidents have attempted to address the police's weaknesses head on. Carlos Mesa, who assumed the presidency after Gonzalo Sánchez de Lozada was ousted in October 2003 (partly as a result of police strikes), focused on police corruption, while his successor, Evo Morales, has been attempting to make the police more accountable to human rights standards.

Corruption is the most serious problem: many top officials view it as "profound" and "systemic." Since 1982, when Bolivia began to democratize, the country has had nearly one commander per year. Of them, eighteen were forced out because of involvement in criminal activities, cover-ups, or related malfeasance. Top officials have covered up crimes, tortured detainees, organized burglaries, and extracted money for speeding up or slowing down court cases. Forced entry without warrants, illegal confiscation, extrajudicial shootings—implicitly allowed by edicts and anti-drug laws and tolerated by police superiors—are common, as is police extortion, kidnapping, and trafficking in drugs, arms, and vehicles. The extent of corruption was demonstrated in 2003: after the Interior Ministry purged the 290 officials running the Palmasola prison for taking money from prisoners to leave the prison, an entirely new staff had the same practice up and running a day later. Most inquiries into such abuses lack teeth: investigations into twenty-five of the country's seventy-seven senior police commanders have not been concluded. Efforts to strengthen Internal Affairs in 2002 did not go far.[44]

The greatest source of corruption is police control over its own finances, which is "not known" to outsiders.[45] The retirement fund processes illicit funds, budget chiefs often overcharge contracts by "up to a million dollars,"[46] and the Customs Police (Unidad de Control Operativo Aduanero, COA) has paid officers after they have been fired.[47] The police's National Identification Directorate (Dirección Nacional de Identificación Personal, DNIP) each year earns millions of dollars—only about 15 percent of which is given to the Government Ministry—from fees to citizens to issue and replace about eighteen million identity papers (such as drivers' licenses and identification cards).[48] The "dual" income from legal and illegal sources allows the police to ignore state directives.[49] The police have a generous budget compared to other state agencies (the Government Ministry's budget, 82 percent of which goes to the police, increased by over 50 percent between 2000 and 2004).[50] Even with such increases, budget centralization limits efficiency, forcing regional units to foster compensatory corruption networks. According to the Police Reform Commission, Law 1178 (or the SAFCO law), which promotes transparent state financial management, is not fully applied to the police.[51]

The other main problem has been violence stemming from the anticoca eradication campaign, responsible for most of killings by police since 1990.[52] Economic liberalization in the 1980s made coca one of the more secure sources of income in rural regions. But in 1998, President Hugo Banzer enacted the intensive U.S.-backed anti-coca *Plan Dignidad* with a clumsily applied crop substitution program that eliminated illegal coca in most targeted areas but provided few of the promised economic alternatives.[53] The plan involved creation of many new police agencies, often in coordination with the military and some supported by separate drug courts and prisons. The main agency, the Special Antinarcotics Force (Fuerza Especial de Lucha Contra el Narcotráfico, FELCN), has its own intelligence service, and runs the Rural Area Police Patrol Unit (Unidad Móvil de Patrullaje Rural, UMOPAR). Other new forces were the Joint Task Force (Fuerza de Tarea Conjunta, FTC), a combined police and military operation, and the Expeditionary Task Force (Fuerza de Tarea Expedicionaria, FTE), both funded and trained by the U.S. In both the coca areas and in La Paz, security forces responded to widespread protests with states of siege, mass detentions, and in some cases armed clashes with *cocaleros* (coca growers). As a result of this violence, FTC and FTE forces have been downsized or removed from the coca-growing regions.

There have been some encouraging reforms. Most accusations against police are directed to the Office of Professional Responsibility (Dirección Nacional de Responsibilidad Profesional, DNRP), which investigates them and sends those with sufficient evidence to the Superior Disciplinary Tribunal (Tribunal Disciplinar Superior, TDS), which tries and disciplines the accused. Although the DNRP was considered the place "where complaints die,"[54] prodding by the U.S. led the Bolivian government to modify the police disciplinary code to increase efficiency and more effectively protect the rights of the accused. As a result, in 2004 the TDS processed 70 percent more officials than in 2003, a jump from 550 to 920 cases.[55] The police academy (Academia Nacional de Policía, ANAPOL) was also overhauled, reducing physical preparation from about 50 percent to 10 percent of the time. Encouraged by the government, the Fiscalía has been better able to prosecute high-level cases, including the first-ever conviction of police generals in December 2004 for involvement in the fatal holdup of a truck transporting currency.

Despite these important steps, Bolivia's police reforms have yet to address the causes of poor and abusive policing. Aside from a few high-profile prosecutions, the vast majority of cases handled by the police disciplinary system were for desertion among noncommissioned ranks of the two-tiered structure (about 85 percent of the approximately twenty thousand police personnel), which is rooted in their low pay and poor working conditions. Reflecting the country's sharp ethnic and class divisions, most noncommissioned officials are from the indigenous groups that comprise the majority of the population, and the broader discrimination against indigenous people is replicated within the police, compounding internal divisions. While education has improved, the constant rotation of officials prevents them from developing expertise in their area of work and acquiring the control over an agency needed to monitor and improve it. Indeed, rotation and lack of expertise are the central complaints of the judicial police chief.[56] Entrenched favoritism in the annual promotion process, which a former security minister characterizes as a "total war,"[57] also fuels corruption further by allowing corrupt officers to rise up the ranks.

Reform is limited by inconsistent law enforcement as well. The Organic Police Law (the main legal instrument) does not discuss human rights at length, while edicts and anti-drug laws often encourage abuse, although some of its more controversial provisions were eliminated, for example, the 1988 anti-trafficking law (1008), which violates due process by, for instance, prohibiting pretrial release. Like Colombia and Peru, Bolivia's special courts for drug-trafficking and terrorism often lack transparency or fail to comply with due process. The Ombudsman (Defensoría del Pueblo), the country's main accountability agency, is empowered to challenge such abuses, but has been blocked by a stonewalling executive and by inefficient courts. A former *defensora*, Ana María Romero de Campero, complained of haplessly trying to block unconstitutional state actions such as intrusions on citizen privacy and the use of clandestine agents. Such efforts caught her up in the false division between rights and security, with many labeling her a "*defensora* of Delinquents."[58]

Most generally, police reforms remain unrealistic. Like many of its predecessors, the latest (and now defunct) security reform, the 2003–2007 Institutional Strategic Plan[59] was a compendium of excellent ideas lacking institutional support. It included measures to control corruption with new disciplinary regulations; better education, housing, and health services for the police; economic incentives for police work; improving the public image of the police; and creating a Police Treasury to control police finances. While U.S. support led to improvements in the first two areas, the rest fell by the wayside given the absence of adequate financial, institutional, or political backing. The absence of such support also affected the 1999 penal process code. Despite training of criminal justice officials by UN and U.S. officials,[60] along with steps to increase public access and support,[61] there has been a dire lack of training for police, public defenders, and prosecutors in the code's provisions on gathering evidence, interviewing suspects, protecting crime scenes, and conducting oral trials. The result is a mix of inquisitorial and oral procedures, which, along with a lack of mechanisms to ensure transparency and sharing of information between police and prosecutors, leads to only about one in every five cases going to trial.[62]

As in Honduras and other countries, though, the most effective security reforms in Bolivia are coming from below. Based on legal reforms such as the 1994 Law of Popular Participation (Ley de Participación Popular, LPP) and flourishing citizen-police units such as Neighborhood Security Brigades (Brigadas de Seguridad Vecinal) and School Brigades (Brigadas Escolares), community policing has gained momentum around the country. In 2006, for example, the city of La Paz launched a Neighborhoods of Truth Program (Programa Barrios de Verdad) to stimulate citizen development of security policy in low-income areas,[63] as well as a community police project to build police centers, teach seminars on issues from crime reporting to family violence, and form neighborhood brigades made up of residents and police officers. While the president's popularity will help sustain these efforts, demands by regional government for control over policing may undermine them by increasing instability in police structure and criminal policy. Along with continuing crime, such politics will continue to make long-term change an uphill struggle in Bolivia.

ARGENTINA

Although police reform in Argentina also suffers from similar political, legal, and institutional obstacles, this section describes how they have been minimized more successfully through new laws, initiatives, and community policing programs. Such reforms also show how authoritarian legacies, stronger in Argentina than most of Latin America, can be overcome. Historically, the Argentine police played a central role in repression under democratic and military regimes alike. The 1983 transition to democracy brought with it personnel purges, new rights guarantees, and other reforms in some of the twenty-four provincial police forces as well as in the federal police agency, the Argentine Federal Police (Policía Federal Argentina, PFA), which enforces law in the federal capital and federal law throughout the country. However, in most of the provinces there was continuity in police structure and authority. And when military unrest and economic crisis in the late 1980s sidetracked police reform, the government of President Carlos Menem (1989–1999) built up the security apparatus and gave police agencies broad new powers, particularly allowing them to act to prevent crime at the "precriminal" stage. As crime increased to record levels in the 1990s (along with unemployment, inequality, and poverty) and criminal justice remained slow, public demands for a *mano dura* approach increased.[64] Greater controls over the police tended to come only after specific incidents of abuse.[65]

However, in provinces where a *mano dura* approach failed to work, the public started to believe that the police were too involved in corrupt activities to be effective, and began to support reform. The provinces where such pressure resulted in the most widespread reforms were Buenos Aires and Mendoza. In Buenos Aires, then governor and presidential hopeful Eduardo Duhalde overhauled the notoriously violent and corrupt police in 1997. The force was decentralized into eighteen departments (the same as the judicial districts), each run by an official accountable to the civilian Secretary of Justice and Security of the province. The agency's functional division also changed: it was divided into security, investigative, transportation, and penitentiary agencies. Popular participation was instituted through citizen forums at the community, municipal, and departmental levels. Within a few years, however, the reform collapsed under the pressures of increasing crime rates, police resistance, and opposition from Duhalde's successor.[66] When reformers were elected in 2003, though, the reform was reintroduced and greatly expanded. First, there was a radical structuring that entailed, among other changes, the transfer of most security authority to municipal-level units. Education and internal affairs were strengthened, as was financial transparency and coordination with social services. Most of all, citizen power and participation were increased to levels almost unknown in Latin America through Neighborhood, Municipal, and Departmental Forums authorized to control and monitor policing, evaluate police officers, and develop preventative policies.

The pattern was similar in Mendoza, where an ambitious 1999 police reform was catalyzed in part by that province having the country's second highest crime rate and one of the worst records of police abuse. The provincial security structure was altered through the establishment of a Ministry of Justice and Security to head the police, along with two oversight bodies, citizen forums, and security councils made up of political officials and neighborhood representatives. As in Buenos Aires, however, the reform clashed with political and institutional interests. It met with "ferocious resistance" from the police, which had been left out of planning. The changes were enacted under a Peronist government, and its 1999 successor, the Radical party, failed to follow through. Meanwhile, the two accountability agencies, the General Security Inspectorate (Inspección General de Seguridad, IGS) and the Disciplinary Junta (Junta de Disciplina) became politicized and were starved of resources, which stymied the training for civilians that the reform stipulated. As a result, the vast majority of investigations of police misconduct were carried out by police themselves, which undermined both the unit's credibility and overall accountability.[67]

As most provinces were unwilling or unable to propose serious police reforms, the pressure for change fell on the national government of President Néstor Kirchner, which was elected in 2003. During his first year in office, the president purged 107 top PFA officers and in April 2004 introduced a broad national security plan of sweeping changes in the police, courts, and law. Among other changes, it proposed a new crime mapping system, a Federal Investigations Agency, the replacement of many police chiefs with elected civilians, citizen boards to evaluate police promotions, jury trials for many criminal and corruption cases, new courts for juvenile crime, the relocation of some judges and prosecutors to neighborhoods, and educational scholarships for youth in "critical areas." Although this plan was the most feasible and broadest in Argentina's democratic era, proposing a long-term alternative to the *mano dura*, a range of political, legal, and institutional obstacles emerged in the different stages of its implementation.

A first area of obstruction was political. As the president learned, political support for his administration did not necessarily translate into support for his reforms, as an impatient public was more inclined to support proposals that seem to be "tough" and immediate. In Argentina, kidnappings have come to symbolize the uncontrollable nature of crimi-

nality and police ineffectiveness. In March 2004, the kidnapping and killing in Buenos Aires province of twenty-three-year-old Axel Blumberg
led to a massive two-hundred-thousand-strong protest in front of the
national congress, which responded by enacting a series of hastily drawn-
up laws, including lowering the age of criminal liability and tougher sentences for murderers, kidnappers, and rapists. Although these measures
lacked the detailed coherence and institutional focus of the national plan,
the political upheavals forced the government to revise it—precipitating
resignation of the PFA police chief; the firing of the Minister of Justice,
Security, and Human Rights; and charges that the executive was unas-
sertive and unclear.

A second problem that Argentina shares with other federal countries
concerns coordination. Any national plan requires the cooperation and
coordination of provincial governments, which are notoriously territorial. Indeed, soon after the plan was announced, security officials from
every province complained that it would limit their autonomy and take
up scarce resources. Further, like many countries, the federal government and the province of Buenos Aires that together cover the Buenos
Aires metropolitan area suffer from poor local coordination by the
various police forces operating in a single urban area (such as with agencies working on drug abuse) with highly varying crime rates.[68] Such institutional problems are aggravated by politics, such as the patronistic
alliance between most of the province's mayors with former president
Duhalde, one of Kirchner's biggest political adversaries.

A third problem is control over internal affairs, both legal and financial. As elsewhere, police control over budget and procurements has long
been a source of corruption networks in the PFA. Heads of the suboffi-
cial police academy keep funds earmarked for firearms, while street officers are expected to extort money to pay their commissioners.[69] Police
control over the legal aspects of internal affairs creates similar problems, especially slowing down or preventing investigations into police wrongdoing. In fact, the Chief of Judicial Investigations said that
he lacks the personnel to address the backlog of cases, particularly as
even judges—with a lack of trust in the judiciary—hand over charges
to be investigated.[70] The government developed innovative ways to investigate wayward police officers (creating new citizen channels, for instance, and forcing retirement of accused officers by not assigning them
to a position). But legal and financial branches of Internal Affairs must

be stronger and "civilianized" to address the roots of the problem. More transparent, effective internal affairs would make prosecution more consistent and less politicized (the top echelon of the PFA argued that Kirchner's dismissal of 107 of their colleagues was arbitrary, for example[71]), increase the likelihood of popular support (since the reasons for the action would be public), and free up more officers to police the streets (just one third of all police officers work on the street).[72]

A fourth and more important long-term problem is officer evaluation and promotion. As in Bolivia, Honduras, and elsewhere, promotion in Argentina is rife with favoritism. Moving up in the PFA depends almost entirely on the officer's academy exam score and whether she has caused any problems rather than on positive actions or skill development. Street officers basically monitor a single corner without any real proactive crime prevention,[73] even though improvement in crime fighting calls for promotions based on acquiring expertise in different areas of policing, such as community relations. Argentina's government is moving in this direction with policies that reward *comisarías* that reduce crime, but lasting change requires both broader training as well as evaluations that are more consistent.

A fifth problem obstructing reform throughout the region is the lack of clarity, development, and application of criminal laws and policies. The use of force in Argentina illustrates this. Insufficient training on how its use-of-force guidelines apply in practice leads to the unwarranted use of force and the cover-up of resulting fatalities. In the capital, one in every four killings is attributed to police officers, and between 1996 and 2002, the number of civilians killed by police rose by 89 percent and the killing of officers by 132 percent. As in other countries, formalistic legal education in police academics involves little critical analysis or actual application to activities on the force. Commissioners have become far better at tracking crimes through recently installed COMPSTAT (Computer or Comparative Statistics) programs, which use crime mapping and identification of local crime hotspots to determine the use of police personnel. But their understanding of causes or the development of strategies for high-crime areas (often blanks on police station maps) lags behind.[74] This underscores the need for revamped education curricula and joint policy efforts between the police and social services. But criticizing police training, a topic about which the police are highly defensive, is not politically practical, particularly when restructuring reforms are underway.

But what most clearly underscores the government's new approach is community policing. In Argentina, the core of the government's community policing proposal was to enlarge the Buenos Aires city Community Police with fifteen hundred new officers. But the PFA plan to put these officers in *plazas* and other public spaces condemns community policing to failure by marginalizing it to a particular sector of the police and by not empowering citizens meaningfully. The city of Buenos Aires does already have a functioning program of forums, networks, and coordinators who work with residents to find solutions to conflict and violence. Because the latter already have great support in the neighborhoods, the federal government should work to integrate them with the PFA, establishing joint patrols, for example.[75]

CONCLUSION

Describing the failures of police reform is far easier than formulating successful proposals. In the range of police reform initiatives, from local projects to comprehensive national packages, nearly every government in Latin America has experienced the political, legal, and institutional impediments described above. Pressures to fight crime erode efforts to make the police more accountable, most police forces resist reform as interference or lack the capacity to incorporate change, and "zero tolerance" laws undermine due process and civil rights. In short, as other chapters in this book also demonstrate, actions against escalating crime run counter to the very standards that comprise democracy. But community-oriented policing, by making democratic processes central to criminal policies, can overcome these obstacles by preventing the crimes that trigger them in the first place.

NOTES

1. As reported by the Pan American Health Organization (PAHO), *Health Situation in Latin America: Basic Indicators* (Washington, DC: PAHO, 1997).

2. In the 2007 Latinobarómetro poll of 20,212 people in eighteen Latin American countries, crime was tied statistically with unemployment as citizens' biggest concern.

3. See George L. Kelling and Catherine Coles, *Fixing Broken Windows: Restoring Order and Reducing Crime in Our Communities* (New York: Touchstone, 1996).

4. Patrick A. Langan and Matthew R. Durose, Bureau of Justice Statistics, U.S. Department of Justice, "The Remarkable Drop in Crime in New York City" (paper for the International Conference on Crime, Rome, December 3–5, 2003).

5. Author interview, Security Minister Óscar Álvarez, Tegucigalpa, July 18, 2003.

6. See Casa Alianza, at www.casa-alianza.org.

7. Author interview, youths on the streets of Tegucigalpa, July 16, 2003.

8. Author interview, Víctor Parelló, the human rights commissioner for the northern region, San Pedro Sula, February 20, 2004.

9. Author interviews, warden, officials, and prisoners at the El Porvenir Agricultural Penal Colony, February 23, 2004, and at the Centro Penal of San Pedro Sula, March 1, 2004.

10. Author interview, Ramón Custodio, National Human Rights Commissioner, July 4, 2005.

11. Julieta Castellanos, "El Tortuoso Camino de la Reforma Policial," *El Heraldo,* October 8, 2002.

12. Author interview, María Luisa Borjas, former UAI Chief, National Police, Tegucigalpa, July 18, 2003.

13. Author interview, Aída Estella Romero, July 22, 2003. Eduardo Villanueva, *fiscal* for children, added that "there are neither human nor logistical resources," to handle "the enormous quantity of cases"; author interview, Tegucigalpa, July 15, 2003.

14. Committee meeting (with about twenty-five in attendance), Choloma, February 19, 2004.

15. Author interview, Carlos Chincilla, Executive Director of *Comunidad Más Segura,* Tegucigalpa, July 22, 2003. Prosecutors and human rights commissioners estimate there have been thousands of unreported vigilante attacks since 2002. Author interview, Eduardo Villanueva, Tegucigalpa, July 15, 2003. In an author interview on February 26, 2004, Walter Menjivar Mendoza, the head prosecutor for the northern region, agreed that vigilantism had become uncontrollable, but did not want to estimate the number of cases.

16. Author interview, anonymous, Confite, Honduras, February 25, 2004.

17. Survey in 2002 and 2003 of 237 residents of community policing areas in the cities of Tegucigalpa, San Pedro Sula, Danlí, and Choluteca. Carried out by City University of New York "Community Policing in Latin America" project and the Centro de Documentación de Honduras (Cedoh).

18. Observatorio de la Violencia, *Boletín Enero-Diciembre 2006,* no. 5, February 2007, Tegucigalpa: Universidad Nacional Autónoma de Honduras.

19. "Venezuela es el sexto país con mayor índice de homicidios," *El Nacional,* August 31, 2002; "President of Venezuela Fires Deputy and Interior Minis-

ter," *New York Times,* January 5, 2007, A6. Crimes documented by the judicial police rose from 175,855 in 1986 to 261,630 in 1996. As in other countries, these statistics vary widely, with the morgue often reporting over 50 percent more crimes than the police.

20. OCEI, *Anuario Estadístico de Venezuela,* 1993, 1996, and 2000.

21. "Los crímenes se han vuelto cada vez more violentos," *El Nacional,* July 23, 2001.

22. "El crímen disparó más de 150 porciento," *El Universal,* January 13, 2003.

23. "Sistema de drogas y reciclaje de químicos eran las funciones del cuerpo parapolicial," *El Nacional,* February 13, 1988.

24. Author interview, Congressman William Tarek Saab, Fifth Republic Movement (*Movimiento Quinta República,* MVR), February 27, 2003.

25. "Asesinadas 30 personas en el mes de octubre," *Últimas Noticias,* November 7, 2002.

26. Author interview, Luís Enríque Oberto, President of the Legislative Commission, June 29, 1998; Inter-American Development Bank (IDB), *The Código Orgánico Procesal Penal* (Washington, DC: IDB, 1998) 5–15.

27. Author interview, Dília Parra, Director of the Institute of Superior Studies of the Fiscalía, February 25, 2003; and Omar Jiménez, Public Prosecutor in the state of Guarenas, February 26, 2003.

28. "La Ley Antidroga es una patente de corso de jueces y policías," *El Nacional,* September 9, 1988; "PTJ: un cuerpo que vive entre la enfermedad y la depuración," *Diario de Caracas,* June 21, 1989; author interview, Carolina Oliva, Office of the Attorney General Liaison with Congress, April 6, 1995.

29. Author interview, Amram Lazes, Commissioner of the Judicial Police, the PTJ, July 2, 1998.

30. Author interview, Jerssen Mojica, Inspector of the CICPC, February 26, 2003.

31. Citizen deaths jumped from nine per police officer in 2000 to twenty-eight in 2001.

32. In 2001, six hundred GN officers were deployed in key parts of the DF, partly to take over areas unprotected by striking local police. Using checkpoints and seizing narcotics, vehicles, crime suspects, and weapons, it lowered the crime rate in the first six months of 2001 by 16 percent. "Hubo sólo 5 homicidios en áreas cuidadas por el GN," *El Nacional,* July 18, 2001.

33. For officers convicted of homicide, the average sentence is over five years less than citizens guilty of the same crime. Fiscalía General, *Informe del Fiscal General al Congreso de la República,* 1998, p. 13.

34. "El avance fue muy escaso," *El Universal,* July 23, 2001. Between 2000 and 2003, the mayor of Baruta municipality invested 33 percent of municipal income in security and reduced the crime rate by 30.9 percent.

35. In one poll, only 22.1 percent of respondents expressed confidence in the police. See Richard Hillman and Elsa Cardozo de Silva, "Venezuelan Political

Culture and Democracy: 1996 and 1997 Survey Results," (paper presented at the Caribbean Studies Association, Antigua, 1998).

36. Author interview, Valmore Leegos, CICPC officer, February 26, 2003.

37. See Luís Gerardo Gabaldón and Daniela Bettiol, *Presencia policial en zonas residenciales urbanas.* (Mérida, Colombia: Universidad de los Andes, 1988).

38. Author interviews, residents, barrios of Catia, La Vega, and Brisas del Paraíso, 1998 and 2003.

39. "Un hombre fue linchado en Carabobo," *El Universal,* October 1, 2002. In 1995, the Interior Minister met with leaders of some "self-defense" groups to get their cooperation "to better guarantee security"; see "Escovar Salom se reunirá con empresas de vigilancia y grupos de autodefensa," *Ultimas Noticias,* February 2, 1995.

40. "MIJ evalúa a 327 cuerpos policía del país," *El Globo,* November 25, 2000. Like the police, they also benefit from legal impunity. One of the few legal actions against para-police leaders stalled because of the absence of witness protection; "El Defensor no quiere que lo envíen al Rodeo," *Tal Cual,* September 18, 2002.

41. See Juan Ramón Quintana, "Bolivia: militares y policías" (unpublished manuscript, La Paz: Observatorio Democracia y Seguridad).

42. See Franklin González Mendivil, *Doctrina policial* (La Paz, Bolivia: Policía Nacional/Comando General, 1988).

43. Author interview, Coronel Jaime Gutiérrez, Director of Human Rights, National Police, July 13, 2000.

44. "Bolivia: La policía tiene poco interés en el cambio y emite mala señales," *La Razón,* March 20, 2002.

45. Author interview, retired police official José Arancibia Mollinedo, December 15, 2004.

46. This was according to a top Interior Ministry official, on condition of anonymity.

47. "El escándalo no cesa en la Policía, revelan sueldos fantasmas," *La Razón,* September 24, 2004.

48. Movimiento Autonomista Nación Camba, "Policía y Seguridad Ciudadana," January 27, 2002, available at www.nacioncamba.net.

49. Author interview, Luis Ossico Sanjinés, former Vice President of Bolivia, December 16, 2004.

50. Fundación Libertad, Democracia y Desarrollo (FULIDED). *The Budget for State Security in Bolivia, 2004* (Santa Cruz, Bolivia: FULIDED, 2004), 11 and 14.

51. Author interview, Gloria Eyzaguirre, Oscar Molina and other members of the Police Reform Commission.

52. Quintana, "Bolivia."

53. Linda Farthing and Ben Kohl, "The Price of Success: Bolivia's War against Drugs and the Poor," *NACLA Report on the Americas* 35, no. 1 (July–August, 2001): 36.

54. Author interview, Alfonso Ferrufino Valderrama, former government minister and currently Executive Director of the Foundation to Support the Parliament and Citizen Participation (*Fundación de Apoyo al Parlamento y a la Participación Ciudadana*, FUNDAPPAC), December 16, 2004.

55. As stated by Embassy officials requesting anonymity, who also asserted that the time it takes to process complaints dropped from seven to ten years to just two to ten days.

56. Author interview, Colonel Rolando Fernandez, Chief of the PTJ, December 20, 2004.

57. Author interview, Alfonso Ferrufino Valderrama, former government minister, December 16, 2004.

58. Author interview, Ana María Romero de Campero, *defensora nacional*, July 12, 2000.

59. See "7 políticas del Plan Estratégico de la Policía 2003–2007," *La Razón*, May 16, 2003.

60. This was mainly from the UN Office on Drugs and Crime (UNODC) through the U.S. Agency for International Development (USAID).

61. The 1995 Public Defense Program established public defense offices in underserviced neighborhoods, and the proposed Platform to Attend the Public (Plataforma de Atención al Público, PAP) would receive complaints on a twenty-four-hour basis, help victims, and ensure that deadlines are met. There has been a delay in the U.S.-funded program, however, because of problems with fund disbursement.

62. Author interview, Gloria Eyzaguirre and General Óscar Molina of the Police Reform Commission, December 22–24, 2004. One prosecutor stated that the Fiscalía has "no control" over the police, who often send information to their superiors rather than to prosecutors, as required. Author interview, William Alave, Fiscal de Materia, December 17, 2004.

63. "Ultimo día para las propuestas al programa Barrios de verdad," *El Diario*, September 18, 2006.

64. According to the most reliable cross-referenced estimates (by the police, national statistics institutes, and NGOs), homicides rose over 50 percent between 1995 and 2004 (from about 4.0 to 6.3 per 100,000 people) and reported crimes more than tripled between 1983 and 2001 (from 348,780 to 1,178,530).

65. In 1991, for example, the death of a seventeen-year-old in a police station prompted congressional modification of the federal police code to allow detention only for a reasonable suspicion of criminal activity (or inability to produce identification), and to reduce from twenty-four to ten hours the maximum time allowed for such detentions.

66. The country's largest force, the forty-seven-thousand-strong Buenos Aires provincial police continues repressive practices, including extrajudicial killings. Many of its commissioners have been former dictatorship officials, including Aldo Rico, a former military official, who said that "it is necessary to kill [delinquents] in the street without any doubt and without pity." See "El carapintada por la boca muere," *Página/12*, March 10, 1998, 12. During the 1999 gubernatorial campaign, the Peronist candidate, national vice president Carlos Ruckauf, justified police killings and, after taking office, appointed Rico as the province's Chief of Security; see: Eduardo Oteiza, "Consecharás tempestades," *Clarín*, August 8, 1999.

67. Author interview, Gustavo Lucero, Junta de Disciplina, June 3, 2004.

68. The Federal District homicide rate (4.99 homicides per 100,000 as of 2001) is far lower than that of the province (11.48), with 71 percent occurring in the *conurbano*, the poor area surrounding the federal capital. See "Solá anunció que bajó el delito, pero le preocupa la sensación," *Diario La Unión* (La Plata), July 15, 2004.

69. Author interviews, police officials at the Falcón de Oficiales Police Academy of the PFA, May 27, 2004, and the PFA Commissioner, General Alberto Villa of the noncommissioned officers (NCO) school, May 28, 2004.

70. Author interview, Alejandro Hayet, Chief of Judicial Investigations, May 24, 2004.

71. Author interview at a meeting with the Plana Mayor of the PFA, May 26, 2004.

72. Author interview, Fernando Simón, Under-Secretary of Coordination and Innovation, May 26, 2004.

73. Author interview, commissioner, under-commissioner, and two sub-commissioned officers of *Comisariado 32*, May 25, 2004.

74. Author interview, Father Farinello of the Farinello of Quilmes Foundation, Buenos Aires province, May 22, 2004; author meetings with neighborhood groups in the working class Illia district and the Ciudad Oscura *villa* (shantytown) in the city of Buenos Aires, May 22, 2004.

75. Based on the author's observation of the community policing program, Morón, Buenos Aires province, May 27, 2004; author interview, Claudio Suárez, head of the security program of the Buenos Aires City government, May 26, 2004; author interview, four coordinators of the safety program of the city of Buenos Aires.

CHAPTER FIVE

Public Opinion and the Police in Chile

HUGO FRÜHLING

During the past twenty years, a number of governments in Latin America have undertaken police and criminal procedure reforms to improve the efficiency of their criminal justice systems and make them more accountable. Many of these attempts at police reform resulted from corruption scandals and the indiscriminate use of lethal force by the police.[1] Twenty years later, many questions remain about what has been achieved. In a number of countries, reforms have not had an impact on the low esteem in which the general population holds the police. As an example, results of the Latinobarómetro survey, a poll conducted in eighteen Latin American countries, reveal that in recent years confidence in the police and the judicial system remains much lower than confidence in the armed forces and other institutions, although confidence in the police showed an increase in 2007. In 2003, 62 percent of those surveyed expressed much or some confidence in the Catholic Church, while only 29 percent had much or some confidence in the police, and a mere 20 percent said they had much or some confidence in the judicial system. In 2007, trust in the armed forces and the police showed an increase, with 51 percent saying they had much or some trust in the armed forces and 39 percent saying the same about the police. When it comes to perceptions of corruption, figures from the 2004 Latinobarómetro survey indicate that 65 percent of survey respondents in México, 58 percent in Paraguay, and 57 percent in Argentina believe that in their country it is possible to bribe a member of the police. The lowest percentages of support for this statement are found in Chile (22 percent) and in El Salvador (20 percent).

Although the results of police reforms have been modest in some countries, certain police forces, such as those of Chile, Colombia, and Nicaragua, have been able to improve substantially their image, reinserting themselves fully into democratic systems.[2] In Chile, support for the police has been increasing since the return to democracy in 1990, despite a significant rise in the crime rate in the country during that time. Surveys carried out in 2003 confirm this, revealing high levels of subjective insecurity and significant rates of victimization, particularly of property crimes. At the same time, however, Chileans manifest substantial support for police forces, particularly the Carabineros de Chile (CC), which are mainly responsible for preventative public safety.[3] The level of support for the police is noticeably higher than that for institutions of the criminal justice system, such as the courts or the government, as public security provider. This chapter compares the situation in Chile with that of other Latin American countries that have undertaken police reforms in the recent past. Chile is an anomaly in the Latin American context: while many of the police forces of the region have undergone administrative reforms to improve efficiency and counteract declining prestige in the eyes of the citizenry, the Chilean police have, by contrast, only experienced gradual changes under democracy.

The aim of this chapter is to use the above mentioned public opinion surveys to analyze why there is public support for the police in Chile. The first part offers a description of the organizational changes affecting various police forces in Latin America as a result of democratization processes initiated two decades ago, and of the need to improve efficiency and control police abuse and corruption. The second part examines the situation of the Chilean police from the period of transition to democracy in 1990, and the changes introduced to bring the forces closer to the public. Finally, there is an assessment of the results of the surveys to draw some conclusions about the challenges facing the Chilean police. Survey results show that there is strong support for the police because the public understands that the police are not responsible for rising crime rates, and because they see them as committed to their doing their job and invaluable when the country faces natural catastrophes. However, the surveys also reveal a series of challenges facing the police: lower income sectors clearly have a less positive view of the police, and, furthermore, the problems that appear to worry the majority of people are precisely those that have led to a questioning of police effectiveness, such as drug trafficking in residential areas.

POLICE REFORMS IN CHILE AND LATIN AMERICA: COMPARING REALITIES

Latin America

There were myriad police reform initiatives in many Latin American countries in the 1990s that aimed to curb a notable rise in violent crime in the region and to address the lack of public faith in police probity. One major reform was to establish the autonomy of the police vis-à-vis the armed forces. El Salvador, Guatemala, Honduras, and Panama established new police forces with this goal in mind. The Salvadoran police reform integrated combatants from both sides of the civil war, and involved the creation of a General Police Inspectorate (Inspectoría General de la Policía, or IGP), independent from the Director General of the Police, with the power to investigate violations of the law by police officers. There was a separation of the police academy, responsible for recruitment and training, and the police force to ensure that the curriculum reflected democratic values rather than police corporativism.[4] Given a continually rising crime rate, however, particularly of crimes committed by youth gangs, the organic law of the National Police changed in 2001, bringing the Inspector General under the aegis of the Director of Police. More recently, a police officer was nominated director of the police academy, which put an end to the institutional autonomy of that body as well.[5]

The reforms of Guatemala, Honduras, and Panama have been less successful than those of El Salvador in terms of achieving significant levels of democratic policing. In these three Central American countries, the functioning of police academies is seriously deficient, control over police corruption and abuse falls short, and adequate equipment is lacking. On average, these police forces have a still short, ten-year history, and they have a long way to go in terms of the kind of institutional development that enables officers effectively to address crime waves. In Guatemala, there is strong evidence that organized crime has penetrated the police. In early 2007, members of the police participated in the killing of four Salvadoran members of Congress visiting Guatemala, apparently under orders from organized crime. Prompted in large part by the failure of police reform, in 2006 the government signed an agreement with the United Nations to form an international Anti-Impunity Commission that will assist the Guatemalan government with its investigation of particularly significant crimes.[6]

In the Dominican Republic, the National Police underwent legal reforms to curb militarization. The new legislation stipulates that active military officers may not have a career in the police.[7]

These above mentioned reforms to transform the police into a civilian force have certainly led to an improvement with respect to the previous situation in which many police forces were subordinated to the armed forces or emulated their values and organization. However, as is the case in El Salvador, there have been partial reversals because of the need to deal with rising crime. In other cases, the police force has remained a weak institution that has not been modernized.

Various countries have attempted to strengthen police accountability mechanisms. In several cases, there has been reform of internal disciplinary systems because of the key role they play in preventing and controlling abuse. These disciplinary systems typically face a number of shared problems. They tend to focus on breaches of internal discipline, rather than on incidents of police abuse. Sometimes they suspend decisions regarding crimes committed by officers until after the adoption of a judicial decision, which can take a long time. Punitive action rather than preventative measures preserve internal discipline, which can be counterproductive in terms of ensuring voluntary adherence to the law by police officers; in addition, procedures are secret and complainants have little access to them. Offices of Professional Responsibility in charge of investigating these cases are usually located only in the capital cities and are not truly accessible to the public at large.[8] All of these characteristics usually make it difficult for external observers to determine whether incidents of police misconduct are in fact decreasing and whether the efficiency of the system is improving.

In El Salvador, the police reform created an internal system under the authority of the police Director General, which was comprised of a disciplinary investigative unit, a disciplinary tribunal, and a control unit. These entities reviewed compliance with internal regulations, quality of police operational procedures, and use of resources. An external Inspector's Office supervised the entire system, reporting to the Vice-Minister of Public Security. By the end of the 1990s, the system was overwhelmed by cases and the slow rate of progress in addressing them, creating a serious backlog. In 1999, an additional Internal Affairs Unit was set up to work with the prosecutor's office investigating possible criminal acts committed by police. In August 2000, a change to the police organic law was approved which specified the disciplinary powers and duties of supervisors and local chiefs of police, and emphasized the disciplinary powers and duties of the local police chiefs. In mid-2000, in response to media revelations about police involvement in organized crime, 1,568 policemen were fired in accordance with extraordinary powers vested in police authorities to remove police officers on suspicion alone.

In 1999 in Rio de Janeiro, state governor Anthony Garotinho created a model police station program in order to improve the productivity and quality of service to the general public by the state's civil police. The program included changes to the physical structure of the stations, the division and assignment of work among employees, officers' behavior, and the supervision of individual officers.[9] Evaluations of the program have indicated that it has great potential to improve the quality of policing and compliance with human rights. However, the program has yet to be implemented fully within the civil police of Rio de Janeiro, partly because of informal internal opposition on the part of officers who are poorly paid and not motivated to change. This internal opposition was strengthened also by a view that is apparently widely held among the ranks, namely that initiatives of this kind may be abandoned once a new state governor with a different political view takes office.[10]

Many countries have undertaken community policing programs to improve police-community relations as well as police efficiency. These programs have garnered public support but have not persisted over time because of political changes that often lead to an emphasis on *mano dura* policing, which contradicts the goals of community policing.[11] In his analysis of community policing in Sao Paulo, Túlio Kahn compares public perceptions of traditional forms of policing and community policing, arriving at the conclusion that there are significant differences: 56.9 percent of those surveyed said that the community policing model is accessible, while 10.5 percent said the same about traditional policing. Just 0.6 percent of those surveyed considered community policing corrupt— for traditional policing the figure rose to 42.1 percent. Only 0.6 percent believed that community policing is violent, while 60.2 percent said the traditional police are violent. On the other hand, only 14.5 percent of survey respondents said that community policing is more efficient than traditional policing.[12]

The perception that corruption is widespread, that the police are unable to deal with crime or that they disregard the law in pursuit of criminals fuels lack of trust in the police. A recent public opinion study on the Federal Police in Buenos Aires conducted by the University of San Andrés shows that only 12.8 percent of those surveyed agree that the police are honest.[13] Other surveys regarding police agencies mentioned above show that the public often does not believe that police reforms work. With the exception of isolated cases such as Chile and Colombia, Latin America's citizens still do not trust the police. Lack of trust in the courts is also very high. A 2003 international Latinobarómetro survey covering eighteen Latin American countries showed that 62 percent of respondents trusted the church, but only 29 percent trusted the police and 20 percent the judicial system. A 2004 survey by the same organization showed that 65 percent of respondents in Mexico, 58 percent in Paraguay, and 57 percent in Argentina believed it was possible to bribe a police officer in their country; the lowest percentage scores for this question were in Colombia (3 percent), Chile (22 percent), and El Salvador (20 percent). A 2006 study by the Instituto Universitario de Opinión Pública of the Jose Simeon Canas University shows that 38.4 percent of respondents had much or some confidence in the police.

The Case of Chile

In Chile, police reforms have been more gradual than elsewhere, and quite rapidly gained significant levels of public support. The Chilean police have a long institutional history. The Carabineros de Chile was established in 1927 with the definitive unification of the state and municipal police and the Army corps of Carabineros.[14] The Investigative Police (Policía de Investigaciones de Chile, or PI) was set up in 1933. The Investigation Service and the Identification and Passport Service were separated from the Carabineros, and placed under the direct aegis of the Ministry of the Interior. The Carabineros were put in charge of on-the-street policing and the maintenance of public order, while the PI took responsibility for the investigation of crimes.

Under the military regime installed in 1973, the CC underwent significant changes, with the participation of its General Director in the military junta. New institutional norms increased its autonomy vis-à-vis the political ministries and reinforced its military attributes. The imposition of public order was emphasized, and hostility toward the Communist Party and left wing parties in general was widespread, as evidenced by the discourse and policies of the institution.[15] With Decree Law 444, the CC was placed under the aegis of the Ministry of Defense in April 1974 and the PI followed suit in September of that year. The decree justified the change with the argument that coherent CC activity and technical efficiency called for freedom from control by politically motivated state secretariats.[16] This institutional change, however, actually consecrated a relatively high level of operational autonomy because the Defense Ministry lacked public order and safety powers. Moreover, amendments to the Code of Criminal Procedure passed in 1989 and 1991 allowed the CC to carry out criminal investigations in geographic areas where the Investigative Police has no presence, or when instructed to do so by a judge. Today, a military ethos still dominates the CC in terms of its discipline and training and its personnel remain under military judicial jurisdiction.[17] The CC is a 41,409-strong force.

The PI is a much smaller civilian body made up of 6,514 people, of which 3,444 are investigative police officers. Its primary function is to investigate crimes, although the PI is also in charge of controlling cross-border movement of people. Before the military regime, the PI was responsible for any activities that might threaten political stability, and with the exception of the period between 1992 and 2007, the director has always been an "outsider" who is politically trusted by the president of the country.[18]

Both the Carabineros and the PI have undergone reforms to respond to the growing importance of criminality in the national debate, and they have received strong budgetary and political support from democratic governments to regain public trust. Relations between the newly elected civilian government and the Carabineros were initially difficult after the end of the military regime in 1990,[19] for two fundamental reasons: First, the CC opposed a government proposal that would remove the police force from the Ministry of Defense and place it under the supervision of the Ministry of the Interior, on the grounds that such a move would encourage political interference in police operations. Second, relations between the government and CC suffered further strain when a number of police officers were tried for human rights violations committed during the military regime. However, by the mid-1990s, relations between the government and CC had improved considerably. The rising importance of public security doubtless was a contributing factor. In addition, the CC undertook a series of changes to improve police management and strengthen relations with the community. Incidents of human rights violations also declined probably because of the implementation of criminal procedure reforms that strengthened the rights of those accused of a crime.

Citizen Security and Police Reform in Chile

From the beginning of the 1990s onwards, and with the reestablishment of democratic rule, there has been increasing public demand for improved security for citizens and their property in association with the perception that criminality has reached unprecedented levels. Like Bergman's analysis of Mexico and Buenos Aires in this book, surveys by CEP-ADIMARK (1992–1993) and CEP (1995–1999) in Chile consistently show that criminality is one of the top three problems that governments must address in Chile. In addition, the 2003 national urban victimization survey shows that, together with drug-trafficking, criminality is the second most important national problem identified by respondents. The same survey also reveals that many respondents feel that crime has risen significantly: 80.5 percent said they believed that crime had risen in the country, while only 44.6 percent said the same about their own neighborhood. This is evidence of the distance that surveys often reveal between perceptions of reality and experience. Of respondents, 30.3 percent said they had been the victim of one of the following crimes: car theft, the theft of objects from their car, robbery with the use of violence, muggings, theft, injury, economic crime, or corruption. An Interior Ministry study comparing levels of victimization in Chile and abroad concludes that Chilean rates are particularly high in the case of the theft of objects from cars and home burglary.

The only way to assess the increase in crime levels is to look at crimes reported to both police institutions, because there are no published series of national victimization surveys. According to an Interior Ministry assessment in 2003,[20] reports of the most socially significant crimes (*delitos de mayor connotación social,* or DMCS)[21] have tended to rise since 1982 and, following a slight decline and stabilization in both 1987 and 1995, have tended to increase significantly until now. Among these crimes, home burglaries have shown a clear tendency to increase (reports of such crimes increased fourfold by 2003, to 902.1 cases for every 100,000 inhabitants).[22] The homicide rate, which is a key indicator for the purposes of cross-national comparison, is not valid for Chile because the way it is reported leads to underestimation.[23]

Another important indicator is public fear, a phenomenon that accompanies criminality. In the National Urban Citizen Security Survey of 2003, 45 percent of respondents said that they or a member of their family had been the victim of a crime in the preceding year, and 89 percent felt that it was "very probable" or "probable" that they would be the victim of a crime over the following twelve months; 83 percent of the 54.4 percent who indicated that no member of their family had been victimized felt the same way. This means that fear of victimization exists among both those who have personally experienced victimization or been close to a victim, and those who have not. According to Latinobarómetro, in 2004 only 14 percent of Chileans "entirely agreed" or "agreed" that "the battle against crime is being won." Together with Argentina, this is the lowest percentage for the region.

Changes in the Police

Over the past decade, the Carabineros and the PI have undergone changes to adapt to democratic conditions. The PI began to make efforts to improve normative controls over its staff in the 1990s. A significant number of detectives were dismissed, there were important curricular changes, including the introduction of teaching about human rights, and the Fifth Department was established to investigate cases of corruption or abuse of the rights of citizens.[24] However, there is insufficient information available to evaluate the improvements in internal police control. The CC has changed more gradually. It maintained a relatively high degree of autonomy from political authorities for some years after the transition to democracy, in part because the legislation that governs the institution (which entered into force four days before the inauguration of the first democratic government in the post-Pinochet era) gave broad powers to the Carabineros' Director General. Article 10 of the law states that, as with the armed forces, only the Director General can propose promotion and retirement of officers, which must then be confirmed by presidential decree. Thus, the President of the Republic did not have the power to dismiss officers or promote them without the prior approval of the Director General. Further, both police forces report directly to the Ministry of Defense. As noted above, this accentuates the autonomy of the Carabineros by freeing the institution from the control of the Ministry of the Interior, which is responsible for citizen security. However, a constitutional amendment passed in 2005 gave the president the power to dismiss the Director General of Carabineros. Moreover, the amendment mandated that both police forces will report in the future to a Ministry or Vice-ministry of Security, still awaiting formal legal creation. This amendment created conditions for improved governmental oversight over the police.

In response to greater citizen insecurity, the Carabineros undertook a streamlining process from the late 1990s onwards in order to increase the number of personnel engaged in operational activities. As a result, the institution has ceased to carry out twenty-four of the sixty-seven legally mandated tasks for which it is responsible.[25] In addition, since the return of democracy and reflecting the tone of government and municipal officials, the "community" has become part of the discourse of the Carabineros. In 1999, the CC began implementing the Quadrant Plan (Plan Cuadrante), the primary aim of which has been to increase the street presence of the police. To implement this plan, the national territory was divided into small sectors (*cuadrantes*), each overseen by a police station (*comisaría*) under the command of a major. The aim was to allocate more efficiently vehicles and human resources to meet the needs of each sector. According to official Carabineros information, a delegate and subdelegate, whose responsibility it is to address and solve problems presented by the residents, was assigned to each sector. Within each police station there was established a small unit dealing with community relations to liaison with neighborhood associations and assess their security needs. The CC also began to hold public hearings to present statistics on policing activities, to which neighborhood leaders and sector authorities were invited.[26] This practice was suspended but may be reinstated in the future. A recent Ministry of Finance evaluation by a panel of three independent experts found that the Quadrant Plan has been effective in terms of the management of preventative patrolling and in defining management tools that help determine the resources needed by each police station. However, the panel suggested that the plan did not adequately consider community participation in defining priority security problems. Moreover, the panel found that there was insufficient information needed to manage the plan, as data on its implementation was not gathered systematically. The panel recommended that resources allocated to the Quadrant Plan be separated from Carabineros' general budget, in order to discern its cost-effectiveness.[27] However, the undersecretary of Carabineros within the Ministry of Defense disagreed with some of the panel's findings, objecting to the recommendation that Carabineros coordinate crime prevention efforts with municipal agencies and social programs. Instead, the undersecretary stated, such coordination efforts should occur through Carabineros' participation in municipal safety committees.[28]

In order to improve internal oversight of its efficiency, Carabineros developed performance indicators in 2000. In 2005, new indicators were proposed based on information from victimization surveys. These indicators were designed to measure progress towards achieving the performance goals set in response to the Public Security Strategy announced by the government in 2006. With the new indicators, Carabineros tried to identify more clearly the security needs that its officers respond to. Since Jose Bernales' arrival as General Director of Carabineros in 2006, there is also greater emphasis on the quality of services provided by the police, including the establishment of a new program, "Quality Improvement Program for Police Services to the Community." For a six-month period in 2006, Carabineros asked people who either visited police stations or called the police to fill out a questionnaire, which included questions about the promptness of the attention they received, how well they were treated, and the quality of police responses.

To complement the design of new indicators, targets were established associated with many of the performance measures that were considered top priorities. The Carabineros' Office of Planning and Research to the General Director proposed the targets, and the office distributed them to the Carabineros' Council of Generals in April 2007. The targets were defined in accordance with the commitment made by the institution to contribute to the government's goal of reducing crime victimization rates by 10 percent for 2010.

Despite the changes introduced in both forces, there are still reports of police abuse. A study by Claudio Fuentes on cases in the military justice system shows that reports of unnecessary violence by CC officers increased during the 1990s, although reports of homicide, attempted homicide, and bullet wounds tended to decrease after 1992. Death of detainees in Carabineros prisons also tended to increase (there were sixteen reported cases in 1990–1994 and thirty-six in 1995–2000). Fuentes asks why police violence is not an issue in the Chilean public debate when human rights played such an important role under military rule. Among the various possible explanations, he highlights the absence of effective external control over the Carabineros, the fact that civil society is not organized, and the fact that the public is more concerned with crime than with the rights of individuals.[29]

Both police forces have been the subject of criticism as a result of rising crime rates. But their legitimacy, particularly of the Carabineros, has not come into question, despite the fact that the Carabineros' internal organization has not undergone any major reforms in recent years. The main reasons for that are the public's overarching concern about crime and its level of trust that the police are addressing the issue. Moreover, gradual changes undertaken by the police have likely played a part in convincing the public that the CC is an institution capable of improving its effectiveness. But the underlying reasons for public support for the police are more profound. Because Chile was characterized by political polarization and conflict from the 1960s through the 1980s, Chileans now place a high value on stability and the rule of law. Almost half of the electorate has consistently voted for parties that supported the previous military regime. Moreover, Carabineros, as well as the armed forces, have come to be seen as permanent state institutions that have successfully reinserted themselves into the democratic system. Carabineros is perceived as playing an important role in attaining compliance with the law. In a 2004 Latinobarómetro report, Chile ranks second only to Colombia in positive responses to the question, On a scale of one to ten, do you believe that in your country the state is able to make people obey the law? A ranking of ten would mean that people obey all laws, while one means that there is no obedience. While Chile obtained a 5.37, Argentina obtained only a 4.05.

PUBLIC PERCEPTIONS OF INSECURITY AND THE POLICE: ANALYSIS OF KEY RESULTS

The analysis below explores public perceptions of the police in Chile, as well as reasons for them and is based on the results of surveys undertaken by the Interior Ministry and the National Statistics Institute in 2003: the first national victimization survey (based on face-to-face interviews and available to the public) carried out in September–November 2003, which surveyed 16,289 people over the age of 15, and covers urban centers throughout the country and the 77 most populated municipalities (comunas); and a survey from October 2003, "Perception and Evaluation of the Work of the Carabineros of Chile," conducted in three regions: the Santiago Metropolitan Region and the Fifth and Eighth regions. Since each survey covers a different universe, their results are not strictly comparable, so any conclusions based on a joint analysis of the two needs further testing.

Perceptions of Police Crime Control

As noted above, crime and drug trafficking together constitute priority issues for respondents. When asked about the possible causes of crime levels in the country, respondents of the national urban survey opted for the following general explanations: unemployment and other social circumstances, insufficient police patrols, and failings in the judicial system, such as overly light sentences by the courts. When asked about the possible causes of crime in their neighborhoods, interviewees placed insufficient policing after unemployment. This shows that the public places heavy emphasis on the role of the police in controlling crime. A closer look at the responses by socioeconomic group, particularly those regarding lack of police patrolling and light sentencing by the courts, shows that it is clearly the lower-income sectors that attribute the most importance to insufficient police presence, while higher-income sectors tend to emphasize the importance of light sentencing by the courts. Lower-income sectors, which express lower levels of satisfaction with police protection than higher-income groups, attribute a high level of importance to police presence in crime control (with higher-income groups supporting more severe sentences).

The importance attributed to the police in combating crime by all social sectors in Chile is corroborated by the fact that only 1.4 percent of respondents believed that the lack of community organization was the cause of crime in their neighborhood. In Chile, all social sectors seem to believe that only the state, and the police in particular, can ensure lower levels of criminality. The fact that 32.5 percent of those interviewed for the national urban survey stated that the CC is the most responsible for citizen security, followed by the government (26.1 percent) and the courts (20.8 percent) also confirms the importance of police action. In summary, the public attributes a great deal of importance to police work in controlling crime, which explains the strong demand for a greater police presence. The following section examines why rising crime has not had a negative impact on the positive image of the police.

Trust in the Police

Different results emerge from the various surveys undertaken regarding the level of public trust in both police forces. In the survey focused on perceptions of the Carabineros, 82 percent of respondents said they trusted the institution, while 35 percent said they trusted judges, and 31 percent members of the national congress. For the Carabineros, these are high levels, but they decrease as one goes down the socioeconomic ladder. The national victimization survey shows different results: when asked how much trust they had in the named authorities, 32.6 percent of respondents said that they had a high amount of trust in the CC, while

50.4 percent had little trust, and 15.5 percent stated they did not trust the CC at all. Although negative, these figures are still more favorable than those for members of the Supreme Court, senators, and the Ministry of the Interior. In other words, although levels of trust vary from survey to survey, trust in the Carabineros is above average when compared with other public authorities. As regards the PI, 30.4 percent stated they had a high level of trust in the institution, and 18.3 percent said they did not trust the institution at all. Levels of trust in the Carabineros vary according to age, socioeconomic status, and whether the respondent was a victim of crime in the twelve months preceding the interview. Thus, while 25.50 percent of youths between nineteen and twenty-four years of age trust the *Carabineros* considerably, 44.61 percent of those over sixty feel this way; and while 41.37 percent of higher-income respondents express significant trust in the Carabineros, only 30.27 percent of lower-income respondents do so. Furthermore, 29.7 percent of people who had been the victim of a crime over the preceding twelve months said they trusted the Carabineros very much, while the percentage for those who had not was 35.0. Table 5.1 contains a fuller presentation of these results.

There are many reasons why Chileans show such high levels of trust in the police. One is that people believe that the two police forces are efficiently addressing citizen insecurity. The CC was the third most valued institution among those listed in the national victimization survey, preceded by the National Women's Service (Servicio Nacional de la Mujer, or SERNAM), and the National Service for Minors (SENAME). The PI came after the CC. While the numbers are average, they are much higher than those obtained by political institutions. The survey on attitudes toward the Carabineros validates the institution even more: only SERNAM comes out ahead, and 50 percent of respondents had a positive or very positive view of the institution. Results differ according to socioeconomic status in this survey as well: while 70 percent of higher-income respondents (ABC1) were positive, only 38 percent of lower-income respondents (E) were. It is worth noting, however, that respondents belonging to sectors C2, C3, and D (middle-income) had mostly favorable opinions about the Carabineros. The largely positive response elicited by the question of whether the respondent believed that the institution had adopted adequate measures to address crime confirms this.

Table 5.1 Trust in *Carabineros*

	Level of Confidence According to Gender (%)				
	Much	*A little*	*None*	*NS/NR*	*Total*
Men	33.20	49.86	15.52	1.42	100
Women	31.98	50.84	15.44	1.75	100
Total	32.56	50.37	15.48	1.59	100

	Level of Confidence According to Age (%)				
	Much	*A little*	*None*	*NS/NR*	*Total*
15–18 years	27.13	52.24	19.23	1.40	100
19–24 years	25.50	55.21	18.36	0.93	100
25–29 years	28.17	54.10	17.03	0.70	100
30–45 years	29.23	51.91	17.63	1.24	100
46–60 years	36.70	48.64	12.62	2.03	100
60 and over	44.61	42.60	9.97	2.82	100
Total	32.56	50.37	15.48	1.59	100

	Level of Confidence According to Income Level (%)				
	Much	*A little*	*None*	*NS/NR*	*Total*
ABC1	41.37	51.18	7.08	0.37	100
C2	45.43	43.86	8.78	1.93	100
C3	35.42	50.67	12.39	1.52	100
D	28.63	51.76	18.01	1.60	100
E	30.27	46.54	21.52	1.67	100
Total	32.56	50.37	15.48	1.59	100

Note: ABC1 refers to higher-income status; C2, C3, D, to middle-income; and E, to lower-income.

Thus, as the above figures show, most citizens feel that the Carabineros are acting effectively to deal with crime, even though the results they have achieved fall short of expectations, given the increasing crime rates. The significant support for the police is not a product of closer relations with the community as a result of the Quadrant Plan. Indeed, most of the population (the percentage is particularly high among lower-income sectors) is unaware of the plan. The survey on perceptions of the Carabineros is complemented by the question about whether people are aware of the public hearings initiated by the institution three years ago: 95 percent are not, and only 4 percent have heard about the initiative; further, only 9 percent of those who answered affirmatively had actually attended a hearing. Trust in the police depends on the perception that the officers act with probity and not for personal gain. The survey on perceptions of the Carabineros asks whether respondents have been victimized by or a witness to any action undertaken by the Carabineros that used his or her position for personal gain: 88 percent of respondents said that this was not the case, 6 percent had witnessed such an incident, and 2 percent claimed that they had been a direct victim. The national victimization survey confirms the relatively low levels of police corruption compared with other Latin American countries, with 1.2 percent of respondents saying that a public servant had asked for or demanded of them the payment of a bribe; in 21.7 percent of cases in which this happened, the person implicated was a Carabinero. In a study conducted in the city of Buenos Aires in 2003, 5.7 percent of respondents said they had been asked for bribes over the previous twelve months, and in 72.2 percent of cases, the person involved was a police officer.

The Quality of Police Work

The national victimization survey asks respondents who have visited a police station in the previous twelve months to evaluate how well they were attended to; in 2003, 69 percent rated the attention "good" or "very good." The figures for a comparable question regarding the PI are similarly high. A positive image of an institution depends fundamentally on people having a positive image of its members. The national urban survey asks respondents whether they agree with a series of statements about the Carabineros. The statements that respondents most agreed with

were: the Carabineros were helpful (78.9 percent), disciplined (73.9 percent), efficient (66.2 percent), polite (65.1 percent), and treat people well
(63.2 percent). Much lower levels of agreement were shown for a statement to the effect that the Carabineros are corrupt (39.3 percent agreed
and 38.8 percent disagreed).[30] There was also a notable difference between the response of the more affluent (ABC1) and the poorest (E)
socioeconomic groups to the question of corruption and appropriate
treatment by the Carabineros.

The most positive responses pertain to the existence of a military ethos
or culture that emphasizes discipline, serving the public when the problems at stake are the kinds that call for a social role for the police, polite-
ness when dealing with civilians, and overall levels of efficiency probably
associated with the institution's military organization. At the same time,
the percentage of people that disagree with each question increases as
one descends the socioeconomic ladder. Thus, only 15.3 percent of ABC1
respondents disagreed that the Carabineros were educated, compared
with 34.3 percent of E group respondents; at the same time, 61.1 percent
of ABC1 group respondents disagreed with the statement that the Carabineros are corrupt, and only 35.5 percent of the E group disagreed with
the statement. More notable in terms of the gap is that 10 percent of
ABC1 respondents disagreed with the statement that the Carabineros
treat civilians well, compared with 34.9 of E respondents. The view that
the Carabineros do not act impartially among lower-income groups is
also apparent: 59 percent agreed that the Carabineros obeyed the law,
57 percent that they were committed to their job, and 52 percent that
they were honest. However, the percentage of people with a positive view
of the impartiality of the Carabineros is lower (48 percent), and that of
those responding negatively to the question is higher (13 percent).
Equally notable is the fact that a significant percentage of those who agree
that the Carabineros act with partiality associate that view with excessive
use of force by the institution.[31]

The survey also shows that people view the Carabineros' service to the
public very positively, while there is a much more negative view of their
crime control work. Thus, while 78.9 percent agreed that assistance and
rescue efforts by Carabineros during natural disasters was "good" or
"very good," only 57.3 percent were positive about the response to home

emergencies (people being locked in, gas leaks, and others), and 60.7 percent were positive about traffic monitoring. The police work that the population considers most important received the worst marks (32.6 percent for combating drugs and 33.8 percent for combating crime). The national survey also evaluated the performance of the PI when carrying out certain tasks, but because the public has much less contact with this institution and because many of the questions require a level of knowledge that the public may not possess, there is no analysis of this data.

Public Demands With Regard to the Police

In the survey on perceptions of the Carabineros, there were questions that aimed to identify the specific demands of the public vis-à-vis the institution and to assess the quality of police action to satisfy those demands. These questions seek to establish the gap between expectations and perceptions of actual police work. This kind of study is useful because it sheds light on the specific demands of the public regarding the Carabineros. The ranking of demands should lead to changes in police work and to changes in the priorities established to guide police work. Further, this type of analysis makes it possible to establish which kinds of actions the public views as responding to their demands and its assessment of those actions.

The first question asks the respondent to rank the problems that call for CC intervention in order of importance. The sale of illicit drugs ranks first, followed by the consumption of alcohol by minors, then burglaries of homes and shops and other locations, traffic accidents, youth gangs, robberies, and street muggings. The responses confirm the profoundly disruptive effect that the sale of illicit drugs has on social networks and daily social relations, particularly among the poorer social sectors. The second most mentioned problem is not crime-related, but rather has to do with the perceived lack of control over the sale of alcohol to minors. The third issue is that which the Chilean press pays most attention to: burglaries of homes, shops, and other establishments.

Concerns vary considerably according to socioeconomic sector and region, which should increase pressures for decentralization of police work so as to enable the forces to respond to different demands. The

Table 5.2 Do you think that concrete actions by the Carabineros respond to the aforementioned problems in your neighborhood?

Type of Incident	TOTAL (%) Yes	No	ABC 1 (%) Yes	No	C2 (%) Yes	No	C3 (%) Yes	No	D (%) Yes	No	E (%) Yes	No
Traffic accidents	60.3	29.7	78.9	14.2	57.4	29.9	65.9	24.7	57.3	32.0	46.5	47.2
Theft/burglary of homes, shops	45.5	56.8	30.2	42.0	31.5	52.6	31.7	54.3	29.5	60.6	29.8	67.0
Car theft, or theft of objects in cars	38.6	52.8	38.6	49.0	40.0	47.0	39.5	51.1	36.6	53.6	27.3	68.4
Street robberies	37.4	53.7	39.7	44.5	37.8	46.6	37.1	50.8	29.8	58.3	33.2	62.7
Minors' alcohol consumption	37.3	46.3	51.8	27.3	43.1	41.4	42.1	42.9	33.1	51.1	33.7	59.2
Street fights	35.7	44.2	70.2	22.7	49.5	38.3	49.5	39.5	38.3	51.2	39.0	54.8
Youth gangs	34.2	51.1	64.8	24.3	39.1	45.7	43.5	46.1	28.7	58.6	33.0	63.1
Family violence	31.9	44.5	28.2	38.2	23.3	38.2	34.4	40.7	33.8	47.9	33.4	57.8
Illicit drugs sale	30.6	46.3	24.9	43.0	31.5	43.1	42.0	40.4	35.0	49.6	33.3	59.2
Street prostitution	22.4	45.3	26.2	31.3	18.2	40.0	22.6	44.3	22.7	47.4	25.6	58.4
Stopping cars or persons and charging them for transiting streets	19.1	45.4	9.2	29.7	18.2	33.0	21.3	45.8	18.3	50.9	23.8	53.8

Source: Estudio Percepción y Evaluación de la labor de Carabineros de Chile (Ministerio del Interior–Carabineros, 2003).

increase in the sale of illicit drugs is a much more serious problem for the lowest-income groups (D and E), the consumption of alcohol by minors is a key problem for middle-income groups (C2 and C3), while traffic accidents are essentially a concern for high-income groups (ABC1). Respondents were asked whether they felt the Carabineros undertook specific actions to address these problems in their neighborhood. Table 5.2 presents the answers to that question, and shows that responses are mostly positive only with regard to two problems: traffic accidents and burglaries. For all other problems or crimes, the responses are mostly negative. The percentage of mostly negative responses is concentrated in the answer to questions that refer to CC action to combat the sale of illicit drugs, youth gangs, and alcohol consumption by minors.

Table 5.3 compares public demands of the Carabineros and the ranking of concrete actions taken by the institution to address each particular problem. The ranking of perceptions of concrete action results from subtracting negative from positive responses.

The greatest discrepancy between the importance of demand and perceptions of effective CC action emerges with regard to controlling the sale of illicit drugs. The survey then asks how interviewees rate the activities undertaken by the Carabineros to address the aforementioned issue. Table 5.4 ranks the views of respondents according to the net importance of each issue or according to the difference between the percentage of those that declare a given action as very important for their neighborhood and those that say it is not very or not at all important.

The survey on perceptions of the *Carabineros* asks respondents how they evaluate a set of actions, among them those mentioned above. By comparing the positive evaluations, and making a net assessment between the percentage of people that judge those actions positively or very positively, and those that view them negatively, one arrives at an evaluation that coincides in many ways with the results of the victimization survey, insofar as the most positive evaluations concern action to assist the public (namely, assistance and rescue during natural disasters, traffic accidents, the maintenance of public order during mass events, and domiciliary emergency assistance). The lowest scores are for actions such as protecting crime victims and operations against drug traffickers. Table 5.5 presents this information.

Table 5.3 Ranking of Priority Demands and Assessment of CC Performance

	Importance (%)	Rank	Action (%)	Rank
Sale of illicit drugs	38	1	-15.7	7
Public alcohol consumption by minors	19	2	-9.0	3
Theft/burglary of homes and shops	13	3	-11.3	4
Traffic accidents	9	4	30.6	1
Youth gangs	7	5	-16.9	9
Street holdups	6	6	-16.3	8
Theft of cars or objects in cars	4	7	-14.2	6
Intrafamily violence	2	8	-12.6	5
Street fights	1	9	-8.5	2
Street prostitution	1	10	-22.9	10
Stopping cars and charging them for transiting streets	0	11	-26.3	11

Source: Author elaboration based on the *Estudio Percepción y Evaluación de la labor de Carabineros de Chile* (Ministerio del Interior–Carabineros, 2003).

CONCLUSION

For the past two decades, various Latin American countries have implemented police and criminal justice reforms. Police reforms have covered three main areas: those aiming to ensure the autonomy of police from armed forces and to establish civilian police agencies; those seeking to strengthen internal accountability mechanisms; and those aiming to improve service delivery and relations between the police and the community. While some programs have been successful, there have been various political and institutional obstacles. Consequently, public opinion has remained distrustful of the police in many countries. But Chileans clearly value their two police forces more than other Latin Americans. This is partly the result of higher levels of institutionalization and professionalization on the part of the Carabineros. After an initial period after the transition to democracy in which Carabineros clashed with civilian governments, the institution successfully modernized its management, cre-

Table 5.4 Evaluation of Importance of Carabinero Action

Type of Action	Evaluation (%)
Visible street patrols, especially at night	95.2
Speedy dispatch of vehicles in response to emergency calls	94.7
Detention of criminals	94.2
Operations against drug traffickers	91.9
Detention of people consuming alcohol or drugs in public	90.9
Protection of crime victims	90.6
Control of sale of alcohol to minors by bars and liquor stores	90.5
Respect for the rights of individuals	89.2
Provision of information to prevent robbery of people and shops	88.3
Community relations	83.7
Problem-solving with neighborhood groups	82.4
Monitoring compliance with traffic rules	82.0
Monitoring identity of "suspicious" people on the street	81.8
Regular hearings with the participation of residents	79.0
Detention of street prostitutes	76.1
Combating the detention of vehicles or persons to charge them for transiting streets	72.1

Source: Estudio Percepción y Evaluación de la labor de Carabineros de Chile (Ministerio del Interior–Carabineros, 2003).

ated new programs such as the Quadrant Plan with government support, and essentially kept its doctrine and organization intact. Thus, Carabineros integrated fully with the democratic system without altering their militarized and centralized organization.

Public support for the force does not seem to depend solely on fear of high crime levels (which could explain increased public dependence on the police); instead, it appears to reflect a positive assessment of police service and Carabineros' levels of discipline and education. The surveys analyzed here tend to show that the public values these attributes and is less concerned about transparency. The demand for community policing programs and for public information about crime figures and police

Table 5.5 Evaluation of the Performance of the *Carabineros* by Type of Action

Type of Action	Negative (Bad/Very Bad) (%)	Positive (Good/Very Good)(%)	Net Evaluation (Pos./Neg.)(%)
Traffic accidents assistance/rescue	3.8	69.2	65.4
Natural disasters assistance/rescue	4.3	69.5	65.2
Monitoring compliance with traffic rules	7.6	62.9	55.3
Search for missing persons	5.4	58.2	52.8
Home emergency assistance	6.3	58.2	51.9
Safeguarding public order in mass events	9.5	58.8	49.3
Frontier control	4.1	50.2	46.1
Control and safety during marches or public demonstrations	10.8	55.3	44.5
Detention of criminals	14.0	51.1	37.1
Repression of vandalism	10.6	47.6	37.0
Respect for individuals' rights	15.6	45.3	29.7
Addressing intrafamily violence	13.0	42.2	29.2
Patrolling of central streets on foot	22.4	46.1	23.7
Protection of victims of crime	18.3	39.4	21.1
Visible street patrols, especially at night	24.1	42.3	18.2
Community relations	20.0	37.0	17.0
Criminal investigation	16.0	32.3	16.3
Economic crime investigation	15.0	30.9	15.9
Monitoring identity of suspicious people on the street	19.7	32.4	12.7
Operations to combat drug traffickers	24.1	35.9	11.8
Detention of people consuming alcohol or drugs in public	25.9	35.4	9.5
Detention of street prostitutes	21.0	28.9	7.9
Speedy dispatch of vehicles in response to emergency calls	28.2	35.3	7.1
Prevention of drug consumption activities	29.6	32.4	2.8
Control of sale of alcohol to minors in liquor stores and bars	29.4	30.5	1.1
Action against the detention of vehicles or persons to charge them for transiting streets	24.0	22.9	-1.1
Provision information to prevent robbery of residents and shops	29.6	28.3	-1.3
Working with neighborhood groups to solve problems	39.3	22.1	-17.2
Regular public hearings with resident participation	37.5	20.2	-17.3

Source: Estudio Percepción y Evaluación de la labor de Carabineros de Chile (Ministerio del Interior-Carabineros, 2003).

activities does not seem to be very high on the public agenda. Thus, the lack of radical changes within the Chilean police forces accurately reflects the attitudes of the population. However, the surveys also show that the police are not equally trusted and valued across the board. Generally, lower-income sectors view the performance of the police less favorably, particularly with regard to their impartiality, and also show significant levels of mistrust and the perception that the police do not provide sufficient protection for them. The available information indicates that the police, particularly the Carabineros, face significant challenges, notably, a large gap between priority problems for the public and the perception of CC taking actions to address them. At the same time, the surveys show that concerns vary according to social class or geographic sector, which suggests that police work should be much more decentralized to respond to local concerns. However, decentralization would require major changes in the present organizational structure and is likely to face opposition from the institution's top echelons.

NOTES

1. See Mark Ungar, "*La Mano Dura:* Current Dilemmas in Latin American Police Reform," in this volume.

2. Hugo Frühling, "Dos décadas de reforma policial en América Latina: factores para su éxito o fracaso" ("Two Decades of Police Reform in Latin America: Factors for Success or Failure"), in Erik Alda y Gustavo Béliz, *¿Cuál es la salida? La agenda inconclusa de seguridad ciudadana (What Is the Solution? The Unfinished Agenda of Public Security),* ed. Erik Alda and Gustavo Beliz, 281–310 (Washington, DC: Inter-American Development Bank, 2007).

3. Ministerio del Interior-Carabineros, *Estudio de percepción y evaluación de la labor de Carabineros de Chile de octubre de 2003* (Santiago: MI-Carabineros, 2003); Ministerio del Interior, *Encuesta nacional urbana de seguridad ciudadana* (Santiago: Ministerio del Interior, 2004.)

4. Rachel Neild, "Sustaining Reform: Democratic Policing in Central America" *Citizen Security Monitor,* October 2002, p. 3 (Washington, DC: Washington Office on Latin America [WOLA]); Gino Costa, *La Policía Nacional Civil de El Salvador, 1990–1997* (San Salvador: UCA Editores, 1999.)

5. Fundación de Estudios para la Aplicación del Derecho (FESPAD) and Centro de Estudios Penales de El Salvador (CEPES). *Estado de la seguridad pública y la justicia penal en El Salvador, julio 2002–diciembre 2003.* El Salvador: FESPAD-CEPES, 2004.

6. In December 2006, the UN and the Guatemalan government signed an accord to create an International Commission Against Impunity in Guatemala (CICIG) to support the Office of the Public Prosecutor and other state institutions to investigate and dismantle these illicit organizations. Its broad goal is to assist the Guatemalan Public Prosecutor and National Police to investigate and prosecute a limited number of very difficult, sensitive cases. The Guatemalan Congress ratified the CICIG agreement on August 1, 2007.

7. Institutional Law of the National Police no 96-04, Article 39, Paragraph II.

8. On changes in the disciplinary system in the Peruvian police, see Carlos Basombrío and Fernando Rospigliosi, *La seguridad y sus instituciones en el Perú a inicios del siglo XXI: Reformas democráticas o neomilitarismo (Security and Its Institutions in Peru in the Early 21st Century: Democratic Reforms or Neomilitarism)* (Lima: Institute for Peruvian Studies, 2006), 220–33. For an analysis of two provinces in Argentina, see Gustavo Palmieri, Josefina Martínez, Máximo Sozzo, and Hernán Thomas, "Mecanismos de control interno e iniciativas de reforma en las instituciones policiales argentinas: Los casos de la Policía Federal Argentina, la Policía de la Provincia de Santa Fé y la Policía de la Provincia de Buenos Aires" ("Internal Control Mechanisms and Argentine Reform Initiatives: The Cases of the Argentine Federal Police, the Provincial Police of Santa Fé and the Provincial Police of Buenos Aires"), in Hugo Frühling and Azun Candina, *Policía, Sociedad y Estado: Modernización y Reforma Policial en América del Sur (Police, Society and the State: Modernization and Police Reform in South America),* ed. Hugo Frühling and Azun Candina, 177–220 (Santiago, Center for Development Studies, 2001).

9. Saima Hussain, 'Na guerra, que morre nao é innocente': Human Rights Implementation, Policing, and Public Security Reform in Rio de Janeiro, Brazil" (Ph.D. dissertation, Netherlands School of Human Rights Research, Utrecht University, 2007), pgs. 148–78.

10. Ibid., 171–78.

11. Hugo Frühling. "Policía comunitaria y reforma policial en América Latina: ¿cuál es el impacto?" (Serie Documentos del Centro de Estudios en Seguridad Ciudadana, Santiago, Universidad de Chile, 2003); Hugo Frühling, ed., *Calles más seguras: estudios sobre policía comunitaria en América Latina* (Washington, DC: Inter-American Development Bank, 2004).

12. Tulio Kahn, "Policía comunitaria: evaluando la experiencia de Sao Paulo" ("Community Policing: Evaluating the Sao Paulo Experience"), in *Participación Ciudadana y Reformas a la Policía en América del Sur (Citizen Participation and Policing Reforms in South America),* ed. H. Frühling and A. Candina (Santiago de Chile: Center for Development Studies, 2004), 214.

13. "Victimización en la Ciudad de Buenos Aires," Universidad de San Andrés, Buenos Aires, 2007.

14. Carlos Maldonado Prieto, "Los Carabineros de Chile: historia de una policía militarizada," *Nordic Journal of Latin American Studies* 20, no. 3 (1990): 3–31; Hugo Frühling, "Carabineros y consolidación democrática en Chile," *Pena y Estado* (Buenos Aires) 3, no. 3 (1998): 81–116.

15. Frühling, "Carabineros y consolidación 88–92.

16. Decree Law 44, May 4, 1974.

17. The military courts have broad jurisdiction over the Carabineros, covering crimes committed by its members as well as those committed by civilians against CC officers. See Jorge Mera Figueroa, "Hacia una reforma de la justicia militar, delito militar, régimen disciplinario, competencia y organización" (Cuadernos de Análisis Jurídico, Escuela de Derecho, Universidad Diego Portales, October 2002).

18. Under the military regime (1973–1990) the directors general of this force were retired army generals. Nelson Mery, who made his career within the institutions, was director general between 1992 and 2003. He was replaced in 2003 by Arturo Herrera, former head of police education.

19. Hugo Frühling. "Carabineros y consolidación."

20. This diagnosis was undertaken by a Forum of Experts, which compiled data from various sources to describe tendencies in criminality between 1977 and 2003, since the Ministry of the Interior only has homologated data on the Carabineros and the PI since 1999.

21. Among these are included theft with force, violent robbery or robbery with intimidation, theft, homicide, injuries, and rape, to which is added intrafamily violence.

22. See Ministry of the Interior, Forum of Experts on Citizen Security, "Diagnóstico de la seguridad ciudadana en Chile" (working paper no.1, Santiago de Chile, 2003).

23. When the Carabineros find a body it registers it as "discovery of body" rather than a homicide, since only a judge can determine whether there has been a crime or not.

24. For an analysis of institutional changes in the PI see Azun Candina and Alejandra Lunecke, "Formación en derechos humanos y control institucional: los cambios en la Policía de Investigaciones de Chile, 1992–2002," in *Participación ciudadana y reformas a la policía en América del Sur,* ed. Hugo Frühling and Azun Candina, 119–66. Santiago: Centro de Estudios del Desarrollo, 2004.

25. "Plan antidelictivo: Carabineros deja de cumplir funciones extra policiales." *El Mercurio,* January 12, 1999, A1 and A10.

26. Hugo Frühling. "Policía comunitaria y reforma policial," 12 and 13.

27. Ministry of Finance, Budget Division, "Executive Report: Quadrant Plan of Preventive Security" (Santiago: 2007.)

28. Ministry of Defense, Undersecretariat of Carabineros, "Comments and Observations on the Evaluation Made by the Responsible Institution" (Santiago, 2007).

29. Claudio Fuentes, "Denuncias por actos de violencia policial," FLACSO-Chile, 2001.

30. The two surveys are not strictly comparable but can be used to compare consistently citizens' perceptions of police corruption. My hypothesis is that the percentage of people personally affected by acts of corruption is relatively small and lower than the perception that members of Carabineros are corrupt, particularly among the poor.

31. Forty-one percent of the sample said they had witnessed a member of Carabineros using unnecessary force.

CHAPTER SIX

The Weaknesses of Public Security Forces in Mexico City

ELENA AZAOLA

This chapter outlines some of the results of a qualitative study conducted between 2001 and 2005 on the preventative police in Mexico City. One of the key goals of this study has been to "give a voice" to police officers so as to understand their views and their understanding of their job, as well as the obstacles they face when doing their work. The premises of the study are that police officers must know about and be willing to carry out any police reform project if it is to produce profound changes (see Bayley 2001); that if reform is to have the backing of the police, it must take their needs into account and respond to their problems; and that to know and understand the problems that are most important for police officers, it is necessary to listen to their points of view.

The study underpinning this chapter consists of an analysis of the testimony of 280 police officers in all ranks of the hierarchy. One hundred and seventy of them were interviewed at police headquarters, and 110 are eight-page autobiographies written by police officers of different ranks and career lengths who responded to an invitation from their institution to write the story of their life as a policeman.[1]

The preventative police supposed to protect Mexico City's nine million inhabitants consist of seventy-six thousand officers.[2] Half are employees of the Secretariat of Public Security (Secretaría de Seguridad Pública, SSP), and the other half (auxiliary and bank police) have an irregular status, so that while they are members of the force, their labor rights are not fully recognized, and they operate autonomously and according to arbitrary and rather opaque criteria (Arroyo 2003; Varenik 2005). Of the total, including auxiliary forces, 20 percent are traffic police (policía de vialidad). Belonging to the traffic police is considered a privilege, even though not all officers have access to a patrol car or a motorcycle. This is because traffic cops have the most opportunities to extort people who violate the traffic code, and the income they receive from extortion far outstrips their wages (Pérez 2004).

The preventative police is not only the most numerous force in Mexico City but also in the rest of the Mexican Republic, as can be seen in Table 6.1; it accounts for 91 percent of the state force at the national level. The mandate of the various preventive police forces is to preserve public order, respond to citizens' needs, protect their lives and goods, and control motor traffic; the judicial or ministerial police and the Federal Agency of Investigations are in charge of criminal investigations, although the preventative police can also detain people caught committing a crime in flagrante delicto.

Table 6.1 National State Forces in Mexico, 2006

Police	Force	Percentage
Municipal Preventative	144,276	37
State Preventative	190,730	49
Judicial or Ministerial	25,495	7
Federal Preventative	19,597	5
Federal Investigation Agents	5,945	2
Total	386,043	100

Source: Information supplied by Secretaría de Seguridad Pública Federal, January 2007.

MAIN FINDINGS

It is a known fact that the inhabitants of Mexico City are dissatisfied with the performance of the police (see, among others, Zepeda 2004; López Portillo 2003; Arango 2004). It is a perhaps less-known fact that there is also deep and widespread job dissatisfaction among the police. High levels of uncertainty prevail, as there is no consistent application of norms in the contractual relationship between the Public Security Secretariat and the police. There is also widespread vertical (inter-rank) and horizontal (inter pares) lack of trust within the institution, which constitutes a significant obstacle to the adequate performance of police work. Because norms and procedures are not consistently applied, a parallel informal or paralegal regime governs relations among officers. Deplorable working conditions have also generated a sense of abandonment or lack of protection among police officers, leading to their growing loss of interest in properly fulfilling their duties. Another important problem is what the rank-and-file describes as a continual lack of citizen respect and recognition.

There are some recurring issues that emerge in both the interviews and the autobiographies. First among them are the problems related to deficient working conditions. Second, there is the problem of corruption and the way in which the police address the issue. Other issues that come up frequently are: relations with police chiefs, a negative self-image and the image citizens have of the police, problems related to lack of training, the way officers feel they are treated by the institution, and alcohol and drug consumption among officers. The following section uses a small sample of the collected testimonies to examine these issues.[3]

DEFICIENT WORKING CONDITIONS

Police officers often refer to a set of issues related to deficient working conditions. There is broad consensus on this matter, although there are nuances and differences depending on rank, seniority, or the sector or grouping to which officers belong. The problems are related to wages, material conditions, working hours, and promotions.

Wages

There is great dissatisfaction with wages among the rank-and-file. It is commonplace to hear officers of all ranks say that low wages promote and even justify corruption. They also say that poor police performance is related to low wage levels.

> This job is not valued in our society. In any other country, a policeman is well paid, but a policeman is not well paid here and so he can't do his job properly

> To improve [the situation of] corruption, they would have to pay us a good salary. They pay us three thousand pesos every two weeks, minus the deductions . . . This is not enough for the family . . . if we have no stimulus, well, we look for another way to get ahead . . . if we got a decent wage, we would do our work more carefully and we would not risk things for the 100 or 200 pesos that drivers give us.

Strange as this may seem, some police officers have gone so far as to suggest that if it is not possible to pay them a better wage, their employer should help them to find another job.

> I think that a policeman should be helped, or the corporation itself should help him, to find an extra job, to improve his living standard . . . I would like to be called into the office someday and that they would find us another vocation other than this one of being a policeman, so that there would be more opportunities for the people who have a real service vocation.

> If I were the head of the police, I would reduce the number of effective police officers in order to improve training and raise wages. I would take good care of my police officers and would recognize their achievements publicly.

The rank-and-file do not express dissatisfaction just because of the poor wages they are paid, but also because rules and procedures that would make their jobs more secure are not consistently applied, there is a lack of recognition for their work, there are no other incentives and benefits, and many of the promises made to them are never fulfilled. Thus, one of the major causes of discouragement is that they do not know what they can count on.

> The main problem is resignation among most of the elements and a great disillusionment because they feel deceived because of so many promises that for whatever reason are never fulfilled . . . clear rules are needed for this to work properly . . . rules that chain up the corrupt one who wants to be a chief and will not allow him to be one. Recognition of higher ranking colleagues is very important when good work is done. We are greatly lacking in self-esteem, to the point of sometimes thinking about suicide because of the feeling that no one cares about us as human beings. We need people to listen to us and to take an interest in what is happening to us.

> The great majority of the elements fulfill their work more out of obligation than conviction. Our job lacks of something: motivation and acknowledgment.

As these testimonies show, the problem is not just that officers are very low paid, but also that their efforts are not valued or appreciated, and that they are not able to express their points of view. This is why they repeatedly insist on the need for their superiors to listen to them and to take their opinions into account. Indeed, they often describe situations in which, far from gaining recognition for undertaking important work, they were further discouraged by inadequate responses.[4]

Equipment and Uniforms

Police officers are almost unanimous in their discontent with lack of equipment and with their uniforms, which are either inadequate or of very bad quality.

> We the police lack equipment, we don't have it because of the corruption at the higher levels. They have not given us uniforms for two

years . . . Our flak jackets are not part of our uniform and we have to buy them ourselves, the quality of the uniforms is very bad, and we are not given good equipment.

Because we are a special group, we suffer from many unmet needs. We have to buy our own flashlights, batteries, everything we need to go into an alley. We are aware that we have to buy something, but we do not have enough means to buy uniforms only to have them stolen.

The top administrative ranks have not given us uniforms or credentials for over ten years. The majority of delinquents carry better weapons than we do. We even have to pay for bullets, they charge us ten pesos, and most of the times we shoot into the air just to scare people.

Regarding equipment, the problem is not just that they are not given the minimum equipment necessary to do their job properly, but also— as the testimonies show—that equipment is distributed discretionally, or stolen, or that police officers are forced to pay for it, be it access to a weapon, a motorbike, or a patrol car. And they are also charged if they want to work in certain (less dangerous and more profitable) areas. According to the testimonials, they must pay for bullets, flashlights, batteries, and also for the repair of patrol cars, and that, as shown below, they prefer to pay rather than to limit their source of "income." It is notable that the issue of the uniform is more relevant than that of equipment, or at least is mentioned more frequently. This is because the uniform is not only an important personal presentation element for officers, but also a part of what constitutes the identity of the police. Indeed, the identity of the police seems to be tied up with or embodied by their uniform, which explains why, when they are given a bad quality uniform, they feel offended.

I want to go on serving with this uniform, that is my life and thus honor the name of the Secretariat . . . I'm not thinking of turning in this uniform, I am not shamed of being a policeman . . . I love this uniform and wouldn't change it for anything in the world.

Working Hours

The working day is predominantly a cause of complaint among the higher (superintendent) and mid-level ranks (officers and inspectors), as shown by these testimonies:

> We get no family or social life, no working hours . . . We have not had a holiday for more than fifteen years. Many of us are single because we destroy any chance of having a family . . . We do not get to see our children grow up. Sometimes we see what we gain but we don't see what we lose: family and health.

> We get up at 4 o'clock in the morning and at 22:30 we get home, annoyed, exhausted, tired, angry . . . everything on the street is a noisy confusion . . . we only want to get home so that we can begin to get comfortable. The family sees us from 11 o'clock at night until 4 in the morning . . . We cannot enjoy our family.

> Chiefs and sub-chiefs should do shifts and work only 8 hour days, and not work for the long hours that we do because it feels horrible to fall asleep when we get into the patrol car.

> We never get holidays, never. In seven or eight years, we have not missed one day [of work]. Having a post in the structure means we cannot miss work, get ill, nothing. If we get ill, we are fired.

> We are always at work at 5:30 in the morning until 11 at night. So the people who run the Secretariat are tired, exhausted. A mid-level officer is not allowed to go on holiday or take sick leave. This is an attack on the family, not only on oneself, and this has an effect on the discontent of commanding officers.

Although working hours appear to be a greater source of discontent among the upper ranks, there are many reasons why it also concerns police officers with no leadership positions. The main one is probably that the area where they live is not taken into account when assigning them to a sector or group, which often means that the journey to and from work prolongs their working day by up to three or four hours. Indeed, officers cannot request reassignment for this reason. Other reasons why the working day might be prolonged is when police officers are punished with eight to thirty-six hours of arrest, which usually happens for minor or innocuous misdemeanors (such as not wearing their helmet, for instance), or because of arbitrary decisions by their bosses. Even when interviewees say that the time and the conditions of arrests have improved, they still claim that conditions are far from complying with clearly established rules and procedures.[5] Indeed, almost every police officer says that they have suffered unjustified arrest.

Another issue addressed by many interviewees is the bad quality of the food they get at police barracks or when they are on the street, as well as the difficulties they face when trying to satisfy their most elementary necessities while at work. Many officers said their bosses were indifferent to or insensitive about their basic necessities, and that the same was true of citizens who make fun of them or berate them for eating in the public space to the point that there is no recognition of their humanity.

If you are a policeman, it is as though you were not a human being: you can't go to the bathroom or eat; citizens don't like it when they see you eating some tacos. When they see us eating, people shout at us asking if that is what they are paying their taxes for.

There are no proper facilities at the barracks, good toilets, a dining room, a library . . . There would be no need for a policeman to go out and get [money] to have lunch if there was a good dining room with even just some coffee and bread. A human being with a nice bellyful would go out to work happily . . . If they want better security, they have to improve the barracks, the toilets, dining facilities, otherwise in what conditions do we leave the barracks to go out on the street?

There is something that is very fundamental: people have to realize that we police are human beings, not robots. We cannot work like robots . . . Society does not trouble to think that we also think and feel like they do, that we are not made of steel and that we are not supermen either.

I would ask for more psychological support because sometimes we need to know that we matter to somebody.

The image of the robot, the machine of steel, or the superman emerges when they refer to their condition and their human necessities, and this clearly shows how they feel ill treated.

Promotions

Another main cause of discontent is lack of respect for procedures and norms that regulate careers and promotions. There is a broad consensus about this within the rank-and-file (not among the top ranks). The testimonies include frequent references to disappointment because promotions fail to materialize even when the requirements stipulated in the regulations have been met.[6] There are also references to the innumerable arbitrary decisions that ignore the requirements and lead to the practice of giving jobs to family members, friends, or people that are recommended, without recognition of the efforts made by officers who have served for years without ever being promoted.[7]

There have been no courses for promotion in ten years. I was promoted twice during the first eight years, but over the last ten years I have not been able to rise up the ranks . . . There are so many obstacles in our way, and when you do not find the right way, you lose heart. When you prepare for something and you don't succeed, you get frustrated . . . What has happened to all those promises?

There are people that prepare themselves and rise up the ranks, but there are others that ascend just because they are someone's relative. Everyone wants a motorbike or a patrol car, but only chosen relatives get a look in. There are no places other than for the mounted police or in the grenadiers (*granaderos*).

Various testimonies pointed in the same direction: loss of motivation due to repeated attempts to make rules work that are never applied; lack of trust and uncertainty that generate a sense of insecurity when rules exist but are flouted; and finally, a sense of apathy and paralysis caused by these situations. Table 6.2 compares opinions about working conditions according to rank.

CORRUPTION

This section looks at the different explanations that policemen offer for corruption and at some of the corrupt practices in which they are involved. It also offers an overall view of the issue and raises some questions about it. First, there is the simplest explanation that low wages among the rank-and-file cause corruption.

> Policemen are corrupt because what they get paid is not enough.

> If they paid us a good wage, corruption would be solved. What happens right now is that with the infractions we are paying ourselves for the salary that we are not given.

By contrast, others think that people become officers because they intend to obtain income through corruption.

> The uniform is used to get rich: 95 percent of the policemen come in with the idea that they will get rich.

For others, the problem is the lack of institutional support they receive at the onset of their professional careers, which becomes a decisive factor in the corruption of police officers. Some policemen refer to the time they started the basic training course given at the police academy as the moment when they began to have close contact with corruption.

> [T]he teachers and instructors themselves were part of the much hated corruption because some teachers with no ethics would sell exams and ranks, and some instructors, for a certain amount of money, would let people off when they were arrested.

Table 6.2 Views of Working Conditions among Police Officers by Rank

Top Ranks	Mid-Level Ranks	The Rank-and-File
I have been on the job for forty-five years and I earn a good wage, I cannot complain. Things have gone well for me, so what I have I owe to the police. I have not paid for my rise up the ranks; I have earned it with my work. The regular policeman works an eight or twelve hour shift, but we who have a post in the structure have no personal life and because of my age and seniority I hold on to this, I do my job carefully because it is the only thing that sustains me. If I retire they give me a pauper's wage of five thousand pesos, and I lose my rank. And do you know what this has cost us? Our life . . .	The street is a jungle; you have to cross yourself to go out. It is not our judgment but that of our bosses that counts on the street, or we risk being arrested. For them everything is wrong, if they find us eating or if we go to the toilet, you have to ask permission for everything. They don't care what we eat or if we drink, they don't care about what time we go home, so what rights has a policeman got? Only a few of us enjoy this job, we do it because we need to, because as we say, where shall we go at our age? I prefer to risk dying here, to go to jail or to be kicked out, than to be . . . unemployed.	I took exams to be promoted and they even gave a rank to those who failed, and those of us who passed were told there were not enough posts. They tell me the same thing at every examination session (*convocatoria*). It would be better if they told me how much I have to pay for a rank rather than making me go round in circles. I've been in service for twenty-two years and have taken the exams several times; they always say the same thing, there are no open posts. They demoralize you and even lower your wages. They should be fair and not have preferences, because they promote their friends and their secretaries. It is traumatizing to be in service for so many years and always remain a lowly policeman.
It is harder to be a boss now because the elements talk to you as an equal (*se te ponen al tú por tú*). Arrests used to last eight to fifteen days, but not anymore, there was more discipline before. They did not know as much before, and now they read the regulations and know that arrests can only last 36 hours. They have lawyers advising them. We should not let them to be advised like this.	One feels bad because there is no work security, if a new superior comes along one is fired, or one loses ones position. Effort is not rewarded.	We are not given the chance to ascend honestly. We have been here for so many years and I have not even been thanked, we don't even get the medals we used to receive every five years. Now they just give us two additional pesos for every five years and thirty-four pesos for meals for the family (*despensa*).

Source: Interviews by Elena Azaola and Esperanza Reyes, secretariat of Public Security.

We went to the shooting range three times, but as we were not given bullets, the teacher would tell us that if we wanted to shoot we would have to pay him to buy them . . . This is when I realized that it is in the academy that the spirit of corruption of the policeman is formed.

Yet others stated that corruption began when they were assigned to a specific sector or group.

You get to the sector and the bosses begin to ask you for money. They force the policeman to get money off people. There are policemen who say that if they go out with five pesos, they have to come back with a thousand; that's what they say.

As soon as you set foot in the sector, you get asked for money for everything: the uniform, notebook, not to get sent here or there or not to have to do this or that job, and most of all for a patrol car . . . As soon as you get in, it's a begging spree (*pedidera*). I give the money, if I have it, because you get a benefit . . . There is consent at all levels.

It is hard to add anything else to the above testimonies. In any case, it is important to emphasize the common element among them: the ease with which people admit their own and others' participation in corruption, as well as the absence of a framework in which legality is the frame of reference and the acceptance of a parallel order or paralegal regime that in fact governs the institution. Equally, the lack of questioning corruption and the sense that one is confronting something inevitable, is striking.

Some women police officers said that they also participate in corruption.

There is more corruption among the men than among us women, which is why they say that the police are corrupt. We also take what we can, we don't ask for money but if we are offered it, we accept it. What happens is that we are not offered it as openly and unashamedly because some of us get offended and kick up a fuss, but others don't.

Those who have held administrative posts also mention cases of corruption.

> There are lots of irregularities, for example, according to a staff list I had twelve hundred officers in my charge, but in reality there were only two hundred; the others were seconded to politicians and I didn't even know them and nor have their files. The DF government itself would give them leave and would send them out with journalists, former presidents; a crime of diversion of human resources . . . Some were seconded for as long as fifteen or twenty years and I never knew where they were; but they had a rank and received a wage.

> Before, there were also journalists and actors who received the rank of police officers and would receive a wage corresponding to their supposed rank. The wives of the chiefs got them as well. So there were actors who were captains, colonels, etc.

The above quotes show how the ties of corruption are woven between institutions through informal agreements to such an extent that this leads to the predominance of a paralegal order. This system operates on a personal and political basis that includes the higher and middle management of the police organization. In other words, on the margins of and above existing laws, a number of officers have ceased to carry out their public security functions, so that they can protect the private security of civil servants and their family members, members of the governing party, friends, or journalists. On the other hand, there are groups within the institution, such as the patrols on motorcycles or cars that are particularly desirable since they are considered to be the best sources of "income." It is therefore said that not just anyone can enter these groups, since posts are reserved for family members or people recommended by the chiefs.

> Patrol car duty brings in quite a lot of money . . . some colleagues repair their patrol cars or buy parts when the cars break down, because if they wait for them to get fixed, they stop earning . . . they prove that it is best to invest their money in the institution than in any other

business . . . In the police, you can invest and gain juicy benefits, although the fault is partly that of the population that does not report this.

We get charged one hundred pesos for not coming in to work, five hundred for getting in the patrol car, and I could go on like this listing the infinite number of acts of corruption that exist within the corporation.

Some officers hold their chiefs responsible for corruption. Various testimonies mentioned the existence of what is known as the Brotherhood (*Hermandad*) among the chiefs.

The top ranks are part of a power group, of the so-called corrupt Hermandad that does not allow trained young policemen to take up leadership posts, since those posts have not only cost them years of service but also money, and they do not think that one should rise up the ranks without paying the price. They own this Secretariat and between them they rotate sectors with the help of a godfather (*Jefe Halcón*). There have been sector chiefs that have been removed for corruption, but instead of being punished, they have been put in another sector.

The famous Hermandad has to end, that mafia that does so much damage to the corporation and the only thing it does is rotate posts . . . But a chief has never been fired; that really would be a notable thing.

We all go in wanting to be good policemen, but our aspirations are cut short by some chiefs who, instead of supporting us, send us out to work so that they can demand quotas from us.

All of us who have been career officers get caught up in the game of receiving money [from people] to give to the commander and [in this way] receive privileges . . . it is a chain that reaches up to the top.

The above quotations provide another different and contradictory reason for corruption: according to these latter testimonies, corruption is not a result of insufficient wages among the rank-and-file but the result of pressure that the top rank officials put on lower ranking officers to raise for them certain amounts of money. This operation is also portrayed as unchangeable even though most of those interviewed report that, in one way or another, they are victims of such a system. Other testimonies mention that ranks can also be bought and that many are chiefs because they paid for the post they occupy.

There are still personnel whose ranks were given or bought under past administrations.

That is the first link in the chain of that old corruption: everything has a price here.

Here you can ascend through your wallet (*bolsillo*), buying posts. I have never had that opportunity because I never came across any of the influential ones . . . they would have to be my acquaintances for me to do it.

Another form of corruption is to earn money by protecting criminals.

One of the things that aids corruption is fear, because when we get a criminal, we know who they are and we know they will get out and sometimes even offer us money . . . and since wages are very bad and we do not get promoted, well, sometimes we take it.

Another source of corruption relates to the distribution of benefits. For example, the contribution of the police to build houses, which is allocated through a lottery system, is flawed and biased. Various officers testified to the fact that their chiefs often win the lotteries.

Here, the police do not get given houses, but they say that there are police chiefs with three or four apartments they receive because they have "won lotteries."

Yet another corruption problem that is often mentioned is the management of the police force savings bank, a problem that has not been resolved despite having been the object of a criminal investigation and prosecution a few years ago.

Another view is that police corruption cannot be explained without taking into account the participation of the citizenry, although in some cases the emphasis on citizen responsibility appears to be an attempt to exonerate the police. In addition, some policemen cover up corruption saying that they do not extort citizens but rather the latter give them "gifts" to show their gratitude and appreciation for their services.

> Corruption is often the fault of citizens who offer us [money] to sort out a problem. Other times it is a gift because they are grateful for our work . . . So we don't know if it is right or wrong to accept what citizens give us out of gratitude, which is a gift . . . I don't think there is anything wrong with it, it's not as if we extort them.

> People think that all police officers are corrupt, but corruption starts with the citizens because it is easier for them to speed up their business and save time with money. The government allows many things, the city is engulfed in corruption, and since we do not get good social benefits because of the economy of the country, the policeman allows himself to be corrupted.

> I would like to ask citizens and the mass media: why are they so keen to put the blame on us if there is corruption everywhere in this country? [Even] various government authorities and leaders have stolen money from the Mexicans.

> There are others who steal millions and get immunity. But when the policeman steals four pesos, he is persecuted.

The above testimonies are worrying because, in addition to referring to gifts as a way to cover up or justify corruption, they appear to suggest the following argument: if politicians can steal, why should the police not? Or, if there is impunity for politicians, why should the police not benefit from it as well? This seems to suggest that police corruption is justified or minimized by pointing out that others are corrupt. There is also a rather widespread view that it is not possible to put a stop to corruption or even to address it with any degree of success.

Corruption within the police is an evil that cannot be exterminated . . .
At the rank-and-file level, when a policeman is efficient, corruption
should not be seen negatively.

People say that if we were paid better wages there would be no more
extortion (*mordida*). I don't think so; there would be extortion and
wages.

Finally, others testify that corruption is not just a mark of the relationship between police officers and citizens, but also that it profoundly alters
the relationship that police officers have among themselves. This is apparent in the following testimony.

Discipline has to be imposed, but what breaks the chain of command
is corruption, since we cannot look at our chiefs in the same way after
we have given them money and after they have accepted it. If I am
going to apply corrective measures to someone for not doing their job
and if the chief has received money from someone, then he will not be
able to apply that corrective [measure] because the subordinate will
not respect him anymore, so that is how the chain of command is lost,
because of corruption.

Corruption, then, not only alters or subverts the relationship between
police and citizens, but also irremediably distorts relations among police
officers. The testimonies suggest that most officers cannot escape corruption. This not only exposes them to citizen opprobrium but also
breaks down police self-confidence. If chiefs ask their subordinates to
pay dues, and if the latter, in turn, ask citizens to do so; if anyone who has
attained a certain rank is suspected of having bought their post; or if
every person knows about acts of corruption among their colleagues, and
the latter, in turn, know about one's own acts of corruption, then nobody
is immune and nobody can trust anyone else or be trusted by anyone
else. This is perhaps the greatest weakness of the police institution. This
being the case, corruption is probably more damaging to the police than
to citizens. In sum, police officers cannot escape corruption, which leaves
them exposed, makes them vulnerable, and puts them in such a weak position that their capacity to carry out their duty properly is extremely

limited. It is as though they become unable to act other than from a position of vulnerability, a position that does not allow them to escape corruption: theirs, that of their chiefs, and that of their peers. A situation like the one just described is clearly unsustainable or places a heavy burden on the functioning of the organization, and so it appears that the only way to counteract vulnerability is to subscribe to a sort of tacit pact that forces officers to protect themselves and cover up for one another. This pact, however, only serves to establish a precarious equilibrium that is under constant threat of breakdown. This explains the growing number of officers who are reported, investigated, or sent to prison.

As regards corruption among the citizenry, it seems that the procedures in place to ensure compliance with traffic rules are so ineffective that, as pointed out in various testimonies, everyone finds it advantageous—even if only on the surface and in the short-term—to violate the rules and find a way around them through corruption. In this case, it is necessary to think about the kinds of procedures that might favor rule obedience and allow for the reestablishment of bonds of trust between the police and the citizenry.[8]

IMAGE AND SELF-IMAGE

One of the issues that has received little attention in the specialized literature is the self-image of the police. However, this issue is relevant when trying to understand the way they view themselves, the way they think others see them, and how their language and their categories reflect this. It also seems important to see whether there have been changes in the way officers viewed the institution before they became members, and how they see themselves after they have become members, as well as the way in which they think citizens view them, and how they view citizens from their own vantage point. This set of "images" is important insofar as it can tell us how policemen feel about everyone who is not an officer, the perceived constraints to their work that emerge as a result of their image, and the way in which this affects their performance.

By collecting the views of officers on these issues, I have attempted to understand how they see themselves and how they feel others see them, which is another way of looking at how they relate with others once they have adopted the identity of an officer. This work is also an attempt to relate or integrate a subjective dimension (self-perception) and an objective reality (relations with other agents or sectors). As we know, both dimensions are always present, and interact and condition one another.

Self-Image

Most testimonies presented below aim to answer the question of how officers viewed the institution before they became officers, and how they see it and themselves now.

> Just hearing the word "police" would leave a bad taste in my mouth . . . I thought that all these people did was rob or extort people who had the misfortune of falling into their hands. Six years on the other side has not changed my view of the police much, there is no end of justifications, some very valid, others less so, but what is certain is that the police does not work as it should.

> Before I entered the corporation, the opinion I had was the same as the one many people have today: I thought that being a policeman was the worst thing, that policemen were crooks, extortionists. I was one of those people who would hurl insults when I saw a patrol detaining a driver . . . I thought that it was degrading to be a uniformed police officer, that these were people who were not educated enough. I was against the police in every way. When I entered the institution, I was insulted and attacked and even beaten on many occasions by people who think like I used to think.

> For normal people or civilians, the police have always been a source of fear, repression, beings from another world, illiterate, drunkards, drug addicts, thieves, etc. Obviously, I could not think differently; when seeing an armed officer, I would imagine being detained so that they could rob me or put me in the police car.

> Before I entered the corporation, I thought that they were going to treat me badly to train me, that they were going to scorn me for making a mistake or for not doing well in my training.

The idea I had was that the police lacked academic training, which was apparent in the way they spoke; that they were careless with themselves (dirty); that they were thieves and all the other synonyms that society uses to label us, abusive and even murderous.

Before becoming a member of the institution, I thought that being a policeman was degrading, that it was a job that did not live up to the sacrifice I had made to study for my degree . . . When I used to see policemen on the street, they never symbolized security, but rather inspired my mistrust. However, the need for economic income led me to overcome my prejudices and to apply for admission to the mounted regiment.

Initially, I had a deplorable and very negative view of the police, perhaps because I had never had any dealings with them or maybe because of their reputation for corruption and arrogance, but experiencing the inclemency and arbitrariness faced by a good police officer such as myself, I realize how wrong I was.

In my opinion, 80 percent of policemen are negative and only 20 percent want to serve society.

The above testimonies provide a lot of information about how officers see themselves and how they feel others see them. Some of the characterizations made are that officers are thieves, abusive, arrogant, ignorant, dirty, alcoholic, corrupt, rude, addicted to drugs, and aggressive. Although not all the testimonies mention these traits, as a whole the sample transmits a predominantly very negative view of the force before admission to the institution. In some cases, that image became more positive after admission, at which point some officers report some change in their perception. In other cases, officers say that becoming members of the institution did not change but rather corroborated the negative image they harbored. It is relevant to ask what kind of relationship can be established with the citizenry on this basis, or how officers are able to perform with such a low self-image. The following section addresses these questions.

Image Police Have of Citizens

Having looked at how officers view themselves and how they think others observe them, this section now looks at how policemen view citizens and what they would like to say about the created image of the police.

Everyone, from the highest politician to the lowliest of citizens, uses the police as a shield to hide the bad things they do. They say we are corrupt when in fact it is the citizen who is corrupt, and the first thing he does is to offer us money to get rid of the problem after infringing a law or a regulation.

Citizens make demands of us, and I feel angry with the citizenry because it complains, for example, that I am a drunkard but they themselves don't start by changing things. It is not just the police who is corrupt, but the citizen who is willing to give [us money] as well. Necessity breeds corruption. Citizens do not support us; they shout at us, they throw stones at us.

I would like a society that would not stigmatize us for our humble origins. In fact, it is true that we lack a certain economic status, but we do have a strong fighting spirit and enough courage to give our lives for someone who we don't know.

I am aware and know the problem that surrounds us perfectly, because of the pressure that citizens especially submit us to . . . I think that everyone knows that we the police are not loved or supported by anyone. Everyone calls us thieves, conmen.

As regards the citizenry, my experience, like that of any colleague, is of aggression, as well as insults and the classic threats that they will put me in jail for doing my work, but, even with all this, I have a good view of society since in the end we are there to serve it.

When we try to impose order, we get insulted. They have no idea what it is like to spend eight hours standing at a crossroads . . . There are crazy people on the street who insult us for no reason. Sometimes you get into arguments with people and even when a citizen attacks us, he is always right. Sometimes you have to shout at people.

We are the scum of the earth for society because they say we are evil and corrupt and it does not occur to them that we are part of that same society and we are as corrupt as it is. The whole of society has lost its values . . . It is not worth talking to a society that is more corrupt than we are.

For the police officer, citizens are also arrogant, corrupt, and incapable of respecting the rules. Officers seem to feel they are scapegoats, who must purge the evil that others do. Their anger comes across in many ways. They feel scorned, made to look ridiculous, abused, and some even refer to a desire to get revenge on the citizenry. Others adopt a more resigned attitude as if they had no choice but to tolerate the abuse of citizens. Whatever the case, although their relationship with the citizenry is theoretically not confrontational, it is characterized by a fear of being insulted, scorned, and mistreated. It would seem that officers must engage in two types of battles when they go out on the street: on the one hand, they must combat crime and deal with accidents and disorder; on the other hand, they must defend themselves from the mistrust of citizens. Under these conditions, officers are unlikely to offer protection and security given the way citizens regard them.

Institutional Image

The following testimonies refer to the way in which officers view their institution, how they see themselves as members of that institution, and how they compare with other police organizations in the world.

We are at a disadvantage internationally, but only in terms of equipment and installations because in terms of courage, aptitude, of what we call esprit de corps (*espíritu policial*), we are at the level of any other country, if not in first place.

I think that there is no comparison that can be made with international institutions because we are so far below any that one might mention, not because we despise ourselves but we must know our place and try to overcome [our situation] and improve so that one day we can be counted among the best police forces in the world.

The SSP is among the best public security forces in the world, and what we lack is better training to optimize our performance, legal support when we carry out our duties, and to improve the quality of life of police officers with better salaries and benefits.

I think that the police corporations in our country suffer from great deficiencies, not only economic, to acquire the whole infrastructure that would allow us to be better equipped, trained, to be professionals when combating crime; but also deficiencies related to culture, conscience, commitment, royalty, and honesty.

The testimonies above contrast with those in the previous sections because they show that while there is recognition of the institutional deficiencies that put the police at a disadvantage in relation to their foreign counterparts, one also pays a price for being a member of the institution. This is true to such a degree that many testimonies underline what officers consider to be their greatest virtues: bravery, commitment, esprit de corps, which in the eyes of some compensates for what are mostly material deficiencies and puts them on a par with other police forces abroad. However, what prevails and is apparent in the testimonies are very high levels of tension and lack of trust between citizens and the police. Statements devaluing or denigrating them appear constantly in their self-portrayal. What is clear is that whatever the means adopted to confront that reality (including identification with the image that denigrates them, rebelling against it, considering that such an image is better applied to corrupt citizens, or expressing the hope that police-citizen relations will improve in the future), the ability of the police to perform their duty and to provide citizens with security and protection is presently compromised.

CONCLUSION

This chapter has focused mainly on the obstacles that the preventative street police in Mexico City face when attempting to fight crime effectively. As shown, the deficiencies and weaknesses of the police organization, which have become more visible lately, are key obstacles to improved performance. These shortcomings are not new, but seem to have worsened as demands on the institution have increased. As regards crime fighting and democratization, the consolidation of democracy and the rule of law clearly call for more solid and better managed organizations, with higher levels of trust and credibility.

This becomes particularly clear when one sees that in Mexico, as compared with other Latin American countries, the chances of being a victim of a crime are very high. In 2006, 20.2 percent of Mexicans reported being victims of crime, rates nearly as high as Peruvians (26.2 percent), and Chileans (23.1 percent). It is worth mentioning that the 2006 rate of victimization in Mexico increased 3 percent compared with 2004 (Parás and Coleman 2006, 73).

It is important to note that there has been no comprehensive police reform process in Mexico City, although if one compares the institution today to what it was twenty-five years ago it is clear that there have been modest improvements and slow progress in the right direction. Civilian control over the police is practically consolidated, although efficient police administration is still absent.

We must remember that corruption has been identified as a significant challenge to the process of democratization, because it involves deviations from the rule of law (Ambos, Colomer, and Volger 2003; Frühling 2001; Parás and Coleman 2006). At the same time, however, in 2006 almost two-thirds of the Mexican population (64.9 percent) admitted to being seriously worried about the impact of delinquency on citizen well-being now and in the future. In particular, crime victims were less inclined to think that government officials always act according to the law (Parás and Coleman 2006, 82, 86).

Human rights accountability is only just beginning to emerge on the institutional agenda, and the organizational changes to ensure greater respect for human rights have yet to be implemented. Over the last decade, public institutions have begun to supervise compliance with human rights standards. Many complaints were lodged against the police, which is one of the institutions that has resisted such scrutiny most fiercely.[9]

Finally, we need to remember how difficult it is to reform an institution with seventy-six thousand officers. There are significant obstacles to improve working conditions and to elaborate incentive programs for officers. At the same time, constant changes at the top undermine serious efforts to implement long-term reforms and policies. The design of new policies calls for high-level expertise, and the dearth of policing experts has been a liability. As for corruption, there is a complete collapse of mechanisms and procedures to ensure accountability at all levels of the institution. Likewise, there is no strategic plan to combat the culture of corruption and the predominance of the paralegal regime within the police force.

NOTES

1. The interviewer told police officers that they had permission from the authorities to carry out the interviews, which were for strictly academic purposes and would have no impact on their work situation or professional advancement. Interviews lasted for about two and a half hours and covered groups of eight to ten police officers of the same rank, encompassing the ten ranks of the hierarchy. Autobiographies were written freely and voluntarily by police officers who agreed to tell their story as part of a competition held by the Secretariat of Public Security.

2. Although the metropolitan area of Mexico City has nineteen million inhabitants, the Preventative Police of Mexico City can only act within the perimeter of the Federal District (*Distrito Federal*), where nine million people live.

3. Findings from this work are consistent with those found by Suárez de Garay (2006) in a study carried out in the Police Department of the City of Guadalajara. See also the works of Ríos (2004) and López Ugalde (2003).

4. These findings match those of studies by Yañez (1999), López Ugalde (2003), and Tello (2005).

5. Article 42 from the Law of Public Security of the Federal District of 1993, in force at the time of the study, states that: "the arrest or detention of a subordinate officer for significant misdemeanors or for accumulating five warnings within a calendar year can last up to thirty-six hours." However, the law does not stipulate what kind of conduct merits such punishment, which gives bosses ample margin for discretion.

6. The norms regulating contractual police relations can be found in Secretaría de Seguridad Pública (2000, "Reglas para el establecimiento") and (2001).

7. See "Reglas para el establecimiento y operación del Sistema de Carrera Policial de la Policía del Distrito Federal," Gaceta Oficial del Departamento del Distrito Federal, February 28, 1994, 5–8.

8. Other studies also confirm that corruption is one of the main problems of the Mexican police, although levels of corruption are comparable to those in

other Latin American countries. The 2006 Latinobarómetro, for instance, shows that Mexico comes second (after Paraguay) in Latin America in terms of corruption, as almost one-third of the population (31 percent) asserts they had to pay a bribe in the preceding twelve months. The percentage rises to 47 percent in the case of Mexico City. Similarly, the Mexican police obtained the lowest qualification (3.3, in a ranking of 1 to 7) in terms of citizen trust in police institutions (Parás and Coleman 2006, 56, 61, and 79).

9. See Centro de Derechos Humanos Miguel Agustín Pro (2005), and Comisión de Derechos Humanos del Distrito Federal (2003; 2004a; 2004b).

CHAPTER SEVEN

The Pursuit of Efficiency and the Colombian Criminal Justice System

ELVIRA MARÍA RESTREPO

Colombia is different from most countries in Latin America in that the most recent criminal reforms did not originate from a transition of a dictatorial regime to a democratic one nor from a sudden uprise of crime. It is also singular in that it has experienced the longest irregular war in the whole continent (almost fifty years), almost four decades of drug trafficking, and unparalleled levels of hard crime, such as homicides and kidnapping.

Parallel to the country's high criminality and partly as a response to it, Colombia has had a striking record as far as the number of substantial reforms to the system of criminal justice is concerned. In less than four decades, from 1971 to the present, there have been reforms in almost every area of the criminal system, which itself has been transformed from an inquisitorial to an adversarial system in two different periods.[1] The evidence shows that the executive ordered the above-mentioned reforms, which represented important or substantial changes to the system of criminal justice, through exceptional legislation until the passage of the

1991 constitution.[2] Many analysts have shown that excessive reformism
has contributed greatly to the enormous judicial backlog because of the
inefficiency that it generates.[3] Over the years, reformism clearly has contributed to excessive judicialization and to the criminalization of activities that are best addressed beyond the scope of the system of justice.
Similarly, an excess of new laws and reforms also indirectly threatens impartiality since it makes legal procedures unpredictable, and the adjudication of cases can become subject to the personal criteria of presiding
prosecutors or judges.

Based on existing empirical data, I argue that the 1991 judicial reform
in Colombia made the criminal system more efficient, that is, cases are
closed in shorter periods of time. Thus, one can claim that the rule of law
was strengthened. But I also argue that many of the gains in efficiency
may be the result of arbitrary practices, particularly the indiscriminate
use of preventative detention. This contradicts a fundamental underpinning of democracy. Since existing data limitations inhibit deeper
analysis of the true extent of impunity under the new system, it remains
unclear whether increasing efficiency when the rule of law is weak (as
it is in most countries in the region) reduces or deters crime. Impartial adjudication—which, ultimately, is what sustains judicial system's
legitimacy—is clearly still not in place.

In the first section, I discuss briefly the main characteristics of the
1991 criminal reforms, claiming that they increased the efficiency of the
system but also introduced greater arbitrariness. In the second section, I
analyze the main characteristics of the reforms to the criminal system
comparing the performance of the new and old systems (judicial backlog, length of proceedings, and levels of impunity). In the third section, I
ask whether the new system has increased or decreased arbitrariness, focusing on four indicators for which there is data: the duration of pretrial
detention among the national prison population; two different indicators on the percentage of pretrial detentions that can be considered arbitrary; and the number of tort cases against the FGN for unfair or arbitrary
detention. In the fourth section, I argue that the lack of credibility of the
system of justice (which is clearly the result of poor performance and
perceived arbitrariness) must be discussed in the broader context of a
fear of accusing and prosecuting in Colombia. Judges have reasons to be
fearful, and this fear affects their impartiality; citizens, in turn, experi-

ence a high level of fear, which often inhibits their cooperation with the system. The precariousness of the Colombian state and the ongoing armed conflict fueled by illegal drug profits means that the causes of fear are still present, and in many parts of the country alternative "systems of justice" coexist with the official judicial system.

PURSUIT OF EFFICIENCY AND THE NEW FISCAL GENERAL DE LA NACIÓN

The search for efficiency has been a constant factor in the reforms of the Colombian system of justice at least since the 1970s. Consequently, most judicial policy in the last three decades has favored efficiency above all else, with the aim of clearing the judicial backlog of the courts. The old criminal justice system was inquisitorial and relied on judge-based written investigations similar to that of most Latin American countries before the reforms. The new criminal system was drafted in the 1990s and incorporated into the 1991 constitution.[4] The main reform to the new criminal justice was the creation of the Fiscal General de la Nación (FGN),[5] which is responsible for the investigation and prosecution of all crimes (akin to the U.S. Attorney General, albeit with Colombian particularities), and the introduction of a "semi-adversarial" criminal system of justice for the first time in the history of the country.[6]

The creation of the FGN as part of the new "semi-accusatorial" system of justice constituted a major change in the administration of criminal justice in Colombia. The FGN has been criticized for various reasons, notably its incorporation into the judiciary[7] and the amount of power it has accrued without any judicial controls.[8] Whereas the FGN has no fixed jurisdiction and the guidelines defining its competence are flexible, judges have a fixed jurisdiction and the norms that determine their competence are strict, thereby guaranteeing a certain degree of impartiality.[9] Moreover, unlike judges, public prosecutors lack stability or independence since they are agents of the Attorney General and as such can be appointed or removed by the incumbent Attorney General at any time.[10] Thus, the enormous powers of the FGN and the semi-accusatorial system apparently leave the way open for greater efficiency (compared to the old system) but also for greater arbitrariness.

COMPARING THE OLD AND NEW SYSTEMS: WHAT RESULTS?

How do the old and new systems compare in terms of efficiency and perceived degree of fairness? The FGN has increased its powers enormously to achieve efficiency, even at the expense of guaranteeing the rights of the accused. But has this led to more effective administration of criminal justice, and has the new system contributed to the reduction or containment of crime?

It is very difficult to quantify the efficiency of and determine an "efficiency threshold" for a criminal justice system (should it be 100 or 50 percent?). Nonetheless, statistical data on proceedings and investigations can be used as efficiency indicators (the term "indicators" is used here because of the uncertain reliability of existing statistical data, which are often incomplete). Since 1971 two additional factors have accounted for statistical uncertainty: first, a set of mainly executive-led judicial reforms have distorted the information supplied by the National Administrative Department of Statistics (Departamento Administrativo Nacional de Estadísticas, DANE), which fails to factor in many crimes; second, Colombia's prolonged armed conflict has also made the collection of data difficult. With these caveats in mind, the following indicators of efficiency are used here: judicial backlog, the length of the judicial proceedings, and different types of impunity (cases closed due to procedural issues rather than the resolution of the crime). When possible, there is a comparative analysis of these indicators for the old and new systems.

The Judicial Backlog

The Old System

Data from accumulated criminal proceedings in Colombia from 1958 to 1968 reveal a strong pattern of accumulation (239,561 in 1958) that reached critical levels by the end of the 1960s (832,119 in 1968).[11] In response to this excessive and ever-increasing backlog and seeking to increase efficiency above all, in 1971 the executive introduced a new statute of criminal procedure that divided criminal investigation into two phases: instruction and judgment.[12] As shown in Table 7.1, this appears not to have affected accumulation.

The figures for 1982–1993 show that the percentage of accumulation decreased. This decrease coincides with, and is possible to interpret as a consequence of, reforms in the criminal statutes and changes in crime recording practices of relevant agencies. First, after 1987 a reform changed DANE recording of investigations.[13] Second, Law 23 of 1991 decriminalized many minor offences and assigned their prosecution and judgment to police inspectorates. Third, the FGN, which became responsible for the prosecution phase of all criminal investigations after 1992, relieved the backlog of most criminal courts. Finally, Decree 2790 of 1990 excluded kidnapping, extortion, and terrorism from DANE data. Since it was precisely in 1989 that these three crimes increased dramatically due to the "war on drugs" against the Medellín and Cali cartels, the criminal system of justice appeared to become more efficient.

Table 7.1 Flow Rate of Criminal Proceedings, 1972–93

Year	Number of investigations	% of accumulated proceedings
1972	198,400	79
1974	264,200	85
1976	278,600	81
1978	249,100	76
1980	296,800	80
1980*	296,817	95
1982	304,389	96
1984	240,615	91
1986	403,607	94
1988	251,343	83
1990	235,568	82
1991	191,420	78
1992	175,640	82
1993	109,023	72

Sources: Colombian SER Research Institute (1972–1980) and DANE, 1980*–1993.
Note: The difference in the statistical data for 1980 arises due to its two different sources, the SER Research Institute (a think tank that works on justice issues) and DANE.

The New System

Data from the FGN shows a sharp decrease (from 80–90 percent to an average of 43 percent) in the backlog that occurred under the old system after the introduction of the FGN. There has also been an increase in the number of criminal investigations since 2000 (table 7.2) that may create new backlogs, but the data shows that the new system is certainly more efficient than the old.

Length of Proceedings

The Old System

Research conducted by the Universidad Externado de Colombia[14]shows that the average length of criminal proceedings in the 1970s exceeded

Table 7.2 Judicial Backlog under the New System

Year	Number Fiscales*	Evacuation Average per Public Prosecutor	Accumulated + New Proceedings	Finished Proceedings	Accumulation (%)
1992	1,598	89	388,641	141,611	63.60/82*
1993	1,778	180	478,726	319,481	33.30/71*
1994	3,015	199	1,096,604	600,432	45.20
1995	3,323	247	1,561,198	821,728	47.40
1996	3,124	284	1,511,447	886,148	41.40
1997	3,192	264	1,518,802	842,397	44.50
1998	3,190	288	1,606,920	917,516	42.90
1999	3,158	306	1,656,720	967,510	41.60
2000	3,248	312	1,689,471	1,014,422	40.00
2001	3,329	360	1,967,288	1,199,563	39.00
2002	3,301	385	2,171,342	1,271,858	41.40
2003	3,060	422	2,201,602	1,290,742	41.40

Sources: FGN and *DANE.
Note: Data from FGN differs from that of DANE for the two years they coincide (1992 and 1993), partly because the FGN data only includes the first two phases of the criminal proceeding, but also and greatly for reasons I explain in the text when talking about the atypical ways of finishing a proceeding.

statutory time limits.[15] It showed that proceedings lasted for an average 202.9 percent over and above legal limits. The range of excess length for the sample set was between 89 percent and 86.1 percent.

The New System

Graph 7.1 shows the duration of proceedings in 1996, and reveals that although criminal proceedings under the new system last longer than the legal limit by less than a third, the situation is better than under the old system. Overly long proceedings is one of the factors contributing to the judicial backlog, and also has the effect of making proceedings too costly, and may even lead people to bypass the system of justice to resolve a conflict.

Levels of Impunity

The data on backlogs and overly long criminal proceedings suggest that levels of impunity are significant. However, further analysis is necessary

Graph 7.1 Length of Proceedings under the New System

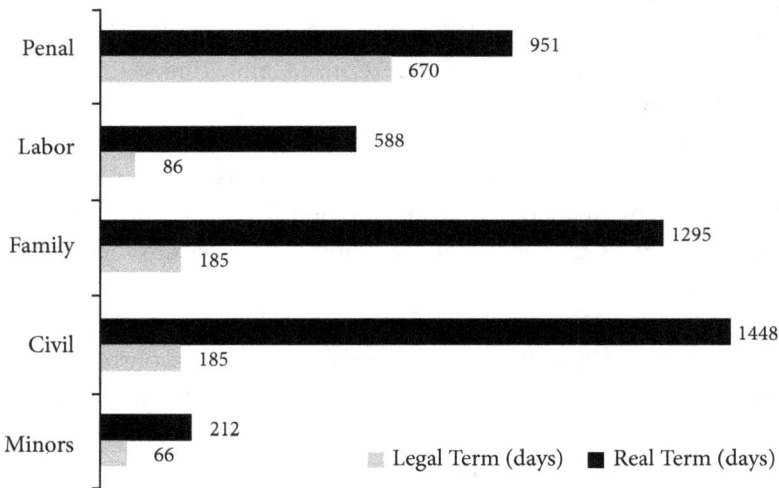

	Legal Term (days)	Real Term (days)
Penal	670	951
Labor	86	588
Family	185	1295
Civil	185	1448
Minors	66	212

Source: Superior Council of the Judiciary (CSJ) data, 1996. The CSJ, created by the 1991 constitution, is the agency of the judiciary in charge of judicial statistics.

to understand the extent of the phenomenon. For decades, and certainly in the period under review, the common wisdom has been that the levels of impunity oscillate between 95 and 99 percent.[16] Until very recently, this went unquestioned and there was no attempt to research the claim with rigor. The fact is that if such high levels of impunity were real, the justice system would be irrelevant. The argument here is that this is a dangerous myth.[17]

Victim surveys and official crime statistics (reported crimes) are the main sources to study crime. Recent empirical research supports the view that most crimes investigated by the Colombian criminal system involve known or captured offenders.[18] It also shows that the probability of finding culprits is limited when organized crime is at stake. It is important to note that there is a perverse incentive effect arising from the fact that police performance has been measured generally by the number of detentions made. It is certainly easier for the police to capture petty thieves than organized criminals such as kidnappers, terrorists, or white-collar offenders. Public prosecutors corroborate this when they claim that it is very difficult to find witnesses to prosecute organized crime successfully.[19]

As in Britain, the U.S., and most Latin American countries, recent victimization surveys in Colombia show that there is a large universe of unreported crimes (see also the chapters by Bergman and Dammert in this book). Four such surveys carried out since 1985 in Colombia[20] show that there is an average of 76 percent of unreported crimes per year. This coincides with the findings of a recent National Police report, of a report by the National Planning Department (*Departamento Nacional de Planeación*, DNP), and of a private survey undertaken in 1997.[21] Confirmation of the figures by many different sources, both public and private, suggests that only 20–25 percent of the criminal offences are reported in Colombia.

An average of 218,033 crimes is reported each year according to the total number of crimes recorded by the police over the last two decades. If one factors in unreported crimes, approximately 1,100,000 crimes are committed every year. And if one adds misdemeanors—the average for the same period is 586,566 misdemeanors per year—the total number is about 1,686,566 (see graph 7.2). It is hard to credit this number in a country with so much crime. If one accepts that people report between 70 and 75 percent of crimes to the police, one can only conclude that police criminal statistics in Colombia are far from reflecting reality.[22] If the un-reported crime figure that emerges from victimization surveys is about 80 percent, this means that the police (as shown in the cases of Argentina, Mexico, and Chile in the other chapters of this book) underrecord and fail to discover many crimes.

The linearity of police crime figures over two decades also casts doubt on their validity. It seems rather implausible that the total number of reported or recorded crimes has not changed over two decades in a country with statistically established sharp crime waves. This means that the police are limiting the capacity of the system to administer justice, which is not surprising given the small fraction of the national police force dedicated to crime control.

As in other countries, Colombian victim surveys also fail to register serious crimes such as homicides or kidnappings. Sexual crimes, family abuse, and crimes against property generally are excluded as well. Moreover, unlike the British Crime Surveys (BCS), Colombia's victimization surveys only cover the country's main cities. This limits their value, as violence and crime are not exclusively urban problems. Together with incompetent crime detection and recording by the police, these deficiencies lead to the conclusion that very little is actually known about the real quantity and nature of criminality in Colombia, with the possible exception of homicide[23] and car theft (for insurance reasons).

Graph 7.2 Crimes and Misdemeanors Registered by the Police, 1980–2002

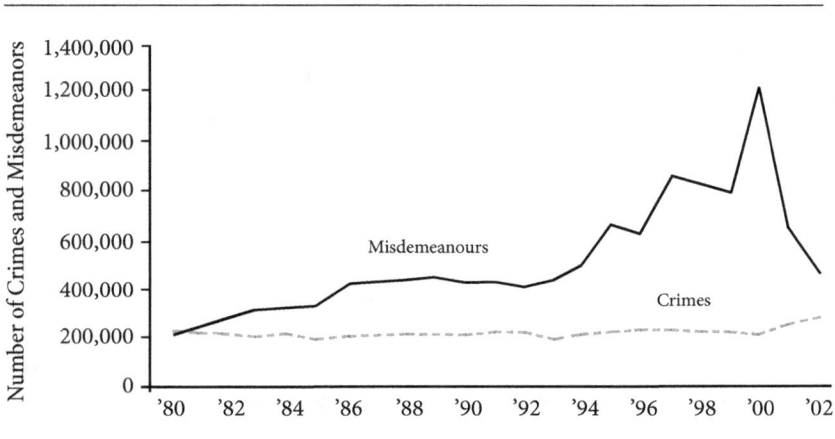

Source: National Police (*Policía Nacional*, PNC).

In short, neither police statistics nor DANE judicial data are reliable instruments to measure impunity: there may be 95 percent of impunity or there may be less, but at this stage it is not possible to know. However, one cannot hold the system of justice entirely responsible for impunity when cases never reach the courts. Improved statistical gathering and victimization surveys are crucial, and, more importantly, police discovery and recording must be improved.

There are qualitative limitations inherent in comparing a country like Colombia with Britain, but it is worth stressing the fact that in Britain there have been over five million offences recorded by the police every year since 1995 and that only 10 percent of these actually came under police jurisdiction or were sentenced (came under court jurisdiction). In 1995, for instance, 203,000 or about 4 percent of over five million offences came under police jurisdiction, and the courts sentenced 301,000 or 6 percent.[24] This does not mean that there is 90 percent impunity in Britain. A recent model of representative data for 2000 shows that in Bogotá 4.7 percent of cases reaching a preliminary phase at the local and sectional levels of the FGN culminated in sentencing,[25] a percentage that is very similar to that of Britain. Irregular ways of closing proceedings that reach the criminal system under the old and new systems represent another form of impunity.

The Old System

Under the old system, a judgment in a criminal proceeding was either final (resolving the essence of a conflict) or atypical (meaning that a case is dismissed as a result of a procedural failing,).[26] Atypical case closures generate two kinds of impunity—relative and total—and are the responsibility of the criminal system. Prescription generates total impunity since a case ends because of system inaction and prescribed cases cannot be tried again (*res judicata*). Relative impunity occurs when cases are filed temporarily until new evidence emerges. The term "relative" is appropriate since it is not possible to know how many filed cases are reopened and successfully closed, and how many simply prescribe.

Under the old system, impunity occurred mostly because of the prescription of criminal proceedings or because they were temporarily filed,[27] each atypical result generating total and relative impunity, respectively. Data for 1958–1968 show that an average of 72 percent culminated in prescription and therefore total impunity.[28] In 1976–1980, the average was still a high 65 percent, some of them culminating in relative impunity (atypical decisions, mainly writs of filing) and some in total impunity (proscription).[29]

The decrease in prescriptions in the early 1990s (to an average of 52 percent) was probably the result of the 1987 Penal Process Code (*Código Procesal Penal,* CPP), which separated the preliminary investigation and prosecution phases.[30] Since DANE registered only prosecutions, all investigations that died at the preliminary stage were omitted (impunity occurs mainly at the preliminary phase). Many cases that would have prescribed (because offenders were not identified, for example) were not recorded, which accounts for the overall reduction in the number of prescriptions in 1990–1993.

The New System

Under the new system, a criminal proceeding is finalized when there is an accusation, preclusion,[31] a plea bargain sentence (*sentencia anticipada*) during the prosecution phase, and a conviction or a "not guilty" finding in the trial phase. Atypical resolutions are similar to those under the old system, although there are many more case closures that are atypical in the new system. As with the old system, atypical results generate relative and total impunity. Diagram 7.1 shows the different types of impunity that may occur at each stage of new criminal proceedings. Whereas under the old system, prescription was the main atypical outcome, under the new system there are many other atypical ways of concluding proceedings (shown by the dotted lines in Diagram 7.1) leading to impunity, both relative and total.

The term relative impunity is appropriate given the high level of discretionality of hierarchically superior public prosecutors and the high number of cases reassigned (an average of 25 percent for the period), as well as the perception among public prosecutors removed from particular cases.[32] The term also applies to *inhibitorios* and *preclusiones,* common atypical ways to end proceedings that extinguish penal action when the crime is inexistent or the accused did not commit it. Although both are legally regular ways to end proceedings, they allow for great discretion as they occur when the public prosecutor deems that "the

Diagram 7.1 Structure of the New Criminal Proceeding and Types of Impunity

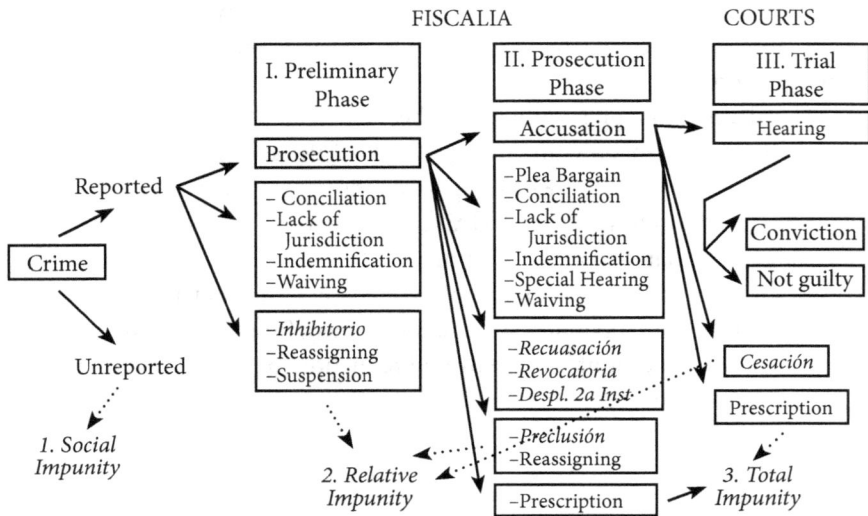

FISCALIA   COURTS

| I. Preliminary Phase | II. Prosecution Phase | III. Trial Phase |

Accusation → Hearing

Prosecution

Reported

- Conciliation
- Lack of Jurisdiction
- Indemnification
- Waiving

Crime

- Plea Bargain
- Conciliation
- Lack of Jurisdiction
- Indemnification
- Special Hearing
- Waiving

Conviction

Not guilty

- *Inhibitorio*
- Reassigning
- Suspension

Unreported

- *Recuasación*
- *Revocatoria*
- *Despl. 2a Inst·*

Cesación

Prescription

1. Social Impunity

- *Preclusión*
- Reassigning

- Prescription

2. Relative Impunity

3. Total Impunity

Source: Restrepo and Martinez (2004).

proceeding could not be initiated or continued."[33] Further, *inhibitorios* and *preclusiones* do not always resolve the essence of the case. Recent empirical evidence shows that many *inhibitorios* occur because there is insufficient evidence to prosecute, or because existing evidence is misused or misinterpreted, or because it is impossible to identify suspects that belong to guerrilla or other illegal groups.[34]

Finally, in contrast to the old system, not all atypical case closures necessarily generate impunity. Reassignment, for example, may delay a proceeding, but a competent court can take up the case again at a later stage. The same can be true for *inhibitorios* and *preclusiones* when these occur because there was no crime, or when there was a justifiable cause precluding liability. Thus, in diagram 7.1 these new forms of atypical closure of proceedings are classified as relative impunity.

Graph 7.3 shows preliminary phase criminal proceedings in 1996–2003 in accordance with the impunity classifications proposed above.[35] Graph

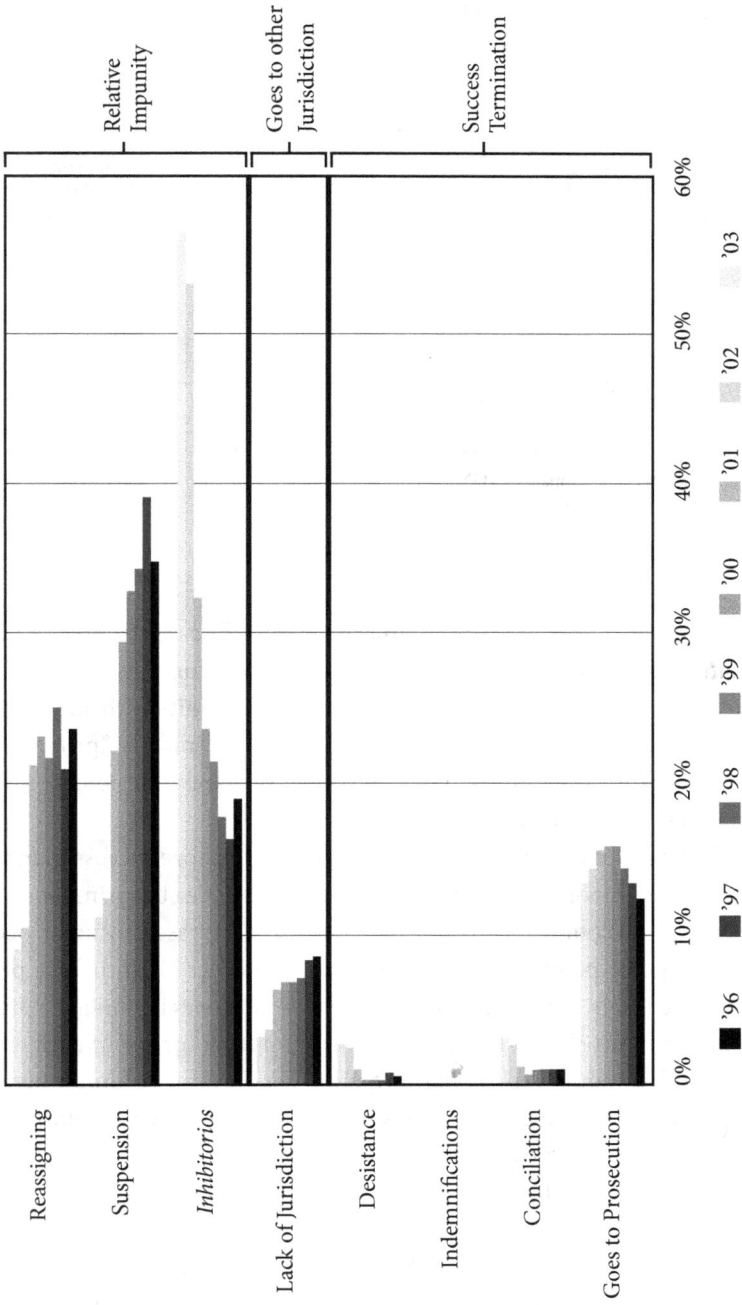

Graph 7.3 Preliminary Phase Terminations, 1996–2003

Relative Impunity

Goes to other Jurisdiction

Success Termination

Reassigning

Suspension

Inhibitorios

Lack of Jurisdiction

Desistance

Indemnifications

Conciliation

Goes to Prosecution

0% 10% 20% 30% 40% 50% 60%

■ '96 ■ '97 ■ '98 ■ '99 ■ '00 ■ '01 ■ '02 ■ '03

Source: FGN data.

Graph 7.4 Impunity in the Preliminary Phase, 1996–2003

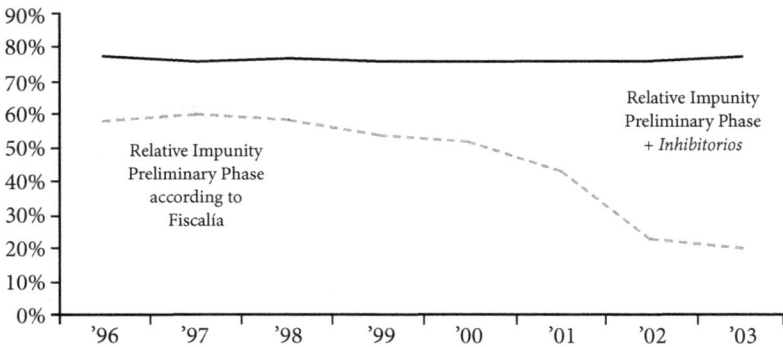

Source: Own calculations and FGN data.

7.4 shows that during the preliminary phase most case closures result in relative impunity and that *inhibitorios* account for most of these (as shown by the two different curves for relative impunity with and without *inhibitorios*). In contrast, successful case closures (mainly "prosecuted," "conciliation," and "desistance") account for barely 20 percent of the total in the best years.

Graph 7.5 shows that the prosecution phase is more successful mainly because an important percentage of accusations, plea bargains, and conciliations (accounting for almost 35 percent of case closures) occur. However, the percentage of *preclusiones* is still very high in this phase (approximately 30 percent). The effect of *preclusiones* is similar to that of *inhibitorios* (as shown by the two different curves for relative impunity with and without *preclusiones* in graph 7.6). In terms of impunity, approximately 25 percent of cases are reassigned (relative impunity), but there is a great decrease in prescriptions (total impunity)—they almost cease at the end of the period under analysis.

Finally, during the trial phase, it is possible to consider a large percentage of case closures as being successful.[36] The percentage of convictions has been increasing significantly (there were two times more in

Graph 7.5 Prosecution Phase Terminations, 1996–2003

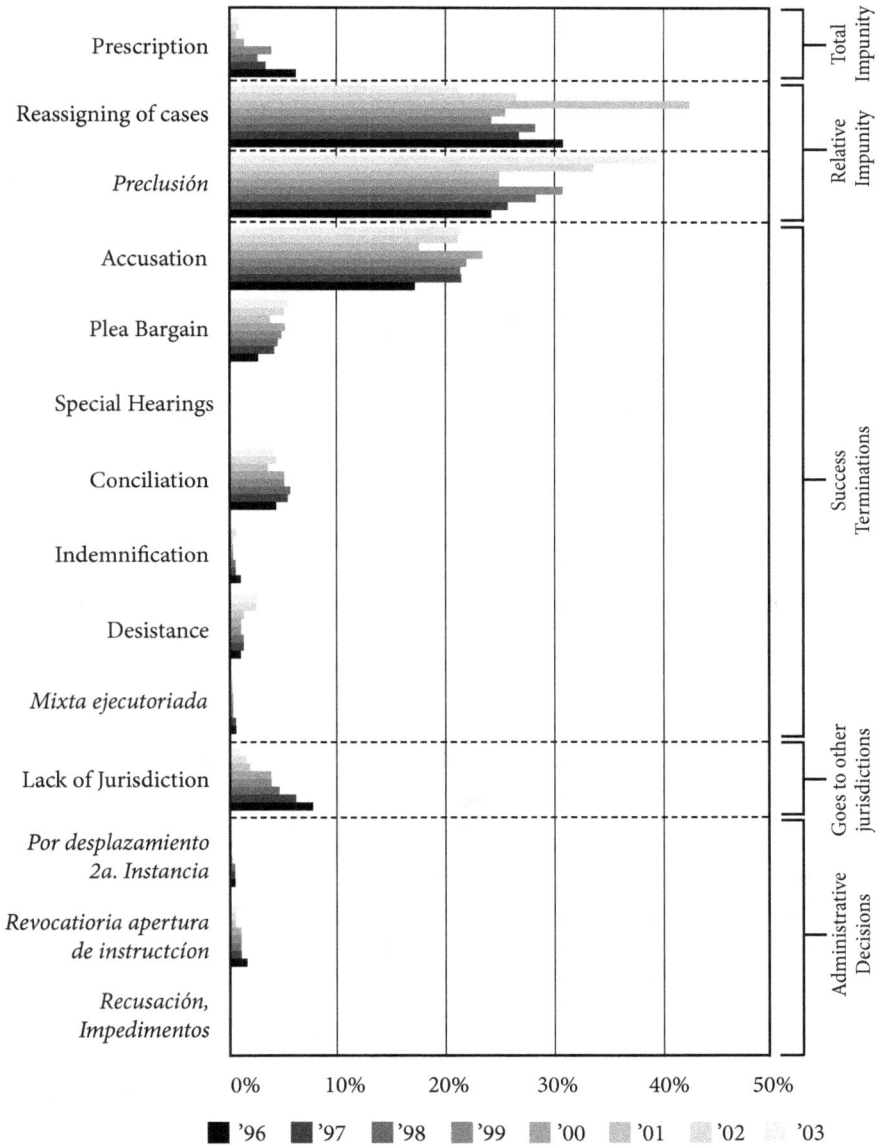

Graph 7.6 Impunity during the Prosecution Phase, 1996–2003

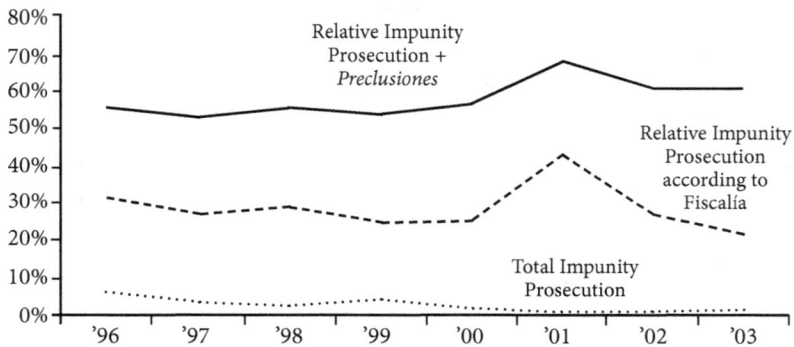

Source: Own calculations and FGN data.

2002 than in 1996, and even more in 2003), which indicates that there has been great improvement under the new system. Also increasing in frequency since 2002 are plea bargains, although they are still few compared to convictions. Total impunity has decreased significantly from 30 percent of all case closures in 1997 to 8 percent in 2003. Relative impunity has also decreased as shown in graph 7.8. All this indicates that the new system is more efficient than the old.

All this suggests that, during the trial phase of criminal proceedings, the level of efficiency of the courts is very good and levels of relative or total impunity are quite low. Similar claims can be made about *cesaciones,* which in this phase make up an important percentage of all case closures, as for *preclusiones* in the second phase, or *inhibitorios* in the first. However, unlike the latter two, *cesaciones* have been constantly decreasing to their lowest levels since 2002. Overall, the greater level of success in the third trial phase is to be expected because by then there is usually a confirmed accused and solid evidence. This is why impunity from this phase should not be compared with those for the preliminary and prosecution phases.

Graph 7.7 Trial Phase Terminations, 1997–2003

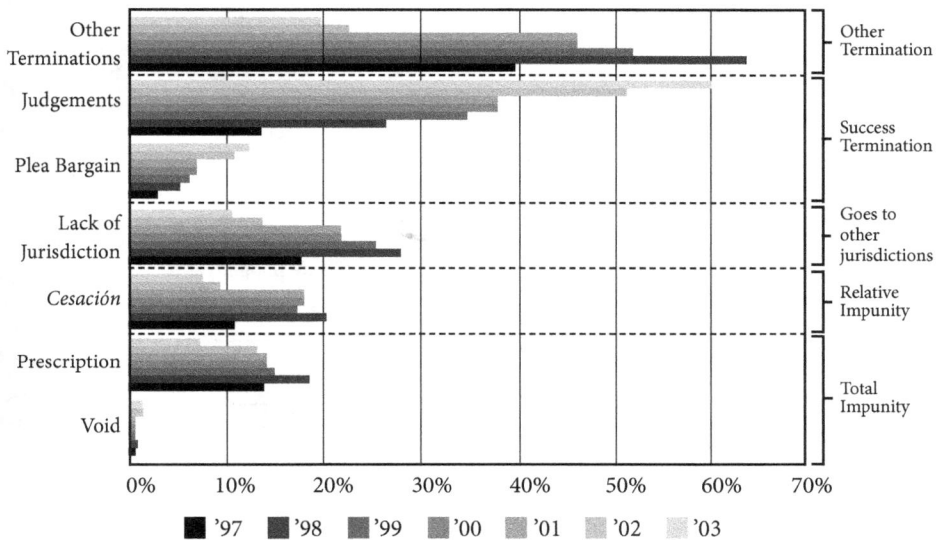

Source: CSJ data.
Note: It is unclear from the data of the Superior Council of the Judiciary (CSJ) what "other closures" means. One hypothesis is that it refers to robberies that go directly to court and bypass jurisdiction of the FGN. It is estimated that these represent an average of 30 percent of the crimes processed by the criminal justice system, although the officials working the data at the CSJ were also unsure about this!

IS THE NEW SYSTEM MORE ARBITRARY?

So far, we have shown that the new system has increased efficiency, but is it fairer? There are several ways to measure whether the existence of the FGN increased or decreased arbitrariness. Based on available data, the focus here is on four indicators: the duration of pretrial detention among the national prison population, two indicators of the percentage of pretrial detentions that can be considered arbitrary, and the number of tort cases against the FGN for unfair or arbitrary detentions.

As regards the length of pretrial detention, a DNP analysis of the prison system data shows that most pretrial detainees stay in prison for an average of 5 months, as shown in table 7.2.[37] Table 7.3 also shows that

Graph 7.8 Impunity during the Trial Phase, 1997–2003

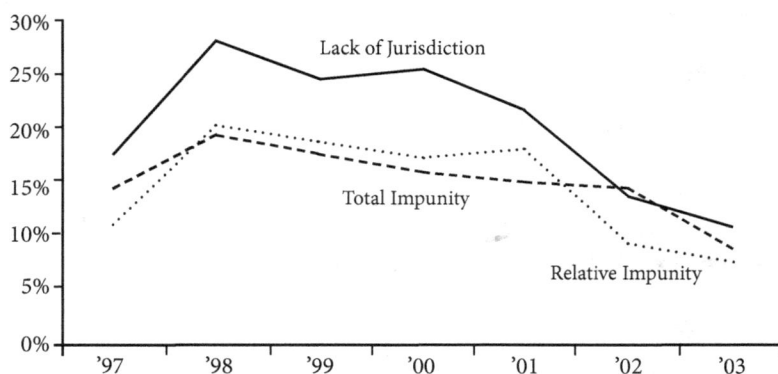

Source: Own calculations and CSJ data.

of an average of 5,000 prisoners entering the national prison system every month, only 1,000 remain there. (Colombia will be an average case in the region. See chapter 9 for other countries' prison admissions and length of imprisonment before trial.) This increase can mean that there has been a huge increase in unjust preventative detentions since the FGN began its work, and consequently that more than 80 percent of those imprisoned must be released according to *habeas corpus* provisions for lack of evidence.

In terms of arbitrary pretrial detentions, it is only possible to compare the old and new systems for three years because there is no data available for the 1980s. Graph 7.9 shows that since the creation of the FGN, pretrial detentions have increased by an average of 34.9 percent per year, while the opposite is true for detentions ordered by judges (these have decreased by an average of 5.3 percent per year). What is worrying is the great and progressive increase of detentions ordered by public prosecutors and the gap between those detained and those formally accused.

Preventative detentions have increased by 176.8 percent since the FGN started to operate in 1992. By contrast, the accused population in 1992–1995 remained relatively stable (increasing gradually by 30 percent

Table 7.3 Months of Detention for National Prison Population until
October 1999

Region	0–5 Months	6–10 Months	11–15 Months	16–20 Months	21–25 Months	> 25 Months	Total Months
Central	2,592	812	797	606	577	852	6,236
Percentages	42	13	13	10	9	14	100
West	1,866	998	580	387	233	176	4,240
Percentages	44	24	14	9	5	4	100
North	1,016	363	238	185	152	182	2,136
Percentages	48	17	11	9	7	9	100
East	643	390	192	147	103	113	1,588
Percentages	40	25	12	9	6	7	100
Northeast	601	847	685	675	538	811	4,157
Percentages	14	20	16	16	13	20	100
Coffee region	991	543	224	154	90	120	2,122
Percentages	47	26	11	7	4	6	100
Total	7,709	3,953	2,716	2,154	1,693	2,254	20,479
Participation	38%	19%	13%	11%	8%	11%	100%

Sources: National Penitentiary and Prison Institute (*Instituto Nacional Penitenciario y Carcelario*, INPEC), and DNP.
Note: The national prison system is divided into six regions.

Graph 7.9 Increase in Detentions, 1990–2000

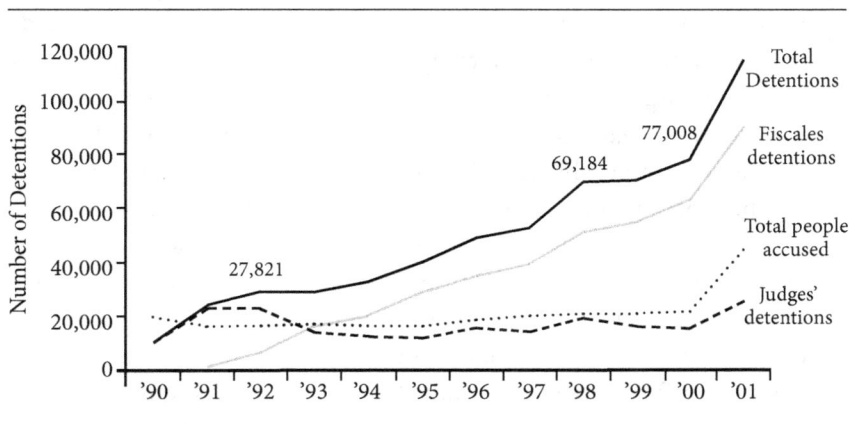

Sources: FGN and INPEC.

per year until 2000). However, the growth of the prison population does not correspond to the increase of post-FGN detentions. The lack of a correlation between the percentage of detentions and the prison population in 1992–2000 indicates that a large number of detentions are not enforced, probably because the police are unable to do so or because they lose legal validity (namely, unfair detention orders that appear as valid in the system as shown in graph 7.10).

One can glean another indicator of arbitrariness from a sample taken by the FGN at the entrance of its main building in Bogotá. This corroborates earlier findings that there is an excessive number of detention orders under the new system that are active but have in fact been cancelled or invalidated for different reasons. Graph 7.10 illustrates the disorderly and arbitrary nature of detention orders handled by the FGN. The fourth indicator of arbitrariness is illustrated by graph 7.11, which shows that the highest number of tort cases filed against the FGN is for unfair or arbitrary detention.

This section has shown that the new system is more efficient in clearing up the backlog (an average of 86 percent, compared with 43 percent under the old system). It has also reduced the time to resolve cases that are actually adjudicated, which is important given the constant increase of cases entering the system. It is less clear whether efficiency is actually reducing crime or increasing deterrence. The new system has definitely reduced total impunity, but unfortunately this has been achieved at the expense of increasing a form of impunity (relative impunity) that is hard to define, since one cannot ascertain the percentage of it that finally leads to total impunity and the percentage that is successfully adjudicated. It is possible to argue that the new system is undertaking far more criminal investigations than the old one. But again, based on existing data it is hard to determine whether it is resolving more crimes or simply diverting them because the system allows for too many atypical case closures. The 2003 victimization survey shows figures similar to those of the prior two decades, which casts doubts on the true "efficiency" of the new system in terms of crime reduction or deterrence. The inability of the police to detect crime is arguably far more problematic in terms of impunity than the performance of the criminal justice system. It is quite unbelievable that police crime detection statistics and data collection have re-

Graph 7.10 Sample of People Detained Entering the Main FGN Building in Bogotá

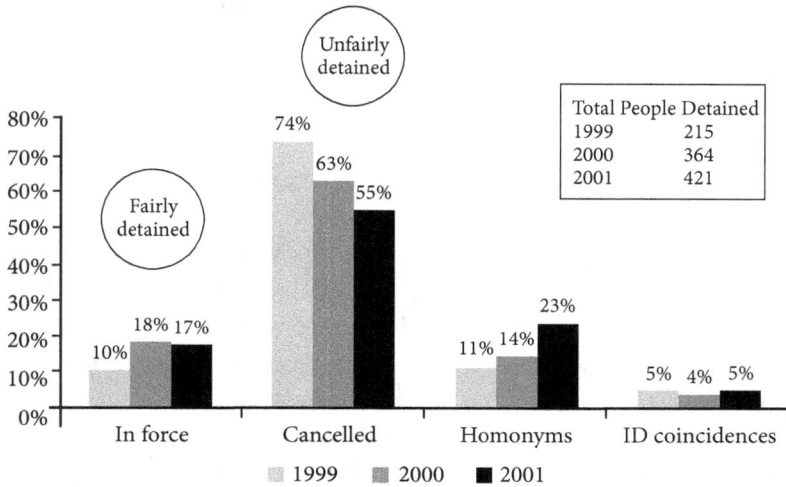

Unfairly detained

Fairly detained

Total People Detained	
1999	215
2000	364
2001	421

■ 1999 ■ 2000 ■ 2001

Source: FGN.

Graph 7.11 Facts Generating Torts, 1998–2001

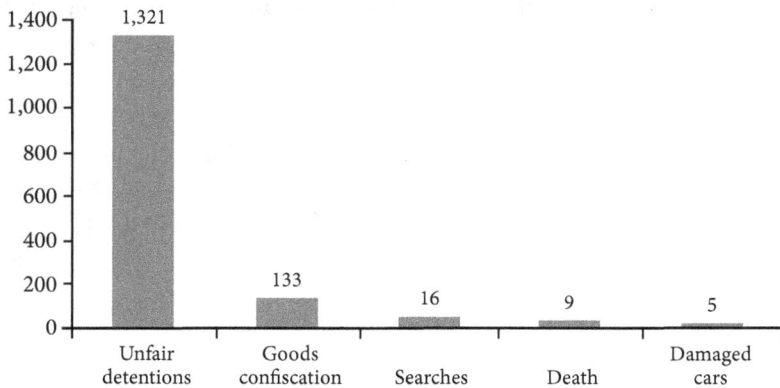

Source: FGN.

mained unchanged over two decades when crime has risen so sharply (caused by wars against the different cartels, intensity variations in armed conflict, or high and low levels of unemployment, among other possible factors). One could argue, therefore, that the poor police performance has inhibited the ability of the criminal justice system to reduce crime.

FEAR TO ACCUSE AND PROSECUTE

A generalized and growing fear of crime has spread in most Western countries and in Latin America (see, for example, chapter 2 in this book, on Chile) since the 1990s. But in Colombia, fear has another dimension: recent research suggests that fear prevents people from resorting to the criminal justice system or from collaborating with it. There is a fear to accuse and a fear to prosecute.[38] Several surveys reveal the lack of trust in the administration of justice since the 1980s and its main causes.[39] Lack of trust and a tendency not to use the system has two important consequences: either people do nothing (which implies that "crime pays," a situation that is probably similar in many Latin American countries), or they take justice into their own hands (which implies that crime generates more crime, and is probably more common in Colombia than elsewhere in the region). Fear is even more perverse than lack of trust. In a best case scenario, a crime is reported or discovered, but there are no witnesses to testify and hence the case is dropped for lack of evidence. Far worse is when fear among judges (including public prosecutors and investigators) makes it impossible to prosecute crimes, as they either absolve those responsible, or condemn the culprit but pay with their life or at the cost of the safety or tranquility of their families. "Unhappy is the land that needs heroes," as Brecht once claimed. It is hard to see how justice can work in a climate of fear and distrust, and the danger is that it becomes an irrelevant institution. (This happened at the end of the 1990s when drug traffickers managed to silence judges by telling them to choose between two metals: silver or lead.)

This brings us to a more general claim, namely, that inefficiency or impunity cannot be divorced from weak rule of law and democratic limitations, and without addressing the latter issues, the justice system can do little to address common crime and hard criminality. This section, therefore, shows how the system of justice is not entirely responsible for inefficiency and impunity, although its poor performance is the cause of its shaky legitimacy. Survey results serve to show that impunity results in large part from the fear of the victims to accuse, of the witnesses to testify, and of judges (public prosecutors and investigators) to prosecute. A 1997 survey shows perceptions about the efficacy of "private justice"[40] as compared to formal channels to pursue justice, and the inhibiting power of fear.

When organized crime is at stake, fear is all the greater. Even when publicly known hard criminals are caught, there is often no evidence to prosecute them. The extreme vulnerability of judges is apparent in the 1997 survey as well, as demonstrated in graph 7.13.

Equally catastrophic is the proportion of respondents who claimed to know who was responsible for a homicide but still preferred to do nothing about it (one out of three for the general population and the judges, and one out of two for members of the armed forces). This shows that

Graph 7.12 Users of the Criminal System vs. Other Alternatives

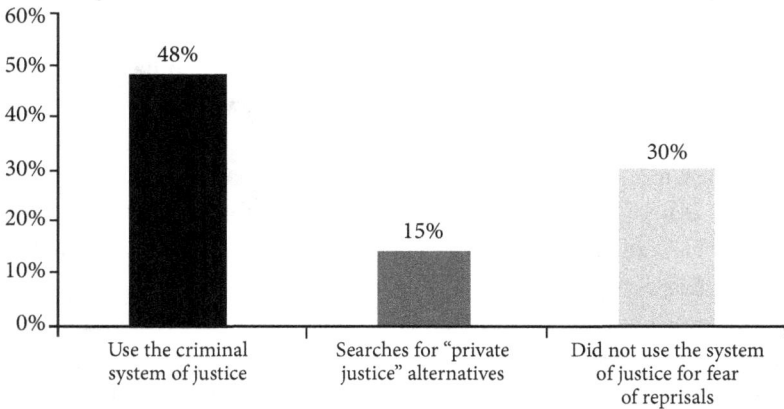

Source: M. M. Cuellar, *Colombia: Un proyecto inconcluso; Valores, instituciones y capital social,* 2 vols (Bogotá: Universidad Externado de Colombia, 2000).

Graph 7.13 Judges Affected by Homicides and Carrying Arms

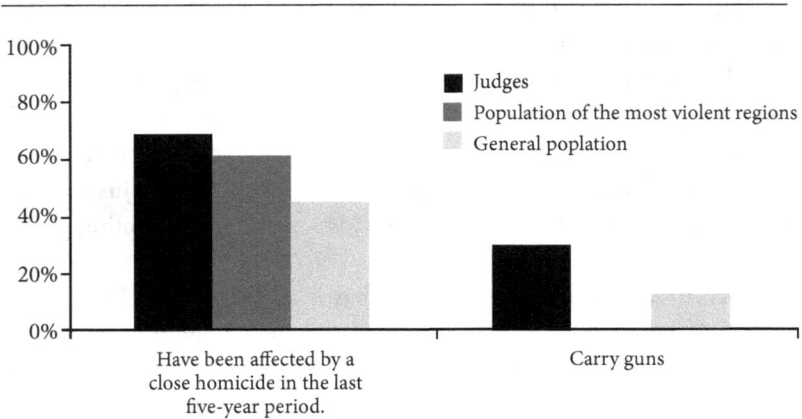

■ Judges
■ Population of the most violent regions
▨ General poplation

Have been affected by a
close homicide in the last
five-year period.

Carry guns

Source: M. M. Cuellar, *Colombia: Un proyecto inconcluso; Valores, instituciones y capital social,* 2 vols (Bogotá: Universidad Externado de Colombia, 2000).

impunity feeds on the fear to accuse. Fear is greater in areas of the country where there are guerrillas, paramilitary groups, or drug traffickers, as shown by perceptions of performance of the criminal system in graph 7.14.

The 1997 Survey also shows that "private justice" competes with the formal administration of justice and, what is more worrying, is not only efficient but has become quite credible among a not so insignificant percentage of the population, including judges. Equally seriously, it also shows that many homicides go unreported when the identity of the perpetrator is known. This indicates both lack of trust in the system of justice *and* fear of reprisal.

The same kind of phenomenon affects judges, as shown in graph 7.15. Violence against them was very high in 1979–1991. During this period, forty judges per year were the victims of violence. The dramatic decline in life threats and murder of judges subsequently in 1991–1998 was the result of the *justicia sin rostro* (faceless justice) statute, which ensured the anonymity of judges and public prosecutors responsible for prosecuting

Graph 7.14 Impact of Armed Conflict on the Criminal System

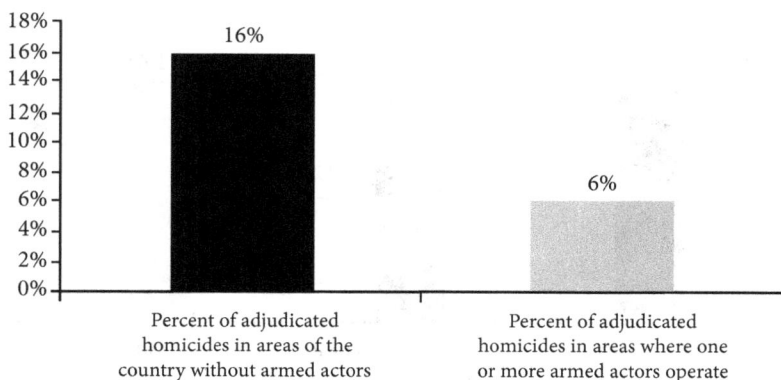

Source: M. M. Cuellar, *Colombia: Un proyecto inconcluso; Valores, instituciones y capital social,* 2 vols (Bogotá: Universidad Externado de Colombia, 2000).

serious crimes.[41] Nevertheless, the level of violence against judges in Colombia is still high by international standards.

In sum, the lack of credibility of the system of justice is clearly the result of poor performance and perceived arbitrariness, but this must be discussed in the context of the fear to accuse and prosecute. Fearful judges are less likely to be impartial. The precariousness of the Colombian state and the ongoing armed conflict fueled by illegal drug profits means that the causes of fear have not been removed, and in many parts of the country alternative systems of justice emerge. Fear still rules societal exchange in some important areas of the country.

CONCLUSION

Systems of justice play an important role in legitimizing states. The legitimacy of state authority rests on the ability to support and uphold just institutions. A state with a system of justice that fairly administers the law is bound to have a high degree of authority over its citizens. At the

Graph 7.15 Violence against Judges

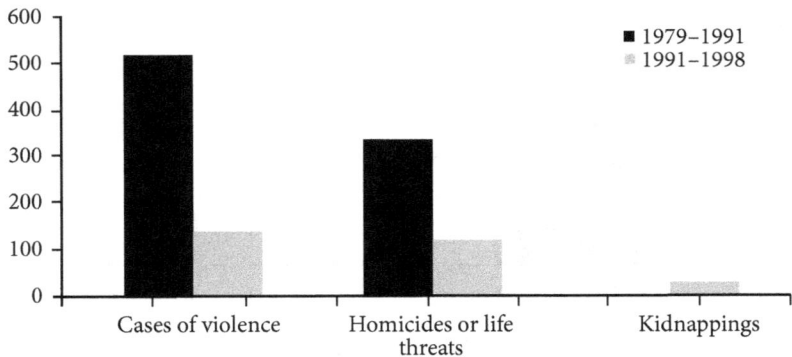

Source: M. M. Cuellar, *Colombia: Un proyecto inconcluso; Valores, instituciones y capital social,*
2 vols (Bogotá: Universidad Externado de Colombia, 2000).
Note: The evidence for 1979–1991 includes data on violence against judges and lawyers, as
it is impossible to disaggregate it. There was also no available data on kidnappings for the
period.

very least, citizens that take their disputes to court are entitled to expect
equality of treatment, a neutral and impartial attitude, and an objective
procedure. Even when a particular judicial decision is unfavorable, it will
be accepted, or legitimate grounds for complaint will be eliminated, if
the rules underlying legal proceedings are fairly implemented and decisions are impartial.[42] Fairness, equality, and impartiality are therefore
what sustain the authority of a system of justice. But this is only possible
if systems of justice are efficient. I have shown that in Colombia the new
system performs better at this level (more cases are closed in shorter periods of time). But as was discussed in the third section, there are too
many arbitrary detentions and hence some of the principles of justice are
sacrificed. The lack of trust in the system of justice has negative effects in
the deterrence capacity of the system. Added to this, the particularities of
fear analyzed in the fourth section also account for the limited impact of
this efficiency in the reduction of impunity, precisely for some of the
most violent actors of society.

The general question that remains is whether criminal justice in Latin America should strive for judiciaries that are more efficient, and the extent to which efficiency can be obtained with impartiality in order to deter and reduce crime. Ideally, one will want both. The question remains as to whether weak rule of law and limited democracies, characteristic of the region, can actually achieve both. Moreover, one must ask whether greater efficiency inhibits impartiality or if one excludes the other, and, if one does exclude the other, which should prevail. This chapter suggests that in Colombia increased efficiency does not necessarily enhance the quality of case-by-case decisions. The latter is problematic because it has a negative impact on peoples' willingness to cooperate with the system—which is crucial for the success of a criminal investigation. Perhaps at issue is the extent to which a society is willing to make trade-offs between quantity and quality. It seems doubtful that the system will be able to achieve both. The latest adopted reforms in Colombia entered into force in January 2005 and abolished the judicial powers of the public prosecutors, which immediately reduced the number of arbitrary pretrial detentions. It will be interesting to see what happens to the formerly achieved efficiency and which system is more effective in reducing and deterring crime.

NOTES

1. For a more detailed account of the reforms see Elvira María Restrepo, *Colombian Criminal Justice in Crisis: Fear and Distrust* (New York: Palgrave, 2003), 34–37.

2. Due to specific restrictions of the 1991 constitution, the executive indirectly interferes in the drafting of the criminal law but no longer drafts it directly.

3. See J. Giraldo et al., *Reforma de la justicia en Colombia* (Bogotá: Instituto SER de Investigación, 1987), 78; Mauricio García-Villegas and Rodrigo Uprimny Yepes, "El nudo gordiano de la justicia y la guerra en Colombia," in *Armar la paz es desarmar la guerra,* ed. Álvaro Camacho Guizado and Francisco Leal Buitrago, 33–72 Bogota: (FESCOL, 1999).

4. When I say "new" I refer to the semi-accusatorial system that has existed since 1991 and which, since 2005, has gradually been replaced by a more orthodox accusatorial system.

5. An analysis of the functions of the FGN may also shed some light on its role in initiating one of the most serious corruption crises in Colombia with the infamous *Proceso 8000*. See Lawrence Boudon, "Party System Deinstitutionalization: The 1997–1998 Colombian Elections in Historical Perspective," *Journal of Inter-American Studies and World Affairs* 42, no. 3 (Fall 2000): 33–57.

6. In 1979 a failed constitutional reform also tried to introduce the accusatorial system of justice.

7. See C. Lleras de la Fuente et al., *Interpretación y génesis de la justicia en Colombia* (Bogota: Cámara de Comercio, 1992), 428.

8. The public prosecutors, for instance, could issue arrest warrants and any other intrusive preventive measures without judicial order. See Rodrigo Uprimny, "Fiscal General o General Fiscal?" *Revista del Colegio de Abogados Penalistas del Valle* 29–30 (1995): 15–23. These judicial functions have been removed with the latest reforms in 2005, with the adoption of a more orthodox accusatorial system of justice.

9. See articles 119, 121, and 250 of the Criminal Procedure Code (Código Procesal Penal, CPP), and Uprimny, "Fiscal General."

10. Article 19, *Estatuto Orgánico de la FGN.*

11. Giraldo et al., "Reforma de la justicia"; and Department of National Statistics (DANE).

12. Before the 1971 statute, each judge was in charge of both the instruction and the judgment of a criminal case.

13. DANE, *La justicia colombiana en cifras, 1937–1994.* (Bogotá: Imprenta Nacional, 1996).

14. J. Muñoz, "La duración del proceso penal," *Derecho Penal y Criminología* 6, no. 15 (1980): 198–222.

15. A judicial process can last a decade, mainly because the lawyer of the defendant has the right to contest practically every step of the process.

16. The 99 percent figure for impunity is calculated based on the National Household Survey (*Encuesta Nacional de Hogares,* ENH) 1995 survey data. The number of estimated crimes per year (3,500,000) was divided by the number of convictions per year (approximately 36,000) resulting in levels of impunity of the order of 99 (funnel calculations). Funnel calculations lead to similar percentages of impunity in countries around Latin America, the United States, and the United Kingdom, a situation that suggests that measuring "impunity" in this way is certainly misleading.

17. See Elvira María Restrepo and Mariana Martínez, "Impunidad penal: mitos y realidades" Documento CEDE, no. 24 (Universidad de los Andes, Bogotá), June 2004.

18. A significant sample of kidnapping, terrorism, and embezzlement proceedings corroborates this trend. See Elvira María Restrepo et al., "Impunity or

Punishment? An Analysis of Criminal Investigation into Kidnapping, Terrorism and Embezzlement in Colombia," *Global Crime Journal* 2 (Summer 2006): 179–99.

19. Author interview with public prosecutors and with former Attorney General Alfonso Gómez Méndez, May 2000.

20. DANE 1987; ENH 1991 and 1995, in DANE 1996, p. 256.

21. DNP 1994; M. M. Cuéllar, *Colombia: Un proyecto inconcluso; Valores, instituciones y capital social,* 2 vols. (Bogotá: Universidad Externado de Colombia, 2000).

22. ENH 1991 and 1995, and DANE, 1996, p. 103.

23. *Medicina Legal,* which is in charge of homicides data, covers the whole country and has a very trustworthy recording system.

24. Mike Maguire et al., "Crime, Statistics, Patterns and Trends," in *The Oxford Handbook of Criminology,* ed. Mike Maguire, Rod Morgan, and Robert Reiner (Oxford: Clarendon Press, 1997), 173.

25. Consejo Superior de la Judicatura and Universidad Nacional de Colombia, *Modelo probabilístico para cuantificar la impunidad* (Bogotá: Imprenta Nacional de Colombia, 2000), 52–53.

26. This is usually the inability to identify the accused or lack of evidence.

27. Filing means that after two years of prosecuting a criminal case without finding the possible offenders, the case is temporarily closed until new evidence comes to light. Random samples of filed cases show that many prescribed.

28. J. Giraldo et al., "Reforma de la justicia."

29. SER research institute data from 1983.

30. DANE data, from 1992.

31. A *preclusión* is a way of ending a criminal case during the prosecution phase. *Preclusión* occurs for reasons similar to those leading to *cesación* (the crime did not take place, the accused did not commit it, or the public prosecutor states the case cannot continue).

32. Author interview, public prosecutors and members of the FGN, May 2001.

33. Article 36 of the CPP.

34. For more details, see E. M. Restrepo et al., "Impunity or Punishment."

35. FGN data is only available from 1996.

36. Notice that data for the trial phase comes from another source, the CSJ, the judicial entity responsible for statistics after 1997.

37. DNP, 2001, p. 24.

38. See Restrepo, *Colombian Criminal Justice in Crisis.*

39. See ibid. for details on the perception of the Colombian criminal system.

40. Judges were obviously the least critical of their own inefficiency (23 percent compared with 35 percent for the population as a whole).

41. Its abolition in 1999, however, certainly increased the number of crimes against them.

42. H. L. A. Hart, *The Concept of Law* (Oxford: Clarendon Press, 1994).

CHAPTER EIGHT

Criminal Process Reform
and Citizen Security

LUIS PÁSARA

Wherever the rule of law reigns supreme, a high level of rule compliance provides the backbone of citizen security both objectively (respect for the rights of others does in fact grant citizens more security) and subjectively (people derive a sense of personal safety when rules are obeyed). But if a society disregards rules, and if such disrespect coexists with high levels of impunity, the state (the entity presumed to have a monopoly on the use of force) fails to guarantee citizen security objectively and, what is more, as citizens realize how widespread are impunity and the breaking of rules, subjective insecurity increases too.

Thus, citizen security is linked to the relationship between punitive action and impunity. Given that where people obey rules there is a repressive apparatus to punish violators with some efficiency, people tend to believe that when people ignore rules, all that needs doing is to make punitive mechanisms more efficient. Thus, the problem of flouting rules or violating laws is shifted to the judicial arena, which "common sense" tells us is in the best position to promote rule enforcement, as the hypothetical enforcer of the rule of law and therefore a decisive factor in citizen security.

In Latin America, crime levels are rising in a context where the rule of law is imperfect at best, and rights and duties are very imperfectly enforced. The reform of criminal proceedings, *reforma procesal penal*, or RPP, has been proposed as the most efficient way to deal with the resulting citizen insecurity. Most countries of the region are debating, have passed, or are implementing such a reform. Rather than evaluate the results obtained thus far (already started by Riego 2002; Baytelman 2002; Riego and Santelices 2003; J. E. Vargas 2005; Riego 2007), the question addressed in this chapter is whether or not changes in the criminal trial system can decisively increase levels of citizen security, or whether the state needs other, better instruments to achieve this goal.

The main argument made here is that there is no evidence to answer the first question positively. Indeed, when RPP is seen as a variable that can decisively influence criminality, a conceptual error is being made; further, given a series of peculiarities of the most recent RPP, as many or more cases are never tried (or punished) as were left without punishment under the old system. Despite this negative view, there is no denying that RPP has brought about some positive changes, namely the speedier processing of cases and their resolution (albeit of a minority) within the system;[1] and the provision of a set of guarantees that, even though enacted long ago, are now more likely to be enforced, and that offer the accused a clearer understanding of their rights and how to defend them. However, these important improvements are not related causally with fighting crime, and they certainly do not contribute to improving objective citizen security.[2]

This chapter is divided into three parts. The first examines the relationship between criminality and justice. The second highlights the main points of RPP and examines some studies evaluating it. And the third focuses on the key question of how reforms in the criminal justice system may contribute to citizen security.

CRIME, LAW, RULE OF LAW, AND THE JUSTICE APPARATUS

In Latin American, there is a widespread belief that there is a causal relationship between norms and reality, even though experience belies this. Thus, people assume that when a law or a regulation changes, there will be a corresponding change in reality (Pásara 2004, 530). In terms of criminal law, this translates into the view that the harsher the penalty established by law, the less inclined individuals will be to disobey the law; and moreover, the more efficacious the punishment, the lower the incidence of criminal conduct. It is hard to disagree that increasing the enforcement of punishment increases the cost of disobedience; but it is less clear that such an increase, in and of itself, results in less crime. Let us examine this assertion more closely.

Increased instances of punishment alone do not have any discernable effect if the coercive system does not make provisions for people to obey legal norms. There is an aspect of the coercive system that is internal to individuals, keeping them from engaging in illegal activity, be it because of adherence to moral or social principles, or because they fear punishment. An external aspect supplements the internal aspect, coming into play when a norm is violated, via prosecution and enforcement in accordance with the existing legal provisions. There are two further points to be made here. First, the punitive mechanism (or what we are calling the external aspect of the system) cannot be efficient if the majority of the population decides to transgress a given norm. This happens in many third-world countries with various traffic rules, for instance: the sheer volume of violations undermines punitive mechanisms, so that the rules themselves lose their power. Second, and related to the first, when the majority complies with a norm, this does not depend fundamentally on the external aspect of the coercive system functioning efficiently; rather, it is individual self-control that inhibits people from committing a crime or disobeying the law. This is when the rights and obligations of the citizen have been "internalized rather than imposed" (Whitehead 2002, 166).

So we need to think about which factors inhibit individuals from behaving in ways that contradict criminal law, and to reassess the role that the justice apparatus may have in controlling criminal acts. In many Latin American societies, there are powerful economic and social systems of exclusion, and low levels of formal employment and high percentages of poverty, on the one hand, and ongoing processes of fragmentation and social dissolution, on the other. In this context, the sites of primary socialization such as the family and the school have to operate under such difficult conditions that it is hard for them to convey the importance of adhering to established norms or even basic rules of coexistence.

Not only are there high levels of poverty in Latin America, but the region also has the highest levels of inequality that have existed worldwide in the past twenty years (Inter-American Development Bank 1998, Facing Up to Inequality). Most countries in the region face a high level of social exclusion affecting important sectors of society, which deprives people of value as workers or consumers (Zúñiga 2005, 586). Unemployment, a verifiable manifestation of exclusion, is strongly associated with criminal behavior as is demonstrated by several statistical indicators. Studies acknowledge that "criminality is a product of society" (Zúñiga 2001, 252), and reference is made to "criminality of poverty" in contrast with the "criminality of well-being" (Roxin 1998, 443). In the Latin American case, the data reveal that high levels of crimes against property and the retail distribution of drugs characterize the former. British criminologist Robert Reiner argues that four factors must be present for a crime to be committed: "someone with a *motive* to commit a crime, with the *necessary means* to carry it out, with the *opportunity* created by a vulnerable victim, and finally, the absence of *external control*—police or security systems—or *internal controls*—conscience and values—the presence of which would impede the delinquent from acting" (quoted by Frühling 1997, 8; my translation from the Spanish). To what extent do these four factors emerge "socially" in the case of Latin America? Poverty is the adequate framework for the creation of motives and for the relaxation of internal controls, and also generates the social conditions that exacerbate conflict. As observed by Frühling: "poverty is not only an incentive for criminality to the extent that the crime grants access to certain goods, but also because it accelerates social disorganization, thus creating barriers for the social standing of generally accepted norms, it deteriorates the socialization and education processes of the young, and weakens the social controls that induce self-discipline" (Frühling 1997, 11). Thus, the possibility that, at any given time, all individuals become aware of the relative benefit of any given self-restriction and the higher cost of transgression is not likely in the conditions peculiar to underdevelopment.

Criminality, but much beyond it as well, is affected by the difficulty of establishing a law-based social equilibrium and a functioning legal system that gives positive feedback. Thus, "the space of formal social control, represented by the state justice apparatus, is disputed, challenged, and even substituted from outside legal formality in the context of Latin America" (Gabaldón 2004, 6). Not only is the reach of formal legality extremely limited, but other rules of the game are efficient, namely, those established for the benefit of other "orders" distinct from that nominally represented by the state, in which the law of the strongest tends to prevail. In most of Latin America, such "orders" are expanding vigorously.

This constitutes an obstacle to the construction of democracy. Without the rule of law and without real citizens' rights and duties in force, democracy gradually becomes no more than a set of ritual practices, rather than institutions, constellated around periodic elections and their formal result. In this context, criminality "constitutes a serious obstacle in the process of democratic consolidation in Latin America as it precipitates an increase in public and private violence as an answer, and increases citizens' distrust of State institutions and authorities" (Frühling 1997, 1). Uncontrolled criminality makes citizens mistrustful and restless (Whitehead 2002, 183), which debilitates the political regime as a whole.

The next question we address takes this real context into account: to what degree can there be the effective application of norms in Latin America? In a classical study, O'Donnell (1993) says it is a question of the state: its coverage, efficacy, and action in the public interest. When private interests colonize the state apparatus, then they will also control the application of norms. When the state bureaucracy practices discrimination, the latter taints the application of law. As regards the justice apparatus in particular, the main problems that emerge are access, how quickly and efficiently it works, and how impartially it applies the law. But these possibilities do not concern the justice apparatus alone; rather, they are conditioned by social circumstances, not only in terms of the resources dedicated to the judiciary, but also because of the biases and forms of discrimination that penetrate the system. Justice is also a social product, and so the actual enforceability and impartial application of norms may not depend, mainly or exclusively, on the voluntary acts of judges.

In this context, the question that follows is the degree to what the justice system does may be decisive. There are those who believe that "effective punishment is a powerful crime deterrent" (Buvinic, Morrison, and Shifter 1999). But this requires deeper empirical examination, which usually establishes a correlation so that "to the extent that the probability of being arrested, condemned, and imprisoned becomes greater, the rates of crime decrease" (Zúñiga 2001, 40). This correlation is apparent in a cross-national comparison, such that in static terms, greater efficacy with repression corresponds with less crime in any given country, as is usually the case in the developed world. That the variables correlate does not mean that the link is causal. It may be that these variables depend on a third factor that is not included in the analysis, as attention is focused only on those two. There is definitely no evidence that increases in the efficacy of punishment leads to decreased crime in any society.[3]

Assuming that the performance of the justice system has some role in increasing or decreasing crime, one must still determine how powerful an agent of dissuasion this factor might be. Clearly, the empirical answer will vary from country to country. In states with a greater capacity for investigation and adjudication, the dissuasive power of the justice system is likely to be higher. But the challenge lies in determining the extent to which this dissuasive factor becomes determinant in countries such as those of Latin America, determining whether individuals commit or do not commit crimes.

One very serious difficulty is the complexity of measuring criminality.[4] In the case of Latin America, we must add to complexity the incompleteness, or unreliability, of statistical information. Conceptually, however, we can construct a six-level pyramid of each country (diagram 8.1). The bottom level represents the actual number of crimes committed in any given period (a figure hard to ascertain in most cases, or one that is subject to coarse estimation via survey techniques). The next level up, which is somewhat more reliable—although its proportionality to the previous level may not be so—represents the number of crimes reported to the authorities. The third level represents investigated crimes (again, there is a "black hole" here, as it is impossible to distinguish actually investigated cases from those ignored after a first report). The final three upper layers do rely on precise statistics, and refer to cases submitted to trial, cases ending with a verdict or sentence, and, finally, cases for which a penalty was imposed.

It is possible to illustrate how the pyramid works in the case of Mexico, using the data provided by Zepeda (2006). As regards the links between the first two tiers, surveys suggest that only 1 in every 4 crimes are reported. As regards the third tier, only 18.5 percent of reported cases lead to a completed investigation. As regards the fourth tier, only 11.4 percent of reported cases (those in the second tier) are presented to a judge. Finally, three out of every four people that are sentenced (fifth tier) are condemned (sixth tier). According to Zepeda, this means that 3.3 percent of Mexicans who have committed a crime stand before a judge.

Since the first tier is estimated based on surveys, there is insufficient information to estimate levels of impunity, because it is not possible to compare with any certainty for a given type of crime the cases that ended with a sentence with the whole universe of cases. Clearly, it is not possible to know whether it was actually the guilty who was punished, or whether punishment was applied regardless of culpability, as is known to happen in some cases.[5] What is more, we do not know what happens with cases that are reported but never reach trial or are never "legally" solved (a huge number in Mexico and all other countries for which there is information). Some explanations for this are lack of resources or professionalism, irresponsibility, and corruption.

It seems clear that in Latin America most criminal cases (even if we talk only about reported cases) are never resolved by the justice system. The margin would probably increase substantially with a qualitative analysis of what happened with cases that were apparently resolved by the judiciary, and about which one would probably be able to prove that

Diagram 8.1 Pyramid of Impunity

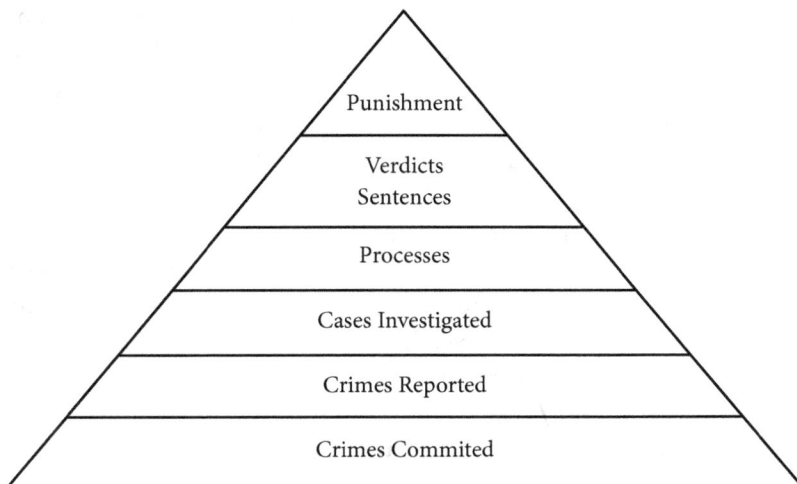

"cultural traits connected with affiliation, clientilism and group coalitions facilitate behavior that often ensures that all kinds of victimizers are immune and in a privileged position vis-à-vis the victims" (Gabaldón 2004, 8). Such cases, as much as cases that punish innocents, are also forms of impunity that undermine the dissuasive capacity of the justice apparatus. The efficient application of the law is severely limited by the above-described factors, which correspond in good measure to social characteristics that the justice apparatus adopts "by contagion" (Pásara 2002, 385) and which cannot for that reason be eradicated only from the latter by means of one or another institutional reform.

Let us now examine the solution adopted to address these problems with the reforms to the criminal prosecution process adopted by over half the countries of the region since the beginning of the 1990s. While these reforms have been implemented in different ways, they follow a single model—the shift from an inquisitorial system to a prosecutorial one.

THE PROMISE OF REFORM

Latin America is a region where one in every five thousand inhabitants per year is a victim of homicide. This rate is three times that of the U.S. and six times that of the European Union (Duce and Pérez Perdomo 2003, 80). The level of criminal activity generates objective insecurity, which aggravates the social perception of insecurity.[6] This has many consequences, not least of which are political and economic. The reform of the criminal process was promoted as the answer to this problem: "Confronted by social pressure, politicians and people in power are moving towards an institutional answer in order to solve the problem: to reform the procedures of criminal justice" (Duce and Pérez Perdomo 2003, 84).

How can the reform of criminal proceedings constitute a response to insecurity? Although not always explicit, the message has been that when criminal proceedings are more efficient, it is possible to combat crime more effectively. As noted above, there is insufficient evidence to prove the link between efficient punishment and crime reduction. What is more, it is a risky claim because it increases social expectations regarding the role of the criminal courts, and may therefore increase dissatisfaction when the results are modest, and thus also increase subjective insecurity.

Whatever the case may be, this reform initiative is part of a broader package. Reform of the criminal process is part of a system change that has received significant U.S. foreign aid since the late 1980s (with support from the model code approved in 1988 by Instituto Iberoamericano de Derecho Procesal). According to Blanco Escandón (2004, 227), since the 1980s, the U.S. "has invested more than $200 million in projects related to criminal justice." The reformed procedural codes have been in force since 1994, when Guatemala inaugurated the wave of RPP (followed by Costa Rica and El Salvador in 1998; Venezuela and Bolivia in 1999; and Ecuador, Honduras, Chile, Paraguay, Bolivia, Peru, Colombia, and the Dominican Republic since then; similar blueprints are under debate in Mexico).

To be sure, there is no homogeneous "Latin American reform of the criminal prosecution process" (Ambos and Woischnik 2000, 837). Equally, however, the reforms introduced "in the different countries are not independent of each other. The central ideas are the same" (Duce and Pérez Perdomo 2003, 77). Further, as Riego and Santelices stress (2003, 36), we are not only facing "reform proposals that are so similar in their purposes and the instruments they use," but there "has also been much similarity with respect to the deficiencies that the processes show in the various countries involved." Indeed, there is a shared external supporter (the U.S.), and the reform has even been promoted by the same key actors in several countries.

For the most part, RPP has been presented as a replacement of the "traditional inquisitorial system inherited from colonial institutions by a process closer to the prosecutorial type with strong influence from the North American model" (Blanco 2004, 272). Concretely, there is a dramatic change in the actors involved in the criminal justice process as a result of the reform. Whereas the judge was at the heart of the traditional process (having investigative as well as sentencing functions in some instances), the prosecution and defense become central in the new adversarial system, with one judge overseeing the fulfillment of norms and another (or others) issuing the sentence. Moreover, "the reformed criminal process is based on the principles of orality, contradiction, and continuity, with core importance attributed to the principle of immediacy" (Ambos and Woischnik 2000, 873). These principles take shape in the most visible characteristic of the new procedure: the oral trial. The promoters of RPP, however, have claimed many other things about the reform, such as making "judicial systems accessible so that they receive the reports and demands of all persons, especially the weaker; so that they are fast in resolving the matters at stake; so that they are predictable in their decisions; so that they are efficacious in controlling crime; so that they are respectful of judicial guarantees and that they repress those who transgress against human rights; so that they are efficient in their administrative procedures; that they are efficacious in determining property rights; that they control corruption; that they are transparent and contribute to the legitimization of the democratic system" (Riego 2002, 14).

Thus, to RPP were attached multiple goals. Two deserve special mention. On the one hand, there is the link with increased criminality, in such a way that "the legislator finds himself obliged" (Ambos and Woischnik 2000, 888) to search for new ways to administer criminal justice. On the other hand, there is the link with a general reform of justice, "to ensure the juridical security of citizens and, more specifically, of investors" (Duce and Pérez Perdomo 2003, 78). So RPP aspires to more than mere technical improvement. Indeed, it is strongly value laden: "The 'prosecutorial' concept tends to refer to characteristics such as progress, modernity, and rule of law. By contrast, the definition 'inquisitorial' is applied to a process which the observer considers traditional, or conservative and therefore, as a function of a personal point of view, of concern with respect to the rule of law. It is in this way that, frequently, unilateral arguments are made in favor of an Anglo-American procedural structure" (Ambos and Woischnik 2000, 867).

The values attached to RPP were very prominent in debates in the countries where the reform has been proposed. Its advocates made skewed comparisons between the way the traditional system worked (full of vices and shortcomings) and the new model in the abstract (not as it actually works). In other words, a familiar reality is compared to an intention, so that any comparison obviously favors the latter. Actual experience with the new model introduces surprises and new difficulties, of course. Prominent among the surprises is that oral trials, the centerpiece of the new proceeding, is used only in very few cases, as it is in countries that have had the adversarial system for a long time. And among the difficulties, the submission of proof in a form that is adapted to oral trial (a requisite of the new procedure) makes it more difficult to reconstruct the truth. As Blanco says, "Proof in the oral trial renders procedural truth as a contingency" (2004, 283). Further, according to the reform design, the prosecution becomes a central player.[7] Indeed, once a secondary, almost negligible player in the traditional system, the prosecutor has gained very important capacities: normally, he has a monopoly on starting criminal proceedings, except in cases where the interest of the victim becomes preponderant (usually, only the prosecutor can report a crime to a judge and thus initiate proceedings); is in charge of the investigation of the crime; and has the authority to determine whether there are insufficient elements to go ahead with the prosecution of a case.

The discretionary powers of the prosecutor to determine whether a case is tried are characteristic of the new model, and can be contrasted with the "model of absolute legality that existed before the reform" (Blanco 2004, 287), in which each case had to be reviewed by a judge. In the post-RPP context, a judge may never get to see a varying but significant number of cases.

Depending on the system established by the codes adopted in each country, the prosecutor receives the report and considers if the case has sufficient merits to initiate criminal prosecution. The prosecutor can: (1) reject a case reported to him by a private party or the police when he believes no crime has occurred; (2) provisionally shelve the case even if there is a crime because he believes there are insufficient elements to undertake a proper investigation; or (3) close the case, using the so-called principle of opportunity, because he considers that the facts, although clearly constituting a crime, are not grave enough to be of public interest. In addition, if the crimes are of lesser gravity, the prosecutor can (1) opt for the provisional suspension of the procedure, subjecting the accused to certain obligations; and (2) negotiate reparatory agreements between the perpetrator and the victim of the crime (Baytelman 2002, 50; Blanco 2004, 287, 290). National legislation establishes in which cases the prosecutor must submit his decision to the approval of a competent judge, but whatever the case, it is the prosecutor who is familiar with the facts of the case, and who drafts the decision that a judge must confirm in some instances.

A Chilean study about how public prosecutors used their powers using 2003 official statistics showed that three out of every four cases submitted to prosecutors were resolved without trial. Using samples

Table 8.1 Discretionary Powers, Alternative Solutions, and Procedural Simplification in RPP Codes

Country	Discretionary powers			Alternative solutions		Simplification	
	Shelved	*Denial of case*	*Principle of opportunity*	*Suspension under conditions*	*Agreement on reparations*	*Conciliation mediation*	*Shortened procedure*
Arg/Buenos Aires	yes	no	no	yes	yes	yes	yes
Arg/Córdoba	yes	yes	no	yes	no	yes	yes
Bolivia	yes	yes	yes	yes	yes	yes	yes
Chile	yes	yes	yes	yes	yes	yes	yes
Colombia	yes	yes	yes	yes	yes	yes	yes
Costa Rica	yes	yes	yes	yes	yes	yes	yes
Ecuador	yes	yes	no	no	no	yes	yes
El Salvador	yes	yes	yes	yes	yes	yes	yes
Guatemala	yes	yes	yes	yes	yes	yes	yes
Honduras	yes	yes	yes	yes	yes	yes	yes
Nicaragua	no	yes	yes	yes	yes	yes	yes
Paraguay	yes	yes	yes	yes	yes	yes	yes
Dominican Rep.	yes	yes	yes	yes	yes	yes	yes
Venezuela	yes	yes	yes	yes	yes	yes	yes

Source: Riego 2007, 27.

from various countries, the same study maintains that 64 percent of cases in Costa Rica never went to trial, and that in Bolivia two of every five cases reaching the prosecutor's office did not culminate in a process conducive to punishment (Riego 2005, 215).

There is no question about the central role of the accuser in the new model, which is the same as the role of prosecutors in Mexico (for many years) and Colombia (since the 1991 constitutional reform) within the inquisitorial systems of both countries. These countries show that prosecutors with such ample power will opt for the bureaucratic route when deciding whether to accuse: they opt to investigate cases with more evidence for proof because these are more likely to end in punishment when taken to trial. So trials are the result of cases that prosecutors anticipate they will win. In Chile, a few months after the reform, an evaluator noticed prosecutors were apprehensive about taking "to trial cases which investigations had not been tuned to perfection" (Baytelman 2002, 55). Usually the easiest cases (not necessarily the most important) are tried. The principle of opportunity, although legally designed to dispose of unimportant cases, can obscure the bureaucratic vice of working on easy cases that contribute to indicators of success.[8]

The prioritization of certain crimes without regard to the gravity of the facts also influences the principle of opportunity. Thus, drug related crimes get special attention from prosecutors in some countries because they have the incentive offered by international aid resources (on Colombia, Blanco 2004, 279).

Finally, strong discriminatory elements existing within the judicial system can contaminate the discretionary latitude of the prosecutor. In one evaluation of the Dominican Republic, for example, an interviewee observed that the principle of "opportunity did not pass the test of cronyism, political clientelism, and corruption" (Riego 2007, 227).

Some researchers suggest that prosecutorial decisions within the broad framework of competences of prosecutors generate social dissatisfaction and citizen protest (Baytelman 2002, 46) because "their" case does not reach the judge and the perpetrator is not punished and the case is "closed" in accordance with prosecutorial discretion. In Chile, which is considered a successful case of reform, it has been observed that "alternative solutions, mainly the temporary suspensions of process, are perceived by public opinion as judicial solutions of very low quality and even as a form of impunity" (G. Vargas 2006, 6).

There is not enough information about the results of RPP. As Hammergren (2002, 63) notes, cases that are reported but do not go to trial (the majority) must be researched empirically. This means focusing on cases that are not adjudicated rather than those that are, which would allow us to understand how the investigation works and how the prosecutor uses his legal capacities. This is the way to evaluate the true effects of RPP. There is evidence to suggest that the number of untried cases is increasing. As regards the crime of kidnapping in Colombia (which has an inquisitorial system in which the prosecutor has power typical of those in the adversarial or prosecutorial model), "a drastic decrease in the rate of arrests can be observed," stabilizing at the level of 0.14 apprehended for each kidnapping that has occurred (Restrepo, Sánchez and

Martínez 2004, 12). More generally, Blanco indicates that "the probability of a crime being investigated in Colombia has been reduced to one fourth the level previous to the reform" of 1991, which transferred the capacity to investigate from the judge to the prosecutor" (she does not cite his sources for this claim). The same author maintains that "because of the discretion that the new law allows the prosecutors, the probability that a criminal will be subject to trial has decreased dramatically" (Blanco 2004, 279).

It is interesting to review the data on the duration of proceedings in the few studies that exist of RPP. Although it has been stressed that "statistics point towards a significant reduction in the duration of the criminal process" (Blanco 2004, 277), the study by Riego and Santelices present data that are inconsistent with what one might expect from reformed criminal proceedings (see table 8.2).

Only in Chile and Ecuador do trials take place within a year; in Guatemala the process takes two years, somewhat more in Córdoba (Argentina), while in Costa Rica it takes about three years. These periods are, of course "too long" (Riego and Santelices 2003, 48). If the overly long duration of proceedings was the main complaint against the traditional model, although there is no information about this that is reliable, it does seem clear that the new system is hardly a major improvement in this area.

It would be premature to draw conclusions about RPP at this point, but the studies available suggest that "these efforts always have a streak of incompleteness; there are important areas where there were not sufficient resources or innovations to modify old practices of the inquisitorial model" (Riego 2007, 15). As a result of these shortcomings, citizens feel that there has not been a significant improvement: "From the point of view of the users, the system is still massively opaque. The decisions still appear distant and their perception of the judiciary does not change substantively just because some trials take place. The daily experience with the system is still very similar to that undergone with the old system" (Riego and Santelices 2003, 42). One of the most active promoters of RPP in Chile has admitted that "we cannot keep sending the message that there are no costs to committing crimes" (J. E. Vargas 2006, 22). In sum, "there is a certain discrepancy between the more concrete objectives that the reform proposes and the transformational capacities that the countries really have" which, in this case, expresses itself as a "struc-

Table 8.2 Comparative Duration of Criminal Proceedings after RPP

Country	Average Number of Days between Commission of Crime and Oral Trial	Average Number of Days between Formal Accusation and Oral Trial
Argentina (Córdoba)	500	240
Costa Rica	900	820
Chile	196	46
Ecuador	268	135
Guatemala	732	490
Paraguay	368	190
Venezuela	566	350

Source: Riego and Santelices 2003, 48, 49.

tural difficulty of our judicial system with respect to promoting innovation" (Riego 2007, 16, 21). And all this despite important increases in public expenditures and in personnel dedicated to criminal proceedings in most RPP countries. If this goes on, the result will not be only disappointment (failed expectations[9]) but also increased subjective insecurity, given the ambitious claims made about RPP.[10]

SEARCHING FOR NEW ANSWERS

So, as Riego asks, "to what extent can the model of judicial reform be independent of the type of state where it is inserted" (2002, 49). Duce and Pérez Perdomo remind us that this reform is not a panacea, and that it is important to maintain a deliberate distance from the proposition that "the reforms will make it possible to punish more criminals faster, thus increasing the cost of crime and reducing the rates of transgression," as promised in the explanatory introduction of the Venezuelan code. They conclude that "the reform has a limited capacity to resolve social problems that surround citizens' security, given that the causes of these problems are clearly beyond the reach of the criminal justice system" (Duce and Pérez Perdomo 2003, 84, 85).

We have returned to reality. The reform of criminal proceedings in Latin America by itself cannot combat crime and address citizen insecurity because "the problems of citizen security are also the result of several social variables that transcend the limited sphere of the criminal social system" (Duce and Pérez Perdomo 2003, 88–89). The basis for this conclusion is not simply theoretical, as is that for the conclusions examined in the first part of this chapter; the basis is also practical, stemming from the experience of countries that have implemented RPP and have not experienced a dramatic transformation in the working of the justice system.

Having returned to real life, we can ask what such reform *can* achieve. According to Duce and Pérez Perdomo, "the reform can make important contributions, within the limited sphere of action of the criminal justice system, to combat problems of citizens' insecurity and crime," but "judicial reform by itself, or even in conjunction with police reform and other specific reforms, . . . cannot be expected to have a decisive impact on problems related to a high incidence of violent crimes or their social construction" (Duce and Pérez Perdomo 2003, 86, 89). This answer is reasonable but it does not solve the fundamental problem of where exactly the boundaries are of the "limited sphere of action of the criminal justice system," and thus of the specific reach of its reform.

That a clear answer is necessary is all the more obvious when we consider the levels of investment in RPP. In the case of Chile, starting in 2005, the state was to assign US$212 million per year for the new criminal trial system to work (Baytelman 2002, 19), which means that "the participation of the judicial system in the public sector budget would be doubled" (Mohor Bellalta and Covarrubias 2006, 2). Hence the demand that RPP produce results better than those of the traditional system, and that it should do so "in a way that would justify having multiplied several times the criminal justice budget in Chile" (Baytelman 2002, 15). In view of the high level of investment in RPP in various countries, it is reasonable to ask if "the same funds and efforts put into an inquisitorial system might have had the same or better results" (Hammergren 2002, 62).

This leads us to consider the ways in which we may measure reform "success." For example, it is troubling to find that, in a study undertaken in the first months of implementation of RPP in Chile, all conditionally suspended or dismissed cases were considered "solved" (Baytelman 2002,

21, table 3). Of course, the victims of the crimes will not consider these case closures as "solutions" or as successful instances of combating crime. Also notable is the fact that there is no assessment of the quality of judicial decisions. A study on Colombia (Restrepo, Sánchez, and Martínez 2004) considers a case successful if the defendant is convicted. But if we are to know whether such hefty investment is worth it, we need studies evaluating the quality of convictions,[11] which means knowing whether the condemned were actually guilty. Given the available evidence, and given that RPP is a reality in over half of the countries of Latin America it is prudent to call for a more complete evaluation of the results of RPP. Broader and deeper quantitative data than that gathered to date is necessary, and qualitative aspects need studying, to establish whether RPP provides better justice and to establish where the limits of its application lie. In other words, it is important to ascertain whether we can resolve current problems with better follow-up measures and correctives, or whether the solution does not depend on the reform of judicial systems at all but on social transformation.

Given the links between poverty, exclusion, and criminality, the social dimension of criminal justice is directly relevant. Clearly, efficiently meeting demands for citizen security transcend criminal justice. To begin with, we must correct the mistaken parallels drawn between security and prevention, and punishment of crimes, as observed by Gabaldón (2004, 1). This involves debating and analyzing public policies (to promote growth, employment, or social investment, for instance) as generators of security or insecurity, rather than leaving it all up to the coercive system.

As regards the prevention of crime in particular, the task is in large part that of implementing "programs that aim at identifying the physical and social conditions that facilitate the commission of crimes, programs aimed at risk groups that develop strategies that would keep them from becoming habitual criminals, and programs of preventative control" (Frühling 1997, 1). Unfortunately, "there is only a handful of preventative programs" in Latin America, at the same time that "prevention measures, of comparatively low cost and high potential returns, have been woefully lacking" (Buvinic, Morrison, and Shifter 1999, 23).

If one also considers public policies that address the conditions leading to criminal activity in Latin America, it is possible to assess properly what the criminal justice system can do to address the crime phenomenon. So there must be reform of public policies affecting crime. Alongside this, the justice system should focus first on prioritizing and giving differentiated attention to two types of crime: organized crime and violations with the most damaging social consequences (such as abuse of power and economic transgressions), deploying an organic intelligence component in the investigative phase, something that is currently weak or non-existent in the region. Second, the justice system must respond to other crimes in a way that takes into account victim expectations.

Organized crime (involving mostly kidnapping, drug trafficking and trafficking of persons, and car theft, among many other offshoot transgressions) is a vastly different criminal activity compared to ordinary or traditional criminality. It employs full-time, specialized people and significant resources, including advanced technology. Depending on its scale, it affects citizen security in a way dramatically different from the activities of minor criminals. However, the justice apparatus, be it police or judges, still treats organized crime in a relatively undifferentiated way, with organized criminal activity considered simply as an increasing legal responsibility. But the nature of organized crime is different, and the means to address it must vary accordingly.

At the same time, making organized crime or crimes with a major social impact a priority must not lead to the neglect of other crimes.[12] It is necessary to deal with ordinary and minor crimes too, in a way that takes into account the interest of the victims. It is necessary to punish minor theft or manslaughter in a way that leaves no room for doubt about impunity, upon which citizen insecurity thrives. Responses must be commensurate with the crimes and certainly different from those necessary to address organized crime.

From the standpoint adopted here, procedure is not as important since it is subject to a criminal prosecution policy wherein resides the fundamental orientation of the justice system. But whatever the case, when shifting from a traditional to an alternative criminal process system one must take into account carefully the costs of the change, the human and financial resources required for change, and a study of whether the cost is justified by the improvements one can expect (in the case of countries yet to undertake RPP). The transformation of the criminal justice system in the region should be judged in these, rather than ideological, terms.

NOTES

1. The fastest reported change is the Chilean, where the reform led to "a reduction of 60 percent . . . in the average time of processing of a criminal case when compared to the old system" (Duce 2006, 3). As we will see later, this has not been replicated elsewhere.

2. Nevertheless, it should be noted that faster adjudication tends to improve citizens' sense of security. So, while speedy trials and prompt punishment do not improve the objective security of a society, they do strengthen the subjective sense of security.

3. As we know, decreased levels of crime have followed harsher punishment in some states in the U.S. But it is questionable whether this implies a causal relationship between one and the other (note that the U.S. imprisoned one out of every 120 inhabitants nationwide in 2006, including habitual offenders, which may have prevented, rather than punished, some violations of the law). If so, this is a case of increasing repression and reducing crime that does not prove the dissuasive capacity of punishment.

4. Despite the difficulties of measuring criminality, which are even more pronounced in cross national studies, specialists agree that citizen security in Latin America has been declining steadily (see Basombrío 2007).

5. For the case of Mexico D.F., see Pásara (2006). The imposition of sentences on persons that should not have been condemned has caused scandal in the U.S. over the last few years, when DNA tests were given only to inmates in death row. Innocence was established in hundreds of cases. Special attention should be paid to this qualitative aspect of sentences because a groundless sentence lacks dissuasive power and, on the contrary, it discredits the system.

6. Under Latin American social conditions, many of which contribute to a sensation of security loss—in employment and in conditions of life—the perception of being threatened from different angles easily becomes concrete through the danger—both real and imagined—of crime. It must be noticed that, occasionally, increases in subjective insecurity do not seem to correspond with increases in objective insecurity. For the case of Chile, see Mohor Bellalta and Covarrubias (2006).

7. In spite of the legal design, those who have studied the process empirically conclude that prosecutors "have tended to behave according to criteria from the old system, even becoming the main agents of reproduction of the inquisitorial system," given that "it is more convenient for them to keep a low profile, and not assume a central role that may result in important criticisms for which they do not get to identify efficacious instruments" (Riego 2007, 26, 27).

8. "The only ones that move are the flagrant cases," said a Colombian prosecutor interviewed in a study evaluating RPP in his country (Riego 2007, 120). This is because when the accused is arrested while committing a crime, or

immediately thereafter, proof is simple and, as happens under the inquisitorial system, requires no further investigation.

9. Evidence that RPP creates social expectations appears in the Chilean case where it was found that the implementation of the reform resulted in increases in the number of crimes reported. However, this change tended to disappear after the first year that the RPP was in force, which suggests a decrease in expectations (CESC 2006).

10. In the case of Chile, given that the implementation of RPP incrementally covered the various regions of the country, it was possible to confirm increases in the perception of insecurity in the regions where the reform had been implemented. The fact that the perception was related to increases in crime, but not in the surroundings of the interviewee, has given way to the hypothesis that the increase may be due to the way the media deals with the issue of crime.

11. Evaluating sentencing quality is to enter difficult and risky terrain, but it is indispensable if we are to address the needs of justice reform and not just the criminal justice system. We must avoid any formal or hierarchical criteria (like the overturning of decisions in courts of appeal), and to evaluate the quality of a decision is not to produce a new judgment on the case. Clearly, the goal is to evaluate the internal consistency of judicial decisions, particularly the treatment of proof and the legal arguments deployed. To this we must add that making sentences public and accessible is indispensable to ensure that society exerts some control over quality.

12. This seems to have happened even in cases where, it is claimed, RPP has had satisfactory results in general. In Chile, it has been admitted that RPP "has had problems in dealing with a great mass of light cases. There is the sensation that these cases, that are the majority of those that reach the system, are not properly dealt with. This happens in circumstances such that the quality of life of many people is linked to these matters and that, generally, the public perception of citizens' insecurity relates more to these types of crimes than to the more serious" (J. E. Vargas 2006, 19).

CHAPTER NINE

Latin America's Prisons

A Crisis of Criminal Policy and Democratic Rule

MARK UNGAR *&* ANA LAURA MAGALONI

Latin America's prison populations are swelling to record levels. The increase reflects the weakness rather than the strengths of the region's efforts to impose law and order. Most of all, conditions in the penitentiary systems of the region provide evidence that patterns of discrimination are entrenched, criminal justice systems are in disarray, and tolerance of human rights abuse is an ongoing reality. Killings, overcrowding, disease, torture, hunger, corruption, and the abuse of due process that occur under the twenty-four-hour watch of the state belie the principles underlying contemporary Latin American democracy. Even the measures being adopted to improve prison conditions, such as reformed criminal codes and new conditional release laws, are undermined by inconsistent and ineffective policy, slow judicial processes, and, above all, a rising crime rate that fuels arrests, prolonged preventative detention, and incarceration (see the chapters by Pásara and Restrepo in this volume).

Various national and international organizations have documented and condemned the state of Latin America's prisons, issuing specific recommendations for improvements. But there are few studies that have explored the underlying causes of the ongoing deterioration of Latin American prisons, even as they are the object of growing attention. The argument presented here is that the penitentiary crisis is steeped in political dynamics and institutional practices that are very difficult to alter. This view is expounded over five sections: the first three provide a general overview of the situation of Latin America's prisons, describing overcrowding, the extent of violence, and food and health deprivations, followed by a description of the institutional structure of prisons to identify the primary deficiencies in policy and administration. Section four consists of a case study of the type of offenders the system imprisons, with a focus on the Mexican penitentiary system (the one about which there is most information). The criminological and socioeconomic profile of inmates is outlined, and the efficacy of due process standards in the criminal justice system is examined. With some caveats, the conclusion drawn from this case study applies to most other penitentiary systems in the region, and we hope our work inspires further scrutiny of prison systems in other countries. The final section examines the applicability in Latin America of the usual kind of justifications offered for penitentiary systems.

OVERCROWDING AND VIOLENCE

Latin American incarceration rates rose sharply after the early 1990s, as shown by table 9.1. Increases began in the 1980s, but shot up in the following decade. Every Latin American country has overcrowded prisons, following an overall increase in prison population of 79 percent over the past decade.[1] Twenty countries have reached a critical level of over 120 percent occupation rates.[2]

The regional average of 161 prisoners per 100,000 inhabitants is comparable to the average rate in Africa (188 per 100,000) and central-eastern Europe (184 per 100,000), but far higher than that for North America, Oceania, and Western Europe.[3] Less than 15 percent of this growth is attributable to population increases—the remaining increase is primarily the result of resorting more frequently to incarceration as a response

Table 9.1 Latin America's Prison Population

Country	Population[1] (Reported Year)	Per 100,000	Increase since 1992 (%)[2]	Overcapacity[3] (%)	Unsentenced[4] (%)
Argentina[5]	56,313 (2002)	148	134	Prov. av. 40	Av. 70
Bolivia[6]	7,207 (2005)	76	Est. 33	62*	75
Brazil[7†]	330,642 (2004)	183	145	State av. 81*	45
Chile[8]	36,374 (2004)	212	58	47*–50	51
Colombia[9]	68,545 (2004)	152	102	39	43
Costa Rica[10]	7,619 (2004)	19	114	28*–67	Moderate
Cuba[11]	55,000 (2003)	487	n/a	Aprox. 175	Moderate
D. Republic[†]	13,836 (2004)	157	28	156*–215	74
Ecuador[†]	13,045	100	63	40–43	Severe
El Salvador[12]	12,117 (2004)	184	113	7*–35	75+
Guatemala[13]	8,307 (2003)	69	n/a	13	62
Honduras[14]	11,236 (2004)	158	97	109*	90
Mexico[†]	191,890 (2004)	182	109	State av. 33	Varies by state
Nicaragua[15†]	5,610 (2004)	100	n/a	13*	17
Panama[16]	10,630 (2003)	354	120	51*–212	Moderate
Paraguay[17]	4,088 (1999)	75	n/a	24*–26	80-90 %
Peru[18]	32,129 (2004)	114	85	41*	55
Uruguay[19]	7,100 (2003)	209	117	86	65+
Venezuela[20]	21,342 (2003)	83	-32	13*–60	70+

1. Figures on overcrowding and prison population increases are from the "World Prison Brief" of the International Centre for Prison Studies. Briefs for each country can be found at http://www.kcl.ac.uk/depsta/law/research/icps/worldbrief/.

2. *Agence France Presse*, March 1, 2000; *Penal Reform International Newsletter* 40 (March 1999).

3. The source of estimates marked * is ILANUD.

4. Observatoire International des Prisons at www.oip.org, and prison associations from each country.

5. In federal countries with separate provincial penitentiary systems, differences can be wide. The table presents averages for some figures.

6. Ministry of Government, General Directorate of the Penitentiary Regime (Ministerio de Gobierno, Dirección General de Régimen Penitenciario, DGRP).

7. *The Economist*, "Tackling the Chaos in Brazil's Prisons," February 24, 2001, 37; and Julita Lemgruber, "The Brazilian Prison System: A Brief Diagnosis" (published for *Prisons in Crisis Project Report*, Latin American Studies Association, February 2005).

8. Lúcia Dammert, "El sistema penitenciario en Chile: Desafíos para el nuevo modelo público-privado" FLACSO-Chile, 2006.

9. Roy Walmsley, *World Prison Population List* (London: International Center for Prison Studies, February 2005). The original source for these figures is the Colombian National Penitentiary and Prison Institute (Instituto Nacional Penitenciario y de Prisones, INPP).

10. Population estimate from the Ministry of Justice, Costa Rica.

11. Nils Christie, *World Prison Population List* (Oslo: International Center for Prison Studies, 2006).

12. Population estimates from Walmsley, *World Prison Population List*.

13. *Penal Reform International Newsletter* 53 (December 2003).

14. Population estimates from Walmsley, *World Prison Population List*.

Table 9.1 Latin America's Prison Population (*cont.*)

15. Percentage of unsentenced prisoners from Justice Studies Center of the Americas (CEJA), *Reporte de la Justicia, Segunda Edición (2004–2005)* (Santiago de Chile: CEJA, 2005).
16. Walmsley, *World Prison Population List.*
17. Population estimates from ILANUD.
18. National Penitentiary Institute (Instituto Nacional Penitenciario, INPE); Reuters, "Peru Admits Jails Packed with Un-sentenced Inmates," April 24, 1996. In that article, the Justice Viceminister said the rate of unsentenced inmates was around 90 percent. Also see Ximena Sierralta, "Cárceles en Crisis: El Caso de Perú" (published for *Prisons in Crisis Project Report*, Latin American Studies Association, February 2005).
19. Enrique Navas, "Apreciación de la situación penitenciaria uruguaya" (published for *Prisons in Crisis Project Report*, Latin American Studies Association, February 2005).
20. This drop was due almost entirely to the 1998 Penal Process Code reform, which led to the release of many detainees. Since then, the population has risen back to average levels. Author interviews, Office of Information and the Press Department of the Office of Defense and Civil Protection, Ministry of Justice, 1998 and 2003; and Alistair Dunning, "Prison Brief for Venezuela," International Centre for Prison Studies, at www.prisonstudies.org.

to rising crime. Moreover, with the exception of situations such as the antiterrorist crackdown under President Alberto Fujimori in Peru, the majority of incarcerations are for minor drug charges. In fact, the Inter-American Drug Abuse Control Commission (CICAD) of the Organization of American States (OAS) estimates that up to 80 percent of detentions are drug related.[4] The Latin American Office of the United Nations Center for International Crime Prevention (ILANUD) asserts that the 300 percent increase in imprisonment in Panama between 1981 and 1995 was the result of mandatory sentences for drug-trafficking and drug-related offences. Only a few countries, such as Costa Rica, have functioning drug rehabilitation programs. Many people are also imprisoned for minor property offenses. In Guatemala, for instance, about 50 percent of prisoners are charged with or convicted of petty offences;[5] and in Mexico City, two out of three newly admitted offenders were charged with petty crimes.[6]

Overcrowding has reached unprecedented levels because the increase in incarceration rates has far outstripped any increase in physical capacity. In Venezuela, where the official capacity is for 15,500 inmates, the penitentiary system in the 1990s held between 24,000 and 27,000 people.[7] In Brazil, in the state of São Paulo alone, a thousand new inmates enter the system every month. The Chilean prison population increases by 20 percent every year, so that up to sixteen people have to share cells built for six. In many countries, overcrowding of up to four times the intended capacity is concentrated in a handful of prisons. Officially, the maximum capacity of Honduras's Central Penitentiary is five hundred people, but it actually holds over three thousand, with some cells holding over forty-five individuals. In Peru, official total capacity is twenty thousand but the system holds over thirty thousand people (almost all the excess is in the Lima Lurigancho prison, built for eighteen hundred persons but normally housing around seven thousand).[8] In Cuba, double occupancy cells for many political prisoners measure ten by four feet.[9]

Overcrowding is usually worse at pretrial centers and police jails, which sometimes hold more detainees than the prisons. In 1996, the Argentine Justice Ministry estimated that there were twenty-eight thousand to thirty-one thousand of the country's fifty-five thousand to fifty-eight thousand prisoners held in pretrial holding facilities, which, as in most countries, regularly hold over one hundred detainees in cells measuring about twenty by two hundred feet.[10] Slow processing of these prisoners leads to the systemic violation of pretrial detention limits and the right to speedy trial.[11] As table 9.1 shows, in nearly every country most inmates are awaiting trial, while about a third complete the maximum sentence for their alleged crimes. Even after the post-Fujimori prison reforms, over half of Peru's detainees awaited trial for more than two years. In Venezuela and elsewhere, the time between arrest and sentencing regularly reaches four years. Reported percentages of unsentenced prisoners vary widely, in some countries ranging from 60 to 90 percent. In countries for which there are no reliable reports, the estimate is that the unsentenced percentage ranges from "moderate" (fewer than 50 percent) to "severe" (over 50 percent).

As overcrowding has increased, so has prison violence (with the exception of Chile and Mexico). Indeed, Latin America has been the site of the most deadly incidents of prison violence in the modern era: riots killed 244 prisoners in Peru in 1986, 111 in Brazil in 1992, and kills over 100 people almost every year in Venezuela (460 were killed in 1999 alone).[12] In the Argentine province of Mendoza, there have been 22 uninvestigated deaths since February 2004. In many prisons, violence is such that guards do not patrol large areas, and crackdowns and prisoner relocation do little to improve things. Riots triggered by overcrowding, and the nature of responses to riots, fuels further violence. In Uruguay, for example, the police have beaten or tear-gassed inmates, or used other violent means in response to regular prison riots,[13] and in a February

2000 riot in the maximum security Yanamayo prison in Peru, imprisoned Sendero Luminoso (SL) guerrillas demanded better conditions and an end to delayed court proceedings.[14]

Violence amid rival factions and gangs is also common in many countries, and is often encouraged or tacitly approved by prison officials. Colombian prisons reproduce conflict between guerillas and paramilitaries, and in Central American prisons the Salvatrucha and Mara 18 youth gangs continue their gang wars. In the state of São Paulo in Brazil, where yearly prison riots increased from a few dozen in the early 1990s to nearly two hundred by 1997,[15] inmates form criminal organizations such as the First Capital Command (*Primeiro Comando da Capital,* PCC), which includes an estimated twelve thousand inmates serving their sentences and over six thousand released prisoners. The PCC demanded that it share responsibility for prison administration and for the relocation of its leaders in the riots that engulfed twenty-nine prisons in February 2001. Inmates, including children living in prisons, receive weapons from visiting lawyers and family members.

INSTITUTIONAL STRUCTURE

In most countries, penitentiaries are tiered systems organized according to the gravity of offenses. Thus, while Chile divides its penal centers into closed, open, and semi-open facilities, countries like Honduras and Cuba have high-security prisons and minimum-security *granjas.* Systems are part of, and administered by, national or provincial ministries of justice, of the interior, or of security. In Brazil, the state justice secretariats run most state systems, although the prisons secretariat and the police under the Secretary of Public Security administer others. Policy, budgeting, and administration are in the hands of whichever ministry is in control, and approaches vary widely depending on which ministry is in charge. Justice Ministry aegis, for instance, helps to prioritize due process, but in many countries, prisons are part of the security apparatus to ensure better physical control.

In an effort to standardize and improve conditions, many countries have created special penal entities with trained specialists either within or separate from the police. Argentina has a Penitentiary School and a Penitentiary Studies Postsecondary Academy, for instance, and the Mexi-

Table 9.2 Prison Administration

Country	Responsible Institution[1]	Admin. Responsibility
Argentina[2]	Varies by province; nationally: MJ, SPF	
Bolivia	DGRP; MG	PN
Brazil	State Secretaries of Justice, Secretary of Prisons or Public Security	
Chile	MIJ	Gendarmería
Colombia	MIJ	INPC
Costa Rica	DAS; MJ	
Cuba	DCP; MJ	
Dom. Republic	MI; DGP	PN
Ecuador	PN	DRS
El Salvador	MG	
Guatemala	DGSP; MI	
Honduras	Secretariat of Security	PP
Mexico	DGPRS	
Nicaragua	MG	
Paraguay	DGIP; MJ	PN and DGIP
Panama	MGJ	
Peru	INPE; MJ	PN and INPE
Uruguay	DCPCR	
Venezuela	MJ	

[1] See list of acronyms for full titles of institutions.
[2] There can be great differences among provincial penitentiary systems in federal countries.

can state of Baja California gave specialized courses to train Security and Penitentiary Custody agents in 2002.[16] In Peru, the decentralized National Penitentiary Institute (*Instituto Nacional Penitenciario,* INPE) has eight regional offices with financial and policy autonomy governed by the Penal Execution Code and the President of the INPE. Many countries also have watchdog bodies to oversee and advise the penitentiary authorities. El Salvador has an ombudsman to investigate prison conditions, and Costa Rica's National Commission for the Improvement of the Administration of Justice (*Comisión Nacional para el Mejoramiento de la Administración de Justicia,* CONAMAJ) has helped to introduce plans such as that to halve sentences and offer prisoner work programs.[17] Guatemala has an independent Commission for the Transformation of the Penitentiary System (*Comisión Nacional para la Transformación del Sistema Penitenciario,* CTSP), and the 1997 peace accords included the training of prison directors under the auspices of the UN Mission to Guatemala (MINIGUA).

Specialized prison agencies or police forces handle day-to-day operations. Directors and guards are the main authorities within prisons. Most directors have a background in prison administration, but they tend to be transferred regularly (usually every two years), which limits their ability to implement change. Guards are usually police officers and are normally rotated in from other policing tasks. In Brazil, over 80 percent of states employ staff to do work for which they were not hired, often sending trained guards to undertake health services, social work, and other activities where staff shortages are chronic. The increasing deployment of soldiers often scuttles plans to add personnel or to replace police with civilian guards. Colombia has a military unit for prison custody and re-socialization,[18] Cuba staffs many prisons with soldiers,[19] and in Chile the Gendarmerie charges military officials with security and civilian officials with administrative and research tasks. Nearly half of Brazilian wardens are members of the Military Police (Polícia Militar, PM), military policemen direct nearly two-thirds of prisons, and in four-fifths of all states the Military Police handle all external security and transport. In Honduras, the Secretariat of Security (in charge of all police forces) took over administration of the prison system from the Ministry of Governance and Justice in the late 1990s. Because the Security Secretariat heads the police and has cracked down violently on crime, the prisons too have become part of this repressive policy—with more rights abuses and less legal protection than inmates would have had under the Justice Ministry.

Whether they are police or military officers, most guards engage in corrupt or criminal activities, ranging from the harassment of family visitors to collaboration with prisoners in multimillion-dollar cocaine and heroin trafficking networks.[20] In the Palmasola prison, Bolivia's largest facility, the government minister fired nearly three hundred staff members in December 2003 for giving "holiday passes" to prisoners paying hefty bribes, but within twenty-four hours the same system was up and running under an entirely new staff.[21] Not only do these and other forms of prison corruption allow for great disparities in conditions for prisoners—forcing the majority lacking resources to live in subhuman conditions—they also help abusive prison officials avoid punishment.

Physical crackdowns are irregular and intense. Guards often raid cells and destroy inmate property without provocation. In Honduras, prison security agencies have engaged in irregular and unannounced mass transfers, triggering violence in 2003 and 2004 that led to the death of 185 detainees. In most countries, some prisoners have permission to maintain internal discipline and are often responsible for the worst beatings and sexual abuse. The violation of minimal standards is a common occurrence as a result of chronic misadministration and creeping militarization, along with malfunctioning judiciaries, anemic budgets, and weak oversight. While international guidelines recommend there should be a 1:3 guard-prisoner ratio, the Latin American ratio ranges from 1:7 in Chile to 1:120 in most Andean and Central American countries. Most prisons lack even information systems to keep track of detainees or, more seriously, fail to separate inmates in accordance with national and international law provisions, so that convicted and pretrial prisoners, youths and adults, petty offenders and convicted murderers live together. Officially, most prisons have work and education programs. In Chile, all prisoners are required to complete high school or learn a trade, for example. But most such programs are underfunded and poorly run, which further aggravates levels of violence.

Specialized administrative bodies, oversight agencies, and national laws often lack financial and political backing. The INPE in Peru has insufficient resources, and its personnel lack opportunities to specialize because they get transferred within the system according to the discretion of prison directors. Violence and neglect cause "one or two deaths each day" in the prisons of Buenos Aires province in Argentina, but investigation of complaints by federal or provincial prison ombudsmen are not taken up for budgetary reasons.[22] In Honduras, the Penitentiary Cooperation and Control Councils (Consejos de Cooperación y Control Penitenciario, CCCP), made up of local and national penal officials, and the Juridical Commission of the Penitentiary System, which is supposed to facilitate releases, have no real power. The Brazilian penal and penal execution laws, meant to standardize and regulate prison administration and prisoner rights for the twenty-seven state prison systems, are not complied with because half of all states lack basic administrative manuals, only nine have career plans for prison staff, and only six states have penitentiary schools to train personnel. Chronic fund and expertise shortages also hinder the work of the National Penitentiary Department (Departamento Penitenciário Nacional, DPN), which assists states financially and technically, and of the National Council for Criminal and Penitentiary Policy (Conselho Nacional para a Política Criminal e Penitenciária, CNPCP), which formulates prison policy and monitors conditions in the states. Furthermore, the large number of people detained in police and pretrial facilities fall beyond the purview of laws and official oversight in most countries.

LIVING CONDITIONS

Living conditions are abominable in all of Latin America's prisons. The food served is often rotten and rarely provides minimal nutritional requirements, so that most prisoners depend on family and visitors (who must pay "tax" for the privilege) because prices for additional items are highly inflated (up to US$8 for a liter of milk).[23] In some Paraguayan and Uruguayan prisons, there is no fruit or vegetables on offer, and "totally insufficient alimentation" causes continual hunger.[24] The Guayaquil prison in Ecuador cooks for only 1,500 people although it holds 2,650,[25] and Lurigancho prisoners have actually starved. Prisoners often eat without utensils or plates, and often in rooms with toilets.

Basic hygiene conditions are equally appalling. Many inmates have no access to potable water or functioning plumbing. The Bluefields prison in Nicaragua, for instance, only has two showers and four toilets for more than a hundred detainees. Most Venezuelan prisons lack clean water, proper plumbing, and are rat and cockroach infested. Loose electric cables have caused several deaths at El Rodeo prison, and El Dorado prison cells (where one bed is shared by four inmates) are infested with vermin. Inhuman conditions are exacerbated by the fact that in nearly every country cells are packed to the point of suffocation, with up to ten inmates crammed into six by ten foot areas. Inmates in Bolivia's San Pedro Prison are known to "buy" cells, but most are crammed into tiny airless spaces or sleep on stairs and in hallways.[26]

Many prisoners are ill, and there is insufficient medication and medical care. Typhus, cholera, tuberculosis, and scabies run rampant in many facilities. In Argentina, an estimated 30 to 40 percent of prisoners are

HIV-positive or have AIDS,[27] and the absence of basic medical attention frequently provokes riots. In many Peruvian prisons, more than half of prisoners have no access to health care, as there is one doctor per 885 inmates.[28] Honduras's San Pedro Sula Penal Center has plenty of aspirin, but little medication to treat specific conditions.[29] In Brazil, most states report regular distribution of clothing and hygiene items, but this is actually neither regular nor does it cover all inmates.[30] One Paraguayan inmate reported that "a simple medical examination, test or radiography requires both cunning and personal connections. There is no medication, not even painkillers. Orthodontics is non-existent, and the majority of [dental] professionals only do extractions. Attention for the mentally ill . . . is inhuman. There are many farm animals in Paraguay that live better than these inmates."[31] Throughout the region, moreover, authorities accuse prisoners of pretending to be ill, or punish prisoners for asking for medical attention or reform. In 1990, Venezuela packed off a group of 239 prisoners carrying out a hunger strike in protest against conditions to the notorious Amazon penal colony of El Dorado.

Under growing pressure, many countries are taking steps to address these problems. In Costa Rica, psychiatrists visit prisons regularly, and both Chile and Costa Rica are expanding contracts with private businesses for the provision of food, medication, and rehabilitation services. Agricultural penal *granjas* provide inmates with the chance to work outdoors and engage in self-sufficient cultivation. Nongovernmental organizations (NGOs) like the Prison Fellowship and Penal Reform International have also helped inmates throughout the region. But tightening budgets delay long-term plans and infrastructural expansion. Although Colombia's prison population increased by 17,000 during the latter half of the 1990s, there were only a few prisons built in that time. In Brazil, many prisons have gone without decent medical facilities and work programs because of a 52.45 percent reduction of the federal penitentiary fund since 1995.

Table 9.3 shows reported expenditures on health and food. Most countries do not calculate or publish how much they spend on these items, so the only reliable estimates are those given by administrators of specific prisons. Governments that do report numbers often calculate per-prisoner expenditures by dividing entire budgets by the number of prisoners. This is deceptive because most spending is on administration. The

Table 9.3 Food and Health Expenditures

Country	Spending per prisoner[1]
Argentina	Varies by province
Bolivia	US$26 per prisoner per month
Brazil	Varies by state
Chile	n/a
Colombia	US$1.44 (food only)
Costa Rica	n/a
Cuba	n/a
Dom. Republic	n/a
Ecuador	n/a
El Salvador	n/a
Guatemala	n/a
Honduras	US$0.40 (food and health)
Mexico	Varies by state
Nicaragua[3]	US$0.58–5.34 (food only)
Paraguay	n/a
Panama	n/a
Peru	US$0.75 (food only)
Uruguay	n/a
Venezuela	US$1.50[3]

[1] Spending per prisoner varies because it covers a different range of expenses in different countries. When a country does not categorize those expenses, a general number is provided. When it does, the categories are mentioned in the table.

[2] Edgard Barberena S., and Sergio Aguirre A. "Revisen presupuesto del SPN," *El Nuevo Diario*, January 1999.

[3] The amount was 1.64 Bolívars, about US$1.50. See: PROVEA, *Informe Anual,* 2001–2002; *El Universal,* March 21, 1995, B-1.

2000 federal prison budget in Argentina, for instance, was US$32,000 per prisoner, but 80 percent of that went to salaries. Most of the 75 cents that Peru spends to feed prisoners per day actually goes to administration.

MEXICAN PRISONS

The substandard living conditions of the inmate population in Latin America is all the more appalling when we analyze the type of offenders that inhabits these prisons, and particularly how the judicial system determines the culpability of offenders. In this section, we provide an in-depth analysis of the composition of the inmate population and the legal process (the period between detention and sentencing) to which inmates are subjected in Mexico. This sheds light more generally on the target population of the Latin American criminal justice system, and how that system adheres to standard practices of human rights and the rule of law.

The Inmate Population

The police and prosecution offices charged with detaining offenders and taking them to court are inefficient: an estimated meager 10 percent of the reported offenses are prosecuted, and for an estimated 44 percent of these cases there are no trial proceedings because the police never issue an arrest warrant. Even if we account for the valid concerns raised by Restrepo in her chapter on Colombia, it is safe to assume that impunity is high in Mexico. Only 6 in every 100 reported offenses are actually tried,[32] so that the rate of impunity is 94 percent of reported offenses (96.7 percent if one takes into account crimes that are never reported).[33] Once an offender stands in a criminal court, however, the probability of conviction is very high, with eight in every ten cases ending in conviction.[34]

The high rate of impunity highlights the ineffectiveness of the Mexican criminal justice system. But closer analysis means undertaking a more detailed study of the kinds of people who are convicted and inhabit the prison system. The best way to measure the effectiveness of the system is by the types of offenses that do not go unpunished, since there is no criminal justice system that can apprehend all those who commit crimes. A criminal justice system is more effective when it concentrates on seizing the most dangerous delinquents. Accordingly, a system that has a very low impunity rate for kidnapping is more effective than one that effectively punishes petty thieves. The type of offender convicted in Mexico shows which crimes are detected and prosecuted. Table 9.4 shows the distribution of convicted offenders by type of crime.

As shown in Table 9.4, 24.8 percent (2002) and 28.6 percent (2005) of inmates are incarcerated for petty theft or larceny, and the remainder for a felony (violent robbery and assault), or for serious crimes like homicide or kidnapping. At first glance, it appears that a little less than a third of inmates are not "dangerous" criminals, and more than two thirds are convicted for a felony. But a closer look at the data suggests this is not the

Table 9.4 Distribution of Convicted Offenders by Type of Crime

Crime	2002	2005
Simple theft and larceny	27.7	29.9
Robbery	31.2	28.1
Injuries	1.9	1.8
Homicides	10.6	10.0
Manslaughter	5.0	6.2
Kidnapping	4.2	4.7
Sexual crimes	8.9	7.3
Use of firearms	1.6	1.7
Fraud	1.7	1.6
Drugs and health crimes	5.5	7.2
Others	1.7	1.5
Total	100.00	100.00

Source: Inmate surveys, 2002, 2005.

Note: Figures represent percentage of the inmate population in the Federal Disctict and the state of Mexico.

case. First, the information in table 9.4 is based on inmate surveys, so it shows the crimes that inmates were being punished for at the time of the survey rather than the distribution of convicted crimes. In other words, it shows the stock and not the flow. Second, because the severity of punishment (the length of sentences) depends on the type of crime committed, the gravest offenses tend to be overestimated, and those accused of petty theft or larceny, who serve shorter sentences, tend to be underestimated in the survey (indeed, some offenders convicted for petty theft and larceny a year before the survey had already served their sentences at the time of the survey). In short, the data underestimates inmates incarcerated for petty theft and larceny and, what is consistent with scattered reports from other countries, shows that the system overwhelmingly detains people responsible for petty offenses.[35]

One could claim that the prison population simply reflects the distribution of crimes given that the majority of crimes in any society are petty offenses. We examined two surveys collected almost four years apart in order to get past the problem of data validity. Between the surveys, the government of the Federal District (DF) and the state of Mexico launched public security initiatives and penal code reforms inspired by the zero tolerance initiative proposed by the team headed by Robert Giuliani. Clearly, despite major policy changes, the evidence shows that petty offenses continued to predominate within the system.

Another way of estimating the severity of offenses committed is by looking at the severity of the sentences issued by judges. Graph 9.1 shows the severity of the sentencing in Mexican criminal trials. As seen in the graph, 63 percent of offenders convicted nationally received sentences of three years or less, and only 8 percent received sentences of more than eleven years. At least six out of ten convicted offenders serve time for petty offenses, which suggests that most inmates have not committed serious crimes. In all likelihood, offenders serving three-year sentences were convicted for nonviolent theft. Moreover, as Azaola and Bergman show,[36] the number of sentences remained stable at approximately 120,000 for the whole country despite rising crime throughout the 1990s, while the time served for these convictions increased in length by an average of 10 percent. In short, the district attorney and the criminal courts did not increase productivity in terms of apprehensions and sentencing; rather, they just "packed" the prisons by raising the severity of sanctions for (mostly petty) crimes. Again, this reveals the incapacity of the criminal system to focus on dangerous and predatory crimes.

Graph 9.1 Distribution of Sentencing, 2002

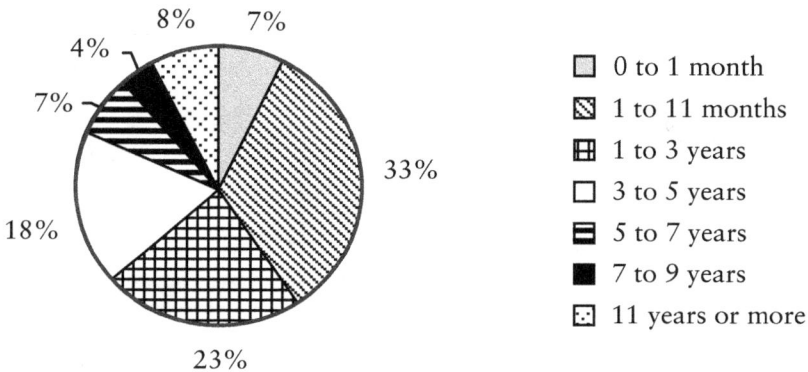

Source: Guillermo Zepeda, *Crimen sin castigo* (Mexico City: FCE, 2004).

There is also indirect but powerful evidence in the Inmate Surveys which suggests that convicted offenders held in prison are not "professional offenders," but those who are apprehended most easily. As shown in Graph 9.2, 58 percent (2002) and 66 percent (2005) reported being detained within three hours of committing the offense, or *in flagrante*.[37] The data also show that the probability of detecting and capturing an alleged delinquent declines dramatically as time passes. This also reveals that Mexican penal institutions are unable to carry out criminal investigations of professional criminality, so that it is less likely that professional criminals are apprehended: the leaders of kidnapping gangs, auto-theft ring leaders, and drug lords are not caught *in flagrante*. In this sense, it is likely that the people apprehended by the system are petty criminals at the bottom of the criminal chain.

The CIDE (Centro de Investigación y Docencia Económicas) Inmate Survey of 2002 supports this claim. Some of those incarcerated for drug-related crimes (*delitos contra la salud*), for instance, were prosecuted for selling narcotics. The average amount of drug sales ending in conviction was US$110, ranging from US$4 to US$300. Only in 10 percent of drug cases did the amount exceed US$3,900. Thus, it is consumers and petty dealers rather than serious drug traffickers that tend to get apprehended.

Graph 9.2 Time between Commission of Offence and Capture, 2002 and 2005

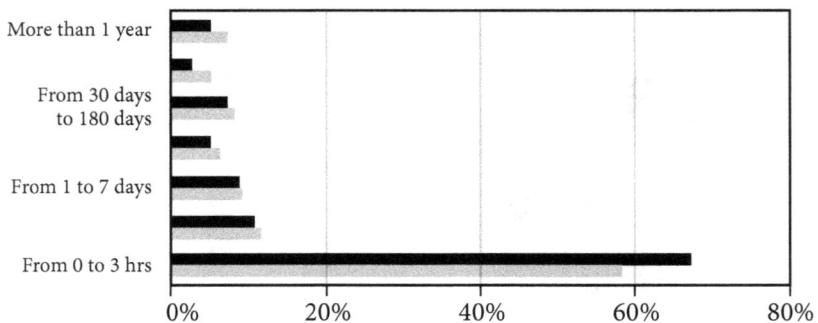

Source: CIDE Inmates Survey, 2002 and 2005.

The same occurs with kidnappings: a third of those jailed for kidnapping reported that they had acted alone or with one partner, and that they had obtained US$3,000 or less for half of the abductions they had carried out. This suggests that many of those sentenced for kidnapping are not really "professionals."

In sum, the data suggests that Mexican prisons do not house the most dangerous delinquents, but those who are easy to apprehend. Authorities have yet to focus their efforts on the most professional and dangerous criminals. As things are, the prison system serves to punish the lowest ranks of the criminal chain.

From Apprehension to Prison

Due process is crucial in legal procedures if defendants are to have fair trials and to minimize the scope for judicial error (and the conviction of innocents). There is legal recognition in Mexico of internationally recognized rights—including the right to be heard by a competent, independent, and impartial court, to be free from torture and not to be held incommunicado, to be immune from arbitrary detention, to be informed at all times of the reasons for the detention, to be presumed innocent until proven guilty beyond a reasonable doubt, and to have legal advice from the time of detention, among others. Theoretically, this should mean that authorities act fairly, impartially, and rationally when depriving someone of their freedom. But what actually happens with due process rights between apprehension by a police officer and sentencing by a judge? This section addresses this question, primarily using CIDE Inmate Surveys that provide information from inmates about how they are treated by the authorities. This data presents advantages and disadvantages: on the one hand, the only way to collect data on the fate of detainees during judicial proceedings is through self-reports because that information is not found in case files; on the other hand, like anyone else in the system, including judges and prosecutors, defendants are biased. However, the similarity of responses suggests a pattern of recurring unlawful practices. In what follows, there is information about each stage of the criminal justice process and the actors involved, starting with the police and ending with prosecutors and trials.

Detention or Arrest

The first contact between the authorities and defendants occurs at the time of apprehension or detention. The street police carry out detentions taking place in the hours immediately after a (flagrant) crime.[38] Since 60–65 percent of offenders report being apprehended almost immediately, this means that the street police are responsible for most detentions. It is necessary for a judge to issue an arrest warrant a few days later after arrest, at which point the DA police (*policía judicial*) becomes responsible for detention.[39] The street police are legally obliged to take a detainee immediately to an agency of the office of the DA. If the detention occurs with an arrest warrant, the DA police must take the defendant to a judge. However, the time of *transportation* seems to be less than "immediate." According to the inmates, the police hold 23 percent for three to six hours, 13 percent from seven to twenty-four hours, and 8 percent for more than twenty-four hours. In sum, the police hold 44 percent of offenders for longer than a reasonable time for transporting them to the DA or judge. This time lag is crucial, since this is usually when police abuse occurs, as detainees have no access to lawyers and are unable to control or limit police brutality. According to inmates, it is during this period when threats or torture are most likely to occur. Table 9.5 shows how often defendants report they were threatened, humiliated, mistreated, or tortured by the relevant authorities.

As Table 9.5 shows, abuse of authority and brutality occur mainly when defendants are in the detention stage, in the custody of the street or DA police. It is also clear that the DA police are the most abusive and violent. Once defendants are with the prosecutor or in court, the occurrence of abuse or brutality diminishes significantly. Finally, as regards the right to prompt information about the accusation and charges, 69 percent of inmates reported that the police failed to inform them.

The Indictment Process

According to Mexican law, it is necessary to transfer to the agency of the DA a person detained *in flagrante*. The prosecutor at the office of the DA prepares the case to file a formal indictment, which must be completed

Table 9.5 Inmate Reports of Abuse by Authorities

	2002		2005	
Authority	Threatened/ humiliated	Beaten/ Tortured	Threatened/ Humiliated	Beaten/ Tortured
Street policeman	16	24	17.1	21.0
Judicial policeman	32	41	29.1	35.4
Prosecutor	6	3	9.5	4.3
Prison warden	4	4	10.1	8.7
Judge's Clerk	1	1	1.7	0.2
Judge	1	1	2.1	0.2

Source: Inmate surveys, 2002, 2005.
Note: Numbers represent percentages of inmates responding positively to questions on the surveys.

within forty-eight hours of detention. Until then, detainees have a right to legal counsel by an accredited lawyer, to make a telephone call, and to be informed about the process. Detainees can make a first statement before the prosecutor or remain silent and make a statement only when brought before the judge. Several studies document "law in action" in Mexico. The initial case file presented with the onset of the indictment process (*averiguación previa*) includes all the evidence and relevant written testimony for the trial.[40] Lack of adequate defense provisions means that no further relevant information is submitted during the trial. Penal procedural rules state that all evidence compiled by the prosecution in the accusation stage constitute *prima facie* evidence at the trial even when the judge has not verified whether that evidence was legally obtained. The point here is that rather than an investigation of facts to be evaluated by a judge, the indictment phase is the most determining stage, which is why ensuring respect for due process rights is crucial at this stage: so that errors are avoided and innocent people are not wrongly convicted. The survey data shows that the offices of the DA consistently subvert due process. One example is the lack of information provided at this stage of the process reported by defendants.

Table 9.6 Respondent's Lack of Information about Basic Rights

The defendant was not informed about...	2002	2005
The difference between the accusation stage and the trial	91	87.1
The right to remain silent	80	68.2
The right to make a telephone call	72	65.7

Source: Inmate surveys, 2002, 2005.
Note: Numbers represent percentages of inmates responding positively to questions on the surveys.

Regarding the right to have legal advice from a lawyer, 70 percent of the inmates interviewed in 2002 reported that they did not have a lawyer when they were at the prosecutor's office in the indictment stage. The remaining 30 percent said they had had a lawyer, however, 70 percent of them reported they never had the opportunity to consult with the lawyer privately, nor did they receive legal advice before making their statement. In addition, 65 percent of the inmates said that their defense lawyer did nothing to defend them. Respondents' answers show high levels of that arbitrariness. The evidence suggests that the DA offices lack clear guidelines to safeguard the rights of suspects. The reason appears to be a lack of incentive to improve performance. The violation of the rights of defendants—not informing them of their rights, not naming the defense counsel, among others—does not mean that conviction is less likely. Given the absence of supervision of the DA office by weak judges, abuse and arbitrariness among the police and prosecutors become standard practices.

The Trial Phase

After prosecutors have filed charges, detainees come under the jurisdiction of a judge. This marks the start of the trial, the legal *battle* in which either the prosecutor must prove the penal responsibility or the defense upholds the innocence of the accused. As noted above, 85 percent of judicial decisions in Mexico favor the prosecution and result in convictions. The data show a slight improvement in the protection of some defendants' rights at this stage. In 2002, for instance, the share of defendants that were not informed of their right to remain silent fell 14 percent, although two-thirds reported not having being informed of this right at the trial stage. Likewise, respect for the right to a defense attorney at trial stage improved significantly: 27 percent of defendants in court claimed that they had no lawyer when they made their statement, compared to 70 percent that had no lawyer in the prior phase, at the DA office. Although present at hearings, the quality of defense council is very poor: 64 percent of inmates said that their lawyers did not provide legal advice while making their statement in court, and 53 percent asserted that their lawyer did nothing to defend them.

The lackluster quality of legal defense limits the scope for a fair trial, but this is not the only element that affects due process. In the 2002 CIDE Inmate Survey, 71 percent of interviewees reported that the judge was not present when they made their statement during the trial phase, and 80 percent stated they were never able to speak to the judge. When asked who was in charge of the court hearings, only 8 percent of inmates identified the judge (51 percent chose the court clerk, 20 percent the prosecutor, and 21 percent the typist). Thus, conditions to ensure fair proceedings are frequently absent in the Mexican criminal system. Not only do defendants suffer from arbitrary treatment, but there is a strong likelihood of incarceration of innocent people. In other words, the scope for error is high because of low standards. Moreover, the high rate of convictions of the DA in the absence of significant investigative efforts generates a perverse incentive to apprehend "easy" targets rather than professional or dangerous offenders. The distribution of the inmate population reflects this.

It is possible that the Mexican case is one of the most serious and extreme in the region, since, compared with other Latin American countries, the reform of the criminal justice system in Mexico was postponed until 2007. Nevertheless, the emphasis and central argument drawn from the Mexican case is that the weak criminal justice institutions that characterize the new democracies in Latin America produce prison systems overpopulated by the poorest and weakest links of the criminal chain. As analyzed below, this presents a serious challenge to the justification and social function of the penitentiary system in the region.

WHAT IS THE LATIN AMERICAN
PENITENTIARY SYSTEM FOR?

By providing an overview of prison conditions in Latin America and by analyzing the Mexican case in depth, this chapter has shown the degree of perversity of a system that primarily incarcerates the underclass and less predatory offenders, placing them in poorly run and overcrowded facilities that fail to either rehabilitate offenders or even hold the most dangerous criminals. Indeed, this description reflects what is an improvised policy response to the rising crime in the region, which is seriously undermining due process and the rule of law in the region. It also reflects the region's unstable socioeconomic conditions, characterized by high levels of violence and inequality. Unstable democratic regimes often respond by marshalling state institutions into tough responses, staving off political crisis and social chaos through short-term measures but doing little to address the structural weaknesses.

Prisons are the last link in the chain of proceedings whereby authorities seek to control crime. The end product of the criminal system (which involves police, judges, prosecutors, and lawyers), is the defendant, or the prison population. One way of evaluating the use of public resources allocated to the criminal justice system is by examining the purposes attributed to the penitentiary system. What is it for? Should the state provide the criminal system with large sums of public resources? This section assesses how the problems raised by these questions reflect on the penitentiary systems of Latin America.

Prisons as Instruments of Dissuasion

One of the most widespread justifications for penal systems is that the threat of severe punishment through imprisonment deters potential delinquents from committing a crime. But for the system to work as a deterrent, citizens and potential delinquents must perceive that the detention and punishment of offenders is likely. Penal institutions in Latin America are unable to apprehend dangerous delinquents efficiently, which means that the deterrence does not work well in that region. In Mexico, for example, where the impunity rate is approximately 96 percent, the likelihood of deterrence is very low.

Prisons as Instruments of Incapacitation

A second, less ambitious justification for prisons is incapacitation or the inability to participate in further crimes as a result of incarceration. To validate this justification in the case of Latin America, however, prison institutions must be able to find and detain professional and dangerous criminals, those committing numerous felonies, serial criminals, or those for whom crime is a way of life. The overwhelming majority of inmates would have to be career criminals and highly predatory offenders. But most prisons systems house a large percentage of petty offenders. Arguably, petty criminals could become professional offenders and prisons could therefore play an incapacitation role. But as long as penal institutions do not apprehend professional criminals, the incapacitating effect is nothing more than a probabilistic speculation.

Prisons as Instruments of Rehabilitation

A rather idealistic justification for penitentiary systems is rehabilitation, according to which prisons provide offenders with the means to reintegrate into society successfully upon their release. Regardless of whether this is possible, as this chapter documents, conditions in Latin American prisons cannot achieve this objective.

Prisons as Instruments of Retribution

A final justification is just punishment, social vengeance, or retribution. Latin American prisons may be fulfilling this objective to some extent, but while penal institutions remain open to corruption, and as long as only a small percentage of real offenders are actually incarcerated, punishment remains selective and biased against the weakest and least protected segments of society. Consequently, punishment as just desserts is undermined. What kind of social retribution imprisons individuals who stole US$30 from a supermarket? To the extent that penitentiary systems in Latin America are populated overwhelmingly by minor offenders, are overcrowded, and allow torture, corruption, and abuse, it is hard to find any social justification. Latin American prisons epitomize a broader regional problem: increased delinquency under democracy has generated erratic responses by weak institutions and deepened unresolved problems. In this context, the struggle to enforce law and order in the region is challenging indeed.

CONCLUSION

The failure of Latin America's penitentiary systems to achieve any of these core purposes exemplifies the larger problems stressed by this book. As Bergman and Whitehead discuss in the introduction to this volume, above all, crime has exposed the weakness of institutions and accountability throughout the region. Many problems in the prisons, such as overcrowding, originate in the criminal justice and political systems. But penitentiary officials' inability to address those that do not—such as inhumane living standards or a lack of basic rehabilitation—symbolize extreme levels of institutional incapacity. More worryingly, the lack of political pressure and legal mechanisms to rectify such abuses or even carry out enacted programs that would reduce crime (such as better treatment of youth) reflect a very low level of accountability on basic democratic principles.

NOTES

1. International Centre for Prison Studies, *World Prison Population List* (London: Kings College School of Law, 2005).

2. Elías Carranza, "Prison Overcrowding in Latin America and the Caribbean: Situation and Possible Responses" (paper presented at the United National Program Network Institute Technical Assistance Workshop, May 2001), 3.

3. Rates in the Caribbean are higher than in Central and South America. Belize has 545 prisoners per 100,000 people, for example. See *Penal Reform International Newsletter* 35 (December 1998).

4. Author meeting at CICAD, Washington, DC, February 17, 2005.

5. *Penal Reform International Newsletter* 36 (March 1999).

6. Marcelo Bergman et al., *Delincuencia, Marginalidad y Desempeño Institucional: Resultados de la Segunda Encuesta de Internos en Reclusión.* (Mexico City: CIDE, 2006).

7. Overall, about 70 percent of inmates are aged 18–25 and nearly 70 percent have not finished elementary school. Author interviews, Mirna Yépez, Ministry of Justice Director of Information, April 20, 1994; Dirección de Segu-

ridad Penitenciaría officials speaking on condition of anonymity; Office of Penitentiary Security and the Office of Defense and Civil Protection, Ministry of Justice.

8. Author interview, Ximena Sierralta, Instituto Nacional Penitenciario, June 21, 2001.

9. Human Rights Watch, *The Human Rights Watch Global Report on Prisons* (New York: Human Rights Watch, 1992), 76.

10. Author visits to holding cells in Venezuela, Honduras, Bolivia, and Argentina, 2003–2005.

11. Nine international treaties refer to trial waiting limits, including the Pact of San José, which limits pretrial incarceration to a "reasonable time" (two years in most domestic statutes). Law 24.390 in Argentina passed in 1994 limits pretrial detention to two years unless otherwise called for by the complexity of a case.

12. Programa de Educación y Acción en Derechos Humanos (PROVEA), *Informe Annual, 1999–2000* (Caracas: PROVEA, 2000).

13. Servicio Paz y Justicia Uruguay (Serpaj), "El fracaso del sistema penitenciario actual: Realidad y reformas urgentes" (Montevideo: Serpaj Uruguay, December 2003).

14. Amnesty International, News for Health Professionals, Medical Bulletin, vol. 3, no. 1, 11 February 2000, available at www.amnesty.org/en/library/info/ACT84/003/2000.

15. "Overcrowding Main Cause of Riots in Latin American Prisons," *Agence France Presse,* December 30, 1997.

16. Poder Ejecutivo de Baja California, *Primer Informe de Gobierno* (Mexicali B.C., October 1, 2002).

17. *Penal Reform International Newsletter* 36 (March 1999).

18. Decree 537, March 8, 1994; Diario Oficial n° 41.266, March 14, 1994.

19. Human Rights Watch, *Cuba's Repressive Machinery: Human Rights Forty Years after the Revolution* (Washington, DC: Human Rights Watch, 1999).

20. *El Nacional* (Caracas), September 2, 1998, D-2.

21. Author interview, Alfonso Ferrufino V., former Government Minister, December 16, 2004.

22. Author interview, Buenos Aires Province police officer Subalcalde Gustavo Romelio García, who works inside the prison, December 10, 1996.

23. Equipo Nizkor and (*Serpaj*) Paraguay, *Informe sobre los Derechos Humanos en Paraguay* (Asunción: *Serpaj,* 1996).

24. *Diario La República,* September 17, 2004; SERPAJ, *Situación Carcelaria: Noviembre 1996–Septiembre 1997,* at www.serpaj.org.uy/inf97/situacar.htm.

25. Comisión Ecuménica de Derechos Humanos (CEDHU), *Derechos del Pueblo,* no. 26 (Quito: CEDHU, 1985).

26. Author interviews, San Pedro prison, July 19, 2000.

27. The World Health Organization (WHO) reports 30 percent, while some Argentine officials say it is closer to 40 percent. Since only a small percentage of those who are ill receive medical attention, one of the demands of rioting prisoners in 1994 was improved treatment and the release of dying prisoners; Calvin Sims, "On Every Argentine Cellblock, Specter of AIDS," *The New York Times,* March 22, 1996, 4.

28. Author interview, Ximena Sierralta, INPE Official, June 21, 2001.

29. Author visit, Centro Penal San Pedro Sula, March 1, 2004.

30. Julita Lemgruber, "The Brazilian Prison System: A Brief Diagnosis" (published for *Prisons in Crisis Project Report,* Latin American Studies Association, February 2005).

31. Hugo Royg, "Rehabilitación Carcelaria" (June 21, 2002).

32. Guillermo Zepeda, *Crímen sin Castigo* (Mexico City: Fondo de Cultura Económica, 2004), 212–21.

33. Ibid., 220.

34. Ibid., 267.

35. It should also be remembered that most petty offenders are released on bail or are subject to other programs.

36. Elena Azaola and Marcelo Bergman, "The Mexican Prison System," in *Reforming the Administration of Justice in Mexico,* ed. Wayne A. Cornelius and David A. Shirk, 91–114 (Notre Dame, IN: University of Notre Dame Press, 2007).

37. The comparison between the two observations also reflects the Mexican version of zero tolerance policies, as a result of which more petty offenders were caught in flagrance after parts of the initiative were launched in 2003.

38. In Mexico the street police cannot do any kind of criminal or judicial investigation. The main task of this police is crime prevention by patrolling the streets.

39. In Mexico the DA Police is in charge of crime investigation under the supervision of a DA officer or *ministerio público.*

40. Luis Pásara, *¿Cómo sentencian los jueces en el Distrito Federal en materia penal?* (Mexico, D.F.: Instituto de Investigaciones Juridicas, Universidad Nacional Autónoma de México, 2006).

PART 3

Citizen Security, Democratization, and the Rule of Law

CHAPTER TEN

"Security Traps" and Democratic Governability in Latin America:

Dynamics of Crime, Violence, Corruption, Regime, and State

JOHN BAILEY

Above some threshold, crime, violence, and corruption can significantly complicate democratic transitions and degrade the quality of democracy in Latin America. Given their central importance, the theory linking this cluster of problems to civil society and democracy ought to be much more developed than it is. The central puzzle addressed here is: Why do some political units (cities, regions, countries) and not others fall into security traps in which crime, violence, and corruption become mutually reinforcing in civil society, state, and regime, and contribute to low-quality democracy? Questions related to these include: Why is there such a strong inertial quality to security traps? What are the implications of insecurity for democratic governability? And, once in a trap, why do some units find escape routes while most do not?

This chapter describes two basic models, one depicting a "positive equilibrium" set of relationships between public security and democratic governability and another that depicts a "negative equilibrium" set, or a security trap. I go on to suggest hypotheses that might account for a unit's falling into a security trap. Relatively more space is devoted to dynamics of inertia and implications for democratic governability. Given the emphasis of this volume, I focus more on criminal violence than on corruption and nonviolent crime. Also, important as it is, attention to escape routes goes beyond the present scope. This is a heuristic exercise, and the test of success is whether the research strategy suggested here points in a useful direction.

VARIABLES AND RELATIONSHIPS

Because I believe they interact with one another and that they affect government and politics in various combinations, I choose to include crime, violence, and corruption in a set of phenomena that I call "public security." As I use the term, public security emphasizes protection of persons, property, and democratic political institutions from domestic and transnational threats of physical violence, intimidation, or corrupt or predatory government actions, especially by law enforcement and justice officials.[1] I differentiate between crime and corruption because, even though many forms of corruption typically are criminalized in most countries, there is an interesting gray area of ethical misconduct, which—although technically not criminal—may be widely perceived as corrupt. Similarly, I differentiate between crime and violence because various forms of violence—as I use the term—are not considered criminal, and many types of crime are nonviolent.

What are the relationships between public security and democratic governability? Democracy in the Schumpeter-Dahl conception focuses on processes that govern access to power and the accountability of governments to electorates (Dahl 1971, chapter 1). Apart from the protection of key civil rights, that approach has relatively little to say about the functioning of state institutions.[2] But experience teaches that citizens of countries characterized by public insecurity, widespread poverty, extreme inequality, and slow growth emphasize the ability of their governments to promote socioeconomic development and public safety. Thus, coherent state institutions and policy-making capacities are keys to governability, understood as "the ability of a government to allocate values over its society, to exercise legitimate power in the context of generally accepted rules" (J. Bailey and Godson 2000, 7). In sum, democratic governability encompasses not only how power is attained and the rules of the game (democratic regime) but also the exercise of power within a legal framework (governability) (Mazzuca 2000; O'Donnell 1997, 2001).

MODELS AND DYNAMICS OF POSITIVE AND NEGATIVE EQUILIBRIUM

In what ways does public security interact with democratic governability? I posit two basic models as points of departure. The first depicts a positive equilibrium and the second a negative one, my notion of a security trap.[3] As shown in graph 10.1, in a situation of positive equilibrium we begin with three overlapping clusters of complex phenomena (crime, violence, and corruption) and two causal paths (direct and mediated linkages) connecting the clusters to two more complex and interconnected phenomena (regime and state). The public security cluster is regarded as being embedded in civil society (shaded area); state and regime are differentiated from civil society.

My premise is that it is useful to differentiate analytically among types of phenomena in the public security cluster. Thus, some types of violence usually are not considered criminal: parental discipline over children, contact sports, self-defense, earthquakes, or other forms of natural disaster, for example (shown as #1 in graph 10.1). The threat, or actual commission, of many forms of violence is typically criminalized (such as assault, homicide, robbery, rape, or kidnapping; shown as #2). Many other forms of crime may be nonviolent (embezzlement, fraud, and tax evasion [#3], for instance). I shall reserve corruption to the misuse of public office for private gain that occurs within the regime or state, or between these and civil society. Abuse of position or office confined to civil society or private life is not directly relevant. Many forms of corruption are criminal and nonviolent (consensual bribery or profiting on privileged information, as in #4). The notion of violent, criminal corruption

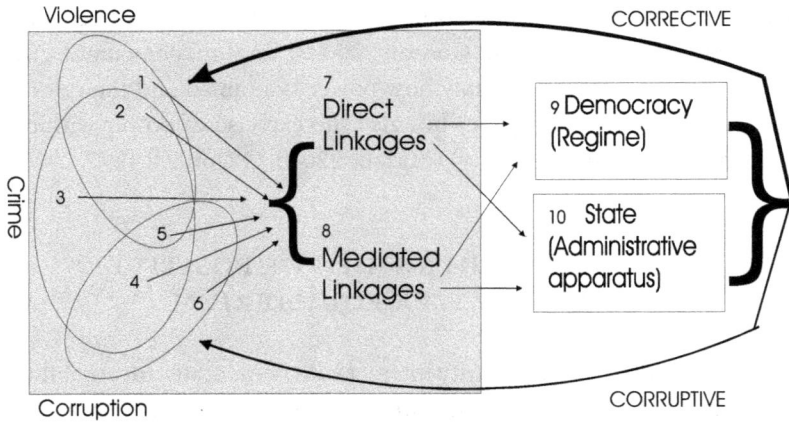

Graph 10.1 Public Security, State, and Regime: Positive Equilibrium

Violence

CORRECTIVE

Crime

1
2
3
5
4
6

7
Direct
Linkages

8
Mediated
Linkages

9 Democracy
(Regime)

10 State
(Administrative
apparatus)

Corruption

CORRUPTIVE

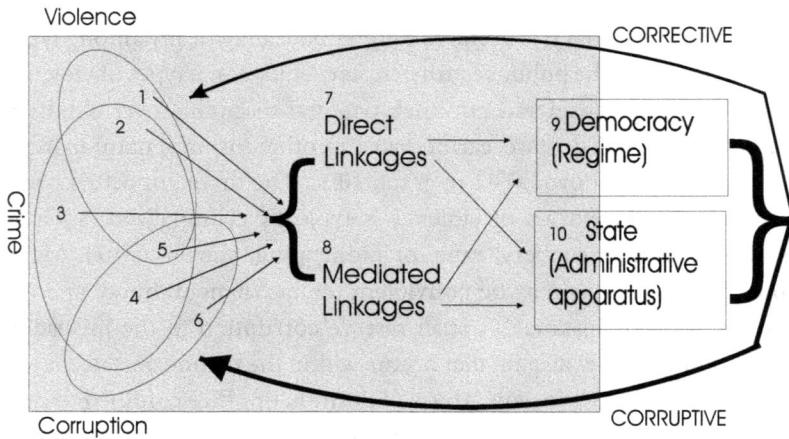

Graph 10.2 Public Security, State, and Regime: Negative Equilibrium

Violence

CORRECTIVE

Crime

1
2
3
5
4
6

7
Direct
Linkages

8
Mediated
Linkages

9 Democracy
(Regime)

10 State
(Administrative
apparatus)

Corruption

CORRUPTIVE

is awkward, because we usually think of corruption as an alternative to conflict. In the positive equilibrium model, we might think of violent, criminal corruption (#5) in the case of rogue state agents who threaten or use force to extort citizens or other state agents. Finally, there are various behaviors one can consider corrupt but are not usually criminalized (exchanging gifts, favors, or information for special treatment, or making campaign contributions for privileged but unspecified access to public officials [#6], for example).

The first causal linkage (#7) depicts crime, violence, and corruption acting directly on state and regime. Tax evasion, intimidation of elected or appointed officials, or bribing a public agent are typical sorts of examples. The second causal linkage (#8) consists of two steps: the first is the impact of crime, violence, and corruption on civil society (not shown in the graph), and the second step is effects of these acts on attitudes held by members of civil society about "the law," about their government (state and regime viewed separately or in some combination), and about one another (especially in the sense of interpersonal trust).

By differentiating among the components of the security cluster and their different linkages to state and regime we can better understand their interactions and patterns of continuity and change over time (corruption is a relatively constant problem, for example, but violent crime has increased substantially) and better grasp the relative importance that citizens attach to one or another problem (street assault or home invasion, for instance, is more feared than consensual bribery).

In a situation of positive equilibrium, the major feedback loop is "corrective"; that is, state and regime operate mostly legally and in the main to ameliorate problems of public security.[4] Some government agents will exacerbate these problems to some extent by, for example, soliciting bribes, violating civil rights, or abusing their authority for personal gain. Some public officials engage in corruption to some degree some of the time. Also, regime or state features themselves may foster crime or corruption.[5] But the main effects are corrective, and the "corruptive" feedback mechanism is of lesser importance. Not shown in the graph, but consistent with the logic, both feedback mechanisms also operate through direct and mediated linkages. That is, state and regime take real actions to reduce public insecurity, and their actions are also filtered by the perceptions of citizens who observe these responses.[6]

Positive equilibrium suggests that crime, corruption, and violence originate mainly in civil society and act on state and regime. Implicit here, but enormously important, is the differentiation between public and private, between government and civil society. The former responds primarily with corrective measures to problems that originate mainly in the latter. Further, notions of law in civil society are relatively congruent with formal law, and citizens generally prefer legal transactions to criminal exchanges. Finally, the regime and state are viewed as relatively effective and legitimate.[7] In sum, this is how we like to think that "developed" or consolidated democracies deal with "normal" volumes of crime, corruption, and violence.

How might we conceptualize the unfortunate state of affairs in which notions of law and norms of behavior in civil society differ markedly from formal law, the citizenry tolerates or promotes formally illegal exchanges, and state and regime themselves act as principal engines of crime, violence, and corruption? This is the case of "negative equilibrium" shown in graph 10.2. The components of public security remain the same, as do the linkages and feedback mechanisms. But there are basic differences. The overall legitimacy of the political unit is weak or absent. Regime-state notions of legality are contested by significant groups, which may ignore, evade or openly violate formal law. In this model, elected and appointed officials, as a general practice, behave unethically and commit crimes or take the initiative to prey upon civil society in a variety of ways in order to extract resources or command obedience outside the formal law. They may do so alone or in coalitions with societal allies. Family life and civil society merge with state and regime. The essential public-private differentiation is blurred or missing altogether; individuals pursue private ends while exercising public duties. In the worst case, the corruption is orchestrated from the top, permeates regime and state institutions, and penetrates deep into the economy and society. The state or regime may intentionally use its instruments of violence (such as the police, army, intelligence service, or paramilitaries) to intimidate society, or rogue state actors can operate independently from political leadership. Though victimized, civil society typically is characterized by apathy, opportunism, and cynicism. In this negative equilibrium, regime and civil society are unable to correct themselves and therefore unable to correct problems of public security. The major feedback loop emanates from civil society in corrupt collusion with state and regime; the "corrective" feedback loop is relatively weaker.[8] Civil society views the state bureaucracy and judicial apparatus as inefficient and ineffective.

The negative equilibrium model implies sufficient order and coherence, however, to differentiate it from a "failed state," or a situation in which state and regime are largely irrelevant and minimal order is lacking. That is, state and regime in negative equilibrium can make the Weberian claim to monopolize violence (whether or not they can effectively exercise it) and exert influence in daily life. Further, I have described polar extremes of positive and negative equilibriums. I suspect we shall find a range of positive and negative equilibriums, and it is more useful to think in terms of a unit's falling into *a* (rather than *the*) security trap.

What sorts of indicators and data might help us identify the thresholds of security traps? Tables 10.1 and 10.2 report data on perceptions and behavior (unofficial economy) for three sets of countries: Latin America, Northern Europe, and a smattering of "large countries." At this stage, the goal is to judge whether the notions of positive and negative equilibrium can pass a minimum credibility test. National-level data are less useful to us than data on subnational units, especially metropolitan areas. Also, police and legal systems are more important with respect to public confidence, as opposed to political actors such as parliament or political parties.

One would expect the Northern European countries to compose a positive profile, and this they do. Also, one would expect the Latin American sample to lean more toward negative equilibrium, and—by and large—this is the case. We see variations within the Latin American sample, with Chile (and Uruguay, to a lesser extent) leaning more positive than the others. The "large countries" also tend to be positive, especially with respect to indicators about their economies, justice systems, and perceptions about their degrees of corruption. I return to these data in later sections.

National-level data mask a good deal of variation, and it is more useful for comparative purposes to focus on subnational units of analysis. It is possible, even not uncommon, to find national governments and capital cities mired in a security trap. It is also possible to find whole nation-states caught in a trap, especially if these are relatively small in size,

Table 10.1 Selected Indicators of Legitimacy: Latin America and Elsewhere

	Armed Forces	Legal System	Police	National Government	Parliament	Political Parties	Civil Service
Latin America							
Argentina	0.31	0.37	0.28	0.35	0.18	0.1	0.08
Brazil	2.5	1.22	0.83	0.95	0.5	0.5	1.45
Chile	1.25	0.81	1.1	1.12	0.62	0.3	0.85
México	1.46	0.7	0.5	0.72	0.76	0.5	0.7
Venezuela	1.5	0.6	0.4	0.36	0.3	0.17	0.45
Peru	0.72	0.2	0.3	0.64	0.18	0.07	0.12
Uruguay	0.56	1.53	1.06	0.68	0.7	0.6	0.8
Colombia	1.58	0.9	0.9	0.57	0.3	0.2	0.48
Dominican Rep.	0.42	0.2	1.4	0.14	0.14	0.1	0.1
Northern Europe							
Finland	4.5	2.19	5.9	0.5	0.45	0.2	0.5
Norway	2.7	2.29	5.9	1.95	2.27	0.5	1.04
Sweden	1.2	1.7	4.3	0.73	0.8	0.4	0.8
Large countries							
Canada	1.3	1.17	5.3	0.6	0.6	n.a	0.98
France	1.29	1.35	2	n.a.	0.93	n.a	0.96
Great Britain	4.29	1.1	3.3	n.a.	0.79	n.a	0.84
US	0.9	1.32	2.9	1.24	0.8	n.a	1.48

Note: The table presents ratios between percentage of respondents somewhat or very confident and the percentage that is somewhat or very nonconfident. A ratio greater than 1 indicates more confidence, while a ratio less than 1 indicates more nonconfidence. Data for Latin America comes from the year 1996, except that for Argentina, which comes from 1995. Data for Northern Europe comes from 1996, while that for "large countries" comes from 1990.
Source: Own estimation based on World Values Survey 1981–1997.

Table 10.2 Selected Indicators of State Capacity, Latin America and Elsewhere

	Unofficial Economy[1]	Economic Freedom[2]	Civil Liberties[3]	Equality under the Law and Nondiscriminatory Access to Justice[4]	Corruption Perception Index[5]
Latin America					
Argentina	21.8	14.0	3	2.5	3.0
Brazil	37.8	7.0	4	0	4.0
Chile	18.2	13.0	2	5	6.8
México	27.1	8.0	4	0	3.3
Venezuela	30.8	7.0	3	0	2.3
Peru	57.9	12.0	4	2.5	4.5
Uruguay	35.2	10.0	2	5	4.3
Colombia	35.1	12.0	4	0	2.2
Dominican Rep.	n.a.	n.a	n.a.	n.a.	n.a.
Northern Europe					
Finland	13.3	14.0	1	10	9.6
Norway	5.9	15.0	1	10	9.0
Sweden	10.6	16.0	1	10	9.5
Large countries					
Canada	10.0	15.0	1	7.5	9.2
France	10.4	15.0	2	7.5	6.7
Great Britain	7.2	16.0	2	7.5	8.7
US	13.9	16.0	1	7.5	7.5

Note: Data for Latin America comes from the year 1996, except that for Argentina, which comes from 1995. Data for Northern Europe comes from 1996, while that for "large countries" comes from 1990.

Sources: Unofficial economy: base estimate provided by E. Friedman et al. (2000); see specific sources and dates. Economic freedom: Freedom House, Freedom in the World Reports, available for multiple years at http://www.freedomhouse.org/ template.cfm?page=15; a higher value means more freedom. Civil liberties: Freedom House, Freedom in the World Reports; a higher value means less freedom. Equality under the law: Fraser Institute, via Gwarney and Larson (1997); a higher value means more equality. Corruption Perception Index: Transparency International, available at http://www.transparency.org/policy_research/surveys _indices/cpi; the index ranges from 1 (more corrupt) to 10 (less corrupt).

[1] Dates, based on sources: MIMIC 1990–93 from Loayza (1996) and reported in Schneider and Enste (1998), table 3.1; Electricity 1989–90 from Lacko (1996) as reported in Schneider and Enste (1998), table 3.1; Currency Demand 1990–93 as used in Johnson, Kaufman, and Zoido Lobatón (1998, "Corruption"; and 1998, "Regulatory Discretion"). There are two different approaches to measuring unofficial economy, the "Currency Demand" method and the "Physical Input (Electricity Consumption)" method. For a full explanation and comparison between these two methods, see Schneider (2006) and Schneider and Enste (2000).

[2] 1995.

[3] 1996.

[4] 1995.

[5] 1998.

relatively centralized, unitary in administration, and dominated by one or another political faction. Some of the Central American and Caribbean countries come to mind. But for the larger nation-states, even those marked by centralism, we can learn more by emphasizing comparisons among the subunits rather than generalizing about whole systems, as we saw in the analysis of regional homicide rates in Brazil (chapter 1, this volume). This is especially so given the nature of federalism and current trends in decentralization.

With these frameworks as orientation, I turn to two sets of questions. First, what explains the origins and inertia of security traps? And second, what are the dynamics of violent crime in contributing to the inertia of security traps?

WHY DO MOST POLITICAL UNITS (BUT NOT ALL) FALL INTO A SECURITY TRAP?

My working hypothesis is simple. With few exceptions, most metropolitan regions in Latin America began their independent existence in negative equilibrium, and subsequent development in the market-insertion periods (from the latter half of the nineteenth century to the depression), and the populist ISI phase (1940s–1980s) maintained, or probably deepened, the negative equilibrium. Though violent crime was a feature of the security traps, the more important dynamic was widespread corruption, passive and complicit civil societies, and weak and inefficient state agencies. The upsurge in violence, especially criminal violence, in the 1980s and 1990s is the result of a particular combination of economic and demographic trends interacting with states with weak legitimacy and with weak or predatory police, regulatory, and judicial capacities.

In a short discussion emphasizing theoretical issues, I cannot explore historical themes at any length. The point to stress is that origins and trajectories figure fundamentally in current contexts of public security. In the case of Latin America, three themes interact to account for weak formal legality: (1) states have been relatively weak in their capacity to extract resources and to regulate behavior;[9] (2) democracy as a continuous regime is the rare exception rather than the rule; and (3) regime legitimacy, whether democratic or authoritarian, has had shallow roots.

The three interact to weaken the creation, continuity, penetration, and societal acceptance of formal law.[10]

Though difficult to define and impossible to measure, corruption was a chronic problem in colonial times (see, for example, Phelan 1967), it probably increased in the early national period, and it took on new forms and dynamics with the insertion of the Latin American economies in global trade in the last quarter of the nineteenth century (McFarlane 1996; Miller 1996). The question here is the usefulness of current European-American notions of corruption in the context of premodern Latin America. As James Scott points out, a variety of premodern practices, such as the sale of offices or the use of public position to acquire personal wealth, were widespread and generally accepted in the Northern European and Anglo-American contexts into the late eighteenth century. As he notes, "The difficulty here simply serves to highlight the fact that much corruption is in a real sense a product of the late eighteenth and nineteenth centuries. Only the rise of the modern nation-state, with its mass participation, broadly representative bodies, and elaborate civil service codes, signaled the transformation of the view of government office, and even kingship, from a private right into a public responsibility" (Scott 1999, 131).

The absence or weakness of modern bureaucracy, representative bodies, civil service codes, and the like throughout most of Latin America implied that practices that Scott terms "proto-corruption" took root in the colonial and independence periods and persisted into the late nineteenth and twentieth centuries. The rise of populism and import-substitution industrialization generated new sources of corruption, with the multiplication of state functions in economic development and social welfare.

Political violence or conflict related to broader issues of power in a community, rather than to wealth alone or to private goals, was a continual problem throughout most of the region in the independence period and continued as a problem in many of the countries up to the present. Criminal violence, on the other hand, is researched much less than political violence, or even corruption. Useful studies are relatively recent; most of these are case studies of cities or subregions, and we lack a broad comparative synthesis that would permit a more nuanced interpretation.[11]

If there is merit to the hypothesis, it leads us to look at the variations. That is, what do exceptions to these patterns teach us? Candidate cases might include Santiago, Chile, and San José, Costa Rica. What contrasts about their origins with respect to state capacity, regime stability, civil society participation, and political leadership are particularly instructive?

WHAT EXPLAINS THE INERTIA OF A SECURITY TRAP?

I speculate here that important aspects of the economy, civic culture, and state institutions reinforce criminality and law-avoidance in most Latin American political units. My overall hypothesis is that corruption and law-avoidance are more deeply embedded than is the recent upsurge of criminal violence, but that a step-level increase in criminal violence takes on its own inertia and deepens the trap. I take up first the issues of inequality, informality, and civic attitudes; then the issue of police, courts, and regulatory agencies; and finally the factors that contribute to criminal violence.

Inequality, Illegality, Informality, and Problems of Civic Lawfulness

Latin America's economies and societies are characterized by profound inequality and extensive informality. Though equally important, informality has not received sufficient attention in the context of crime and democracy. Latin America is the world region of greatest income inequality. Fajnzylber, Lederman, and Loayza (1999, 1) report that, for forty-five developed and developing countries over the period 1965–95, "straight income inequality, measured by the Gini index, has a robust significant and positive effect on the incidence of violent crimes." The causal linkages between inequality and crime are not self-evident, although Merton's "strain theory" is explored amply in the literature.[12] Further, I suspect that acute income inequality undermines the legitimacy of private property. The property of the upper strata may be viewed as acquired through luck, deceit, or other such means, rather than earned through individual labor.

Informality refers to economic and social activity that operates "off book," outside the lawful regulation of the state. The term is used broadly, however, and we need to differentiate among activities that are: (1) *illegal* (common sense criminal); (2) *informal* (menial or marginal economic activities); or (3) *underground* (designed to avoid taxes or regulation).[13] Informal labor, according to the International Labor Organization (ILO), is activity whose primary objective is to generate employment and income to the persons involved. The primary rationale of informal labor units is not to evade taxes or social security contributions. In fact, much informal labor operates below the tax or social security payment threshold. It may be best to view informality on a continuum, ranging from activities that completely evade state regulation of any type to those that evade only some regulations (child labor laws or environmental rules, for instance).

Estimating the size of the informal sector is difficult, but it constitutes a large part of the Latin American economies. Table 10.2 reports estimates for eight Latin American countries that range from a low of 18 percent of GDP (Chile) to a high of 58 percent (Peru), with most of the others in the 30 percent range. Further, the relative proportion of informal employment, particularly in the middle and lower strata, increased substantially in the period 1980–2000 (Portes 1985; Portes and Hoffman 2003).

The implications of illegal and underground activity would seem straightforward. Criminals, including tax evaders, seek to avoid detection by state agents. Informality presents a more complicated problem as some aspects of it overlap illegality (for example, street markets for stolen or smuggled goods) and tax evasion. The problem in many cases is threefold. First, informal labor generally is condoned by society on grounds of practicality and necessity. Where the state's regulatory regime is complex and cumbersome and the formal economy fails to generate enough employment, the informal economy plays a vital role. Second, as we have seen, the informal sector is quite substantial in most Latin American economies. By operating outside the legal regulatory regime, informal activities both deny the state substantial tax revenues and can generate corruption wherever they come into contact with state agents, depending on the ability and disposition of the police and regulators to negotiate bribes. Finally, widespread informality would seem to habituate civil society to operate in ways that ignore, evade, or violate formal law.

The implications of all this are wide-ranging, but at a minimum it would seem to create incentives for individuals to move almost seamlessly between formal and informal exchanges, according equal legitimacy to both (or to neither). In sum, my hypothesis is that extensive informality reinforces negative inertia in at least two ways: (1) it multiplies the points of corrupt exchanges between civil society and the police-justice-regulatory system, and (2) it cultivates a civic and official culture of illegality and extra-legality.

Inefficient or Predatory Police, Justice, and Regulatory Agencies

It far exceeds the present scope to undertake an evaluation of police, regulatory, and justice systems in the various Latin American countries. For my purposes, the key issue is whether these clusters operate with sufficient effectiveness to tip calculations in civil society toward obeying the law voluntarily in cases of negative equilibrium or to reinforce law obedience in cases of positive equilibrium. A systematic empirical evaluation would be quite useful, but perceptions are probably more important with respect to civil society behavior.

Table 10.1 reports data from the World Values Survey for selected countries for the questions: "How much confidence do you have in the legal system/In the police?" With respect to the legal system, the Nordic cases score highest, as expected. France, Great Britain, and the U.S. report less confidence. The Latin American cases report least confidence overall. Uruguay is an exception, with scores above the "large countries." Brazil is a surprising exception as well. But seven of the nine cases report negative scores, that is, the majority reporting little or no confidence. These findings reinforce the data reported in the introduction of this volume and in Restrepo's discussion of Colombia's justice system (chapter 7, this volume). The pattern is reproduced by an outside evaluation of "equality under the law" by the Fraser Institute (table 10.2). Chile and Uruguay score highest in the Latin America sample. Four of the eight cases ranked received scores of zero.

The findings on confidence in the police follow a similar pattern (although Canada joins the high marks of the Nordic cases). Only Chile (as Frühling demonstrates in chapter 5, this volume), Uruguay, and (sur-

prisingly) the Dominican Republic report slightly positive scores, with
the remaining six scoring below one (in other words, a majority responding "little" or "no confidence" in the police).

It is doubtful that the real performance of the legal systems and police
far exceeds perceptions as reported in surveys. Also, we are considering
national-level averages, and there is probably interesting variation at the
subnational level. Even so, these data, along with the various case studies
available, suggest the hypothesis that a significant cause of negative inertia in most of the Latin American examples is ineffective legal systems
and police. Even so, we should recall Pásara's argument (chapter 8, this
volume) that reform of the justice system will have only a limited effect
in solving the challenges of insecurity.

What Explains the Recent Upsurge in Criminal Violence?

Two distinctions are useful here: (1) between risk factors and accelerants,
and (2) among types of national circumstances in the region. A broadly
similar set of "risk factors" emerged in many metropolitan areas of Latin
America in the 1970s and 1980s that contributed to the upsurge of
criminal violence. Different agents or events, in different combinations,
probably served as accelerants. Further, we need to distinguish between
countries affected by internal war (Colombia, Peru, El Salvador, Nicaragua, and Guatemala) and those not. Explanations of the subsequent inertia of higher crime rates go beyond the present scope.

Risk factors abound in the region, in both structural and institutional
forms. I briefly discussed inequality and informality, and weak police
and justice systems, in previous sections. To these we should add demog-
raphy, especially concentrations of young, lower-strata males in urban
areas, high proportions of whom are unemployed, and who lack adequate education or job skills.[14] The growing numbers of single-parent
families also contributes to delinquency.

If risk factors generally increased throughout the region in the 1970s
and 1980s, what served as accelerants for the upsurge in criminal violence? What was new and different? Three general candidates are an
upsurge in drug and weapons trafficking, transitions toward competitive, democratic politics, and the waves of stabilization-structural adjustment policies that most of the governments of the region adopted,

which—at least in the short term—worsened unemployment and income distribution and increased uncertainty. Bergman's analysis of labor markets in Mexico City and Buenos Aires (chapter 3, this volume) is a useful case in point.

One would have to seek causal patterns in comparisons of selected regions (in metropolitan areas, transportation routes, and border zones, among others). It would be useful to be able to differentiate among types of criminal violence in order to "map" their incidence socially and geographically and to analyze their interactions. We could learn from paired contrasts among metropolitan areas, that is, the pairing of regions that are similar in key respects but whose patterns of criminal violence varied significantly. Given sufficient data, one might be able to address the counterfactual: What might be patterns in violent crime in the region in the absence of one or another accelerant, such as significant drug trafficking and consumption? There is a discussion of some effects of violent crime on democratic governability in the following section.

IMPLICATIONS OF A SECURITY TRAP FOR DEMOCRATIC GOVERNABILITY

Recall that there are both direct and indirect linkages between the public security cluster in graphs 10.1 and 10.2 and state and regime. Graph 10.3 sets out direct linkages between types of crime and corruption (violence is implied in many of these) and the society and political system.[15] The horizontal axis (left to right) depicts the political nature of the criminal act. The act may affect civil and economic society (for instance, bluecollar offenses such as auto repair fraud, or violent crimes such as armed robbery) with little apparent political relevance. An act becomes "political" as it affects behavior by public officials in terms of specific decisions or applications of a policy (bribery, for example). Political salience increases as the act affects the regime and state. Thus, in a less obviously political sense crime first affects private citizens in civil society; at the next level it reaches the individual state agent (or agency) and a particular decision (or policy); at a higher level, crime can damage the regime through its effects on the procedural guarantees and accountability mechanisms discussed above; and in its most serious forms, it can undermine the state through its effects on basic state institutions and functions.[16] The vertical axis (top to bottom) depicts the organizational complexity of the act, from simple-individual to complex-organized. Note that graph 10.3 refers to criminal *acts* and not to specific actors. Further, I have in mind here the intended target of the act and not possible wider effects. We shall find a rough correspondence between the nature of acts and types of actors that commit them. Typically, single individuals or small, spontaneous groups carry out organizationally simple acts. This does not suggest that atomized crime is somehow less important for the polity, however. If the behavior is widespread (if there is tax or regulatory evasion or simple corrupt exchanges), its effects can be quite significant. Criminal acts at the middle range of complexity tend to be committed by larger and better-coordinated, continuous groups, taking us into the terrain of organized crime, whether perpetrated by civil society groups or by state agents (such as police). The most complex crimes, in the sense of extension of organization, occur at the national and transnational levels. Also, the graph differentiates between nonviolent financial and regulatory offenses (far left column), and those that suggest violence against persons or institutions (second, third, and fifth columns).

In a security trap, problems of crime, violence, and corruption originate both in civil society and in state and regime. Thus, we need to read graph 10.3 in both directions: first, from left to right, to consider criminality that originates in civil society and affects regime and state actors; then in the opposite direction, to consider how criminal behavior by regime and state actors might affect civil society. The reader can explore graph 10.3 and speculate about which kinds of criminality might be more or less threatening to democratic governability.

This volume emphasizes criminal violence and thus draws our attention to columns two, three, and five. We lack research that evaluates comparatively which types of violent crime suggested here are most injurious to democracy. Setting aside such obvious examples as voter intimidation, guerrilla rebellion, and military *golpe de estado*, which directly attack core functions and processes of democracy, I shall briefly sketch two examples that fit more closely the themes of the volume. These are diffuse violent crime (assault, homicide) and a form of regional-local organized crime (drug distribution). Diffuse violence is interesting because of its

Graph 10.3 Crime, Regime, and State

Political Nature of Criminal Act

Organizational Complexity of Criminal Act	Civil and Economic Society		Public Official / Public Policy	Democratic Regime	State
Simple	Informal- underground (Tax & regulatory evasion) White collar Blue collar	Traffic violations Theft Armed robbery Assault Rape Homicide	Simple bribery Intimidation Police-regulatory extortion & violence	Intimidation Corruption Election violation Civil disobedience	Terrorism Treason Assassination Individual intimidation / corruption of judiciary, army, police
	Informal- underground (Tax & regulatory evasion) Money laundering Corporate crime	Gambling Prostitution Drug distribution Cargo hijacking Carjacking Kidnapping Armed robbery Extortion / Protection	Complex bribery Intimidation Civil disobedience Police-regulatory extortion & violence	Intimidation Corruption Election violation Civil disobedience	Terrorism Sedition/treason Regional rebellion Vigilantism Corruption/intimidation of regional judiciary, army, police
Complex	National / International Cartel-Price- fixing Tax & regulatory evasion Money laundering	Int'l smuggling Extortion/Protection	Complex bribery Intimidation Civil disobedience	Election violation Large scale corruption Intimidation	Terrorism Sedition/treason Vigilantism Mutiny Corruption/intimidation of national judiciary, army, police

mediated effects on civil society support for democracy. That is, perceptions that criminal violence has increased significantly can undermine diffuse support for democracy as regime or for state organizations, such as the police and judiciary. Drug distribution illustrates one of the region's most vexing problems: webs of alliances between police and criminal organizations that reinforce widespread distrust and anxiety in civil society, and flows of corruption that can reach into the upper echelons of regime and state.

Diffuse Violence, Perceptions, and Behavior

Several recent studies identify connections between diffuse violence and democracy. The usual line of reasoning is that increased perceptions of violent crime, coupled with perceptions of inept or corrupt police, produce attitudinal effects (increased anxiety about personal safety, reduced support for government) and behavioral effects (altered personal routines, support for hard-line anti-crime policies). These can reduce support for democracy and formal legality, if people perceive them as ineffective against insecurity. The studies (such as Caldeira 2000; Dammert and Malone 2003; Dammert, chapter 2 in this volume; and Smulovitz 2003) usually establish fairly firmly the tendencies in perception and in the attitudinal and, to a lesser degree, the behavioral effects.

At least two points seem interesting. First, perceptions of personal vulnerability to violence are usually greater than justified by real risk. Mass media, especially television, and other communications networks such as family and friends play complex roles in sensitizing audiences to risk of violence. Also, fear of violence may be a manifestation of varieties of other personal fears and insecurities, and individuals react differently to the same kinds of messages. Second, while the causal linkages from perceived increases in violent crime through behavioral effects are plausible and empirically demonstrated to one or another degree, the effects on regime and state are usually implied. That is, the fear and distrust induced by violent crime probably reduce support for democracy as regime and increase the disposition to consider (tolerate) alternative regime types; fear and distrust probably increase support for extra-legal suppression of crime.

Cruz provides a suggestive comparative effort to assess the effects of insecurity on regime support, in this case in Guatemala, El Salvador, and Nicaragua. He used 1999 survey data that measured the effects of: (1) having been a victim of violent crime, and (2) feelings of insecurity on (3) diffuse political support for the political system (as based on a scale composed from a variety of items that conflate aspects of regime and state as laid out in this chapter). He found that being a victim of a violent crime was a statistically significant negative predictor of regime support in all three countries, but more so in El Salvador and Guatemala than in Nicaragua. Feelings of insecurity are a negative predictor of support in El Salvador and Guatemala, but less so in Nicaragua, where other variables are more important than violence and insecurity in predicting regime support (Cruz 2003, 27–28).

The three countries that Cruz analyzes are interesting, but we should be cautious because they—like Colombia and Peru—may be outliers, that is, post-conflict situations with relatively high crime rates and fragile institutions. Even so, his findings support our intuition that perceptions of violent crime negatively affect support for democracy as regime at the national level. They also support the hypothesis that violent crime reinforces the security trap.

Drug Distribution, Gang Violence, and Corrupt Symbiosis

Drug trafficking and consumption, a growing problem throughout the region, offers a contrasting example in that the phenomenon is geographically concentrated and generates substantial revenue, and its associated violence takes diverse forms. Much of the violence is inherent to the industry (for example, protecting turf and operations, enforcing transactions) and tends to be more concentrated spatially and carried out by varieties of groups—some of which might assume the forms of complex organizations. Also, diverse kinds of drug-related violence are projected into society as well (such as robbery, assault, extortion, or road accidents), along with substantial corruption. The example of interest here is the localized, limited-area trafficking groups.

The gang-society relationship is dynamic, and Peter Lupsha's stage-evolutionary model is useful. Lupsha (1996, 30–33) posits three stages in gang evolution: predatory, parasitical, and symbiotic. Predatory groups are rooted in a particular area and much of their violence is defensive turf protection; their criminal acts are opportunistic rather than strategic; and the gangs are servants of the established order, whose police can exercise control. Parasitical gangs "develop a corruptive interaction with the legitimate power sectors, and meld their control of a territorial base with the power broker's need for illicit services" (31). The gangs corrupt police and justice systems and extend their presence into legal business and social organizations, using these as "fronts." At the symbiotic stage, the established political order comes to depend on the webs of criminal groups to sustain itself. At this stage, "the traditional tools of the state to enforce law will no longer work, for organized crime has become a part of the state: a state within the state" (32). Presumably, then, the most serious effects of organized crime on democratic governability would be seen at the symbiotic level.

An interesting example to explore this line of reasoning is the drug trafficking gangs in the *favelas* (shanty-towns) of Rio de Janeiro. Descriptions by Leeds (1996) and Arias and Davis (2001) suggest situations in some *favelas* in which the regular police, viewed as corrupt and violent by residents, lost effective control to trafficking gangs over considerable periods of time. The symbiosis occurs as the gangs provide drugs to middle and upper strata consumers and votes and resources to municipal authorities. Additionally, the gangs often provide informal policing and alternative dispute resolution to *favela* residents with respect to violent acts (like rape, robbery, and assault) and diverse forms of conflict (such as property claims, or landlord-renter disputes). The image conveyed is that some gangs can gain degrees of legitimacy and can provide different levels of street justice and predictability. Gangs frequently cooperate with and support the local residents' associations. But the image also suggests a kind of perverse volatility of violence, first, as gangs discipline their own members and clients and protect their turf; and, second, as gangs battle the police and—occasionally—the army sent by political authorities to reassert state control (or to appease in some symbolic sense the public's expectation that the state effectively exercise its "monopoly" of violence).

Space prevents a lengthy analysis of the effects on regime and state of the sort of symbiotic situation described above. Further, rather like the Central American cases and diffuse crime, the trafficking gangs in the *favelas* would seem to be outliers with respect to organized crime. But it would seem clear that the violence, illegality, and corruption associated with trafficking, as well as the *ad hoc* nature of street justice, contribute to poor quality neighborhood democracy. And the spillover effects of these forms of organized crime into the broader metropolitan area (as through corruption of elected officials as well as municipal police and justice authorities), strongly reinforce the security trap of the particular area. Whether the negative influences of such an area would have "tipping" or reinforcing effects on the larger political unit would depend on a variety of other variables, such as the size and complexity of the national unit, the strength and coherence of national police and justice systems, and the like.

CONCLUSION

I began with the assumption that crime, violence, and corruption are significant problems for the quality of democracy in Latin America and tried to make a case about how to frame a research strategy. The strategy involves five sets of assertions. First, it is useful to differentiate among crime, violence, and corruption and to interconnect them in a cluster of variables that I labeled "public security." Second, it is useful to distinguish between democracy as a regime type and state as a bureaucratic-judicial apparatus operating in a framework of laws. Third, the nature of civil society and its differentiation from regime and state is a central dynamic. Fourth, the elements of the public security cluster interact with regime and state through both direct effects and effects mediated by perceptions. Finally, relationships among public security and democratic governability tend toward either a positive or a negative equilibrium, which once established demonstrate significant inertia.

If the research strategy passes the plausibility and usefulness tests, the main immediate task is empirical. What are useful indicators and data with which to investigate the various elements and relationships of the general models? Comparative data on crime, violence, and corruption are relatively sparse and difficult to use. Even so, we need indicators to show variation across time and space. Examples of such indicators are an impunity index and judicial coverage.[17] Survey data are becoming much more available, though little is designed directly to investigate the elements of linkages suggested in the models. A practical approach is to focus on the relatively data-rich political units (for example, Mexico City, Bogotá, Rio de Janeiro, São Paulo), recognizing the risks of bias and distortion in selecting mega-cities. If the hints in the national-level data (tables 10.1 and 10.2) are useful, we should include Santiago and Montevideo for purposes of contrast. This said, the practical guide is instrumental opportunism: we go where the available data take us and adjust the concepts and hypotheses as best we can.

I end with two cautionary notes. First, we need to be attentive to particularities and cautious about generalizations. Useful theoretical frameworks that can help us relate particular cases to middle-range generalizations must guide our approach. The nature of the public security problem varies from one unit to another, as do the character of regime and state. For example, forms of organized crime, their activities, their industrial organization, and their capacity to corrupt or intimidate vary substantially. The powerful grip of a mythical image of the Sicilian mafia as a unitary, hierarchical, and disciplined organization has done more to distort than inform political discourse or academic research.

Second, policy prescription is a legitimate end, and useful strategies to find escape routes from security traps are a priority. But description and explanation are an enterprise quite different from policy prescription. The evaluation of policies can be a useful part of description and explanation, and—ideally—policy prescription draws on solid conceptual and empirical grounds. But policy prescription is a little like an agricultural extension service: the extension agent may be well versed in horticulture, but each little plot of ground has its own chemistry, climate, and vulnerability to pests. We need to know a great deal more about the dynamics of public security, and then we need to learn just as much about tools and techniques of intervention before offering advice about problem solving in specific plots of real estate.

NOTES

1. National security, in contrast, is concerned with protection of the state, territorial integrity, and sovereignty, and essential state functions and agencies

from threats by other states or trans-state actors, such as terrorism, organized crime, and the like (J. Bailey 2003). As will become obvious, public security presents difficult boundary problems with its notions of physical violence and intimidation. Assault and homicide, for example, clearly fit within the boundary, but there are many difficult cases, such as the "violence" of hunger, malnutrition, and disease, or the "threats" associated with subsistence farming or hyperinflation. Given the volume's focus, I shall limit the violence component of the security concept to actual physical violence or the overt threat of violence intentionally inflicted by one person or persons on another or others. Physical injury or psychological trauma suffered by a person or persons due to natural disasters, such as earthquakes, fires, floods, and the like, also fit within the arena of public security but lie beyond my present scope.

2. Dahl (1971, 3), however, includes "[i]nstitutions for making government policies depend on votes and other expressions of preference" as a requirement for democracy. Presumably, he implies two things here: (1) that there are institutions that make and implement policies; and (2) that these institutions are accountable to a democratic regime that, in turn, is accountable to an electorate.

3. Two sources are especially helpful in thinking about traps and equilibriums. Bo Rothstein (2005) sets out a useful case about culture, perceptions, and strategic behavior to understand problems of interpersonal trust in social traps. Douglass North (1990) demonstrates the significance of institutions (formal and informal) to understanding what he calls "low equilibrium" and "path dependence."

4. I set aside for the moment the ways in which civil society acts to ameliorate or exacerbate problems of public security.

5. For example, lack of expertise or other resources by auditing agencies may promote corruption; extensive state intervention in the economy creates more opportunities for rent-seeking than minimum intervention; and financing expensive election campaigns invites corrupt exchanges.

6. To simplify, the model depicts a political unit in isolation from the broader national and international contexts.

7. The reasoning here draws on Lipset (1959, 77): "Effectiveness means actual performance, the extent to which the system satisfies the basic functions of government as most of the population and such powerful groups within it as big business or the armed forces see them. Legitimacy involves the capacity of the system to engender and maintain the belief that the existing political institutions are the most appropriate ones for the society . . . While effectiveness is primarily instrumental, legitimacy is evaluative."

8. Bayart, Ellis, and Hibou suggest interesting indicators of what they call the "criminalization of politics." The key idea is "the macroeconomic and macropolitical importance, as distinct from the occasional or marginal role, of [criminal] practices on the part of power-holders and of these activities of accu-

mulation in the overall architecture of a given society" (Bayart, Ellis, and Hibou 1999, 25–26). They do not, however, offer empirical indicators or thresholds.

9. I agree with Centeño (2002, 10): "In summary, using Weber's original language when referring to the state, one cannot speak of states dominating their societies. While generalizations are always dangerous, we may classify most of the Latin American states, even well into the twentieth century, as highly despotic, yet infrastructually weak. They are 'despotic' in the ability of the state elites to undertake decisions without routine negotiation with civil society. They are weak in the institutional capacity of the state, or its ability to actually implement decisions. Despite its reputation for autocracy and repression, the Latin American state has been far less able to impose itself on its societies than its European counterparts. In reality, the Latin American state cannot be called a Leviathan, or the oppressive equalizer of neoliberal myth, or even the overwhelming centralizer of black legends of Iberian culturalism. What has characterized the Latin American state is not its concentration of power, but the very dilution of power."

10. North's discussion of institutions and path dependence is useful here. He uses the North and South American contrasts to illustrate his general theory of institutional change (North 1990, 96–103).

11. Two useful collections are by Aguirre and Buffington (2000) and Salvatore, Aguirre, and Joseph (2001).

12. To oversimplify, strain theory suggests that individual "innovators" resort to criminal acts in order to acquire things such as wealth, power, and status, which the social order unfairly denies them. The theory applies to those in society who cannot compete in legitimate ways. "As a result they often reject societal values and create a new set for themselves. In the process, a criminal subculture can develop in which individuals can achieve success under a different set of rules" (Vito and Holmes 1994, 164).

13. My discussion follows Tanzi (2000, 202–3).

14. Gottfredson and Hirshi (1990) convincingly demonstrate that, across centuries and cultures, the concentration of young males in the population is a powerful correlate of "risky behavior," of which crime is a principal type.

15. The ideas in graph 10.3 have their roots in a project on violence and democratic governability funded by the United Nations Development Program and directed by Professor Marc Chernick.

16. Once again, we confront difficult boundary issues. One can argue that virtually all crimes have political implications. Rape can be about power; theft can be about capitalism and property; tax evasion can be silent treason. Ultimately, the boundary rests on findings from psychological interviews with lawbreakers: What was the motivation and target of the act? Another type of boundary issue is the exclusion of private life (family and friendship groups) from the scope of inquiry. Caldeira (2000) makes a plausible argument that one

must include, indeed emphasize, private life (for example, domestic violence) to understand the nature of crime and violence in civil and economic society. I set these issues aside for the time being, aware that they may need to be revisited in light of empirical findings.

17. An impunity index can be calculated as a ratio between crimes reported in victimization surveys and judicial proceedings completed. Judicial coverage is the geographical presence of courts or hearings officials throughout a country.

CHAPTER ELEVEN

Citizen Insecurity and Democracy

Reflections on a Paradoxical Configuration

LAURENCE WHITEHEAD

In the 1970s and 1980s—and earlier in Central America—military and authoritarian rule became widely associated by local and outside observers alike with the abolition of basic civil and political liberties and the systematic violations of human rights. These came to be perceived by many as the *décadas negras* of torture and disappearance, and of the politics of fear that shrunk the public arena to a bare minimum. Dictatorship may have restored order to polarized societies, but for the majority of citizens the price was finally deemed too high, and the slogan that marked the end of this period was *Nunca Más!* With the return to democracy, human rights organizations—which, in the absence of political parties as the once dominant conduits between state and society and often aided by churches, had become the only voice of protest against authoritarianism in many countries—initially turned their attention to the past, campaigning for accountability and "truth telling" about the human rights violations of the authoritarian period.

But it was not long before it became apparent that the present and future were as much, if not more, of a challenge as backward looking accountability and justice. Democracy had not simply and reliably established institutions and values that guaranteed the protection of human rights. In some countries, such as Brazil, human rights violations actually increased after the demise of authoritarianism. For some sections of the electorate, and in some localities, the authoritarian past came to be remembered in a more favorable light, by contrast with subsequent experiences. At least for those who stayed away from political protest, the past could be reimagined as a period of order and security. In consequence, some politicians and parties with clear ties to the repressive past could hope to prosper in democratic elections by capitalizing on their reputations for imposing effective disciplines.

It also became clear that democratic government, allied with the universal precepts of economic liberalism, was not, in Latin America, creating a virtuous circle of greater wealth *and* distribution. The application of the wisdom of the Washington Consensus may have stabilized inflation and introduced game rules that are more predictable for foreign investors, benefiting the population insofar as the elimination of acute instability helps ordinary people to plan their lives and manage their households. But liberalization as applied in the region was creating many more millionaires than it was contributing to increase the ranks of the middle classes. One estimate is that the per capita product received by the richest fifth of the region's population is more than eighteen times the product received by the poorest fifth, compared with a worldwide average of about seven to one, and an average for all developing countries of about eight to one.[1] Other comparative figures and new time series suggest that Latin American democracies are not likely to bring the region back into a more normal range of income or asset distribution within the near future.

So, if economic liberalization was deemed necessary to ensure competitive insertion into the "global economy," it is proving to be a less than adequate tool to address the dislocations produced by long term structural transformations such as urbanization, youth unemployment, shifting family structures, and the fragmentation and even destruction of traditional community structures of solidarity—all phenomena associated with rising crime rates and citizen insecurity. Indeed, increased social spending and state intervention to "control" the undesirable side-effects of such processes seemed to be incompatible with the strict disciplines demanded by the new liberalism. Thus, just as Francis Fukuyama announced the "end of history," the weight of history began to make itself felt with a vengeance in a newly democratized Latin America: poverty and inequality, embedded undemocratic political cultural traditions and mechanisms of power mediation, and institutional habits inherited from a long history of formalism unmatched by de facto implementation and follow through are blocking even the best designed institutional reforms in the region.

The region-wide shift to civilian constitutional governments with competitive elections and freedom of expression has generated significant *desencanto* rather than adherence to a positive, consensual notion of the kind of democracy societies wanted, and how to achieve it: *nunca más* was followed by an *ahora qué?* There is no consensus on how to frame a new "law and order" model so as to stem citizen insecurity resulting from growing criminality and police responses to it; on how to ensure that well intentioned reforms to the institutions of law and order produce more security and more justice; and given increasing recognition of the links between rising crime and various forms of social exclusion, on how to adapt economic liberalism to social cohesion needs.

DEMOCRACY WITH INSECURITY: A LATIN AMERICAN CONFIGURATION

The return of democracy provided Latin Americans with the opportunity to bridge social divisions and protect human rights, and generate a broader consensus about the kinds of economic and social policies and institutional reforms that were necessary to "deepen" democracy. Twenty years after the first transitions, despite the assumptions of liberal democratic theory and in contrast with the experience of Southern Europe, the weak social integration and lack of public security that once provided the backdrop for episodes of emergency rule are still facts of life. As Guillermo O'Donnell put it, in Latin America "democracies of truncated or low intensity citizenship" replaced the dictatorships of the past.[2] There is evidence of widespread alarm over the often apparently uncontrollable expansion of common, organized, and petty crime. Of all the regions in the world covered by the Pew Global Attitudes project, the "extent of public anxiety about crime is most evident in Latin America. This is seen not only in the high level of personal concern over this issue, but also in the overwhelming perception among people in this region that crime is a major national problem . . . no fewer than 65 percent in any country in the region view this as a major concern . . . Outside of Latin America, only South Africans raise crime as a major personal concern, reflecting that country's high crime rate."[3] In Mexico, crime and insecurity are a key citizen concern, as witnessed by the prominence of the issue in federal and local electoral campaigns, and vividly illustrated by the June 2004 demonstration in Mexico City, in which an estimated quarter of a million people took the streets dressed in white to protest against the failure of the government to address rising crime. In El Salvador, in May 2001, 49 percent of the adult population in El Salvador rated crime and delinquency as the main national problem. Crime and tough crime policies were a dominant theme in the electoral campaign of the winner of the 2004 presidential election. Mass demonstrations in Buenos Aires in 2007 displayed a similar pattern. In Venezuela, anxiety over rising levels of criminality has shifted the policy agenda in directions unforeseen either by President Chávez or his opponents. In Brazil gang warfare and police repression in the *favelas* have shaken the complacency of the second Lula administration.

Survey data, crime statistics, victim reports, and press coverage tend to confirm the legitimacy of such concerns. El Salvador is one of the most violent places on earth, with one of the highest per capita murder rates in the world (59 per 100,000 inhabitants in 2005). An average of ten murders and three car-jackings are reported daily. In 1996–1998, almost 60 percent of urban households were affected by crime.[4] National Civilian Police (PNC) statistics reveal that there were between 2,700 and 2,790 homicides reported in 2004, an increase of around 27 percent relative to 2003.[5] Kidnappings,[6] armed property crimes (the bulk of offences), armed robbery, and car jacking are common occurrences and are still rising. Rape is also endemic and on the rise. The police estimate that only 10 percent of rapes are reported (in 2005, there were 910 rapes reported to the police). In 2003, one study estimated the economic costs of violence in El Salvador to be US$1,717 million (11.5 percent of GDP).[7] In Mexico, the national average for homicides is 11–14 per 100,000 inhabitants, which is above the 10 per 100,000 that the World Health Organization considers "epidemic." Official reported crime declined from the 1940s to the 1970s, but increased sharply thereafter, particularly from 1994 onwards.[8] Between 1997 and 2004, there were 17 reported crimes per 100,000 inhabitants each year nationally. One survey in 2001 showed that during any given year, around one in four people are assaulted, and nearly half of the population has relatives who have been victimized by crime in the preceding three-month period.[9] Mexico also has the dubious honor of having the highest rate of kidnapping worldwide: in 2004, the unofficial estimate was that there had been three thousand kidnappings in 2004.

A recurrent feature of citizen anxiety and discontent is distress over weak or ineffective police forces and judiciaries. To take the example of Mexico, in a 2001 survey of sixty thousand people in the country as a whole, 67 percent of respondents said that they had some or no trust in the supreme court and only 6 percent claimed to have a "lot of trust" in the institution.[10] A 2004 survey indicated that about two-thirds of victims do not report crimes, and only 37 percent of Mexicans believed that the judicial system would punish violators. Ordinary people avoid entanglement in the justice system, which is too slow, expensive, and tilted towards the untouchable *los de arriba,* and they avoid the police whenever they can, as contact invariably means paying bribes.

A clear manifestation of citizens' abandonment of trust in the state institutions that should protect them is provided by the exponential rise in private security companies employed to provide policing services. There is an estimate that Mexicans (particularly the owners of businesses) employ around 75,000 private security guards every year. In Brazil, the Federação dos Vigilantes de São Paulo and the Sindicato das Empresas de Segurança Privada e Cursos de Segurança de São Paulo reported that the number of private security men employed in the state increased from 80,000 in 1993 to 135,000 in 1996, a 68.7 percent increase in four years; and that an estimated 100,000 clandestine vigilantes who were not registered with the Federal Police operated illegally in security related activities.[11] A more recent study by the National Federation of Security and Valuables Transport Businesses (FENAVIST), estimates that between 1999 and 2004 the private security market grew by a further 67.8 percent in the country as a whole, with a growth of one vigilante per 552 inhabitants in 2002, to a projected 1 per 482 people.[12]

Perhaps even more worrying than the proliferation of security firms (which are insufficiently regulated and reportedly often involved in shootings and other rights abuses) is vigilantism. Fear, combined with the sense that the state is unable to respond adequately (and indeed with the strong view that the state is party to crime insofar as state institutions are corrupt) have established the conditions for vigilantism, and there are reports of acts of "rough" popular justice, including mob beatings and lynchings (some even televised) in urban areas, and in rural areas this kind of "justice" is widespread. At present, this does not seem to be undermining faith in democracy, but overwhelming concern with crime and insecurity and institutional inaction or debility can feed perceptions that are liable to stimulate authoritarian and antidemocratic reflexes among significant sectors of the electorate. This means that the public institutions reshaped during democratization processes are the beneficiaries of no more than provisional or conditional popular approval. Their continued authority depends on delivering expected benefits, which is presently far from assured. According to opinion polls in Brazil in 1992, for instance, a large percentage of people questioned approved the killing of 111 detainees awaiting trial in a São Paulo prison by military police on 2 October 1992, as well as the videotaped execution of a criminal suspect in a shopping centre in Rio in 1995.[13] In El Salvador, one survey in 1998 showed that 27 percent of respondents believed the police should be enabled to detain people on the basis of their appearance; 24 percent that it is acceptable to take justice into one's own hands; 16 percent that the police should be allowed to torture suspects in order to obtain information; and 15 percent approved of "social cleansing."[14] In October 2005, almost 64 percent of Brazilians voted against a proposed ban on firearms in the first national referendum on the issue. Although one cannot extrapolate from this a majority inclination towards "private" justice, it certainly reveals a lack of faith in the anti-crime and citizen security policies of the federal and state-level authorities.[15]

Negative perceptions and recourse to "alternatives" appear to be "justified" by the facts. To take the case of Mexico again, the rate of impunity there is estimated to be around 94 percent, so the justice system obviously does not serve as much of a deterrent. A survey of the penitentiary population shows that most people are arrested by the police either *in flagrante* or three hours after a crime has been committed (70 percent of detainees were apprehended within twenty-four hours of the commission of a crime).[16] This suggests that if suspects are not apprehended immediately, the chance of their being caught is very low. Another survey shows that 71 percent of detainees in the Federal District received no legal assistance whilst held in detention, and of the 30 percent that had access to a lawyer, 70 percent were unable to consult them privately; 60 percent were never informed that they had the right to remain silent when taken before a judge; one in every four was not assisted by a lawyer during the preparatory declaration before the judge;[17] 80 percent of detainees never spoke to the sentencing judge; and in 71 percent of cases when the detainee made his or her declaration in court, the judge was not even present.[18] Following a May 2001 visit to Mexico, the UN Special Rapporteur on the Independence of Judges and Lawyers concluded "impunity and corruption" were prevalent (50 to 70 percent of federal judges were corrupt),[19] and that mechanisms to punish corruption were dysfunctional. As crime and insecurity have risen, these failings have become all the more apparent. There have been various instances of convicted traffickers escaping from jail, and, despite efforts to pursue them more vigorously, organized crime groups have become stronger and more consolidated in recent years. Indeed, impunity for drug lords is almost "guaranteed." As described in the chapter by Ungar and Magaloni (chapter 9, this volume), the prisons are populated not with the worst criminals but with the biggest losers, the petty villains least able to avoid the long but selective arm of the law. Police officers are often involved in kidnapping, extortion, and people-trafficking, and it is known that some collude with drug traffickers. Impunity for such activities by state agents is also a reality. As Elena Azaola details in her contribution to this volume (chapter 6), lack of resources, low morale, and high levels of corruption make a mockery of policing in Mexico City.

Why are Latin America's democracies so crime ridden, and why are the responses of states in the region apparently so inadequate? Or, put differently, why do Latin American citizens have a set of well-established formal rights, but only precarious "real rights"? This chapter will not attempt to answer these questions in detail; rather, it will look at the issue of inequality and poverty; the impact of heterogeneity, the gang phenomenon, and the transnational dimension of criminality; the challenges they pose to Latin American states and democracies; and finally the dilemmas of top down policy-making.

Of course, these are all very large questions, and—as the various contributors to this volume demonstrate—experiences diverge over time
and between different countries (as well as *within* most countries). As
broad generalizations we can say that citizen insecurity is acquiring
growing salience as a political issue; that justice system reforms are proving slow and difficult almost everywhere; that both petty and transnational crime is displaying cumulative dynamism; and that consequences
for democratic governance and the reinforcement of a sense of citizenship are troubling. But there is a large analytical gap separating such general and approximate statements from the more specific, empirically
grounded, and contextually limited findings reported by most authors in
this volume. As a partial contribution towards narrowing this void, it
may be helpful to distinguish between macro, meso, and micro levels of
analysis.

The macro level refers to democratic politics and policy making at the
national level. It therefore covers how elected leaders may respond to
citizen concerns over crime and insecurity; it includes top-down aspects
of police and justice system reform; and it could even address the underlying possibility that soaring criminality might destabilize the entire
democratic process. But, for the most part, national politics remains
somewhat insulated from the full impact of citizen insecurity. (After all,
it is not only in Latin America that we find a broadly democratic national
political reform coexisting with rampant criminality lower down—think
of the Mafia in Italy, the U.S., or Yeltsin's Russia).

The meso level of analysis can help here. It directs our attention to
what Guillermo O'Donnell has called "brown areas" of local authoritarianism within nationally democratic parties.[20] Quite large regions, whole
communities, clusters of municipalities, or extensive social groups can
be subjected to parallel structures of social control, even to quite explicit informal provision of order, by crime networks and local gangs. At
meso levels, extra-legal power and enforcement may become sufficiently
stable, authoritative, and well-established within the overall power structure that they penetrate the national level of institutions as well. They
may seek out "their" congressmen, judges, and law enforcement officers,
and these may coexist within the framework of a procedurally minimal
democratic system. On the one hand, such meso level arrangements
could corrupt or destabilize democracy as a national project. But on the
other hand, it is also possible that a fairly stable equilibrium could be es-

tablished, anchoring a "low quality" democracy without uniform rule of law institutions or universal citizenship.

This brings us to the micro level of analysis. Citizens and voters will tend to judge the authenticity of national political rhetoric based on what they perceive to be the case in their local communities. If they observe an important or corrupt justice system, complicity between officeholders and extra-legal powerbrokers, and the absence of basic guarantees for law-abiding neighbors, this will affect both interpersonal trust and confidence in formal institutions. At the micro level, it may be hard to discover the full facts of the case. Citizen insecurity can be a product of alarmist perceptions or a delayed reaction to adverse circumstances that have already been corrected. Thus, the interrelationships between the macro, meso, and micro levels of analysis are not specified tightly, and may not be highly predictable. But the three levels certainly do interact over the medium to long term, which is why democratization scholars need to attend to all three and to disaggregate their explanatory schemas. With this in mind, let us survey the region's heterogeneity.

THE POLITICAL IMPACT OF HETEROGENEITY

Global statistics obscure Latin America's extremely heterogeneous reality. Take poverty and inequality. While in Chile, Costa Rica, and Mexico the US$1 a day PPP poverty headcount ratios are 3.5, 5, and 13.9, respectively; in Haiti, Ecuador, and Bolivia they are 50.9, 30.3, and 27.7 percent, respectively. While Uruguay, Brazil, Venezuela, Argentina, Mexico, Costa Rica, Chile, and Panama have a per capita GNP between US$1,760 and US$2,620 a year, the remaining countries of the region have a per capita GNP between US$620 and US$1,200. Differences are not simply international, but intra-national too: according to the World Bank, income per capita in the poorest Brazilian municipality in 2001 was around 10 percent of that in the wealthiest, and in Chiapas in Mexico, it was 18 percent of that of the capital. In Paraguay and Peru, regional differences account for more than 20 percent of inequality, and in the Dominican Republic and Venezuela for more than 10 percent. In Bolivia, Honduras, Mexico, Paraguay, and Peru, there is more than 40 percent difference in the poverty count among regions, according to the World Bank.

Differences are also marked according to gender or ethnicity, to cite just two categories. The gender gap in average earnings ranges from 12 percent in Mexico to 47 percent in Brazil. The racial or ethnic disparities are even greater. Indigenous people in the region earn an average 46–60 percent of what nonindigenous people earn. In Brazil, blacks and *pardos* earn just over half of white's average earnings. In the informal sector, the proportion of white men is much lower than that of nonwhite men.[21] With the exception of Brazil, over 45 percent of indigenous or Afro-descendant people in the region live in rural areas (in Honduras, Ecuador, and Panama the figure is as high as 80 percent), and because rural areas are poorer and have less access to social goods and infrastructures, poverty among these groups is more persistent.[22] Another divide is between educated and noneducated people. Families headed by high school graduates have poverty rates 25–40 percent lower than families headed by people who have not completed primary education. Globally, less than 10 percent of poor people come from households headed by college graduates. Drop out rates increase substantially for people in houses headed by mothers with only primary education (by 60 percent in El Salvador) or fathers in similar conditions (by as much as 40 percent in the Dominican Republic). And school failure risks for such families ranges from 55 percent in Brazil to 20 percent in Chile.

Similarly, the "dynamics of violence" occur in an extremely fragmented and heterogeneous universe. In Mexico, for instance, the Deputy Minister of Citizen Security reports that about 70 percent of violent crime occurs in 25 percent of the territory.[23] In El Salvador, PNC data shows that 63 percent of recorded homicides in 2004 occurred in 20 of the 262 municipalities in the country. Similar levels of heterogeneity are apparent in Brazil, as Beato and Marinho show in this volume. Also, in relation to Brazil, it has been argued that violence and precarious rights are partly the result of the regional and local survival and readaptation of "traditional" nondemocratic forms of social and political power mediation, which coexist with "modern" democratic modes of state-society relations. Ambiguous attitudes among elites and society to the "modern" concepts of the rule of law, such as equality before the law and citizenship, arise because of the survival and proliferation of an alternative view of justice and rights. In some regions or localities the logic of "the force of the law" is overwhelmed by that of "the law of force," coloring relations between the law enforcement authorities and sectors of the political class, on the one hand, and the "marginalized" or underprivileged, on the other. These nondemocratic forms of power mediation and the ambiguity of attitudes towards citizenship and the rule of law predate authoritarian military rule, but the latter's "authoritarian enclaves," mentalities, and practices have reinforced them.[24] So, within a single country there are enclaves of violence and enclaves of "peace." There are local and state level governments that are "modern" in the sense that power is mediated by the routine application of rule of law principles, and others where clientilism, patrimonialism, and *coronelismo* and variations thereof prevail, or, worse, where the rule of law is entirely absent and criminal gangs have a near monopoly on violence. While some localities or regions live "in crime" and in the absence of the rule of law and the state, in other parts of the same country, criminality is something that appears in the newspapers, reported from recognizable but alien areas of the national territory.

This heterogeneity has crucial political and policy implications. In terms of policy, it limits the capacity of the national or central state to implement effective strategies, to establish secure citizenship rights, and to combat sources of insecurity. This is particularly evident in federal states like Argentina, Brazil, and Mexico, but also applies to countries where the legal and institutional reach of the state is weak or only partial. In political terms, heterogeneity—interspersed "rule of law-free" zones or "brown jurisdictions" to use Guillermo O'Donnell's phrase—makes the issue of crime and citizen insecurity very volatile. For the part of the electorate living under rule of law areas, crime may be a relatively minor concern and not likely to mobilize them; but because crime and insecurity are ultimately national problems—it may be dominant in only some localities, but its consequences, as O'Donnell argues, extend well beyond the "brown jurisdictions"—because they constitute a substratum of instability, incidents of violence or criminality may unleash underlying tensions with potentially explosive effects. Violence may surface—as it has done in Brazil's prisons—and force a new round of public security initiatives. Or a new government lacking a majority in Congress could aim to boost its popularity by making high profile policies on the justice system a top priority. Beneath the political level, social frustration coupled with lack of citizen security and effective law and order institutions can easily erupt. In short, heterogeneity of experiences introduces an unstable equilibrium.

This heterogeneity also presents a challenge to universalistic visions of "one shot" regime change producing a smoothly homogenous new rule of law dispensation, and has implications for social theory and comparative analysis. John Bailey's contribution to this volume, for instance, posits two contrasting models, one that promotes a positive equilibrium that enables states to respond effectively to (avoid) what he calls "security traps," and another based on a negative equilibrium in which state and society are seemingly helplessly caught in a "security trap." While this is a useful heuristic device, it should not be overused, since within a single territory, one may find a complex interaction between the positive and negative equilibria, a combination of partial capacities to avoid or overcome "traps" with the inability to do so. As noted about Brazil:

> Despite earlier assumptions that the ambitious project of economic modernization undertaken by the military would naturally undermine the hold of traditional elites over local and regional politics, "traditional" non-democratic enclaves have continued to exist. Indeed, not only have traditional politics and elites "survived" economic modernization and political democratization but they have adapted their economic practices to the new and "modern" forms of economic activity and have re-shaped their political practices of patronage and clientelism to operate in the changing landscape of democratic politics. This has profound implications on citizenship and attitudes to human rights. The use of state and municipal resources to perpetuate the power of local elites, particularly in the North and North East, is not limited to the traditional exchange of public funds for political support characteristic of the politics of patronage. The power of local elites is also grounded in the selective enforcement of the rule of law. The ability of these elites to place themselves above the law is a core characteristic of traditional politics, as is the blurring of the division between private and state force. Local police forces are often at the service of the landed elites and private gunmen enforce the "law of force" as laid down by landowners. This extra-legal form of social interaction is "rational" in a context where formal, legal and routinized institutional forms of social and political mediation are absent, ineffective or seen to be "biased" towards the privileged, who also feel

that their security is not properly guaranteed through the legal implementation of law and order. Thus, drug gangs in shanty-towns, for example, are often more trusted to "mete out justice" and provide protection than the police; death-squads become part of a parallel social order and system of justice in poor neighborhoods deprived of state protection; sectors of the middle-class, in turn, opt for private security arrangements where the rule of law is almost entirely absent. And in a context of increased violence and criminality, moreover, parts of these more privileged social sectors have reacted against the very notion of human rights which they identify with the protection of delinquents and bandits to the detriment of the rights of their victims.[25]

In short, it is necessary to recognize the diversity and complexity of crime, including threshold, generational, and international contextual effects, and to understand how some types of crime feed into the broader sociopolitical framework, and how these corrupted or criminalized arenas feed back into the phenomenon of crime and change its parameters and meaning. Combating crime and insecurity then, is a long-term and open-ended process, as prone to partial victories and advances as it is to partial defeats or reversals. As argued elsewhere, like many other problems in Latin America, this issue needs to be "interpreted configuratively" if its dynamics, variability, and complexity are to be understood.

ON HETEROGENEITY, FEAR, AND QUICK FIXES

A crucial distinction that appears throughout this volume, and which relates to the above, is that between crime (the objective reality) and fear or the sensation of insecurity at the microlevel among citizens. One has to attempt to gauge the relative distance between the objective reality and subjective perceptions of it, and attempt to pinpoint the reasons why that gap may be narrow in some contexts and very broad in others. There is usually a lag between the realization that reforms have had an impact at the macrolevel and the subsequent impact at the meso and micro levels. Crime may level off, but citizens will respond not to this but to the experience of the past decade. Obviously, the gap is broader to the extent that there is a perception that the forces of law and order are not coping—or are even implicated in—criminality, as the fear is then a fear of "loss of control." Subjective insecurity and fear and perceptions of crime lag behind any momentary decline, or leveling off, of crime rates because the overall sense may be that the state is fighting a losing battle.[26] The balance between efforts at reform and the felt needs and expectations of the citizenry can be slow to improve. Macro level reform results are likely to be patchy, partly because they may destabilize old patterns of behavior without crystallizing well structured new alternatives, partly because more time is needed, and partly because there are many vested interests engaged in resistance and hoping for reversal. A further difficulty for reform arises from the fact that the process aims at a moving target—as the justice system evolves, so do the practices of those who aim to evade it. Their resources remain very large and diverse, and they have more incentive to innovate rapidly than the justice system has to reform quickly.

But the gap may be wider for other reasons. It may be because the press is more yellow, or it may be because democracy in the age of the "communications technology" revolution generates new opportunities for citizen access to information about crime, so that it is often hard to tell whether crime and corruption have increased or whether they have just "come out of the closet." It may be because populist leaders gain some footing (for reasons that have less to do with fear of crime and more to do with other perceived systemic failings of the party or political system). It may be that fears and paranoia are accentuated as citizens feel their states are unable to contain the negative effects of globalization and various other phenomena associated with it: immigration, terrorism, trafficking—particularly in low intensity market democracies or "risk societies" where states are weaker and anxiety and defensive reactions perhaps more common, or more precisely, more likely to have negative reverberations. Or the gap may grow simply because a single criminal incident leaves such a mark on the "collective consciousness" that it prompts disproportionate fears.

It is also important to note here that there is no single "collective subjectivity" but rather a diversity of subjectivities, which may be shaped by myriad factors, including language, literacy, ethnicity, gender, place of residence, social class, and levels of education. Fear among the better educated and better off may produce one view of how to deal with crime, and the same phenomenon experienced by the marginalized or poverty ridden sectors of society may produce quite another. This point comes across in a 1999 survey in El Salvador in which 40 per cent of those with university degrees had reported being victimized over the previous twelve months, but only 10 percent of illiterates had done so.[27] There was a similar gradient according to income levels and also by size of municipality. If crimes affect mostly the better off and more educated in the urban centers, then collective perceptions of the gravity of the situation may be more alarmist than if the reverse is the case. The concerns of the educated can also generate public pressure to tackle the problem more effectively through greater resources allocation or prioritizing crime fighting over other problems. In this case, moreover, it appears that the more educated apparently tend to favor more reformist and less authoritarian strategies of crime control than the uneducated. This contrast emerged clearly when respondents were asked to choose between *mano dura* policing and "participation by all." Among those with no education, 53 percent favored the former, compared to 39 percent preferring the latter. Of those with higher education, only 28 percent endorsed authoritarian alternatives compared to 66 percent favoring participatory responses. Since that survey, Salvadoran public opinion has shifted towards a more authoritarian standpoint on criminality—especially as regards *maras,* or youth gangs.

The distinction between objective crime and subjective perceptions of it, between de facto insecurity and perceived insecurity, has crucial policy and political implications as well. For one, it suggests that policies to combat crime must address citizens' subjectivity as much as real crime. And it suggests that if knee-jerk reactions, such as those that typically lead to the unveiling of new *mano dura* policies, are ultimately inadequate to deal with objective crime, they can have but a momentary "soothing" effect on popular perceptions. A brief meso level vignette from Nuevo Laredo, Mexico, provides an illustration of the dangers of a *mano dura* approach, in this case, militarization. This small border town on the frontier with Laredo, Texas, straddles a major point of exchange, not only for licit commerce but also for drugs, undocumented migrants, and apparently also arms. At the beginning of 2005, high ranking police officials in Nuevo Laredo were gunned down. A very senior replacement was drafted in and was assaulted a week later, after which the army took control. It began patrolling the city as if it were Bosnia. This was patently useless: the locally entrenched drug gangs easily evaded control because they could predict that at ten in the morning every day a military detachment would head down Calle 7. Effective policing would have required breaking military routine and engaging with the population, but top officers were extremely reluctant to switch to such a flexible system for fear that they would lose hierarchical control over their units—and become corrupted, like the police. Instead, they proposed imposing a blockade on the city, checking everyone who entered. By doing so, they effectively "criminalized" a population of 100,000 and drove them into dependence on protection from the drug traffickers. This is admittedly an extreme case. There are many parts of Mexico where the police perform better, and a good proportion of the population has reasonable access to justice. But the vignette is not unique. In Chiapas, in Acapulco, in Atenco, in Sicartsa, there is abundant recent evidence that the subterranean problems of public security are also bubbling below the surface.

In certain high profile cases it may be that highly targeted displays of resolve can boost national morale and citizen confidence and therefore reinforce the legitimacy of a democratic regime. But where such hardline policies are badly implemented or overused, they may well have the opposite effect over the long term. Because of their nature, such hard core approaches may erode what can be already fragile commitments to the rule of law, democracy, and rights based citizenship. Further, such "fixes" may produce a sense that, under democracy (under a regime where citizens are coresponsible for their fates along with their state institutions), nothing works, and thereby increase the appeal of "abdicating responsibility" by handing over power (and the task of resolving social problems) to a persuasive authoritarian politician. Ultimately, this may have an effect exactly contrary to that which is hoped for. Because if a broadly shared ethos of responsibility among citizens and state authorities is what is necessary to counter the pernicious effects of heterogeneity, if what is necessary to actually produce a lived sense rather than a floating notion of universality, then isolated "hard" or other quick fixes and shifting political responsibilities cannot be the solution. Ultimately, as the shifting debate in Brazil described by Beato and Marinho (this volume, chapter 1) on crime (with its concomitant partial policy solutions generated according to the crime-cause *moda* of the day) shows, there is no substitute for long-term state-crafting, a commitment to developing stable epistemic communities, and the gradual construction of an edifice of real and secure citizenship rights.

DEMOCRACY, INEQUITY, AND "SECURITY"

One way to illustrate the complexity of the crime phenomenon is to look at the nexus between crime, insecurity, and extreme levels of poverty and inequality. Although there may be no direct causal link between the two, it is clear that the fragility of rights, violence, and citizen insecurity in urban and rural areas is intimately tied up with poverty and exclusion. When Latin America undertook its transitions to democracy, the prevailing conception of that macro-regime type was of the minimalist variety. Procedural and minimalist conceptions of democracy define this type of regime solely by reference to processes of political selection and the accountability of office-holders. The "outputs" of the political system, to use an earlier language, are not to be used as criteria of identification. This approach is based on the wish to distinguish democracy as an institutional practice from the widespread but imprecise demotic tendency to associate democracy with the "good society." Whether or not democracies tend toward peace; whether or not they deliver superior economic performance; whether or not they satisfy popular aspirations and needs; these are all questions to be investigated empirically once an operational definition of the category has been stipulated. They are not attributes that can or should be built into the definition. That is a central tenet of mainstream comparative politics and of much of the literature on democratization.

In the case of Latin America, this new common sense emerged in the 1980s in large measure as a result of the trauma of left wing contestation and popular mobilization in the face of inequality and authoritarian repressive responses to it. It was considered essential to challenge the widespread tendency to conflate "democracy" with "the good society," and the underlying theme was that "the best was the enemy of the good." Democratic reformists highlighted the distinction between the establishment at a national level of a democratic political regime and the satisfaction of popular aspirations, including to social justice, their procedural focus necessarily excluding—or at the very least pushing to the margins—a host of issues that shape the "quality of democracy" lower down, such as widespread illiteracy, vast pockets of rural and urban poverty, and situations of structural "exclusion." However, popular intuitions and subsequent scholarly reflection have insisted that at least some types of "output" are so contrary to democratic values that they invalidate, or render inoperative, such excessively narrow conceptions of democracy. If levels of poverty and inequality are so high as to render the effective enjoyment of civil and political rights inoperative; if organized crime dominates legal economic activity in a wide enough array of sectors and regions (meso level considerations); or if citizens and voters (at the micro level of analysis) are so bereft of physical security that they dare not openly express their political preferences and cannot be represented by crime-free parties or politicians; then macro democratic procedures are emptied of their content, and all but the most tough-minded of methodological intransigents will concede the need to append some qualifying adjective ("illiberal" or "dysfunctional" or "truncated") to the term democracy. The principle is difficult to deny. There is some limit case beyond which a purely procedural account of national level democracy fails to capture the realities of micro and meso social life and of political decision making. In most of Latin America, most of the time, the relatively larger scope for organized crime in some large regions and domains, or the partial absence of citizen security for a substantial sector of the electorate, does not clearly constitute a "limit case," but these traits are too endemic and widespread to be dismissed as marginal to the political system as a whole.

Just as democracy took a minimalist turn, so too did ideas about how to manage the economy. In other regions, democratization has usually been accompanied by a focus on distribution, even if the area of social policy emphasized in each case varies and is conditioned by different local realities and varying popular demands. In Latin America, by contrast, the decision to embrace political democracy was accompanied by a shift away from redistributive and welfare priorities. From the 1980s onwards, again in part as a reaction to exhausted ISI projects and the perceived failure of state-led growth strategies, the burdens generated by the debt crisis, and the failure of heterodoxy, the region's governing elites—

faithful to the tradition of top-down and outward directed reform—took on board the wisdom of Washington consensus. Rather than raising expectations by promising to right past wrongs, the emphasis was on minimizing "unrealistic" expectations, stabilizing the economy in a climate of state shrinking, and preserving social peace without unnecessary resort to overt coercion by conciliating formerly antagonistic interests, and reducing the stakes involved each time an elected government gives way to another. In short, procedural democracy and economic liberalism became the pillars of a postauthoritarian model of citizenship and project of sustainable development.

The results of this distinctive route to political democratization—one disconnected from direct association with much of the region's traditional substantive social agenda—are plain to see.[28] Latin America can be considered a "world champion" in terms of its rapid and broad experience with transition to democracy, but this considerable achievement has been combined with remarkably little advance—at least until very recently in most countries—as regards the "social requirements" for democracy, or the provision of social "goods" to accompany the restored civil and political rights. Per capita incomes have mostly stagnated, traditional inequalities have not diminished, and the economic welfare of much of the electorate has failed to improve since the transition to democracy. Various indicators show the poor in Latin America have fared worse than the poor in nondemocratic or only semidemocratic areas of the world since the advent of democracy. According to the World Bank, GDP per capita in Latin America fell by 0.7 percent in the 1980s, and increased by around 1.5 percent per year in the 1990s, but with no significant impact on levels of poverty. Around 25 percent of Latin Americans are living in poverty (on less than US$ 2 a day), about the same as in the late 1980s, and about 9.5 percent of these (50 million people) live in extreme poverty (on less than US$1 a day). This contrasts with China, for instance, which grew by around 8.5 percent between 1981 and 2000 and reduced poverty by around 42 percent in that period.[29]

Inequity has also remained a central feature. Latin America and the Caribbean is still the most unequal region in the world after Sub-Saharan Africa, with an average 0.53 GINI coefficient. Its wealthiest one-tenth earns 48 percent and its poorest tenth only 1.6 percent of total income.[30] According to the UNDP report on the millennium poverty reduction goals, "if the countries in the sample were to continue to perform as they did in the 1990s, only 7 of the 18 [will] meet their poverty reduction targets . . . by 2015. These countries are Argentina (pre-crisis), Chile, Colombia, Dominican Republic, Honduras, Panama, and Uruguay. Another six countries would continue to reduce the incidence of extreme poverty, but at too slow a pace. These countries are Brazil, Costa Rica, El Salvador, Guatemala, Mexico, and Nicaragua. The other five countries—Bolivia, Ecuador, Paraguay, Peru, and Venezuela—would actually see higher levels of extreme poverty due either to increases in inequality, decreases in per capita income, or both." The report also notes that a "large part of the reason why recent poverty reduction efforts . . . have yielded disappointing results is that the region's high levels of inequality have proved remarkably intractable."[31] So we confront the paradox of a successful region-wide shift to democratization that makes little or no difference to the subcontinent's notorious poverty and inequality.

Under the recent hegemony of international liberalism the claims of social justice no longer legitimize demands for expropriation or quasi-insurrectionary strike action (to take the most extreme manifestations of the old syndrome), but this does not mean all aspirations for equity have been abandoned.[32] It appears to have become more acceptable to demand justice in the form of equitable treatment for individuals as citizens and consumers, probably as a result of the prevailing liberal orthodoxy. Such demands express a much more privatized and nonconflictive understanding of entitlements, but they are nevertheless quite ambitious and still only erratically and imperfectly met. And while such demands are almost invariably too volatile and incoherent to sustain structured alternatives to the prevailing orthodoxies, they are still strong enough to generate waves of protest that can prove intermittently capable of destabilizing top down reform initiatives, and of generating fear among those who have most to lose from a change in the political and social status quo.[33]

How does this link up with the question of crime, security, and democracy? The point here is not so much to examine well rehearsed debates and claims about the links between inequality, poverty, and crime (these are well explored in other chapters in this volume and are the object of a large body of academic work). Rather, the point that can be made here is that in "low intensity" conditions democracies with a foundational discourse based on containment, prudence, and minimalism, "security" can be understood so broadly that it affects the *acceptable* range of options open to citizens when voicing their demands. In so doing, it makes democracy a more inflexible and fragile project, susceptible to reversals when fear of popular demands takes hold. It is crucial that even low quality democracies allow new voices and new complaints by popular groups to make their presence felt with greater freedom and force. "Popular" protest, blockades, demand for greater participation, and other manifestations of the disruptive power of *los de abajo* may be frightening to middle class groups, and perceived as threatening to their security (particularly when institutions of law and order have proved to be so ineffective when combating "real" crime). Perceptions that violence is increasing may therefore be a reflection of increased freedom in deeply unequal and unjust societies. This makes the whole issue of "security" all the more complex, since the politics of contestation (which are a fundamental aspect of democratic politics) may be conflated with "the security problem," and legitimate popular demands conflated with crime.

The persistent imbalance between the normative promise of macro level modern democracy (citizenship for all, self-realization within a permissive framework of order) and "really existing" meso and micro level inequities and disorder can be considered a key source of contentious politics in the region. So long as electorates are persuaded that this imbalance can be diminished over time by living within the constraints of minimalism, or that breaking with those constraints will only make matters worse, then redistributive reversals can be averted. But at existing levels of inequality, neither of these propositions is beyond challenge.[34]

GANGS: WHERE EXCLUSION MEETS CRIME, AND CRIME GOES TRANSNATIONAL

Although the objective here is not to hypothesize about causal linkages between crime and social exclusion, it is worth looking at the gang phenomenon in Latin America, since this does illustrate how one is connected to the other. Moreover, it serves as an entry point to discuss the transnationalization of crime and its impact on macro level Latin American democracy.

There are criminal gangs in many countries in Latin America, and their number, variety, and scope of activities are increasing.³⁵ They are a key manifestation of the link between micro level social exclusion or inequity and criminality. This section focuses on the cases of El Salvador and Mexico. In the former country, gangs made their appearance in the wake of the civil war, particularly after 1992, when the U.S. responded to the transition to democracy by revoking the refugee status of many Salvadorian families. The children of these immigrant families returned to their country of origin after spending years in the hard school of North America's often violent and gang ridden inner cities. Many changed country but retained membership in their gangs of U.S. origin. There are an estimated 309 street gangs with anything from 10,000 to 40,000 members, the largest being the L.A. based 18th Street Gang and the Mara Salvatrucha, followed by the locally based Mao Mao and Máquina gangs.³⁶ These gangs are involved in all kinds of violent criminal activities (the PNC estimates that 55 to 65 percent of all murders are gang-related), including organized crime. In Mexico there are an estimated two hundred gangs, the largest being the U.S.-based Mafia Mexicana (EME), MS-13, and 18th Street Gang (which also operates in El Salvador), and others like Los Aztecas and the Mexicles. The Public Security Secretariat has estimated that there are five thousand MS-13 gang members in Mexico and fifteen thousand Barrio 18 members operating in twenty-four of Mexico's states.³⁷ While many gangs are involved in petty criminality, there are increasing reports of gangs such as the EME, MS-13, 18th Street, among others, working for the drug cartels and trafficking in people, mostly along the southern border region.

More than half of the gang members who are arrested are under eighteen years of age; around 46 percent are between eighteen and twenty-six years old. In Ciudad Juarez, officials believe that part of the problem is that around 30 percent of twelve to fifteen year olds do not go to school and do not have jobs. Another contributing factor is drug use, including heroin, which is rife and increasing, particularly in the border towns of Nuevo Laredo, Juárez, and Tijuana, partly as a result of the sheer amounts available and partly because youths are being used with increasing frequency to smuggle small amounts of drugs across the border to avoid detection. Another long term phenomenon that has contributed to the rise in youth criminality is the rapid and disorganized process of urbanization that has taken place as a result of the development of the *maquila* industry and the influx of Mexican and other Central American workers to man the *maquilas*. As Marcelo Bergman reports in his chapter on Argentina (chapter 3, this volume), changing family structure also feeds youth criminality. In the case of Mexican gangs in the *maquila* regions, usually both parents work at the *maquiladoras* and so children grow up without supervision.[38]

To date, state responses have tended to be too one dimensional. A case in point is the Salvadorian PNC's *Plan Mano Dura* and the *Plan Super Mano* initiated in July 2003 and August 2004, respectively, which have targeted criminal gangs. As the name unequivocally suggests, the policy is meant to transmit a sense of "zero tolerance" and is therefore likely to generate expectations that, finally, a difference will be visible. But if one takes into consideration the long history and causes of the involvement of youths in violence in El Salvador;[39] the induction of émigré youths into gangs in the U.S. as a means of survival and of gaining respect and a sense of community in what are anomic inner cities; and the option to join gangs after "repatriation" for similar reasons and in a context where there are few opportunities for an honorable place in society;[40] the inadequacy of such *mano dura* policies becomes apparent.

If one looks at the transnational dimension of this phenomenon, it becomes apparent that even with a holistic approach to combating youth crime, a single state on its own cannot effectively deal with this problem. As reported by USAID,

> Gang activity has transcended the borders of Central America, Mexico, and the U.S. and evolved into a transnational concern that demands a coordinated, multi-national response to effectively combat increasingly sophisticated criminal gang networks. Whereas gang activity used to be territorially confined to local neighborhoods, globalization, sophisticated communications technologies, and travel patterns have facilitated the expansion of gang activity across neighborhoods, cities, and countries . . . Gangs such as MS-13 and 18th Street conduct business internationally, engaging in kidnapping, robbery, extortion, assassinations, and the trafficking of people and contraband across borders. Some Central American governments claim that a primary source of the gang problem is the U.S. policy of deporting gang

members without sharing information about these deportees with government officials on the receiving end. They point to the fact that the majority of U.S. annual criminal deportations go to the five countries in this assessment. Gang members who commit crimes in their own countries often flee to the United States to hide, engage in criminal activity, and earn income until they are caught and deported, a cycle that often repeats itself again and again.[41]

Worldwide, international criminal organizations have expanded their activities, and moved into an array of legal businesses to "launder" illegal earnings (the IMF estimates that around US$700 billion is laundered through the international financial system, and that if tax evasion proceeds are included, the figure represents 2–5 percent of world economic activity). These networks have become extremely sophisticated, and their capacity for violence is higher than ever. In addition to being involved with drug trafficking, prostitution, illegal gambling, and loan-sharking, international criminals are also active migrant smugglers and large scale bank, insurance, and tax frauds. Like multinationals, such networks operate in a variety of territories, often forging strategic and ad hoc alliances with other crime groups to ensure economies of scale and a "rational" division of labor. The profits to be gained from such activities are immense.

According to U.S. and UN estimates, drug trafficking generates 300–500 billion dollars per year and serves around 185 million customers (4.3 percent of the world population age fifteen and above). In the U.S. alone, there are about sixteen million regular users spending more than US$160 billion dollars annually on drugs, and they cost the country over US$100 billion dollars a year. Turning to trafficking in people, the UN Office of Drug Control and Crime Prevention (ODCCP) estimates that two hundred million people may be in countries other than their own as a result of human smuggling and trafficking (about four million people trafficked annually across the U.S. border alone, with up to fifty thousand women and children smuggled each year). According to the UN International Crime and Justice Research Institute (UNICRI), criminal organizations earn about US$7 billion every year from trafficking in women and children alone.

As regards illicit trading in weapons, the UN estimates that there are five hundred million weapons worldwide, only half of which are in the hands of governments, largely as a result of the disorderly break up of the Soviet Union, and that illegal weapons kill about five hundred thousand people a year, playing a role in forty-six out of forty-nine major conflicts in the 1990s. Selling illegal weapons is also a multi-billion-dollar business. Add to this the estimated US$10–15 billion earned from contraband in cars, US$20 billion in losses (to the U.S. alone) as a result of electronic piracy, the US$1 billion earned from credit card fraud, and the estimated US$200 billion in losses in the U.S. alone from activities such as advanced fee fraud (the so-called Nigerian scam), falsifying currencies, identity documents, and the illegal electronic transfers of money, and one begins to get an idea of the scale of the problem and the profitability of such activities. Indeed, the U.S. and UN estimate that proceeds from all such criminal activities add up to US$1–1.5 trillion per year, which is more than the GDP of most of the world's countries bar very few.[42]

Transnational trafficking in drugs, arms, people, and illegal migrants across international borders and the laundering of huge monetary flows produced by such activities are a dimension of the citizen security problem in many Latin American countries that is tending to overflow the "national" (or macro) level of political authority.[43] Transnational crime networks are becoming increasingly successful at circumventing national controls and establishing strong linkages with counterparts at the micro and meso levels of society. These powerful informal networks may come to exercise growing power outside the authority of the "democratic" national state, with a demoralizing impact on official justice systems and negative consequences for perceptions of citizen insecurity. Such weakened democracies with inefficient law and order institutions in a context of globalization and increasingly porous borders can provide transnational criminal networks with golden opportunities to expand activities. They also provide national actors with new opportunities and sources of criminality. In the region, the focus of the problem is drug production and trafficking, mainly cocaine (of which Colombia produces 70–80 percent in refined form), but also heroin and other drugs. Since the break up of the historical cartels, Mexican cartels and groups operating in the tri-border region in the Southern Cone have become key players. In Mexico, while the type of crime that has increased most is robbery or theft, criminality has also been boosted by the increase in organized crime, focused on trafficking in people (migrants, but also women and children for prostitution) and, of course, drugs, notably through the El Chapo cartel, the Osiel Cárdenas Guillén cartel in the Gulf, the Benjamín Arellano Félix cartel in Tijuana, and the Carrillo Fuentes cartel in Ciudad Juárez. The northern border with the U.S. is considered to be one of the most dangerous areas of the country, as this is the region where drug lords and gangs are most active.

Closely associated with the drugs trade is the traffic in illegal weapons. This illicit trade not only fuels internal conflicts and criminality but also contributes to a broader climate of lawlessness. Armed guerrillas and paramilitaries in Colombia and the *maras* are prime clients of illicitly trafficked and manufactured arms. In Mexico, for instance, a 2004 UN report ranked Mexico the third country in Latin America in terms of homicides with firearms (approximately 60 percent of homicides nationally are committed with guns). It is estimated that there are 15 million small arms circulating in the country (four times the amount registered with the National Defense Secretariat, which means that the overwhelming majority are illegal). In El Salvador, the estimate is that there are four to five hundred thousand illegal firearms in circulation (with an added unknown quantity of non-decommissioned weapons from the civil war) and about two hundred thousand registered firearms. In 2004, official statistics revealed that 74 percent of the homicides committed were the result of firearms. Another major problem is money-laundering, for which the Caribbean is a haven. The IMF estimates that worldwide offshore accounts grew from US$3.5 trillion in 1992 to US$8–10 trillion today. Money laundering is also becoming an increasingly serious problem in several of the countries of the Mercosur, largely due to the need of Colombian and Mexican drug lords to launder their money, and the proliferation of offshore banks in the subregion (Latin America and the Caribbean together account for 43 percent of the international total). People and migrant trafficking is also a major activity in Mexico and across the Caribbean.

The G8 Summit of 1998 identified transnational criminal activity as one of three major challenges of the twenty-first century. Others have called ours the "age of insecurity," in which "violence could arguably be considered the central—if not defining—problem" of the world today.[44] Certainly, Latin America is paying a high social, political, and economic price for these activities. Criminal groups use weak, ineffective, and imminently corruptible state institutions to set up operations with impunity. Politicians, judges, and journalists are bought (the carrot), and if they cannot be bought, they are killed (the stick). It is increasingly difficult to prosecute individuals, since unlike the old hierarchical mafias new criminal actors operate in a more fragmented, decentralized, and diversified world, forging one-off deals rather than permanent alliances. One of the results of the success of the U.S. in dismantling the more structured Colombian cartels was to force them to decentralize and internationalize operations (involving Mexican and Caribbean groups) so that the many small groups now operating are much harder to identify. Prosecution also becomes much harder as criminal organizations gain a measure of "legitimacy" by making legal investments and charitable and political party donations. Crime lords and those who work for them thus weave themselves into the tapestry of national economic and social life, blurring the dividing line between crime and legal activity.

PROBLEMS OF REFORM IMPLEMENTATION

Given the intensity of public concerns over crime and insecurity, a new democracy can gain in strength or become more fragile depending on how well or badly these new arrangements operate or are believed to operate. As the chapters in this volume show in different ways, the inability of the state to provide citizens with security constitutes a major challenge to democratization, one that could even threaten the survival of liberal democracy in the long run. The governments of the region have attempted to respond to the challenge with a series of broad reforms to police forces and judiciaries, and with the introduction of—albeit limited—rehabilitation programs.

In Mexico, for instance, successive governments have introduced institutional and legal reform measures to attempt to improve the situation. Indeed, the police have been exempted from the general state shrinking trend, as the budget for law and order has increased significantly in the last decade. Under the Zedillo presidency (1994–2000), the focus was on a reform of the federal court system and the involvement of the military in law enforcement on the ground (to get around the problem of police corruption). However, these measure failed to address the serious problems of state and local level courts and police forces, and many feared that involving the military in law enforcement would serve only to corrupt that institution as well (this seems to be happening). Under the Fox presidency (2000–2006), which declared law and order to be a top priority, various other reforms were undertaken: a Secretariat of Public Security (SSP) and a Federal Investigations Police (PFI) to replace the old Federal Judicial Police, and a new Federal Preventive Police (PFP) were established, and the National System of Public Security (SNSP) was restructured. In 2004, the Fox administration announced a ten-point anti-crime plan which entailed an increase in the security budget from US$250 million to US$350 million that year, and half a billion dollars in 2005. The Fox administration continued the policy of militarizing law enforcement, particularly anti-narcotics operations, and made efforts to combat corruption and human rights abuse, and to process those accused of drug trafficking and major corruption through the courts. Fox increased recruitment to about four hundred thousand police officers nationally, including five thousand soldiers working for the PFP to combat the drug trade or cartels. President Calderón further reinforced this policy in 2007.

Overall, then, more resources and expertise have been channeled into specialized sectors of public security institutions, both federal and at the state level, and real efforts have been made to identify the biggest sources of challenge to improve data collection and to coordinate efforts. As elsewhere in Latin America, and detailed in various chapters of this volume, the rules of court procedure are under review, with the aim of cutting down on paperwork, recognizing verbal testimony, making legal processes swifter and more intelligible, and promoting the case study rather than the legal code approach to legal training. Various sources of external advice have been enlisted—most notably from the mayor of New York, Rudy Giuliani, but also from Britain and Spain.[45]

Since 2006, however, the incidence of horrific crimes attributable to organized gangs (mostly involved in drug trafficking) has soared, with atrocities intended to demonstrate the impotence of the police and the impurity of the criminals even in major cities and regional centers. These demonstrations of meso level lawlessness tend to undermine citizen confidence at the micro level, even in municipalities not yet seriously affected by violent crime.

The provision of citizen security figured prominently in the Salvadoran peace process, unsurprisingly given the republic's historical background of both political and social violence. Indeed, as most democracies failed to radically reshape police forces or remove from positions of command officials associated with previous episodes of repression, El Salvador became something of a model of postconflict democratization in which a reformed police force plays a new and more positive role as a guarantor of citizen security. Reform of the forces of law and order in El Salvador occurred in the context of the January 1992 Chapultepec peace accords. As regards police reform, the National Guard, Treasury Police, and National Police, as well as paramilitary rural patrols were dissolved, the military were barred from internal security through constitutional reform, and a new National Civilian Police (PNC) force was established. However, security has failed to emerge, and the driving force behind ongoing efforts to improve citizen security is a result of this unmet demand. Without changing the culture of violence, the ineffective judiciary, a weak economy, and a dearth of police resources needed to fight crime, little will probably change in the levels of violent crime. Indeed, overreliance on high profile "anti-gang" laws seems to have reinforced social tension and reduced the scope for broad-based social cooperation to counter the breakdown of communities and rebuild civility.

CONCLUSION

One dimension of the inability of the state to find effective solutions to the problem of citizen insecurity relates to the policy making style that has long tended to characterize many administrations in the subcontinent. This is a centralizing and often personalist style at the macro level (perhaps an outgrowth of presidentialism, although not an inescapable feature of that form of government). Top-down initiatives and *decretismo* can all too easily lead to the adoption of *mano dura* strategies that, when badly implemented, have a tendency to exacerbate the underlying problems at the meso and micro levels.

Profoundly unequal and poorly integrated societies can be subjected to successive cycles of modernizing reform from above, but these transformations may each remain incomplete and contestable because the underlying requirements for a societal consensus do not exist. Traditionally, in Latin America, this was viewed as a key explanation for intermittent episodes of authoritarian rule, often by the military as the ultimate guarantor of order within the state, sometimes more personalist or more populist. Regardless of form, the basis for this recurring pattern was a widely perceived need to impose order and to define the boundaries within which actors could enjoy security in a context where social divisions might otherwise run out of control. In contrast with the relatively stable and durable despotisms that have arisen in other parts of the world, however, the authoritarian regimes of Latin America mostly neither lasted very long nor succeeded in justifying their existence beyond a more or less prolonged period of 'emergency' rule. They were capable of inspiring fear and of generating acquiescence for limited periods of time, when the trauma of previous disorders was still most vivid in the collective memory, but their initial unity and rationale faded rather fast, and the underlying lack of consensus eventually turned against them.[46]

The transition from authoritarian rule to a macro level democratic political regime raised hope for a more secure and comprehensive system of citizenship rights, and for a different policy style. But, as we have seen, many of the factors that had prompted "emergency rule" responses prior to the transition have persisted since then. Moreover, especially at some micro and meso levels they may have been reinforced. As a result, even under democratic conditions features of the old top down and arbitrary policy style may still be in demand. In quite a few cases there has been a resort to *mano dura* methods of crime control, perhaps even at the expense of overdue but difficult to implement projects of police and justice system reform. This can produce what John Bailey characterizes as a negative feedback loop, with a weakening of rule of law protections and the reinforcement of "low intensity" citizenship experiences that in turn generate more demands for order imposed at any price. Taken to an extreme this can convert a fragile democracy into a *democradura,* in which the security forces are again encouraged to act with heavy handed impunity.

The majority of ordinary voters in Latin America may be entirely receptive to a model of liberal market democracy that grants them consumer sovereignty, personal security, and stable political and civil rights. But what they experience is not this ideal, however compatible with their cultural traditions it may be. Instead, they find that this version of modernity, like the many alternative projects that have preceded it, brings nothing like "end of history" closure, but rather something far more precarious and contested. From this standpoint of the region's median voter or typical citizen, one can highlight three features of the current configuration that contrast with the standard liberal template.

First, rights that are supposed to be guaranteed and to provide secure background conditions for the pursuit of individual objectives are experienced as precarious, unstable, subject to abrupt expansion and then contraction. The consequence of this is that it would be foolhardy to trust in formal institutions: from the point of view of the *indivíduo,* to use da Matta's term, they are not there so much to protect them, but to more serve the interests of the elite.[47] Thus, to the ordinary person it seems that the only way to convert ostensible rights and entitlements into cashable benefits is to practice vigilance (to instinctively mistrust rather than to instinctively assume good faith on the part of authorities); to seek powerful protectors who by virtue of their influence and position can do the "favor" of "trickling down" to their preferred "protégés" the rights they are formally entitled to but can only obtain through "favors"; to participate in groups (that act self-defensively against the state rather than engaging with it as a part of the solution, and that tend, in the absence of widespread social trust or good faith, to withdraw from "national" action, and to prefer mobilization with people who can be trusted because they are not part of the system (such as families, local communities, or grievance-specific groups such as the landless or pensioners whose savings have been depleted by fiscally troubled and predatory states); and perhaps to protest before harm is done. This helps to explain the "direct action" or even "praetorian" component of collective action in the context of "contentious politics." This is the often defensive mobilization of those who do not trust the state and elites to act *de boa fé.*

Second and related to the above, distrust of the state and of experts and elites is not just an expression of weak cohesion and the debility of traditional authority at the societal level. It is also a learned response to entrenched experiences of patrimonialism and partiality at the top of the social hierarchy. For the *indivíduo,* unless you are well connected it may be risky to report a crime to the police, because instead of serving the public good of combating crime you may be inviting the unwelcome and potentially life-threatening attention of criminal circles tied into the security apparatus. Similarly, only the naïve or the foreigner would imagine that an anticorruption campaign could be aimed at fighting corruption in general. The entrenched popular assumption, reinforced by constantly renewed examples, will be that in general the elites enjoy impunity, and that when an exception arises this represents some settling of scores at the top rather than a genuine shift towards equality before the law.

Third, even if the liberal state were to develop a more impartial and rights enforcing stance, this would not necessarily do much to promote increased social cohesion, given the strengthening of transnational forces that accompanies liberalization and globalization. The citizen rights and protections that have been promised, but not delivered, by market democracy are responsibilities that accrue to the nation state. But ordinary people in Latin America are under few illusions about the margin of maneuver available to their respective state organizations in catering to a mass public while also retaining international confidence and the goodwill of the developed west. Remittances from the north often exceed the welfare budgets now available to many national administrations (budgets that are in any case subject to many forms of conditionality and external supervision), and estimates of the proceeds from transnational criminal activities, although hard to quantify with precision, far outstrip the entire state budgets of most Latin American republics.[48]

Asserting legally established rights requires activity and vigilance, not just by individuals but also by groups and communities, and such vigilance is often absent or not sustained. Indeed, even when there is the will and vigilance, it is often hard for citizens to promote accountability. As Anthony Pereira argues about security policies in Brazil, "While in the abstract the electoral system should enable voters to pick and choose from a variety of approaches to public security, punishing poor performance via retrospective voting, a lack of credible information, meaningful distinctions between candidates and parties on the issue, and strong levers of control over police forces by state governors dilutes this potential mechanism of vertical accountability."[49] The state is always liable to default unless pressurized, and extra-legal power groups continue to constrain the unorganized majority from expressing and pursuing the 'public good.'

Thus, what characterizes Latin American democracy is not just stark social inequality, but also the associated prevalence of multiple forms of

citizen insecurity. This affects collective perceptions of the real consequences of top down reform initiatives, however attractive they may
sound in principle, and generates waves of protest and resistance from
below, prompted by the fear of being cheated or excluded by elites that
are better organized. It gives rise to what some have called "praetorian,"
and others have labeled "populist," patterns of political pressure and
inter-group confrontation that exceed the boundaries of conventional
liberal democratic practice, and that can easily destabilize whatever reform projects may currently be in vogue. It helps to explain what I have
typified as a characteristically Latin American lack of institutional integration and social consensus, a recurring tendency found not only under
authoritarian rule but also in many of the region's new democracies.

Despite the importance of recognizing heterogeneity and its potential
political impact, the fact remains that the precarious citizenship rights
and the associated insecurities are pronounced features of Latin America,
and in large part explain why its experience with democratization differs
both from the standard assumptions of democratic theory and from
the template of "democratic consolidation." Citizenship involves an exchange: more security in return for less freedom of action. This presupposes the existence of an effective and impartial justice system, of course,
one that is capable of interpreting legal principles as they apply to the
messy particulars of individual cases. As various chapters in this volume
show, it is hard to find any justice system that comes close to meeting
these conditions in contemporary Latin America. It may be that in due
course, and in favorable conditions, this gulf can be bridged gradually,
but this region's longstanding and distinctive tradition of unstable and
precarious citizenship rights and chronic insecurity is proving remarkably resilient at present. And this will constrain the effectiveness and
credibility of current democratic regimes, just as it undermined their
authoritarian predecessors.

NOTES

1. United National Development Programme, *UNDP Human Development
Report* (Oxford: Oxford University Press, 1998), 206.
2. Guillermo O'Donnell, "Delegative Democracy," *Journal of Democracy* 5
(January 1994): 55–69, at 58. He adds that "effective citizenship is not only un-
coerced voting: it is also a mode of relationship between citizens and the state

and among citizens themselves. It is a continuing mode of relationship, during, before and after elections, among individuals protected and empowered by their citizenship. Citizenship is no less encroached upon when voting is coerced than when a battered woman or a peasant cannot hope to obtain redress in court, or when the home of a poor family is illegally invaded by the police" (58).

3. Pew Surveys, *What the World Thinks in 2002: How Global Publics View Their Lives, Their Countries, the World, America* (December 2002), available at http://people-press.org/reports/pdf/165.pdf.

4. Latinobarómetro 1996–1998, cited in Alejandro Gavíria and Carmen Pagés, "Patterns of Crime Victimization in Latin America" (Washington, DC: IADB, October 29, 1999), available at http://www.iadb.org/res/publications/pubfiles/pubWP-408.pdf.

5. See Pablo Parás, *Crime Victimization Survey,* available at http://usmex .ucsd.edu/research/research_governance_data_indicators.shtml.

6. While some reports say that kidnapping has declined, Kroll Security Consultants reported in 2004 that Mexico had the second most kidnappings in Latin America (where half of world kidnappings occur), after Colombia, with three thousand cases, and rising. See "Crime in Mexico: Fear of Captivity," *The Economist,* June 17, 2004.

7. Sociedad Sin Violencia/PNUD, *Qué cuesta la violencia a El Salvador?* (San Salvador: SSV/PNUD, 2005), 8. This study refutes the results of another study of Latin America from 1998, which put El Salvador in first place, with an estimated 24.9 percent loss of GDP, followed by Colombia (24.7 percent), Mexico (12.3 percent), Venezuela (11.8 percent) and then Brazil (10.5 percent). See Juan L. Londoño and Rodrigo Guerrero, *Violencia en América Latina: Epidemiologia y Costos* (Washington, DC: Inter-American Development Bank, 1999).

8. Londoño and Guerrero, *Violencia en América Latina;* see also Arturo Arango, *Interactive Diagnostic Statistics Database* (with crime data from the 1980s to the present), at: http://usmex.ucsd.edu/research/research_governance _data_indicators.shtml.

9. Pablo Parás, *Crime Victimization Survey.*

10. See María de las Heras, "El imperio de la desconfianza," *Milenio Semanal* (Mexico) 274 (December 16, 2002), 32–33. She notes that the National Survey on Political Culture and Citizen Practises of the Government Secretariat of November–December 2001 showed that only 10.18 percent of those surveyed had "a lot of trust" in the supreme court, citing *Este País,* 137, August 2002.

11. Alexandra Barahona de Brito and Francisco Panizza, "The Politics of Human Rights in Democratic Brazil: 'A Lei Não Pega,'" *Democratisation* 5 (Winter 1998): 20–51, citing André Lozano, "Uso da segurança privada explode em São Paulo," *Folha de São Paulo,* April 20, 1997.

12. Isabella Dutra, "Vencendo o medo: empresas de segurança privada crescem mais no país," *Revista de Negócios, SA, 2005*. These numbers are comparable to those found in countries like the UK and Germany, so the phenomenon is not threatening to the rule of law per se, but the difference is that in Brazil and other low intensity democracies there is a legacy of abusive police and military forces, the industry is insufficiently regulated and often manned by retired former officers.

13. See Paul Chevigny, *Edge of the Knife: Police Violence in the Americas* (New York: New Press, 1995), 177–178.

14. Such severe attitudes can better be understood (but are no more comforting) when considering that 20 percent claimed to have been victims of at least one armed robbery in the previous twelve months; 6.2 percent said they had received death threats; 3.0 percent said they had been mistreated by the police; 1.2 percent said they had been kidnapped; and 1.4 percent had been injured in an assault (0.8 percent by firearms). IUDOP, Normas Culturales y Actitudes Sobre La Violencia: Estudio Activo (San Salvador: IUDOP, 1999), 13.

15. It should be remembered that a 2003 law had made *porte de armas* illegal without a special exam and other limiting conditions. "Rely on Brazil's Police? No Way, Say Most Voters," *Reuters,* October 24, 2005, at: http://today. reuters.com/news/home.aspx, accessed July 12, 2006.

16. See Marcelo Bergman, *Delincuencia, marginalidad y desempeño institucional: Resultados de la encuesta a población en reclusión en tres entidades de la República mexicana* (México: CIDE, 2003), 45.

17. Guillermo Zepeda, *Crímen sin castigo: procuración de justicia y ministerio público en México* (Mexico City: Fundo de Cultura Económica, 2004), 252–53.

18. Marcelo Bergman, *Delincuencia, marginalidad,* 47.

19. *Respuesta al Informe del Relator de la ONU para la independencia de jueces y abogados* (Mexico: Poder Judicial de la Federación, 2002).

20. This term appears as a result of a "metaphorical map" in which the places were national state institutions and legality hardly present or entirely absent are colored brown (O'Donnell 1993).

21. Matías Busso, Martín Cicowiez, and Leonardo Gasparini, *Ethnicity and the Millennium Development Goals in Latin America and the Caribbean, 2005* (Bogotá: CEDE/UNDP/WB/IDB/ECLAC, 2005). The countries covered in the report are Bolivia, Brazil, Chile, Colombia, Costa Rica, Ecuador, Guatemala, Haiti, Honduras, Mexico, Nicaragua, Panama, Paraguay, Peru, and Suriname.

22. Ibid.

23. The departments of Santa Ana, Sonsonate, La Libertad, San Salvador, and La Paz, are particularly violent. See Pablo Parás, *Crime Victimization Survey.*

24. Barahona de Brito and Panizza, "Politics of Human Rights."

25. Ibid., 12.

26. Londoño and Guerrero suggest about El Salvador, for instance, that even though current rates of violence might decline, the stock of those ever exposed to it can continue to increase, producing progressively more adverse perceptions of the overall security situation. Londoño and Guerrero, *Violencia en América Latina.*

27. According to a 1998 IUDOP survey, about 60 percent of the population has experienced some form of violent delinquency at some point in the past decade. IUDOP 1999, 13.

28. See C. Binetti and F. Carrillo, eds., *Democracia con desigualdad?* (Washington, DC: Inter-American Development Bank, 2004).

29. According to the report, over the last fifteen years, poverty fell marginally in Central America (30 to 29 percent), increased from 25 to 31 percent in the countries of the Andean community, and fell more significantly from 24 to 19 percent in the Southern Cone countries. Guillermo E. Perry et al., *Poverty Reduction and Growth: Virtuous and Vicious Circles* (Washington, DC: World Bank, 2006).

30. Ibid.

31. Ricardo Paes de Barros, et al., *Meeting the Millennium Poverty Reduction Targets in Latin America and the Caribbean* (Santiago de Chile: UNDP, 2002), 12. The same report indicates that intergenerational mobility is also lower in Latin America and the Caribbean than in the worst performing OECD countries, and children of poor families with little educated parents are highly likely to achieve low levels of education, get lower returns on their education, and remain poor.

32. See Carol Graham and Sandip Sukhtankar, "Does Economic Crisis Reduce Support for Markets and Democracy in Latin America?" *Journal of Latin American Studies* 36, no. 2 (May 2004): 349–77. As observed in the Pew Survey, "economic anxiety also is widespread throughout Latin America. In that region, general economic problems are cited as the principal national concern in most nations" (along with unemployment); Pew Surveys, *What the World Thinks.* Further, "Latin Americans are among the least hopeful when it comes to perceptions of progress." Luckily, for failing policy makers, Latin Americans are also optimistic about the future: "Significantly, in many countries in which there is general pessimism over current conditions, most people have hope for the future. In these nations, the public may feel that the economy is so bad today it can only get better in the future."

33. As O'Donnell says: "the . . . hard fact is that the poor are politically weak. Their permanent struggle for survival is not conducive, excepting very specific [and usually short lived] situations and some remarkable individuals, to their organisation and mobilisation. Furthermore, this weakness opens

ample opportunity for manifold tactics of cooptation, selective repression and political isolation"; Guillermo O'Donnell, "Poverty and Inequality in Latin America: Some Political Reflections," In *Poverty and Inequality in Latin America: Issues and Challenges*, ed. Victor E. Tokman and Guillermo O'Donnell, 49–71 (Notre Dame, IN: University of Notre Dame Press, 1998), 51.

34. See Graham and Sukhtankar, "Does Economic Crisis Reduce Support."

35. There is an abundant literature on the gang phenomenon, mostly focusing on the U.S. The information which follows is based on the USAID report, *Central America and Mexico Gang Assessment* (April 2006), available at http://www.usaid.gov/locations/latin_america_caribbean/democracy/gangs_assessment.pdf. I have relied especially on the executive summary on pages 5–6 and Annex 4 on pages 105–20.

36. There are also organised crime gangs made up of former police or military officers or former rebels who are now jobless. See ibid., Annex 4.

37. There are an estimated 320 active gangs in Ciudad Juárez with 17,000 members, and an estimated 24 gangs in Nuevo Laredo; ibid.

38. Ibid.

39. Around 80 percent of government troops and 20 percent of FMLN guerilla recruits were under eighteen years old, many of which were never caught in the net of social reintegration programs; ibid.

40. According to a poll by the Institute of Public Opinion at the University of Central America in San Salvador, among former and current gang members, 30 percent claimed that their main aspiration was to find a job, and 46 percent claimed they joined gangs to "have a place to hang out" even at the cost of jail or death, which were recognized as the major disadvantage of that choice by 46 percent; Thomas C. Bruneau, "The Maras and National Security in Central America," *Strategic Insights* 4, no. 5 (May 2005) 1–12.

41. USAID, *Central America and Mexico Gang Assessment*, 5–6.

42. Figures from Melvyn Levitsky, "Transnational Criminal Networks and International Security," October 22, 2003, available at www.spa.msu.ru/e-journal/2/26_1.php.

43. There is a large and growing body of literature on the impact of transnational crime in Latin America. To take just two examples see Tom Farer, ed., *Transnational Crime in the Americas* (New York: Routledge, 1999); Mats Berdal and Mónica Serrano, eds., *Transnational Organized Crime and International Security: Business as Usual?* (Boulder CO: Lynne Rienner, 2002).

44. Diane Davis, "The Age of Insecurity," *Latin American Research Review* 41, no. 1 (2006): 178–97.

45. There was a surprising degree of success, for instance, when women police officers were introduced to deal with traffic offences in Mexico City. Many

motorists felt they were fairer—and less likely to demand bribes—than their male counterparts; "Mexico: Righting the Scales," *The Economist*, October 6, 2005. See also Human Rights Watch, *Lost in Transition: Bold Ambitions, Limited Results for Human Rights under Fox* (Human Rights Watch report, May 2006).

46. There are literally hundreds of case studies and monographs tracing variants of this dynamic. To select one vivid illustration, almost at random, see José Matos Mar, *Crisis del estado y desborde popular* (Lima: Instituto de Estudios Peruanos, 1984). For a more recent compilation with many relevant examples, see Douglas A. Chalmers et al., *The New Politics of Inequality in Latin America* (Oxford: Oxford University Press, 1997).

47. Roberto da Matta, *Carnavais, maladros e herois* (Rio de Janeiro: Editora Guanabara, 1990), 193.

48. In 2002, CNN reported that "money laundering activities already account for between two to five percent of world GDP, while the United Nations has said that people smuggling is the world's fastest growing criminal business, raking in up to $10 billion a year." See "Asian Police Need to 'Act Like Triads,'" March 21, 2002 available at http://archives.cnn.com/2002/WORLD/asiapcf/east/03/21/asia.crime/index.html.

49. Pereira, "Public Security, Private Interests, and Police Reform in Brazil" (paper presented at the 26th International Congress of the Latin American Studies Association, San Juan, Puerto Rico, March 16, 2006).

Aguirre, Carlos A., and Robert Buffington, eds. *Reconstructing Criminality in Latin America*. Wilmington, DE: Scholarly Resources, 2000.

Alvazzi del Frate, Anna. *Victims of Crime in the Developing World*. Interregional Crime and Justice Research Institute (UNICRI), publication no. 57. Rome: United Nations, 1998.

Amaya Cobar, Edgardo, ed. *Estado de la seguridad pública y la justicia penal en El Salvador Julio 2002–Diciembre 2003*. San Salvador: Fundación de Estudios para la Aplicación del Derecho (FESPAD)/Centro de Estudios Penales de El Salvador (CEPES), 2004.

Ambos, Kai, and Jan Woischnik. "Las reformas procesales en América Latina." In *Las reformas procesales en América Latina*, ed. Julio B. J. Maier, Kai Ambos, and Jan Woischnik, 835–96. Buenos Aires: Konrad Adenauer Stiftung/Max Planck Institute, 2000.

Ambos, Kai, Juan Luis Gómez Colomer, and Richard Vogler, eds. *La Policía en los Estados de Derecho Latinoamericanos*. Bogotá: Instituto Max-Planck, 2003.

Andrade, M. V., and M. B. Lisboa. "Desesperança de vida: homicídios em Minas Gerais, Rio de Janeiro e São Paulo no período 1981–1997." In *Desigualdade e pobreza no Brasil*, ed. R. Henriques, 347–84. Rio de Janeiro: IPEA, 2000.

Arango, Arturo. *Sistema de Información Delictiva: La estadística de seguridad pública en México*. Mexico: Instituto Nacional de Ciencias Penales, 2004.

———. "Comentarios al Plan de Acciones de Seguridad, Procuración de Justicia y Gobierno 2004–2006." Unpublished manuscript, 2006.

Arias, Enrique Desmond, and Corinne M. Davis. "The Role of Criminals in Crime Management and Dispute Resolution: Understanding Drug Trafficker Control in Rio's Favelas." Paper delivered at the meeting of the Latin American Studies Association, Washington, DC, September 6–8, 2001.

Arriagada, Irma, and Lorena Godoy. *Seguridad ciudadana y violencia en América Latina: diagnóstico y políticas en los años noventa*. Santiago de Chile: CEPAL, 1999.

Arroyo, Mario. "Assessing the Giuliani Strategy: Zero Tolerance Policing in Mexico City." Presented at the conference Reforming the Administration of Justice in México, Center for U.S.-Mexican Studies, University of California San Diego, May 2003.

Ayres, R. *Crime and Violence as Development Issues in Latin America and the Caribbean*. Washington, DC: World Bank, 1998.

Azaola, Elena. "México." In *Encyclopedia of Crime and Punishment*, ed. David Levinson, 3:1053–56. Oakland: Sage Publications, 2002.

———. "Imagen y Autoimagen de la Policía de la Ciudad de México." Mexico: Ediciones Coyoacán, 2006.

———, and Marcelo Bergman. "The Mexican Prison System." In *Reforming the Administration of Justice in Mexico*, ed. Wayne A. Cornelius and David A. Shirk, 91–114. Notre Dame, IN: University of Notre Dame Press, 2007.

Bailey, John. "Introduction: New Security Challenges in the South-North Dialog." In *Public Security in the Americas: New Challenges in the South-North Dialog*, working document, 2003.

———. "Public Security and Democratic Governability: Theorizing about Crime, Violence, Corruption, State and Regime." Paper delivered at the annual meeting of the Midwest Political Science Association, Chicago, 2004.

———, and Roy Godson. "Introduction." In *Organized Crime and Democratic Governability: Mexico and the U.S.-Mexican Borderlands*, ed. John Bailey and Roy Godson, 1–29. Pittsburgh: University of Pittsburgh Press, 2000.

Bailey, William C. "Poverty, Inequality and City Homicide Rates: Some Not So Unexpected Findings." *Criminology* 22 (1984): 531–50.

Barahona de Brito, Alexandra, and Francisco Panizza. "The Politics of Human Rights in Democratic Brazil: 'A Lei Não Pega.'" *Democratisation* 5 (Winter 1998): 20–51.

Barrón, Martín, Carlos Silva, and José Arturo Yáñez. *Guardia Nacional y Policía Preventiva: dos problemas de seguridad en México*. Mexico: Instituto Nacional de Ciencias Penales, 2004.

Basombrío Iglesias, Carlos. *Delito e inseguridad ciudadana: Lima y otras ciudades del Perú comparadas con América Latina*. Lima: Instituto de Defensa Legal, 2007.

———, and Fernando Rospigliosi. *La seguridad y sus instituciones en el Perú a inicios del siglo XXI: Reformas democráticas o neomilitarismo (Security and Its Institutions in Peru in the Early 21st Century: Democratic Reforms or Neomilitarism)*. Lima: Institute for Peruvian Studies, 2006.

Bayart, Jean François, Stephen Ellis, and Béatrice Hibou. *The Criminalisation of the State in Africa*. London: James Currey, 1999.

Bayley, David H. "Democratizing the Police Abroad: What to Do and How to Do It." U.S. Department of Justice, Washington, 2001.

Baytelman, Andrés. *Evaluación de la reforma procesal chilena*. Santiago de Chile: Centro de Investigaciones Jurídicas, Universidad Diego Portales and Centro de Estudios de la Justicia, and Universidad de Chile, 2002.

Beato Filho, Claudio Chaves. "Determining Factors of Criminality in Minas Gerais." *Brazilian Review of Social Sciences* (São Paulo) 1, (2000): 159–73.

———. "Fontes de dados policiais em estudos criminológicos: limites e poten- ciais." In *Criminalidade, violência e segurança pública no Brasil: uma dis- cussão sobre as bases de dados e questões metodológicas*, Fórum de Debates, ed. Daniel Cerqueira, vol. 1, no. 1, 88–110. Rio de Janeiro: IPEA, 2000.

———. "Toward a Society under Law: Citizens and their Police in Latin America." Working Paper, Woodrow Wilson Center, Washington, DC, 2005.

Beato Filho, Claudio Chaves, and Ilka Afonso Reis. "Desigualdade, desenvolvi- mento sócio-econômico e crime." In *Desigualdade, Desenvolvimento Sócio- Econômico e Crime: Anais do Seminário Desigualdade e Pobreza no Brasil-IPEA*, ed. IPEA, 385–405. Rio de Janeiro: IPEA, 2000.

Beato Filho, Claudio Chaves, et al. "Conglomerados de homicídios e o tráfico de drogas em Belo Horizonte e Minas Gerais, de 1995 a 1999." *Cadernos de Saúde Pública* (Rio de Janeiro) 17, no. 5 (September–October 2001): 1163–71.

Berdal, Mats, and Mónica Serrano, eds. *Transnational Organized Crime and International Security: Business as Usual?* Boulder, CO: Lynne Reiner, 2002.

Bergman, Marcelo. *Delincuencia, marginalidad y desempeño institucional: Re- sultados de la encuesta a población en reclusión en tres entidades de la Repú- plica mexicana*. Mexico City: CIDE, 2003.

———. *Tax Evasion and the Rule of Law in Latin America: The Political Culture of Cheating and Compliance in Argentina and Chile*. University Park: Penn State University Press, 2009.

———, et al. *Delincuencia, Marginalidad y Desempeño Institucional: Resultados de la Segunda Encuesta*. Mexico City: CIDE, 2006.

Binetti, C., and F. Carillo, eds. *Democracia con desigualdad?* Washington, DC: Inter-American Development Bank, 2004.

Blanco Escandón, Celia. "El nuevo proceso penal en América Latina." *Crimi- nalia* (Mexico) 120, no. 1 (2004): 271–93.

Blau, Judith R., and Peter M. Blau. "The Cost of Inequality: Metropolitan Struc- ture and Violent Crime." *American Sociological Review* 47 (1982): 114–29.

Blumstein, Alfred, and Joel Wallman. *The Crime Drop in America*. Cambridge: Cambridge University Press, 1999.

Boudon, Lawrence. "Party System Deinstitutionalization: The 1997–1998 Co- lombian Elections in Historical Perspective." *Journal of Inter-American Studies and World Affairs* 42, no. 3 (Fall 2000): 33–57.

Bresser Pereira, Luis Carlos, and Yoshiaki Nokano. "The Missing Social Contract: Governability and Reform in Latin America." In *What Kind of*

Democracy? What Kind of Market? Latin America in the Age of Neoliberalism, ed. Philip D. Oxhorn and Graciela Ducatenzeiler, 21–41. University Park: Penn State Press, 1998.

Briceño-León, R., and R. Pérez Perdono. "Morir en Caracas." Caracas: Universidad Central de Venezuela, 2002.

Bruneau, Thomas C. "The Maras and National Security in Central America." *Strategic Insights* 4, no. 5 (May 2005): 1–12.

Bursik, Robert J., Jr. "Social Disorganization and Theories of Crime and Delinquency: Problems and Prospects." *Criminology* 26, no. 4 (1988): 519–51.

Busso, Martin, Martin Cicowiez, and Leonardo Gasparini. *Ethnicity and the Millennium Development Goals in Latin America and the Carribean, 2005.* Bogotá: CEDE/ENDP/WB/IDB/ECLAC, 2005.

Butcher, K., and A. Piehl. "Cross-City Evidence on the Relationship between Immigration and Crime." *Journal of Policy Analysis and Management* 17 (1999): 457–79.

Buvinic, Mayra, Andrew Morrison, and Michael Shifter. *Violence in Latin America and the Caribbean: A Framework for Action.* Technical study, Inter-American Development Bank, Washington, DC, 1999.

Caimari, Lila M. *Apenas un delicuente: Crimen, castigo y cultura en la Argentina, 1880–1955.* Buenos Aires: Siglo Veintiuno Editores Argentina, 2004.

Caldeira, Cesar. "Politica anti-sequestros no Rio de Janeiro." In *Violencia, sociedad y justicia en America Latina,* ed. Robert Briceno. Buenos Aires: CLACSO, 2002.

Caldeira, Teresa P. R. *City of Walls: Crime, Segregation, and Citizenship in São Paulo.* Berkeley: University of California Press, 2000.

Candina, Azun, and Alejandra Lunecke. "Formación en derechos humanos y control institucional: los cambios en la Policía de Investigaciones de Chile, 1992–2002." In *Participación ciudadana y reformas a la policía en América del Sur,* ed. Hugo Frühling and Azun Candina, 119–66. Santiago: Centro de Estudios del Desarrollo, 2004.

Carabineros de Chile. *Anuario de estadísticas criminales.* Santiago de Chile: Carabineros de Chile, various years, up to 2002.

Carranza, Elías. "Prison Overcrowding in Latin America and the Caribbean: Situation and Possible Responses." Paper presented at the United Nations Program Network Institute Technical Assistance Workshop, Vienna, Austria, May 2001.

Castro, M., et al. "Regionalização como estratégia para a definição de políticas públicas de controle de homicídios." *Cadernos de Saúde Pública* 20 (2004): 1268–80.

Catterberg and Associates. "Seguridad en el gran Buenos Aires." Unpublished survey, 2000.

Centeño, Miguel Angel. *Blood and Debt: War and the Nation-State in Latin America.* University Park: Pennsylvania State University Press, 2002.

Centro de Derechos Humanos Miguel Agustín Pro. *Seguridad Pública ¿Represión o protección?* Mexico: Centro Prodh, 2005.

Centro de Estudios de Opinión Pública. "La seguridad pública en la Ciudad de México." *Este País* (México) 122 (2001): 45–46.

Cerqueira, Daniel, and Waldir Lobão. "Condicionantes sociais, poder de polícia e o setor de produção criminal." IPEA discussion paper no. 957, Rio de Janeiro, 2003.

CESC. *Impacto de la reforma procesal penal en indicadores de la seguridad ciudadana.* Santiago de Chile: Centro de Estudios en Seguridad Ciudadana, 2006.

Chalmers, Douglas A., et al. *The New Politics of Inequality in Latin America.* Oxford: Oxford University Press, 1997.

Chevigny, Paul. *Edge of the Knife: Police Violence in the Americas.* New York: New Press, 1995.

Chiricos, T. "Rates of Crime and Unemployment: An Analysis of Aggregate Research Evidence." *Social Problems* 34, no. 2 (1987): 187–212.

Christie, Nils. *World Prison Population List.* Oslo: International Center for Prison Studies, 2006.

CIDE. *Inmates Survey.* Mexico City: CIDE, 2003.

———. *Victimization Survey of the Metropolitan Area of Mexico City, 2005.* Mexico City: CIDE, 2005.

Cloward, R., and L. Ohlin. "Differential Opportunity Structure." In *The Sociology of Crime and Delinquency,* ed. M. Wolfgang and F. Ferracuti, 300–18. New York: John Wiley and Sons, 1970.

Comisión de Derechos Humanos del Distrito Federal. *Derechos humanos y policías.* Mexico: CDHDF, 2003.

———. *Derechos humanos y Seguridad Pública.* Mexico: CDHDF, 2004.

———. *Seguridad pública, prevención del delito y derechos humanos: Construyendo alternativas desde la sociedad civil y los organismos públicos de derechos humanos.* Mexico: CDHDF-Insyde-Fundar, 2004.

Comisión Ecuménica de Derechos Humanos (CEDHU). *Derechos del Pueblo,* no. 26. Quito: CEDHU, 1985.

Consejo Superior de la Judicatura and Universidad Nacional de Colombia. *Modelo probabilístico para cuantificar la impunidad.* Bogota: Imprenta Nacional de Colombia, 2000.

Costa, Gino. *La Policía Nacional Civil de El Salvador, 1990–1997.* San Salvador: UCA Editores, 1999.

Cruz, José Miguel. "Violence, Insecurity and Legitimacy in Post-War Central American Countries." Unpublished paper, 2003.

Cuéllar, M. M. *Colombia: Un proyecto inconcluso; Valores, instituciones y capital social.* 2 vols. Bogota: Universidad Externado de Colombia, 2000.

Dahl, Robert A. *Polyarchy: Participation and Opposition.* New Haven, CT: Yale University Press, 1971.

da Matta, Roberto. *Carnavais, maladros y herois*. Rio de Janeiro: Editora Guanabara, 1990.

Dammert, Lucía. "Violencia criminal y seguridad ciudadana en Chile." *Serie Políticas Sociales* 109. Santiago de Chile: División de Desarrollo Social, CEPAL, 2005.

———. "El sistema penitenciario en Chile: Desafíos para el nuevo modelo público-privado." Chile: FLACSO, 2006.

Dammert, Lucía, and Alejandra Lunecke. *Violencia y temor: Análisis teórico y empírico en doce comunas del país*. Santiago: Centro de Estudios en Seguridad Ciudadana, 2002.

Dammert, Lucía, and John Bailey, eds. *Seguridad y Reforma Policial en las Américas*. Mexico: Siglo XXI, 2005.

Dammert, Lucía, and Mary F. T. Malone. "Inseguridad y temor en Argentina: El impacto de la confianza en la policía y la corrupción sobre la percepción ciudadana del crimen." *Desarrollo Económico: Revista de Ciencias Sociales* 42, no. 166 (2002): 285–301.

———. "Fear of Crime or Fear of Life? Public Insecurities in Chile." *Bulletin of Latin American Research* 22, no. 1 (2003): 79–101.

Dammert, Lucía, Felipe Salazar, and Felipe Ruz. *¿Políticas de seguridad a ciegas? Desafíos para la construcción de sistemas de información en América Latina*. Chile: FLACSO, 2008.

DANE. *Boletín Mensual de Estadística* 410 (May 1987).

———. *La justicia colombiana en cifras, 1937–1994*. Bogota: Imprenta Nacional, 2003.

Data Opinión Pública y Mercados, "Inseguridad y evaluación al jefe de gobierno de la Ciudad de México" *Este País* 152 (November 2003): 60–62.

Davis, Diane. "The Age of Insecurity." *Latin America Research Review* 41, no. 1 (2006): 178–97.

DNP (Departamento Nacional de Planeación). *Justicia y Desarrollo*. Bogotá: DNP, 1994.

Drumond, M., Jr. *Vida e morte em São Paulo*. São Paulo: Brasiliense, 2002.

Duce, Mauricio. "Palabras de bienvenida." In *Seguridad ciudadana y reforma procesal penal*, 3–4. Santiago de Chile: Fundación Paz Ciudadana, CEJA, Pontificia Universidad Católica de Chile, and Universidad Diego Portales, 2006.

———, and Rogelio Pérez Perdomo. "Citizen Security and Reform of the Criminal Justice System in Latin America." In *Crime and Violence in Latin America: Citizen Security, Democracy and the State*, ed. Hugo Frühling and Joseph S. Tulchin, with Heather A. Golding, 69–91. Baltimore: John Hopkins University Press, 2003.

Dunning, Alistair. "Prison Brief for Venezuela." International Centre for Prison Studies, 2006.

Eilbaum, Lucía. "La sospecha como fundamento de los procedimientos policiales." *Cuadernos de Antropología Social* (Buenos Aires) 20 (December 2004): 79–91.

Equipo Nizkor and SERPAJ Paraguay. *Informe sobre los Derechos Humanos en Paraguay.* Asunción: SERPAJ, 1996.

Escolá, Marc B. *Eficacia y Sistemas de Calidad en la Policía.* Bilbao: Instituto Superior de Estudios de la Gobernabilidad y la Seguridad, 2000.

Escola de Policia de Catalunya. "Experiencias de gestión de la seguridad: desde los modelos de proximidad al uso de la tecnología." *Revista Catalana de Seguretat Pública* 10 (June 2002).

Fajnzylber, P., Daniel Lederman, and Norman Loayza. "Inequality and Violent Crime." From the research project "Crime in Latin America." Washington, DC: The World Bank, 1999.

———"Crime and Victimization: An Economic Perspective." *Economia* 1 (2000): 220–302.

———"Inequality and Violent Crime." *Journal of Law and Economics* 45, no. 1 (2002): 1–39.

———, eds. *Crímen y violencia en América Latina.* Washington, DC, and Buenos Aires: Alfa-Omega and World Bank, 2001.

Farer, Tom, ed. *Transnational Crime in the Americas.* New York: Routledge, 1999.

Farrington, D. "Individual Differences and Offending." In *The Handbook of Crime and Punishment,* ed. M. Tonry, 241–68. Oxford: Oxford University Press, 1998.

Farthing, Linda, and Ben Kohl. "The Price of Success: Bolivia's War against Drugs and the Poor." *NACLA Report on the Americas* 35, no. 1 (July–August 2001): 35–38.

FIEL. *La distribución del ingreso en la Argentina.* Buenos Aires: FIEL, 1999.

FPC (Fundación Paz Ciudadana). *Anuario de estadísticas criminales.* Santiago de Chile: FPC, various years.

———. *Indice de temor ciudadano, Octubre 2001.* Santiago de Chile: FPC, 2001.

Freedom House. *Freedom in the World Surveys.* New York: Freedom House, various years. (Available at http://www.freedomhouse.org.)

Freeman, Richard B. "The Labor Market." In *Crime,* ed. J. Q. Wilson and J. Petersilia, 171–91. San Francisco: ICS Press, 1995.

———. "Disadvantaged Young Men and Crime." In *Youth Employment and Joblessness in Advanced Countries,* ed. D. Blanchflower and Richard B. Freeman, 215–45. Chicago: University of Chicago Press, 2000.

———. "Does the Booming Economy Help Explain the Drop in Crime." Paper from Perspectives on Crime and Justice: 1999–2000 Lectures Series, U.S. Department of Justice, 2000.

Friedman, E., et al. "Regulatory Discretion and the Unofficial Economy." *American Economic Review* 88, no. 2 (1995): 387–92.

———. "Dodging the Grabbing Hand: The Determinants of Unofficial Activity in 69 Countries." *Journal of Public Economics* 76, no. 3 (June 2000): 459–93.

Frühling, Hugo. "La prevención del crimen: Notas sobre la justicia penal y la reducción de oportunidades para la delincuencia." Paper presented at the Conference Crímen Urbano, Rio de Janeiro, March 2–4, 1997.

———. "Carabineros y Consolidación Democrática en Chile." *Pena y Estado* (Buenos Aires) 3, no. 3 (1998): 81–116.

———. "La reforma policial y el proceso de democratización en América Latina." Centro de Estudios para el Desarrollo, Santiago de Chile, 2001.

———. "Policía comunitaria y reforma policial en América Latina ¿Cuál es el impacto?" Serie Documentos del Centro de Estudios en Seguridad Ciudadana, Santiago, Universidad de Chile, 2003.

———. *Calles más seguras: Estudios sobre policía comunitaria en América Latina.* Washington, DC: Inter-American Development Bank, 2004.

———. "Dos décadas de reforma policial en América Latina: factores para su éxito o fracaso" ("Two Decades of Police Reform in Latin America: Factors for Success or Failure"). In *¿Cuál es la salida? La agenda inconclusa de seguridad ciudadana (What Is the Solution? The Unfinished Agenda of Public Security),* ed. Erik Alda y Gustavo Béliz, 281–310. Washington, DC: Inter-American Development Bank, 2007.

———, and Joseph S. Tulchin, eds. *Crime and Violence in Latin America: Citizen Security, Democracy, and the State.* Washington, DC: Woodrow Wilson Center, 2003.

Fuentes, Claudio Fuentes. "Denuncias por actos de violencia policial." FLACSO-Chile, 2001.

Fundación de Estudios para la Aplicación del Derecho (FESPAD) and Centro de Estudios Penales de El Salvador (CEPES). *Estado de la seguridad pública y la justicia penal en El Salvador, julio 2002–diciembre 2003.* El Salvador: FESPAD-CEPES, 2004.

Fundación Libertad, Democracia y Desarrollo (FULIDED). *The Budget for State Security in Bolivia, 2004.* Santa Cruz, Bolivia: FULIDED, 2004.

Gabaldón, Luis Gerardo. "Análisis y Propuestas, Seguridad Ciudadana y control del delito en América Latina." *Nueva Sociedad* (Caracas), September 2004, 1–8.

———, and Daniela Bettiol. *Presencia policial en zonas residenciales urbanas.* Mérida, Colombia: Universidad de los Andes, 1988.

Gabinete de Gobierno, Seguridad Pública y Procuración de Justicia. *Informe de resultados 2005: Plan de Acciones 2005.* Mexico: Gobierno del Distrito Federal, 2005.

García-Villegas, Mauricio, and Rodrigo Uprimny Yepes. "El nudo gordiano de la justicia y la guerra en Colombia." In *Armar la Paz es Desarmar la Guerra*, ed. Álvaro Camacho Guizado and Francisco Leal Buitrago, 33–72. Bogotá: FESCOL, 1999.

Geldstein, R. *Mujeres jefas de hogar: Familia, pobreza y género*. Buenos Aires: UNICEF, 2000.

Gertz Manero, Alejandro. "Minuta de la comparecencia del Secretario de Seguridad Pública ante el Poder Legislativo." October 2001.

Giraldo, J., et al. *Reforma de la justicia en Colombia*. Bogota: Instituto SER de Investigación, 1987.

Gobierno del Distrito Federal. *Plan de acciones de seguridad, Procuración de Justicia y Gobierno 2004–2006*. Mexico D.F.: Gobierno del Distrito Federal, 2004.

González, José. *Lo negro del negro Durazo: La biografía criminal de Durazo; escrita por su jefe de ayudantes*. Mexico: Posadas, 1983.

González Mendivil, Franklin. *Doctrina policial*. La Paz, Bolivia: Policía Nacional/Comando General, 1988.

Gottfredson, Michael R., and Travis Hirschi. *A General Theory of Crime*. Stanford, CA: Stanford University Press, 1990.

Gudiño, Julián Jesús. "De seguridad pública a seguridad ciudadana," *Este País* (México) (October 2001): 42–51.

Guell, Pedro. "Una construcción social sobre un mapa de disyuntivas." En Foco 40. Santiago: Expansiva, 2004.

Gwarney, James, and Robert Lawson, eds. *Economic Freedom of the World 1997 Annual Report*. Vancouver: The Fraser Institute, 1997.

Hammergren, Linn. "Latin American Criminal Justice Reform: Evaluating the Evaluators." *Sistemas Judiciales* (Santiago de Chile) 2, no. 3 (2002): 59–66.

Hart, H. L. A. *The Concept of Law*. Oxford: Clarendon Press, 1994.

Heras, María de las. "El imperio de la desconfianza." *Milenio Semenal* (Mexico) 274 (December 16, 2002): 32–33.

Hillman, Richard, and Elsa Cardozo de Silva. "Venezuelan Political Culture and Democracy: 1996 and 1997 Survey Results." Paper presented at the Caribbean Studies Association Conference, Antigua, 1998.

Hirschi, Travis. *Causes of Delinquency*. Berkeley: University of California Press, 1969.

Human Rights Watch. *The Human Rights Watch Global Report on Prisons*. New York: Human Rights Watch, 1992.

———. *Cuba's Repressive Machinery: Human Rights Forty Years After the Revolution*. Washington, DC: Human Rights Watch, 1999.

———. *Lost in Transition: Bold Ambitions, Limited Results for Human Rights under Fox*. Humna Rights Watch report, 2006.

Human Security Center. *Human Security Report 2005*. The University of British Columbia: Oxford University Press, 2005.

Hussain, Saima. "One Station at a Time: Professionalizing the Civil Police in Rio de Janeiro, Brazil." Unpublished manuscript, 2005.

———. "'Na guerra, que morre nao é innocente': Human Rights Implementation, Policing, and Public Security Reform in Rio de Janeiro, Brazil." PhD dissertation, Netherlands School of Human Rights Research, Utrecht University, 2007.

INDEC (Instituto Nacional de Estadísticas y Censos). *Estadísticas sociodemográficas del INDEC.* Buenos Aires: Sociedad Argentina de Estadística, 1994–2002.

———. "Proyección de población por edad y sexo, Total país, Años 1950–2025." INDEC-CELADE Serie Análisis demográfico 5. Buenos Aires: INDEC. 1995.

———. "Proyección de población por sexo según quinquinales de edad 1990–2010." INDEC-CELADE Serie Análisis Demográfico 7. Buenos Aires: INDEC. 1996.

———. "Alumnos matriculados por nivel y sector (varios años)." Dirección General Red Federal de Información Educativa. Buenos Aires: INDEC, 1998.

———. "Hechos delictuosos con intervención policial, según tipo de delito para la ciudad de Buenos Aires." Buenos Aires: Dirección General de Estadísticas y Censos, 1999.

———. "Tasa de desocupación especifica por edad, 1980–1999." In *Encuesta Permanente de Hogares, Gran Buenos Aires: Información de prensa.* Buenos Aires: INDEC, 1999.

———. "Tasa de empleo específica por sexo y edad; primera onda del año." In *Encuesta Permanente de Hogares, Gran Buenos Aires: Información de prensa.* Buenos Aires: INDEC, 1999.

———. *Encuesta permanente de hogares (EPH): Tasa de empleo especifica por edad y sexo; Primera onda del año.* Buenos Aires: INDEC, 2000.

Instituto de Estudios Autonómicos. "El modelo policial y sus retos de futuro." Generalitat de Catalunya, Barcelona, 2000.

Inter-American Development Bank. *The Codigo Orgánico Procesal Penal.* Washington, DC: Inter-American Development Bank, 1998.

———. *Facing Up to Inequality in Latin America: Economic and Social Progress in Latin America, 1998–1999 Report.* Washington, DC: Inter-American Development Bank, 1998.

International Centre for Prison Studies. *World Prison Population List.* London: Kings College School of Law, 2005.

IUDOP. *Normas Culturales y Actitudes Sobre La Violencia: Estudio Activo.* San Salvador: IUDOP, 1999.

Johnson, Simon, Daniel Kaufmann, and Pablo Zoido-Lobatón. "Corruption, Public Finances, and the Unofficial Economy." Discussion paper. Washington, D.C.: The World Bank, 1998.

———. "Regulatory Discertion and the Unofficial Economy." *The American Economic Review* 88, no. 2 (1998): 387–92.

Justice Studies Center of the Americas (CEJA). *Reporte de la Justicia, Segunda Edición (2004–2005).* Santiago de Chile: CEJA, 2005.

Kahn, Túlio. "Policía comunitaria: evaluando la experiencia de Sao Paulo" ("Community Policing: Evaluating the Sao Paulo Experience"). In *Participación Ciudadana y Reformas a la Policía en América del Sur (Citizen Participation and Policing Reforms in South America),* ed. H. Frühling and A. Candina. Santiago de Chile: Center for Development Studies, 2004.

Katz, Jack. *Seductions of Crime: Moral and Sensual Attractions in Doing Evil.* New York: Basic Book, 1988.

Kelling, George L., and Catherine M. Coles. *Fixing Broken Windows: Restoring Order and Reducing Crime in Our Communities.* New York: Touchstone, 1996.

———. *No más ventanas rotas: El nuevo paradigma policiaco.* Mexico: Instituto Cultural Ludwing von Mises, 2001.

Kessler. G. *Sociología del delito amateur.* Buenos Aires: Paidós, 2004.

Lacko, M. "Hidden Economy in East-European Countries in International Comparison." Luxemburg: International Institute for Applied Systems Analysis (IIASA), 1996.

Land, Kenneth C., Patricia L. McCall, and Lawrence E. Cohen. "Structural Covariates of Homicide Rates: Are there Any Invariances across Time and Social Space?" *American Sociological Review* 95, no. 4 (1990): 922–63.

Langan, Patrick A., and Matthew R. Durose, Bureau of Justice Statistics, U.S. Department of Justice. "The Remarkable Crop in Crime in New York City." Paper prepared for the International Conference on Crime, Rome, December 3–5, 2003.

Leeds, Elizabeth. "Cocaine and Parallel Polities in the Brazilian Urban Periphery." *Latin American Research Review* 33, no. 3 (1996): 47–83.

Lemgruber, Julita. "The Brazilian Prison System: A Brief Diagnosis." Published in *Prisons in Crisis Project Report,* Latin American Studies Association, February 2005.

"Ley de Seguridad Pública del Distrito Federal." In *Diario Oficial de la Federación,* July 19, 1993.

Lipset, Seymour Martin. *Political Man: The Social Bases of Politics.* New York: Doubleday Anchor, 1959.

Lleras de la Fuente, C., et al. *Interpretación y génesis de la justicia en Colombia.* Bogota: Cámara de Comercio, 1992.

Loayza, N. V. "The Economics of the Informal Sector: A Simple Model and Some Empirical Evidence from Latin America." *Carnegie-Rochester Conference Service on Public Policy* 45 (1996): 129–62.

Lodoño, Juan L., and Rodrigo Guerrero. *Violencia en América Latina: Epidemiologia y Costos.* Washington, DC: Inter-American Development Bank, 1999.

López Portillo, Ernesto. "La policía en el Estado de Derecho Latinoamericano: el caso México." In *La Policía en los Estados de Derecho Latinoamericanos,* ed. Kai Ambos, Juan Luis Gómez Colomer, and Richard Vogler, 389–422. Bogotá: Instituto Max-Planck – Fundación Friedrich Ebert, 2003.

López Ugalde, José Antonio. *Violación de los derechos humanos en el ámbito de la seguridad pública en el Distrito Federal.* Mexico: Comisión de Derechos Humanos del Distrito Federal, 2003.

Lupsha, Peter A. "Transnational Organized Crime versus the Nation-State." *Transnational Organized Crime* 2, no. 1 (1996): 21–48.

Maguire, Mike, et al. "Crime, Statistics, Patterns and Trends." In *The Oxford Handbook of Criminology,* ed. Mike Maguire, Rod Morgan, and Robert Reiner. Oxford: Clarendon Press, 1997.

Maldonado Prieto, Carlos. "Los Carabineros de Chile: historia de una policía militarizada." *Nordic Journal of Latin American Studies* 20, no. 3 (1990): 3–31.

Matos Mar, José. *Crisis del estado y desborde popular.* Lima: Instituto de Estudios Peruanos, 1984.

Mazzuca, Sebastian. "Evolving Conceptions of Democracy: Access to Power versus Exercise of Power." Unpublished paper, Department of Political Science, University of California at Berkeley, 2000.

McFarlane, Anthony. "Political Corruption and Reform in Bourbon Spanish America." In *Political Corruption in Europe and Latin America,* ed. Walter Little and Eduardo Posada-Carbó. London: Macmillan Press, 1996.

Mello, Jorge et al. "Análise dos dados de mortalidade." *Revista de Saúde Pública* 31, no. 4 (1997): 5–25.

Mendonça, M. J. C., P. R. A. Loureiro, and A. Sachsida. "Criminalidade e desigualdade social no Brasil." IPEA discussion paper no. 967, Rio de Janeiro, 2003.

Mera Figueroa, Jorge. "Hacia una reforma de la justicia militar, delito militar, régimen disciplinario, competencia y organización." Cuadernos de Análisis Jurídico, Escuela de Derecho, Universidad Diego Portales, October 2002.

Merton, R. K. *Social Theory and Social Structure.* New York: Free Press, 1968.

Miller, Rory. "Foreign Capital, the State and Political Corruption in Latin America between Independence and the Depression." In *Political Corruption in Europe and Latin America,* ed. Walter Little and Eduardo Posada-Carbó. London: Macmillan Press, 1996.

Ministerio de Gobernación (MG), República de Guatemala. *Presupuestario general de ingresos y egresos del estado: Ejercicio fiscal 2005.* Guatemala City: MG, 2005.

Ministerio de Justicia. *Encuesta de Victimización para la Ciudad de Buenos Aires.* Dirección Nacional de Política Criminal, Buenos Aires, 2003.

Ministerio del Interior de Chile. *Informe anual de estadísticas comunales: Plan Integral de Seguridad Ciudadana.* Santiago de Chile: Ministerio del Interior, 1999.

———. *Encuesta comunal de victimización 2001: Plan Integral de Seguridad Ciudadana.* Santiago de Chile: Ministerio del Interior, 2001.

———. *Informe anual de estadísticas comunales: Plan Integral de Seguridad Ciudadana.* Santiago de Chile: Ministerio del Interior, 2001.

———. *Informe anual de estadísticas nacionales y regionales: Plan Integral de Seguridad Ciudadana.* Santiago de Chile: Ministerio del Interior, 2001.

———. *Encuesta comunal de victimización 2002: Plan Integral de Seguridad Ciudadana.* Santiago de Chile: Ministerio del Interior, 2002.

———. *Encuesta Nacional Urbana de Seguridad Ciudadana.* Santiago de Chile: Ministerio del Interior, 2004.

Ministerio del Interior-Carabineros. *Estudio de percepción y evaluación de la labor de Carabineros de Chile.* Santiago de Chile: Ministerio del Interior, 2003.

Ministry of the Interior, Forum of Experts on Citizen Security. "Diagnóstico de la seguridad ciudadana en Chile." Working paper no. 1, Santiago de Chile, 2003.

Ministry of Justice. *Victimization Survey 1995.* Buenos Aires: Ministry of Justice, 1995.

———. *Victimization Survey 1997.* Ministry of Justice: Buenos Aires, 1997.

———. *Hacia un plan nacional de política criminal (II).* Buenos Aires: Dirección de Política Criminal, 1998.

———. *Court Statistics 1999.* Buenos Aires: Ministry of Justice, 2000.

———. *Victimization Survey of the City of Buenos Aires.* Buenos Aires: Ministry of Justice, 2003.

Mohor Bellalta, Alejandra, and Víctor Covarrubias Suárez. *Reforma procesal penal y seguridad ciudadana: ¿cuál es la relación?* Santiago de Chile: CESC, 2006.

Moser, Caroline, and Bernice van Bronkhorst. "Youth Violence in Latin America and the Caribbean: Costs, Causes, and Interventions." LCR Sustainable Development working paper no. 3, Urban Peace Program Series. Washington, DC: World Bank, 1999.

Movimiento Autonomista Nación Camba. "Policía y Seguridad Ciudadana." January 22, 2002. Available at www.nacioncamba.net.

Muñoz, J. "La duración del proceso penal." *Derecho Penal y Criminología* 6, no. 15 (1980): 198–222.

Nagin, Daniel S., and Raymond Paternoster. "Enduring Individual Differences and Rational Choice Theories of Crime." *Law and Society Review* 27 (1993): 467–96.

Navas, Enrique. "Apreciación de la situación penitenciaria uruguaya." Montevideo, Uruguay: DGCPCR, 2004. Published in *Prisons in Crisis Project Report,* Latin American Studies Association, February 2005.

Neild, Rachel. *External Controls.* Washington, DC: Washington Office on Latin America (WOLA), 2000.

————. "Sustaining Reform: Democratic Policing in Central America." *Citizen Security Monitor,* October. Washington, DC: Washington Office on Latin America (WOLA), 2000.

North, Douglass C. *Institutions, Institutional Change and Economic Performance.* Cambridge: Cambridge University Press, 1990.

O'Brien R., J. Stockard, and L. Isaacson. "The Enduring Effect of Cohort Characteristics on Age-Specific Homicides Rates, 1960–1995." *American Jounal of Sociology* 104 (1999): 1061–95.

OCEI (Oficina Central de Estadística e Información). *Anuario Estadístico de Venezuela.* Caracas: OCEI, 1993, 1995, 2000.

O'Donnell, Guillermo. "Acerca del Estado, la democratización y algunos problemas conceptuales." *Desarrollo Económico* 33, no. 130 (1993): 164–74.

————. "Delegative Democracy." *Journal of Democracy* 5 (January 1994): 55–69.

————. "The State, Democratization, and Some Conceptual Problems (A Latin American View with Glances at Some Post-Communist Countries)." In *Latin American Political Economy in the Age of Neoliberal Reform,* ed. William C. Smith et al., 157–80. New Brunswick, NJ: Transactions Press, 1997.

————. "Poverty and Inequality in Latin America: Some Political Reflections." In *Poverty and Inequality in Latin America: Issues and Challenges,* ed. Viktor E. Tokman and Guillermo O'Donnell, 49–71. Notre Dame, IN: University of Notre Dame Press, 1998.

————. "Polyarchies and the (Un)Rule of Law in Latin America: A Partial Conclusion." In *The (Un)Rule of Law and the Underprivileged in Latin America,* ed. J. E. Mendez et al., 303–37. Notre Dame, IN: University of Notre Dame Press, 1999.

————. "Democracy, Law, and Comparative Politics." *Studies in Comparative International Development* 36, no. 1 (2001): 7–36.

Office of the Presidency of Mexico. *Encuestas cara a cara en viviendas sobre seguridad publica y seguridad en el D.F.* Surveys donated to CIDE.

Orlando, Leoluca. *Hacia una cultura de la legalidad: La experiencia Siciliana.* Mexico: Universidad Autónoma Metropolitana, 2004.

Ortega, Joel. "Informe de actividades de la Secretaría de Seguridad Pública: Marzo 2004–febrero 2005." Mexico: Gobierno del Distrito Federal, 2005.

Palmieri, Gustavo, Josefina Martínez, Máximo Sozzo, and Hernán Thomas. "Mecanismos de control interno e iniciativas de reforma en las instituciones policiales Argentinas: Los casos de la Policía Federal Argentina, la Policía de la Provincia de Santa Fé y la Policía de la Provincia de Buenos Aires" ("Internal Control Mechanisms and Argentine Reform Initiatives: The Cases of the Argentine Federal Police, the Provincial Police of Santa Fé and the Provincial Police of Buenos Aires"). In *Policía, Sociedad y Estado: Modernización y Reforma Policial en América del Sur (Police, Society and the State: Modernization and Police Reform in South America),* ed. Hugo

Frühling and Azun Candina, 177–220. Santiago: Center for Development Studies, 2001.

Pan American Health Organization (PAHO). *Health Situation in Latin America: Basic Indicators.* Washington, DC: PAHO, 1997.

Papadimitriou, Greta, et al. *Derechos humanos y seguridad pública.* Mexico: Instituto Estatal de Seguridad Pública de Aguascalientes, 2001.

Parás, Pablo, and Ken Coleman. "Cultura política de la democracia en México: 2006." Latin American Public Opinion Project, Mexico, 2006.

Pásara, Luís. "Justicia y ciudadanía realmente existentes." *Política y Gobierno* (Mexico City) 9, no. 2 (2002): 361–402.

———. ¿Cómo sentencian los jueces del Distrito Federal en materia penal?" Mexico, D.F.: Instituto de Investigaciones Jurídicas Universidad nacional Autónoma de México, 2006.

———. *La enseñanza del derecho en el Perú: su impacto sobre la administración de justicia.* Lima: Ministerio de Justicia, 2004.

———. "¿Lecciones aprendidas?" In *En busca de una justicia distinta: experiencias de reforma en América Latina,* ed. Luís Pásara, 515–70. Lima: Consorcio Justicia Viva, 2004.

Penal Reform International Newsletter 35. December 1999.

Penal Reform International Newsletter 36. March 1999.

Pereira, Anthony Wynne. "Public Security, Private Interests, and Police Reform in Brazil." Paper presented at the 26th International Congress of the Latin American Studies Association, San Juan, Puerto Rico, 2006.

Pérez, Gabriela. *Diagnóstico sobre la Seguridad Pública en México.* Mexico: Fundar, 2004.

Perry, Guillermo E. Poverty Reduction and Growth: Viruous and Vicious Circles. Washington, DC: World Bank, 2006.

Pew Surveys. *What the World Thinks in 2002: How Global Publics View their Lives, their Countries, the World, America.* December 2002, available at http://people-press.org/reports/pdf/165.pdf.

Phelan, J. L. *The Kingdom of Quito in the Seventeenth Century: Bureaucratic Politics in the Spanish Empire.* Madison: University of Wisconsin Press, 1967.

Piccato, P. *City of Suspects: Crime in Mexico, 1900–1931.* Durham, NC: Duke University Press, 2001.

Poder Ejecutivo de Baja California. *Primer Informe de Gobierno.* October 2002.

Portes, Alejandro. "Latin American Class Structures: Their Composition and Change during the Last Decades." *Latin American Research Review* 20, no. 3 (1985): 7–40.

———, and Kelly Hoffman. "Latin American Class Structures: Their Composition and Change during the Neoliberal Era." *Latin American Research Review* 38, no. 1 (2003): 41–82.

Programa de Educación y Acción en Derechos Humanos (PROVEA). *Informe Annual, 1999–2000*. Caracas: PROVEA, 2000.

Programa Nacional de Seguridad Pública 2001–2006. *Diario Oficial*. Mexico, January 14, 2003.

Quintana, Juan Ramón. "Bolivia: militares y policías." Unpublished manuscript. La Paz: Observatorio Democracia y Seguridad, 2004.

Ramirez, T., et al. "Tendencias y Causas del Delito Violento en el Distrito Federal de México." In Fanjnzylber, Lederman, and Loayza, eds. *Crímen y violencia en América Latina*.

Ramos Souza, Edinilsa, et al. "Análise temporal da mortalidade por causas externas no Brasil: décadas de 80 e 90." In *Violência sob o olhar da saúde: infrapolítica da contemporaneidade brasileira,* ed. Maria Cecília de Souza Minayo. Rio de Janeiro: Editora Fiocruz, 2003.

Recasens, Amadeu. "La seguridad, el sistema de justicia criminal y la policía." In *Sistema penal y problemas sociales,* ed. Roberto Bergalli et al., 287–313. Valencia: Tirant do Blanc, 2003.

Reiss, Albert J. "Delinquency as the Failure of Personal and Social Controls." *American Sociological Review* 16 (1951): 196–207.

Restrepo, Elvira María. *Colombian Criminal Justice in Crisis: Fear and Distrust*. New York: Palgrave, 2003.

Restrepo, Elvira María, and Mariana Martínez. "Impunidad penal: mitos y realidades." Documento CEDE, no. 24. Universidad de los Andes, Bogotá, June 2004.

Restrepo, Elvira María, et al. "Impunity or Punishment? An Analysis of Criminal Investigation into Kidnapping, Terrorism and Embezzlement in Colombia." *Global Crime Journal* 2 (Summer 2006): 179–99.

Restrepo, Elvira María, Fabio Sánchez, and Mariana Martinez. "¿Impunidad o castigo? Análisis e implicaciones de la investigación penal en secuestro, terrorismo y peculado." Documentos CEDE, no. 9. Bogotá: Universidad de los Andes, 2004.

Rico, José María, and Laura Chinchilla. *Seguridad Ciudadana en América Latina*. Mexico: Siglo XXI Editores, 2002.

Riego, Cristián. "Informe comparativo: proyecto seguimiento de los procesos de reforma judicial en América Latina." *Sistemas Judiciales* (Santiago de Chile) 2, no. 3 (2002): 12–58.

———, "Informe comparativo: Tercera etapa." In *Reformas procesales penales en América Latina: resultados del proceso de seguimiento,* ed. Juan Enrique Vargas, 13–31. Santiago: Centro de Estudios de Justicia de las Américas, 2005.

———, project coordinator. *Reformas procesales penales en América Latina: Resultados del Proyecto de Seguimiento, IV etapa*. Santiago: Centro de Estudios de Justicia de las Américas, 2007.

————, and Fernando Santelices. "Seguimiento de los procesos de reforma judicial en América Latina. Segundo informe comparativo." *Sistemas Judiciales* (Santiago de Chile) 3, no. 5 (2003): 34–76.

Ríos, Carlos. *La seguridad pública y la defensa de los derechos humanos en contextos desfavorables.* Mexico: Insyde, 2004.

Roberts, Julian V., and Loretta J. Stalans. "Crime, Criminal Justice, and Public Opinion." In *The Handbook of Crime and Punishment,* ed. M. Tonry, 112–29. Oxford: Oxford University Press, 1998.

Rothstein, Bo. *Social Traps and the Problem of Trust (Theories of Institutional Design).* Cambridge: Cambridge University Press, 2005.

Roxin, Claus. *Dogmática penal y política criminal.* Lima: IDEMSA, 1998.

Royg, Hugo. "Rehabilitación Carcelaria." Coordinador FPQ, Foro Nacional, June 21, 2002.

Salamanca, Fernando. "Análisis comparativo de sistemas de indicadores pertinentes a la relación entre policía y comunidad." Centro de Estudios en Seguridad Ciudadana, Universidad de Chile, Santiago de Chile, 2004.

Salvatore, Ricardo D., Carlos Aguirre, and Gilbert M. Joseph, eds. *Crime and Punishment in Latin America: Law and Society since Late Colonial Times.* Durham, NC: Duke University Press, 2001.

Sampson, Robert J. "Communities and Crime." In *Positive Criminology,* ed. Michael R. Gottfredson and Travis Hirschi, 519–51. Thousand Oaks, CA: Sage Publications, 1987.

————. "Urban Black Violence: The Effect of Male Joblessness and Family Disruption." *American Journal of Sociology* 93 (1987): 348–82.

Sampson, Robert J., and John H. Laub. *Crime in the Making: Pathways and Turning Points Through Life.* Cambridge: Harvard University Press, 1993.

Sampson, Robert J., Stephen W. Raudenbush, and Felton Earls. "Neighborhoods and Violent Crime: A Multilevel Study of Collective Efficacy." *Science Magazine* 277 (15 August 1997): 918–24.

Sampson, Robert J., and W. B. Grove. "Community Structure and Crime: Testing Social Disorganization Theory." *American Journal of Sociology* 94 (1989): 774–802.

Schneider, F., and D. Enste. *Increasing Shadow Economies All Over the World: Fiction or Reality.* Unpublished manuscript, University of Linz, Austria, 1998.

————. "Shadow Economies around the World: Size, Causes, and Consequences." IMF working paper WP/00/26, 2000.

Schuerman, Leo, and Solomon Kobrin. "Community Carreers in Crime." In *Crime and Justice,* vol. 8, edited by Michael Tonry and Norval Morris. Chicago: University of Chicago Press, 1986.

Scott, James C. "Handling Historical Comparisons Cross-Nationally." In *Political Corruption: A Handbook,* ed. Arnold J. Heidenheimer et al. New Brunswick, NJ: Transaction Publishers, 1999.

332   Bibliography

Secretaría de Seguridad Pública (SSP). "Estructura Orgánica." Unpublished manuscript, 2000.

———. "Reglas para el establecimiento y operación del sistema de carrera policial del D.F." Unpublished manuscript, 2000.

———. "Directrices de actuación policial." Unpublished paper. Mexico: SSP, 2001.

Servicio Paz y Justicia (SERPAJ) de Uruguay. *Situación Carcelaria: Noviembre 1996–Septiembre 1997.* Available at www.serpaj.org.uy/inf97/situacar.htm.

Shaw, Clifford R., and Henry D. McKay. *Juvenile Delinquency in Urban Areas.* Chicago: University of Chicago Press, 1942.

Sierralta, Ximena. "Cárceles en crísis: el caso de Perú." Published in *Prisons in Crisis Project Report,* Latin American Studies Association, February 2005.

Sims, Calvin. "On Every Argentine Cellblock, Specter of AIDS." *The New York Times,* March 22, 1996, 4.

Sisetma Nacional de Información Criminal. *Informe Annual, 1999.* Dirección de Política Criminal, Ministerio de Justicia, Buenos Aires, 1999.

Smulovitz, Catalina. "Citizen Insecurity and Fear: Public and Private Responses in Argentina." In *Crime and Violence in Latin America: Citizen Security, Democracy and the State,* ed. Hugo Frühling and Joseph Tulchin, 125–86. Washington, DC: Johns Hopkins University Press, 2003.

Sociedad Sin Violencia/PNUD. *Qué cuesta la violencia a El Salvador?* San Salvador: SSV/PNUD, 2005.

Souza, Edinilsa Ramos, et al. "Análise temporal da mortalidade por causas externas no Brasil: décadas de 80 e 90." In *Violência sob o olhar da saúde: infrapolítica da contemporaneidade brasileira,* ed. Maria Cecília de Souza Minayo. Rio de Janeiro: Editora Fiocruz, 2003.

Souza Minayo, Maria Ceilia de, et al. "Perfil de mortalidade por causas externas no Brasil: uma análise temporal das décadas de 80 e 90; Relatório de pesquisa." In *Violência sob o olhar da saúde: a infrapolítica da contemporaneidade brasileira,* ed. Maria Cecília de Souza Minayo and Edinilsa Ramos Souza, 83–108. Rio de Janeiro: Editora Fiocruz, 2003.

Suárez de Garay, María Eugenia. Los policías: Una averiguación antropológica, Guadalajara: ITESO, Universidad de Guadalajara, 2006.

Tanzi, Vito. *Policies, Institutions and the Dark Side of Economics.* Cheltenham: Edward Elgar, 2000.

Tello, Nelia. "La inseguridad pública desde lo social." Serie Insyde en la Sociedad Civil 7. Instituto para la Seguridad y la Democracia, México, 2005.

Tonry, Michael, and Norval Morris, eds. *Crime and Justice,* vol. 8. Chicago: University of Chicago Press, 1986.

Transparency International, 1995–2005. *Corruption Perception Index.* Berlin: Transparency International. Available at http://www.transparency.org/policy_and_research/surveys_indices/cpi.

United Nations Development Program (UNDP). *Desarrollo humano en Chile 1998: Las paradojas de la modernización.* Santiago de Chile: UNDP, 1998.

———. *UNDP Human Development Report.* Oxford: Oxford University Press, 1998.

Uprimny, Rodrigo. "Fiscal General o General Fiscal?" *Revista del Colegio de Abogados Penalistas del Valle* 29–30 (1995):15–23.

Varenik, Robert O., ed. *Accountability: Sistema policial de rendición de cuentas.* Mexico: CIDE-Insyde, 2005.

Vargas, Gonzalo. Remarks in *Seguridad ciudadana y reforma procesal penal.* Santiago de Chile: Fundación Paz Ciudadana, CEJA, Pontificia Universidad Católica de Chile, Universidad Diego Portales, 2006.

Vargas, Juan Enrique (ed.). *Reformas procesales penales en América Latina: resultados del proceso de seguimiento.* Santiago: Centro de Estudios de Justicia de las Américas, 2005.

———. Remarks in *Seguridad ciudadana y reforma procesal penal.* Santiago de Chile: Fundación Paz Ciudadana, CEJA, Pontificia Universidad Católica de Chile, Universidad Diego Portales, 2006.

Vilas, C. "Linchamiento: Venganza castigo e injusticia en escenarios de inseguridad." *El Cotidiano* 20 (2005): 20–26.

Vito, Gennaro F., and Ronald M. Holmes, eds. *Criminology: Theory, Research, and Policy.* Louisville, KY: University of Louisville Press, 1994.

Wacquant, Loïc. *Las cárceles de la miseria.* Buenos Aires: Manantial, 2000.

Walmsley, Roy. *World Prison Population List.* London: International Center for Prison Studies, Kings College School of Law, 2005.

Warr, Mark. "The Social Origins of Crime: Edwin Sutherland and Theory of Differential Association." In *Explaining Criminals and Crime,* ed. Raymond Paternoster and Ronet Bachman, 182–91. Los Angeles: Roxbury, 2001.

Whitehead, Lawrence. *Democratization: Theory and Experience.* Oxford: Oxford University Press, 2002.

Wilson, J., and R. Herrnstein. *Crime and Human Nature.* New York: Touchstone, 1985.

Wolfang, Marvin Eugene, and Franco Ferracuti. *The Subculture of Violence.* London: Tavistock, 1967.

World Health Organization. *Informe mundial sobre violencia y salud.* Washington, DC: WHO, 2002.

Yáñez, José Arturo. *Policía Mexicana, Plaza y Valdés.* Mexico: Universidad Autónoma Metropolitana, Xochimilco, 1999.

Zaluar, Alba. "Gangues, galeras e quadrilhas: globalização, juventude e violência." In *Galeras cariocas: territórios de conflitos e encontros culturais,* ed. H. Vianna, 180–215. Rio de Janeiro: Editora UFRJ, 1997.

Zepeda, Guillermo. *Crímen sin castigo.* Mexico City: Fondo de Cultura Económica, 2004.

————. *Los retos de la eficacia y la eficiencia en la seguridad ciudadana*, México D.F.: Fundación Friedrich Naumann, Centro de Investigación para el Desarrollo, 2006.

Zúñiga Rodríguez, Laura. *Política criminal*. Madrid: Colex. 2001.

————. "Viejas y nuevas tendencias políticocriminales en las legislaciones penales." In *Derecho penal liberal y dignidad humana,* ed. Fernando Velásquez Velásquez, 579–608. Bogotá: Editorial Temis S.A. 2005.

ELENA AZAOLA is senior investigator at the Center for Advanced Studies and Research in Social Anthropology located in Mexico City. She has a PhD in anthropology from the same institution, and AB and MA degrees from the Ibero-American University. She also graduated as a psychoanalyst. She has published more than one hundred works in Mexico, as well as in other countries (including Holland, Spain, Canada, Argentina, Brazil, the U.S., the UK, and Japan). Most of her research has been in the field of juvenile and women's justice institutions, violent crime, human rights, and violence.

JOHN BAILEY has a PhD from the University of Wisconsin–Madison. He is professor of government and foreign service at Georgetown University. With Lucía Dammert he co-edited *Public Security and Police Reform in the Americas* (University of Pittsburgh Press, 2006). His current research project is "Security Traps and Democratic Governability: Mexico in Comparative Perspective."

MARCELO BERGMAN has a PhD in sociology from the University of California, San Diego. He is a professor at CIDE in Mexico City. He chairs the Center for the Study of Public Security and the Rule of Law (PESED) and directs longitudinal victimizations and inmates surveys. His most recent publication is *Tax Evasion and the Rule of Law in Latin America: The Political Culture of Cheating and Compliance in Argentina and Chile* (Penn State University Press, 2009).

335

CLAUDIO CHAVES BEATO has a PhD in sociology from the Instituto Universitário de Pesquisas do Rio de Janeiro (IUPERJ), Rio de Janeiro, Brazil. He is director of the Center for Crime and Public Security Studies (CRISP) at the Universidade Federal de Minas Gerais. He is the author of more than forty scientific publications concerning the subjects of criminality, violence, and the public politics of security. He is interested in areas such as data analysis and management of information for public security; public politics of security, community, and crime; studies of police organizations; and management processes in public security.

FREDERICO COUTO MARINHO has a PhD in sociology from the Universidade Federal de Minas Gerais (UFMG), Brazil. He is researcher in criminal justice (juvenile justice) and criminology at the Center for Crime and Public Safety Studies (CRISP) linked to UFMG. He teaches a Specialization Course on Violence and Crime Studies. His most recent publication is "Freedom Assisted in the City of Belo Horizonte" (*Educação e Realidade* 33, no. 2, 2008).

LUCÍA DAMMERT is a PhD candidate in sociology at Leiden University, Holland. She has worked in several academic institutions in the U.S. and Argentina, and currently is the head of the Program of Security and Citizenship, FLACSO, Chile. She has published articles and books related to community participation, citizen security, and related urban matters in both national and international journals. Her most recent publications are "Perspectivas y dilemas de las seguridad ciudadana en América Latina" (FLACSO, Ecuador, 2007) and "Seguridad y Violencia: Desafíos para la Ciudadanía" (FLACSO, Chile, 2007).

HUGO FRÜHLING has a JD from the University of Chile, and an LLM and an SJD from Harvard Law School. He is currently a professor in the Public Affairs Institute of the University of Chile, and Director of the Center for the Study of Citizen Security of the University of Chile. He has published extensively on police reform in Latin America. His latest publication is *Police Accountability in a Democracy: A Proposal for Latin America* (INSYDE, CESC, and the Human Rights Commission of Mexico City, 2008, co-edited with Ernesto Lopez Portillo). ·

ANA LAURA MAGALONI has a PhD in law from the Universidad Autónoma de Madrid, Spain. She is currently an associate professor at CIDE, Mexico City, Law Department. Her contributions concentrate on constitutional law and judicial institutions in Mexico.

LUIS PÁSARA is a doctor in law (Pontificia Univeridad Católica del Perú) and has worked as a sociologist of law in Peru, Argentina, Guatemala, and Mexico, conducting empirical research on the functioning of justice systems and justice reforms. He is currently a Ramon y Cajal Researcher at the Universidad de Salamanca, Spain. He has recently edited *Los actores de la justicia latinoamericana* (Ediciones Universidad de Salamanca, 2007).

ELVIRA MARÍA RESTREPO holds a doctorate in politics from Oxford University and an LLM from Harvard Law School. She is currently a visiting professor in the Department of International Studies at the University of Miami. Her current research interests include comparative studies in criminal justice, crime, and conflict. Her latest publications include *Colombian Criminal Justice in Crisis: Fear and Distrust* (Palgrave, 2003) and "Security in Bogotá: Crime or More Fear of Crime" (*Desarrollo y Sociedad* 59, 2007). Forthcoming is a paper on transitional justice in the ongoing Colombian conflict.

MARK UNGAR has a PhD in political science from Columbia University. He is an associate professor of political science and criminal justice in the Graduate Center, City University of New York. His most important publications are: *Elusive Reform: Democracy and the Rule of Law in Latin America* (Lynne Rienner Publishers, 2002); *Violence and Politics: Globalization's Paradox* (Routledge, 2001); "The Privatization of Citizen Security in Latin America: From Elite Guards to Neighborhood Vigilantes" (*Social Justice* 34, nos. 3–4, 2007); "Policing Youth in Latin America," in *Youth and Violence in Latin America* (Palgrave, 2008); and *Policing Democracy: Overcoming Obstacles to Citizen Security in Latin America* (forthcoming).

LAURENCE WHITEHEAD is an Official Fellow in Politics at Nuffield College, Oxford University, and Senior Fellow of the College, and director of the Centre for Mexican Studies of Oxford University. His most recent books are *Latin America: A New Interpretation* (Palgrave, 2005); *State-Crafting Monetary Authority: Brazil in Comparative Perspective* (Brazilian Centre, 2006, with Lourdes Sola); and *Democratization: Theory and Experience* (Oxford University Press, 2002). His most recent edited books are *Unresolved Tensions: Bolivia under Evo Morales* (Pittsburg University Press, 2008, co-edited with John Crabtree) and *Debating Cuban Exceptionalism* (Palgrave 2006, co-edited with Burt Hoffmann).

abuse, 96–98, 109–11, 120, 128, 130, 168, 181, 220, 231, 240–42, 245, 253, 282, 304; of human rights, 19, 98, 223, 230; prosecutorial, 102, 252. *See also* police, abuse by

accountability, 9–14, 20, 96–99, 107, 246, 252, 266, 293, 308; for human rights, 170, 277–78; of the police, 93, 99, 104, 109–10, 113, 122, 140–41, 171

alcohol consumption, 42, 88, 137, 139–42, 149

alternative solutions, 214–15

Argentina, 5, 7, 15, 16, 41, 54–58, 64, 68, 72, 77, 79, 80, 82, 83, 85, 87, 94, 108–13, 124, 127, 131, 144, 217, 225, 228, 229, 231, 232, 234, 258, 259, 285, 287, 296, 299

armed forces, 13, 119–22, 128, 131, 140, 195–96

assault, 32, 33, 49, 65, 235, 253, 255, 267–68, 270–71, 274, 281, 292

Attorney General (Fiscalía General de la Nación), 18, 94, 106, 174–78, 182–93

authoritarian regimes, 2, 4, 9, 10–13, 108, 260, 277–78, 287, 306, 309

black figure, 51, 52

Brazil, 5, 7, 15, 27–29, 31, 32–33, 35, 37–38, 40–43, 58, 225–31, 233, 234, 258–60, 264, 278, 280–82, 285–88, 292, 296, 308

bribe, 13, 120, 124, 135, 172, 230, 253, 255, 264, 266, 268, 281

broken windows, 95

Buenos Aires, 6, 16, 57, 62–83, 85, 87, 88, 89, 96, 109, 111, 113, 118, 124, 126, 135, 214, 231, 266, 280

burglary, 53, 74, 127, 138, 140

Carabineros 17, 120, 124, 140, 141, 143, 145

Caracas, 6, 76, 101, 103, 115, 247, 318, 322, 328, 330

Chile, 5, 7, 10, 15, 17, 41, 47–60, 119, 120, 121, 124–27, 130–33, 140, 143, 181, 194, 211, 213–18, 225–31, 233–34, 257–59, 262, 263, 264, 285, 286, 296

citizenship, 21, 31, 279, 284–88, 292–97, 304, 306, 309

civil rights, 16, 95, 113, 252, 255, 306

civil society, 20, 130, 251–72

Colombia, 5, 7, 17, 31, 41, 56–58,
101, 107, 120, 124, 131, 173–76,
178, 180–82, 190, 194, 197–99,
211, 214–16, 219, 225, 228, 229,
230, 233–25, 258–59, 264–65,
270, 296, 301–3
community breakdown, 3, 8, 27,
81–88, 305
community policing, 16, 94, 96, 100,
108, 113, 123–24, 141
comparative perspective, 3, 9, 14,
48–49, 57, 63, 217, 257, 270,
272, 278
consolidation of democracy, 2–3,
170, 207, 256, 309
constitution, 12, 96–97, 102, 107,
128, 174–75, 179, 279, 305
corruption, 7, 19, 20, 42, 88, 119, 120,
127–28, 156–71, 209, 212, 215,
223, 251–73, 282–85, 290, 303,
304, 308; perceptions of, 120, 124,
257, 259; among police, 17, 81,
99, 104–5, 107, 109, 111, 120, 122,
124, 135, 136, 149–51, 156–64,
166–68; in prisons, 230, 245
Costa Rica, 5, 7, 58, 211, 214,
216–17, 285, 296; penitentiary
system of, 223–24, 225–26, 229
cost of crime, 18, 217
courts, 2, 4, 6, 53, 94, 95, 98, 106,
107, 110, 120, 124, 131, 132,
175, 177, 182, 188, 210, 237,
262, 304
crime control, 9–14; authoritarian
methods of, 291, 306; police role
in, 56, 131–32, 136, 181
crime rates, 16, 17, 42, 47–50, 56, 57,
59, 60, 62, 63, 68, 69, 77, 79, 83,
88, 109, 111, 121, 130, 135, 265,
270, 278, 290. See also violent
crimes, rates of
crime statistics, 4, 180, 280
crime waves, 3, 5, 122, 181

criminal justice system, 2, 10, 12, 14,
17–19, 59, 93–94, 119–20, 175–6,
194, 204, 217–18, 220, 223–24,
235, 243–44
criminal law, 112, 205
Cuba, 225–30, 234, 247, 323

decentralization, 93, 137, 143, 260,
303
delinquency, 29–31, 79, 83–88, 95,
104, 170, 245, 265, 280, 312
democratic regimes, 11, 13, 20, 244,
253, 268, 274, 292, 309
democratic values, 9, 21, 294
democratization, 5, 11, 14, 20, 120,
170, 282, 285, 288, 293–97, 303,
305, 309
Dominican Republic, 122, 211, 215,
265, 285–86, 296
drug consumption, 33, 42, 54, 83, 89,
142, 149, 298
drug trafficking, 41, 42, 89, 121, 131,
220, 300, 304
due process, 16, 19, 93, 96, 107,
113, 223–24, 228, 239, 241,
243–44

economic liberalization, 105, 278–79,
295
Ecuador, 5–7, 58, 211, 214, 216, 217,
225, 229, 232, 234, 285, 286, 296,
311, 336
education, 8, 27, 53, 54, 74–77, 94,
98, 107, 109, 110, 112, 141, 206,
231, 265, 286, 290–91
elections, 9, 11, 207, 278–79, 310
El Salvador, 5, 7, 56, 58, 101, 211,
214, 265, 270, 280, 282, 286, 291;
police reform in, 120–24; prisons
in, 225, 229, 234; youth violence
in, 291, 298–302
extortion, 105, 163, 165, 177, 268,
270, 283, 299

family, 3, 7, 16, 27, 29, 30, 31, 83, 85,
    86, 87, 108, 127, 138, 140, 142,
    153, 157, 159, 179, 181, 205, 228,
    230, 232, 256, 269, 275, 278, 299
fear of crime, 6, 14–15, 27, 48–49,
    53–55, 58–60, 69, 127, 141, 194,
    269, 289–90
firearm homicides, 28, 35–41
firearms, 28, 35, 36, 38, 40, 42, 64,
    76, 87, 98, 102, 103, 111, 236,
    282, 302
Fiscalía General de la Nación.
    See Attorney General (Fiscalía
    General de la Nación)

gangs, 1, 6, 29, 41, 97, 121, 137, 139,
    140, 228, 238, 270–72, 284, 287,
    289, 291, 292, 298, 299, 302, 304
gated communities, 6–7
Guatemala, 5, 7, 58, 121–22, 211,
    214, 217, 225, 226, 229, 230, 234,
    265, 270, 296
guns. See firearms

homicide, 3, 15, 22, 28, 29, 32, 33, 35,
    36, 37, 38, 40, 42, 43, 49, 56, 60,
    64, 66, 67, 71, 77, 127, 130, 181,
    195–96, 210, 235, 253, 260, 267;
    homicide rates, 28, 33, 36, 38, 43,
    49, 56, 77, 260
Honduras, 7, 58, 94, 97, 100, 103,
    108, 112, 121, 211, 214, 225,
    227–31, 233, 234, 285, 286, 296
human rights, 17, 19, 95, 103,
    114, 123, 126, 128, 130, 212,
    277–79, 289; community, 10, 12;
    officials, 98, 100, 111; standards,
    2, 104, 170

imprisonment, 19, 98, 189–90, 226,
    244. See also incarceration
impunity, 10, 12, 18, 42, 116, 122,
    162, 174, 176, 179–96, 198, 209,

210, 215, 220, 235, 244, 272,
    282–83, 303, 306, 308
incarceration, 224, 226, 243, 245, 247
inequality, 20, 28, 30, 59, 109, 206,
    244, 252, 262, 265, 279, 283, 285,
    293, 294, 296, 297, 308
information, 4, 13–15, 31, 48, 49,
    51, 56, 59, 63–66, 72, 77, 78, 80,
    97, 99, 103, 108, 128, 129, 139,
    141–43, 166, 176, 208, 209, 215,
    216, 224, 231, 236, 239–41, 253,
    255, 282, 290, 300, 308
inmates, 13, 89, 221, 224–28, 230–33,
    235–46
inmate surveys, 236–43
inquisitorial systems, 18, 108, 173,
    175, 210–18

judges, 10–13, 97–98, 103, 110–11,
    132, 174–75, 190, 194–97, 207,
    220, 237, 239, 244, 283–84, 303
judicial backlog, 174–79
judicial procedure, 55, 94, 108,
    174–76, 182, 198, 239, 241, 261;
    reform of, 119, 126, 210–14, 220

kidnapping, 69, 71, 110–11, 198, 215,
    220, 237–39, 268, 280–83

labor market, 16, 64, 79–87
law and order, 6, 9, 223, 246, 279,
    287, 289, 290, 297, 301, 303–5
law enforcement, 8, 97, 103–7, 203,
    205, 252, 284–86, 288, 303–4
legitimacy, 14, 18, 20, 130, 174, 195,
    198, 253, 256, 260, 271, 273–75,
    280, 292, 297, 303
longitudinal analyses of crime rates,
    48, 51, 60, 63, 79

mano dura, 2, 13, 94, 95, 97, 98, 100,
    103, 109, 110, 123, 291, 299, 305,
    306

media, 5, 47, 56, 68, 97–98, 123, 162
metropolitan areas, 28–29, 33,
    41–43, 67, 73, 111, 131, 257, 260,
    265–66, 272
Mexico, 5, 6, 7, 15, 16, 17, 22, 23, 41,
    54, 58, 62–69, 71–87, 124, 126,
    147–71, 181, 208, 209, 211, 214,
    225–27, 229, 234–37, 239, 241–44,
    246, 266, 273, 280–87, 291, 292,
    296, 298, 299, 301, 302, 303
Mexico City, 6, 15, 16, 17, 62, 66, 67,
    71, 72, 73, 74, 77, 78, 83, 84, 85,
    87, 147, 148, 149, 169, 170, 226,
    266, 273, 280, 283

new democracies, 9–10, 14, 21, 243,
    303, 309
Nicaragua, 7, 41, 58, 214, 225, 229,
    232, 234, 270, 296
nunca mas, 277, 279

offenders, 64, 87, 183, 224, 240,
    243–45, 248; petty offenders, 13,
    19, 180, 226, 231, 235–38, 245
oral trials, 94, 108, 212
organized crime, 13, 18, 42, 58

Panama, 5, 7, 58, 121, 225, 226, 229,
    234, 285, 286, 296
Paraguay, 5, 7, 58, 120, 124, 285, 296;
    criminal reform in, 211, 214, 217;
    prisons in, 225, 229, 232–34
penal codes, 11, 95, 125, 139, 142, 148
penal process codes, 93–98, 102, 107,
    183
penal reform, 18, 96
penitentiary systems, 13, 19, 109,
    223–26, 229, 231, 233, 243,
    244–46, 282. See also prisons
perceptions of crime, 1, 2, 5–7, 13,
    47, 38, 52, 54, 58–70, 72, 73, 126,
    210, 222, 257, 269–72, 280, 285,
    289–91, 297, 301, 309

personal crimes, 49–50, 57
Peru, 7, 41, 58, 107, 144, 211, 225,
    226, 227, 228, 229, 231, 234, 258,
    259, 263, 265, 270, 285, 296, 311,
    316, 337
police, 2–7, 10–11, 13, 15, 47–49,
    53, 55, 143–71, 180–82, 192,
    194, 206, 213, 220, 232, 242, 256,
    257, 260–65, 267, 269, 279–81,
    284, 288, 289, 291–92, 303–4,
    307–8; abuse by, 95–96, 101,
    107, 109, 110, 120, 122, 130, 240;
    academies, 106, 111–12, 121–22,
    156; data collection by, 32, 33, 48,
    51, 56; detentions by, 239–41; and
    gangs, 140, 271–72; of Mexico
    City, 147–72; military police, 101,
    230, 282; in prisons, 227–28, 230,
    235; reform of, 16–17, 42, 93–113,
    218, 305–6; trust in, 7, 47, 58, 97,
    100, 103–4, 119–20, 124–26, 130,
    132–35, 143–64, 168–70, 264–65.
    See also Carabineros; community
    policing; corruption, among
    police
political parties, 12, 95, 101, 257, 277
poverty, 8, 20, 28, 29, 30, 42, 54, 59,
    62, 79, 86, 88, 109, 205, 206, 219,
    252, 279, 283, 285, 286, 291, 293,
    294, 295, 296
prisons, 11, 19, 42, 99, 105, 164, 174,
    189, 189–92, 223–39, 243–5, 282;
    conditions in, 223–28, 232–35;
    overcrowding in, 223–27, 244–46;
    prisoner health, 224, 233–34;
    populations of, 174, 194, 235–39;
    prisoner rehabilitation, 19, 223,
    226, 244–46
private security, 6–8, 55, 159, 281, 289
property crime, 1, 49, 50, 66
prosecutors, 10–13, 94, 98, 102,
    108, 110, 117, 174, 175, 180, 183,
    194–99, 213–16, 239, 242, 244

public health, 27, 53–54
public order, 11, 95, 125, 139, 142, 148
punishment, 18–19, 55, 204–10, 214,
    219, 236, 244–45

qualitative data, 4, 20
quality of democracy, 9, 14, 20–22,
    251, 272, 294
Quito, 6, 247, 319, 329

rape, 23, 33, 253, 268, 271, 280
reform of criminal proceedings, 204,
    210–20
regimes, 1, 9, 11, 12, 13, 17, 20, 108,
    125, 126, 131, 149, 158, 171,
    173, 207, 244, 251, 253, 255–57,
    260, 262, 263, 266, 267, 269, 270,
    271–73, 288, 292–93, 306, 309
reported crimes, 15, 47–50, 52–53,
    56, 67, 70–71, 180, 209, 281
robbery, 60, 89, 127, 141, 142, 145,
    235, 253, 266, 270, 271, 280, 299,
    301, 311
rule of law, 3, 8, 14, 21, 22, 130, 170,
    174, 194, 199, 203, 207, 212, 235,
    244, 286, 287, 288, 306, 311
rural areas, 6, 43, 67, 105–6, 282,
    286, 293–94

Santiago, 6, 48, 50, 57, 131, 262, 273
Sao Paulo, 32, 33, 36, 43, 57, 124,
    226, 228, 273, 281, 282
semi-accusatorial systems, 18, 175
sentencing, 94, 111, 131–32, 182–83,
    208–9, 211, 226–29, 235–39, 283
social control, 30, 81, 87
social disorganization, 28, 29, 42
state, the, 1–4, 8, 14, 16, 19, 20, 43,
    81, 83, 86, 101, 105, 107, 132, 144,
    148, 175, 197–98, 203, 204, 206,
    217, 218, 223, 228, 229, 234, 251,
    260, 261, 263, 266, 269, 270–75,
    277, 283, 286, 287, 288, 289, 290,
293, 294, 295, 299, 301, 304–9;
    authority of, 2, 4, 94, 98–99,
    292; capacities of, 8–9, 14, 95,
    259, 262; failed state, 20, 257;
    institutions of, 13, 20, 62, 82, 131,
    207, 244, 252–53, 256, 262, 267,
    281–82, 292, 303; intervention by,
    1, 278; officials of, 4, 9, 94, 98–99;
    responses by, 3, 8, 55; rogue actors
    in, 255, 256; strong state, 8, 95;
    weak state, 3, 8; welfare state, 79
Supreme Court, 12, 133, 281

terrorism, 14, 107, 177, 200, 274, 290
theft, 32, 33, 49, 50, 53, 55, 57, 60, 67,
    71, 74, 84, 127, 145, 181, 235–38,
    275, 301; car theft, 52, 57, 220,
    238
torture, 19, 32, 223, 239, 240, 245,
    277, 282
transition to democracy, 12–14, 101,
    104, 120, 128, 140, 173, 251, 265,
    279, 293, 295, 298, 306
truth telling, 277

underclass, 7, 16, 88, 244
unemployment, 8, 16, 28, 54, 64, 71,
    73, 79, 80–87, 109, 113, 131, 132,
    194, 266, 278; youth unemploy-
    ment, 16, 80, 83, 86–87, 278
urbanization, 29, 36, 278
Uruguay, 5, 7, 58, 225, 227, 229, 234,
    247, 257, 258, 259, 264, 285, 296,
    327, 332

Venezuela, 5, 7, 94, 96, 100–103, 211,
    214, 217, 225, 226, 227, 229, 233,
    234, 258, 259, 280, 285, 296
victimization, 4, 31, 47–55, 59, 65,
    73–77, 120, 126–39, 170, 181–82,
    192, 276; rates of, 52, 57; victim-
    ization surveys, 5, 15, 49, 51,
    127–29, 181–82

violence, 1, 4, 15, 20, 22, 29, 30, 32,
43, 47, 50, 60, 67, 103, 104, 105,
106, 127, 130, 181, 207, 251, 252,
280, 293, 305; against judges,
196–97; causes of, 15, 28–29, 32,
41–43, 260, 262, 265–66, 286;
diffuse, 267–70; in the family,
100, 108, 138, 140, 142; and
firearms, 28, 26, 40; and gangs,
41, 228, 270–72, 289, 300, 302;
perceptions of, 13, 27, 31, 52, 269,
297; by police, 100, 104–6, 130,
268; and police reforms, 42, 94,
113; in prisons, 224, 227, 228,
231, 244, 287; relationship to
crime, 253–59; and youth, 29,
40, 87, 299
violent crimes, 15, 16, 28, 29, 32,
52, 55–56, 59, 65–68, 97, 101,
121, 218, 255, 260, 262, 266–67,
269–70, 286, 305; rates of ,
28–29, 32, 52, 56, 65, 57, 97, 101,
262, 286, 304. *See also* assault,
homicide, rape, robbery

zero tolerance, 95, 113, 248n37, 299

www.ingramcontent.com/pod-product-compliance
Lightning Source LLC
Chambersburg PA
CBHW061001280326
41935CB00009B/782

LYRICAL-ANALYSIS

LYRICAL-ANALYSIS

The Unconscious Through *Jane Eyre*

Angelyn Spignesi

Chiron Publications • Wilmette, Illinois

Library of Congress Catalog Card Number: 89-25217

Printed in the United States of America.
Book design by Siobhan Drummond Granner and Nancy R. Snyder.

Library of Congress Cataloging-in-Publication Data:
Spignesi, Angelyn
    Lyrical-analysis : the unconscious through Jane Eyre / Angelyn Spignesi.
        p. cm.
    Includes bibliographical references.
    ISBN 0-933029-54-3 : $16.95
    1. Brontë, Charlotte, 1816-1855. Jane Eyre. 2. Psycho analysis and literature. 3. Subconsciousness in literature. I. Title.
PR4167.J5S65 1990
823'.8 – dc20   89-25217
                                                             CIP

ISBN 0-933029-54-3

For my father, Giro

Contents

Introduction 1

    Language 9

    Metaphysics and the Authority of Legitimization 16

    Transference/Countertransference 26

Chapter 1:   Windowseat 33

Chapter 2:   Mirrored Phantom 45

Chapter 3:   Apothecary 63

Chapter 4:   Black Pillar 85

Chapter 5:   Lowood 113

Chapter 6:   Helen Burns 129

Chapter 7:   Natural Curl 143

Chapter 8:   The Seed-Cake 169

Chapter 9:   Crib White Curtain Covering 187

Chapter 10:   Pillowed Voice of Advertisement 207

Chapter 11:   Thornfield 227

Chapter 12:   Gytrash 249

Chapter 13:   Men in Green 273

Chapter 14:   Restory 291

Afterword I 313

Afterword II 333

Acknowledgments

Writing a work such as this, which is a detailed analysis of the unconscious (exploring its meanings, its language), involves a long solitary stay in the unconscious. The seeds of this project began in 1981, and, since fall 1982, I have been working on this book which required years of living in and traversing through regions of the unconscious. In many ways, I was guarded and guided "spiritually" during these years. I'm fairly certain that Brontë herself was a constant guardian, and for that I'm extremely grateful: it could not have been done without a sort of felt dialogue between us.

Such a work requires much silence and hermetic sealing and is not something in which others really can participate: this one required these seven private years of distillation, coagulation, refinement of word and rhythm, etc. The first people to read the manuscript were the publishers to whom I sent it when it was completed. Yet there were those who witnessed: my family somehow understood that day after day, year after year, I had to write in isolation a text which may or may not be inaccessible and/or misunderstood; also a few close friends were supportive during this work which really could not be shared as well as my loneliness which very often was — and for that I'm deeply appreciative. Also over the years I was given support through reading drafts of singular chapters to the Connecticut Association for Jungian Psychology, a seminar on French feminism at Yale University, the Pittsburgh Jung Society, the National Women's Studies Association at the University of Illinois, and the Wainwright Institute of Depth Psychology.

Once the book was finished, there came unexpected and very helpful assistance in the publishing process. Edward S. Casey reviewed the Introduction sections, Afterword I, and Chapters 1 and 2, suggested that I not alter them, and gave me detailed information concerning publishing houses which was a crucial motivating force in my getting underway the publishing procedure. Patricia E. Sabosik took professional risks in endorsing, in the publishing world, such a work that could not be easily "categorizable," and also offered me much support and guidance throughout the publishing procedure, for which I am very grateful. Nathan Schwartz-Salant, a publisher to whom I sent the manuscript, though a stranger to me and my work, immediately appreciated the findings on the unconscious in the work as well as the place of language in it, and he offered me complete editing rights which was a decisive factor in the choice of a publication route. Both he and Murray Stein have been open and sensitive to the nuances involved in my writing such a book, and helped to make its publication much easier than it could have been otherwise. For her love of the music of language and her overall precision, a bow of gratitude to Siobhan Granner, Managing Editor at Chiron Publications, as well as her assistant Ellen Keith who made most of the editing suggestions. Ms. Granner oversaw the entire publishing project with extreme skillfulness and calm. Imagine what it would be like to type a few pages of this text, and here is the good-hearted fortitude, clear mindedness, and technical ability of Debbie Sestito who typed the entire manuscript.

Introduction

In Brontë-esque fashion, this work begins with its negative, with what it is not. It is not an attempt to construct classifications of the novel in order to displace previous ones; it is not an exploration of the epistemological structures of rhetorical tropes or the development of a system of relations between figure and sign, sign and referent. One can locate here a certain analysis of rhetorical tropes and issues pertinent to "representation," yet its primary attempt is to study the unconscious of a woman in its own terms without appropriating that unconscious to conscious structures, that is, models of conscious thought.

Whose terms? What unconscious? What is a female unconscious? To that arises the now commonplace question: is she one or does she have one?[1] She has been so occupied being the unconscious of Western culture that she has only begun to step out of her position as the "unruffled surface" reflection of man's "Other" and venture into her own.[2]

During the years the Brontës lived, it was particularly necessary that a woman physically extricate herself from men and society to explore her

---

[1] This question — "Is woman the unconscious or does she have one?" — is Luce Irigaray's addressed to Jacques Lacan, which is discussed by her in *This Sex Which Is Not One*, trans. Catherine Porter (Ithaca, N.Y.: Cornell University Press, 1985), p. 60–61, 123ff. His response, in *Encore: Le séminaire XX, 1972-3* (Paris: Seuil, 1975), which in part is translated as "God and the *Jouissance* of the Woman" and "A Love Letter," trans. Jacqueline Rose, in *Feminine Sexuality: Jacques Lacan and the école freudienne*, eds. Juliet Mitchell and Jacqueline Rose, (New York: Norton, 1982), is further discussed by Alice Jardine in *Gynesis: Configurations of Woman and Modernity* (Ithaca, N.Y.: Cornell University Press, 1985), p. 168.

[2] See Lacan's discussion of imago and the "pure mirror of an unruffled surface" in "Aggressivity in Psychoanalysis," in *Écrits: A Selection*, trans. Alan Sheridan (New York: Norton, 1977), p. 15. Also his view of woman as Other in the sexual relation and with regard to what can be said of the unconscious, in "A Love Letter": "By her being in the sexual relation radically Other, in relation to what can be said of the unconscious, the woman is that which relates to this Other" (p. 151). Jane Gallop discusses this "unruffled surface" and the distinction of likeness and mirror in *Reading Lacan* (Ithaca, N.Y.: Cornell University Press, 1985), p. 62.

unconscious, the "unthought"[3] of the philosophical systems governing thought, and articulate the findings. It is not an arbitrary occurrence that all Brontë sisters wrote their novels sequestered and unmarried, not in broad social relation. Charlotte Brontë came the closest to such intercourse, and her (forced) extrication from that became the initiation of her novels, pen to the blank page entry to know it instead of being his.[4]

In this work, I take a different position than do others interested in the "feminine" unconscious. To the question about an unconscious which would be a woman's, Luce Irigaray suggests that since the feminine may be included in the unconscious (that it pertains to what is operating in the name of the unconscious), we first need to determine what the unconscious has borrowed from the feminine before we can arrive at a question of a feminine unconscious.[5] She also raises the issue that since the unconscious is a property of discursive logic, still belonging to that system as do others misrecognized by it (savages, children, insane, women), it remains as an outside-other which that primary system continues to appropriate thematically as "object" without eradicating completely its (inferior) difference.[6]

It cannot be denied that the study of *any* unconscious has to occur within the context of the conscious system of discourse, but from the beginning of this study, I have refused to translate or return the workings of the unconscious to that system of discursive thought or even its syntax. My sense is that to continue to study the unconscious as it is now defined (in Freudian and Jungian schools) in order to ascertain what it has repressed of the feminine is to use the prior as primary. That is, to begin from an unconscious explored by male theorists, the unconscious of the theoretical man, to find what it contains of the feminine (and it must since the unconscious consists of un-conscious, other-gender material), requires essentially keeping it a study of man: the base would still be the classical philosophical tradition, a classical unconscious.

Instead, I have preferred peering strategically into the unconscious of a woman, which I have found to be quite different from a feminine uncon-

---

[3]See Jardine (*Gynesis*, p. 92ff) on the exploration of the "unthought" which master discourses of the West have had to confront since the 19th century.
[4]The biographies on Charlotte Brontë which I read for this study are the following: Elizabeth Gaskell, *The Life of Charlotte Brontë* (Baltimore: Penguin Books, Inc., 1975); Helen Moglen, *Charlotte Brontë: The Self Conceived* (New York: Norton, 1978); Winifred Gerin, *Charlotte Brontë: The Evolution of Genius* (London: Oxford University Press, 1967); Margot Peters, *Unquiet Soul: A Biography of Charlotte Brontë* (New York: Atheneum, 1986).
[5]Irigaray, *This Sex*, pp. 122–23.
[6]Ibid., p. 124.

scious or the feminine component of the unconscious of a man. Therefore, I prefer to call it a female unconscious, an unconscious of those who are literal women.[7] My sense is that those studying the unconscious and its relation to body have been so threatened by the essentialism critique,[8] and of the body's power to literalize (that is, paralyze) psychological thought, that they have not respected the almost commonplace idea that psyches work through bodies and bodies are a manifestation of psyche, not its destiny but its *speaking*, a discourse of the very unconscious we claim to be studying.

I am not, however, suggesting that man and woman exist outside the symbolic register (linguistic, social, aesthetic, theoretical, economic, and political frames of reference), or that they can be excluded from it. Instead, I am indicating that the literal woman and her body must be used as base for formulations of the unconscious and its symbolic registers.

Therefore, my starting point is not the classical unconscious with an attempt to disconnect what is feminine from its current economy, but the unconscious of a woman, the writing of a woman who so precisely articulated her unconscious that she arrived at aspects of *the* female unconscious

---

[7]Note the difference between this question and the one Jardine raises:
"What exactly is the metaphorization process surrounding the term 'woman' in contemporary French theory? While avoiding a certain (primarily American) biologistic psychology, one-to-one correspondence of the sign, as well as the notion of a woman's world as separate cultural space or identity, to what extent can we speak of 'woman' *without* referring to the biological female?" (italics hers), in *Gynesis*, pp. 42–43. Also the difference between it and Irigaray's statement: "They should not put it, then, in the form 'What is woman?' but rather, repeating/interpreting the way in which, within discourse, the feminine finds itself defined as lack, deficiency, or as imitation and negative image of the subject, they should signify that with respect to this logic a *disruptive excess* is possible on the feminine side" (italics hers), *This Sex*, p. 78.

[8]On the animadversion to the biological essentialism of Cixous's *l'écriture féminine* and her response to it, see Sandra Gilbert's introduction to Hélène Cixous and Catherine Clément, *The Newly Born Woman*, trans. Betsy Wing (Minneapolis: University of Minnesota Press, 1986), p. xvff. Ironically, Frank Lentricchia criticizes Gubar and Gilbert's, particularly Gilbert's, feminism as "a new name for essentialist humanism," in "Patriarchy Against Itself — The Young Manhood of Wallace Stevens," *Critical Inquiry* 13 (1987), particularly pp. 773–786. I, too, take issue with some of their work, but the tone of his article is disturbing, next to which the following article of Joan DeJean, "Fictions of Sappho," discussing the Phaethon complex of sons critical of recent feminist theorists, is quite satisfying.

which still informs us over a century and a half later.[9] I begin with the premise that if *Jane Eyre* is the manifestation of *a* female unconscious, which because of its acuity and depth, is informative of *the* female unconscious, a study of *that* female unconscious would require the same royal road as any,

----

[9]The assumption that a classical piece of literature pertains to a study of the unconscious is derived from the work of Freud and Jung. C. G. Jung discussed how the fantasy occurrences which make up the "transcendent function" (which mediates the transition between conscious and unconscious contents) appear spontaneously in dreams and visions and are also the basis of literature, in fact, the productive activity of the unconscious is responsible for major works of creativity. See C. G. Jung, "Symbols of Transformation," in *The Collected Works of C. G. Jung*, vol. 5 (Princeton, N.J.: Princeton University Press, 1976), pp. 3–7, 34–39. Subsequent references to Jung's writings will be to the volumes of *The Collected Works* hereafter abbreviated *CW*. See also, *CW* 6, p. 63; *CW* 7, pp. 80, 96, 175, 180ff, 207, 299; *CW* 8, pp. 84ff, 204. On his discussion of the figures of the unconscious, the *dramatis personae*, see *CW* 14, p. 529, and *The Visions Seminars, Book One* (Zurich: Spring Publications, 1976), p. 56.

Interestingly, a piece of literature was the content of Freud's and Jung's correspondence literally. Jung brought the "Pompeian phantasy" *Gradiva* by Wilhelm Jensen to Freud's attention, and, during the summer of 1906, months before the two met one another, Freud wrote an interpretation of that work ("Jensen's Gradiva" — his first published analysis of a work of literature). In his preface to that work, which he referred to as "genuinely poetic material" (p. 10), Freud states: "For when an author makes the characters constructed by his imagination dream, he follows the everyday experience that people's thoughts and feelings are continued in sleep and he aims at nothing else than to depict his heroes' states of mind by their dreams" ("Jensen's Gardiva," in *The Standard Edition of the Complete Psychological Works*, IX (London: Hogarth, 1959), p. 8. Subsequent references to Freud's writings will be to the volumes of *The Standard Edition*, published by the Hogarth Press between 1953 and 1981, hereafter abbreviated *S.E.* See also pp. 41–44 in the same volume and pp. 91–92, where he states that the creative writer and the analyst draw from the same source and work on the same object: "[The author] directs his attention to the unconscious in his own mind, he listens to its possible developments and lends them artistic expression instead of suppressing them by conscious criticism. Thus he experiences from himself what we learn from others — the laws which the activities of this unconscious must obey" (p. 92).

In a very different context, Jardine states: "For to question figurability, the symbolic status of the image, the paths and impasses of narrative, and so on — to work at the edges of the unnameable — *is* to deal with literature, with the literary substance itself." *Gynesis*, p. 89.

that is, through the dream, so that each chapter will be "read" as a dream.[10]

For about a century now, the tools for dream interpretation have been attained through the meticulous exploration by men of their own unconscious, most notably by Sigmund Freud and C. G. Jung. Could aspects of their tools be used in such a study without confounding those techniques with their findings? It is not a matter of stepping outside their tradition, but of using their tools in exploring spaces "beyond" it. The methodology of dream interpretation employed in this study was a result of an engagement of both Freudian and Jungian schools. From Freudian interpretation, I use the method of segregating the dream-text into its distinct elements and applying free association.[11] Unlike Freudian interpretation, however, I do not consider the manifest text to conceal latent thoughts; rather, the associations themselves reveal the unconscious meaning already residing within the manifest text. The sense is that the dream (or literary) images are not rebuses, arbitrarily connected to one another,[12] but that each image both in its meaningful association to the next and its meaning within itself elaborates the signification of the dream instead of having a dissimilar referent beyond itself to which it latently points.

The latter issue is derived from Jungian methodology, which also advo-

---

[10]Freud, *S.E.* V, p. 608. "*The interpretation of dreams is the royal road to a knowledge of the unconscious activities of the mind*" (italics his). This, of course, is Freud's great discovery. The integrity and thoroughness with which he scrutinized the dream, and through that the unconscious, has been quite important to me particularly at certain crossover periods. I agree with Clément's position regarding him: "It is good enough that, even if unwittingly, he has given us the instruments for thinking of these changes, of their limits, and of something else that may break open these limits." *Newly Born Woman*, p. 49.

[11]Freud, on "free association": "The adoption of the required attitude of mind towards ideas that seem to emerge 'of their own free will' and the abandonment of the critical function that is normally in operation against them . . ." *S.E.* IV, pp. 102-104, 241-242, 280-281; *S.E.* V, pp. 527-532, 635-641; *S.E.* XXII, pp. 10-13.

[12]On dream as rebus that is, "a picture-puzzle" which is nonsensical in itself: Freud, *S.E.* IV, pp. 277-278; Lacan, "Agency of the Letter in the Unconscious," in *Écrits: A Selection*, p. 159; and for an example of a Lacanian dream interpretation based on this principle that the value of the image as signifier in no way pertains to its signification: David W. Stewart, "Lacan's Linguistic Unconscious and the Language of Desire," *The Psychoanalytic Review* 73 (1986), 17-30.

cates the amplification of images.[13] The form of amplification I have employed in this study, however, pertains more to the "intertextuality" discussed by Freudian critics and others;[14] that is, it is taken primarily from other texts to which Brontë referred or actually quoted within her own. Therefore, I am proposing an intertextuality construed as amplification: the positing of an intertextuality which does not preclude metaphysics (to which I will return).

This engagement of Freudian and Jungian schools, which has informed the entire work, not only has resulted in the use of techniques advanced by both Freud and Jung, but also includes the contributions of post-schools: object relations (Guntrip, Winnicott) and Lacanian schools of post-

---

[13]Patricia Berry, "An Approach to the Dream," in *Echo's Subtle Body: Contributions to an Archetypal Psychology* (Dallas: Spring Publications, 1982), pp. 53–79. She discusses how the positioning, repetition, emotion and implication of images matter not as linguistic elements or even a narrative strategy yet as an approach to the "epistemology of the imagination with which to meet the dream image on its own level" (p. 78). See also James Hillman, "An Inquiry into Images," *Spring* (1977), pp. 62–88; and "Further Notes on Images," *Spring* (1978), pp. 152–182. Both Hillman and Berry continually caution against linguistic and conceptual interpretations which distance too far from the expression of the images themselves, though at times this privileges the primacy of image as distinct from language, see Berry, "An Approach to the Dream," pp. 65–66. In my view, such a distinction is impossible: all images imply word and have discourse, even the most numinous and intolerable of them can become (indeed their telos is to become) meaning and even language. On amplification, which is the elaboration of dream-image through parallels from symbology, mythology, history of religion, ethnology, etc., see Jung, *CW* 8, pp. 281–297. For Jung's comparison of psychoanalytic and his constructive dream interpretation, *CW* 8, pp. 75–77. Paul Kugler discusses Jung's positing image as meaning in *The Alchemy of Discourse: An Archetypal Approach to Language* (Lewisburg: Bucknell University Press, 1982) pp. 50–80, and the relation of that to contemporary psychoanalytic positions. However, a semantics of image has not been delineated by the post-Jungians.

[14]For Julia Kristeva's definition of intertextuality as the transposition of sign systems into another, see Leon S. Roudiez's introduction to her study *Desire in Language*, ed. Leon S. Roudiez, trans. Thomas Gora, Alice Jardine, and Leon S. Roudiez (New York: Columbia University Press, 1980), p. 15. Also Julia Kristeva, *Revolution in Poetic Language*, trans. Margaret Waller (New York: Columbia University Press, 1984), pp. 59–60. Also, Michael Riffaterre, "The Intertextual Unconscious," *Critical Inquiry* 13 (1987), pp. 371–385; and his "Textuality: W. H. Auden's 'Musée des Beaux Arts,'" in *Textual Analysis: Some Readers Reading*, ed. Mary Ann Caws (New York: The Modern Language Association of America, 1986), pp. 1–13; and Barbara Johnson's chapter "Les Fleurs du Mal Armé: Some Reflections on Intertextuality," in her *A World of Difference* (Baltimore: John Hopkins University Press, 1987), pp. 116–133.

Freudian thought; classical (von Franz) and archetypal (Hillman, Berry) schools of post-Jungian thought.

This study is the continuation of an earlier work which was founded on the assumption that any study of the female unconscious necessitates a scrutiny of the relation of daughter to mother, of mother to the unconscious, as well as a reexamination of the consistent and seemingly inevitable opposition of mother to the unconscious[15] (the silence of her unconscious and the necessity of extricating from her, repressing her or placing her as object in both Freudian and Jungian thought). Therefore, this study continues and elaborates upon my examination of mother–daughter symbiosis begun in the earlier work, and it also explores the implications for the unconscious of woman–woman relations extending from the original maternal bond.

In the earlier work, I found a particular constellation of unconscious "figures" to be analogous to, if not responsible for, the structure of a symptom: anorexia. I use "figure" here in the sense employed by Jungian/archetypal psychology, to describe the "people" of the unconscious, the people who, for example, are a primary way the unconscious appears to us nightly. The figures examined in that study emerged from the unconscious of actual women, the symptom was studied as *dramatis personae* and the symptom was one generally considered "female." I discovered in that work that it is through a symbiosis with her daughter that mother manifests aspects of the unconscious pertaining to thwarted or culturally repressed ambitions or desires (including rage). Within the symbiosis, daughter is available to the effects of mother's unconscious, in fact, is dominated by them (imaged often as male tyrants) and then becomes their embodiment (an attempt at articulation as well as being its foreclosure). Within the anorexic syndrome, daughter was found to be a manifestation of mother's unconscious desire not to locate need and appetite in physical satiation, but to locate a nonbiological desire beyond human need, pertaining to the precise articulation of images of the unconscious not before delineated.

Anorexia, therefore, was explored as the moment a daughter embodies aspects of her mother's unconscious desire without yet having a language to speak that unconscious. The acquisition of such a language was determined to be the resolution of the syndrome. This acquisition was discussed in

---

[15]Angelyn Spignesi, *Starving Women: A Psychology of Anorexia Nervosa* (Dallas: Spring Publications, 1983). In that work, I gradually entered into a language of the female unconscious upon which I am elaborating in this project.

terms of differentiation and delineation of the figures and landscapes of the female unconscious, indeed dialogue with (and through) them.[16]

Freud acknowledged his failure to recognize the importance of the "pre-oedipal" bond between daughter and mother, and stated that its discovery was analogous to the discovery of the Minoan-Mycenean civilization, and as difficult to grasp.[17] In my earlier study, I drew from a Greek myth, the primary mother–daughter myth (which most likely was derived from aspects of Minoan-Mycenean civilization). As I worked this myth to uncover aspects of the preoedipal bond, the writing in the dominant discourse began to break down, as did the *way* I used traditional sources (not *that* I used them). This work continues that penetration into the preoedipal mother–daughter territory, yet uses a narrative closer to the age of modernity. Though I focus on the encounter of the daughter with the various "male forces" of mother's unconscious, I have found that the classification of that territory as either "preoedipal" (which still places the Oedipus myth as primary) or "animus-ridden" (which is more a reversal of findings on anima and in Irigaray's terms would be Jung's blind spot in an old dream of symmetry) does not apply. This study is as much as reexamination of the concept "animus" as it is of "preoedipal."

The issue of symbiosis returns us to how the female unconscious differs from other unconscious(es). A statement of Irigaray's which has been very confirming is her reply to the question on what the content of a woman's unconscious might be: "I might nevertheless point to one thing that has been singularly neglected, barely touched on, in the theory of the unconscious: *the relation of woman to the mother and the relation of women among themselves*" (italics hers).[18]

A daughter is to a mother in a different relation *to the unconscious* than is a son to a mother. How a daughter is related to the mother affects both of their relation to the unconscious. What is different about a female unconscious is precisely this aspect of symbiosis, which, as I discussed in the

———————————————

[16]On Jung's methodology of the interlocution with "others" of the unconscious, see *CW* 8, pp. 88f; *CW* 9i, p. 5; *CW* 7, pp. 200–205; also his *Memories, Dreams, Reflections*, trans. Richard and Clara Winston (New York: Vintage Books, 1965), pp. 170-199. It is interesting to compare this with Lacan's sense of the unconscious as the discourse of the other, that "the unconscious of the subject is the discourse of the other" ("Function and Field of Speech and Language," in *Écrits: A Selection*, p. 55).

[17]Freud, *S.E.* XXI, p. 226. Luce Irigaray discusses this archaic desire of the daughter–mother relation and Freud's statement about it in *This Sex*, pp. 138-139.

[18]Irigaray, *This Sex*, p. 124.

earlier work, is at once a channel to the unconscious (for mother and daughter alike) as well as serving as a defense against that (articulated) passage. This study explores not only various *sorts of symbiosis* — antipathetic, sympathetic — but also various levels of each, all from the vantage point of the unconscious and the woman's relation to it.

Why the particular novel *Jane Eyre*? The decision to continue my study of the female unconscious through a study of this specific novel arose from pleasure reading during an eye operation that would affect, temporarily, the use of the right eye.[19] In the first chapter of this novel, I was surprised to discover a particular sort of symbiosis, not dissimilar to that of the anorexic syndrome, and there was the mother's "tyrant" whose domination of Jane sends her to another level of symbiosis pertaining more to death and affairs of the unseen, locked further into mother's rule of the unconscious, where indeed she wants to starve herself in the seldom-visited hidden chamber of mother's order.

Because each chapter of my study consists of a close textual analysis of a chapter of *Jane Eyre*, involving an analysis of each image regarded as meaningful in itself and through its association with surrounding images, a brief synopsis of the *Jane Eyre* chapter precedes each analysis. The intricate study of the female unconscious through a close textual analysis (each chapter of the novel being read as a dream) is pertinent to a discussion of (1) language, (2) metaphysics and the authority of legitimization, (3) transference/countertransference, and (4) the specific contributions of certain French feminists (this latter discussion became the first afterword).

Language

The entry to and interpretation of the unconscious of another woman's text began to break down the discourse in which I was writing about that unconscious: no longer was I analyzing that unconscious in discursive syntax but another sort of syntax began to emerge. What is the double syntax? Irigaray is asked. Her reply: instead of subordinating the unconscious to a conscious, Freud might have "articulated them and made them work as two different syntaxes." The discursive syntax is, in her view, a means of masculine "self-affection," requiring in its standard of sameness

---

[19]Later I learned that it was during her father's eye operation for cataracts, for which she alone accompanied him to Manchester, August 1846, that Brontë began *Jane Eyre*. And, of course, there is Rochester's eye problem at the end of the book, the result of his finally grappling with Bertha, to her death.

that female "self-affection" be impossible ("the feminine is never affected except by and for the masculine").[1]

Discussed in her essays, and through some experimentation in two of them, Irigaray attempts to discover/recover a female syntax. Her belief is that women will not know their desire, what they want, and will remain severed from themselves and one another until they return to the syntax allowing their self-affection.

Throughout many drafts, a language began evolving out of my analysis of the unconscious through *Jane Eyre*, a "female syntax" evolved which in itself was closer (than discursive syntax) to the unconscious being analyzed. This study is written, therefore, in a psychological language, a language of the female unconscious which also analyzes the unconscious: the unconscious simultaneously generating its own language and its own analysis.

Although it is not precisely *l'écriture féminine*,[2] I have been encouraged by readings in French feminist theory to continue in the evolving syntax, which clearly was a breaking down of discursivity. Xavière Gauthier:

> And then, blank pages, gaps, borders, spaces and silence, holes in discourse: these women emphasize the aspect of feminine writing which is the most difficult to verbalize because it becomes compromised, rationalized,

---

[1] Irigaray, *This Sex*, pp. 132–137.

[2] *L'écriture féminine* is a writing privileging the female body, emphasizing diffusion, fluidity, nonaggression, and emphasizing sexual difference in language and text, and is primarily from Hélène Cixous, "The Laugh of the Medusa," trans. Keith Cohen and Paula Cohen, in *New French Feminisms*, eds. Elaine Marks and Isabelle de Courtivron (New York: Schocken, 1981). See also Catherine Clément's essay "Enslaved Enclave," (trans. Marilyn R. Schuster) in that volume, as well as the dialogue between Cixous and Clément in *Newly Born Woman* (also the Introduction, pp. xv–xviii). Also, Elaine Showalter, "Introduction," in *The New Feminist Criticism*, ed. Elaine Showalter (New York: Pantheon, 1985), pp. 9–10, and the following essays in that volume: Showalter, "Feminist Criticism in the Wilderness," (p. 249); Nancy K. Miller, "Emphasis Added: Plots and Plausibilities in Women's Fiction," (p. 341); and Ann Rosalind Jones, "Writing the Body: Toward an Understanding of *l'Écriture féminine*." Showalter speaks of *l'écriture féminine* as a significant theoretical formulation though more a "utopian possibility" instead of literary practice. Miller discusses it as a "hope" but not blueprint for the future.

Makward sees *l'écriture féminine* as the emergence of the writing of Monique Wittig ["To Be or Not to Be . . . A Feminist Speaker," in *The Future of Difference*, eds. Hester Eisenstein and Alice Jardine (New Brunswick, N.J.: Rutgers University Press, 1985)]. For many American feminists, the problem is to relate the practice of feminine writing to a theory of femininity. I have found that the latter (a theory of the female unconscious) could only be attained through the emergence of the former.

masculinized as it explains itself . . . . If the reader feels a bit disoriented in this new space, one which is obscure and silent, it proves perhaps, that it is women's space.[3]

Marguerite Duras states that when women write they translate from darkness and from a silence in which they have lived for centuries.

I think feminine literature is a violent, direct literature and that, to judge it, we must not—and this is the main point I want to make—start all over again, take off from a theoretical platform . . . . I know that when I write there is something inside me that stops functioning, something that becomes silent.[4]

She discusses how in writing she lets something take over that flows from femininity and which is prior to her identity as Duras.

For Hélène Cixous, a most urgent question is the experience of pleasure, feminine sexual pleasure, where it takes place, how it is inscribed at the level of a woman's body, her unconscious, and how to put that in writing, a writing that inscribes femininity which is the inscription of the unconscious female body. "Everything will be changed once woman gives woman to the other woman."[5] (Charlotte Brontë gives Jane to me. I give Bertha to Charlotte.) For Cixous, not fearing the risk of writing as a woman is not to defend against the multiplicity of the unconscious, not to leave its spaces and desires unexplored in themselves—then to attempt to see the other woman not for purposes of a narcissistic strengthening or the verification of a master's power or weakness—it is, rather, to make love better, to invent.[6] Women writing as a woman do not hate, she says; yet I would add that one of the results of writing as a woman is to hate better.

Does the development of a female syntax require only lyrical love inventions? I could not stop there, nor do I think that is "female." I was struck by the "split" between the emotional subtext of anger and cynicism in sections of Irigaray's deconstruction of Freudian and philosophical Western traditions (in *Speculum of the Other Woman*) and that of love in her two lyrical

---

[3]Xavière Gauthier, "Is There Such a Thing As Woman's Writing?" trans. Marilyn A. August, in *New French Feminisms*, p. 164.
[4]Marguerite Duras, "From an Interview," trans. Susan Hesserl-Kapit in *New French Feminisms*, pp. 174-176.
[5]Hélène Cixous, "Sorties," trans. Ann Liddle, in *New French Feminisms*, p. 95; and Cixous, "The Laugh of the Medusa," p. 252.
[6]Ibid., pp. 245-264.

essays.[7] Must anger and dissection remain within the classical philosophical masculine economy and the female syntax be one only of love? I was struck again by the white column running down Julia Kristeva's pages in "Hérethique": on one side the lyrical discourse, on the other a theoretical discourse on mothering.[8]

In another place, Kristeva also speaks of blank spaces and ruptures in language, forces not grasped by the linguistic or ideological system. She states that in a culture where the phallic position requires speaking subjects to be conceived as masters of their speech, the rhythmic and nondiscursive text questions that mastery. Although in the majority of her writings she speaks of the nondiscursive text as feminine in a nonbiological specification, in this essay she discusses the two extremes of (literal) women writing experience, neither of which extremities seems desirable: (1) valorizing of phallic discourse, the privileged discourse of mastery of the (privileged) father–daughter relation; or (2) fleeing from all that is considered phallic, "refuge in the valorization of a silent underwater body, thus abdicating any entry into history."[9]

It is such oppositions that this work aims to traverse. But this work could not have been done before Irigaray's two lyrical essays separate from yet pertinent to her more analytic work, or before Kristeva's white column (I will return to their specific contributions). That my work analytically inves-

---

[7]Luce Irigaray, *Speculum of the Other Woman*, trans. Gillian C. Gill (Ithaca, N.Y.: Cornell University Press, 1985). "And the One Doesn't Stir Without the Other," trans. Helene Vivienne Wenzel, *Signs* 7 (1981), 60–67. "When Our Lips Speak Together," trans. Carolyn Burke, *Signs* 6 (1980), 69–79.

[8]Kristeva first published "L'Hérethique de l'amour," in *Tel Quel* 74 (1977), 30–49; reprinted as "Stabat Mater" in *Histoires d'amour* (Paris: Denoël, 1983), and trans. Leon S. Roudiez in *The Kristeva Reader*, ed. Toril Moi (New York: Columbia University Press, 1986).

[9]Julia Kristeva, "Oscillation between Power and Denial," trans. Marilyn A. August, in *New French Feminisms*, p. 166. She adds that most women novelists reproduce their literal history or constitute an identification through their story (the refuge of narcissism). The "suspended states" of Virginia Woolf, in her view, are not the dissection of language in Joyce. "Estranged from language, women are visionaries, dancers who suffer as they speak." Yet Kristeva does locate a change in the work of one current novelist (Sophie Podolski) indicating both "feminine" language and a sensitivity to language. However, as Jardine notes (*Genesis*, pp. 62–63), women writers are absent from not only Lacan's and Derrida's texts yet even more absent from Kristeva's, Cixous's, and Irigaray's (and other women theorists') texts. ["The women disciples of all of these theorists do sometimes mention contemporary women writers (Michele Montrelay mentions Chantal Chawaf, Marguerite Duras, and Jeanne Hyvrard), but such references are not in any way central to their theses" (pp. 62–63)].

tigates the positional and semantic relations of figures and landscapes of the
female unconscious as well as lyrically explores the blank spaces and
silences of the text of that unconscious, lyric as analysis, analysis as lyric, in
the same sentence and on the same page is the (dare I say logical?) continuation of what women in France have been doing for over a decade. And my
work draws toward others of a future where female syntax can be even less
dependent on masculine models of discursive thought (for instance, the
necessity of this introduction and the afterwords questioned).

The American contribution may be just this requirement that the analytical mode not be segregated from other essays or delegated to another
side of the page and exclusively written in discursive language. American
psychoanalytic feminists appreciate how several French feminists have
turned to "the preoedipal relation between mother and daughter for a
narrative of female desire that emerges from the relation to the maternal
body," a discourse closer than discursive to the body, *l'écriture féminine*, rejecting Lacan's model of castration, the component responsible for signification
in his schema, for its effect of the renunciation of mother by women. They
translate and discuss in great detail the possibility of Cixous's and Irigaray's
project of a female poetics, language as diffuse and autoerotic, allowing a
once-fused mother and daughter "to become women and subjects, in and
through language."[10]

Susan Rubin Suleiman worries about the exclusion, however, by French
writers of *l'écriture féminine*, of a certain kind of writing pertaining to a "male"
discourse of power which could result in a (mere) codification of woman's
writing or a fetishization of the female body (privileging of body, voice and
lyric over meaning).[11] Ann Rosalind Jones states that resistance to culture
always is built on bits and pieces of that culture however they are "disassem-
bled, criticized and transcended."[12] Nancy K. Miller declares that it is
pointless to deny the effects of culture on female writing or for women to
look for "*uniquely* 'feminine' textual indexes" apart from that culture.[13]
Elaine Showalter advises not to exclude from feminist criticism a variety of

---

[10]See the introduction in *The (M)other Tongue: Essays in Feminist Psychoanalytic Interpretation*, eds. Shirley Nelson Garner, Claire Kahane, Madelon Sprengnether (Ithaca, N.Y.: Cornell University Press, 1985), particularly pp. 22–23. Also see *The Future of Difference*, eds. Eisenstein and Jardine; the Intro-duction and Ann Rosalind Jones's essay in *The New Feminist Criticism*, ed. Elaine Showalter.

[11]Susan Rubin Suleiman, "Writing and Motherhood," in *The (M)Other Tongue*, p. 371.

[12]Jones, "Writing the Body," in *New Feminist Criticism*, p. 374.

[13]Miller, "Emphasis Added," in *New Feminist Criticism*, p. 342.

intellectual tools; whereas a male text is fathered, she says, a woman's is parented and we have to deal with both parents (without women imitating male predecessors or trying to reform them).[14]

Yet, consider Christiane Makward's poignant statement: "If neofeminist thought in France seems to have ground to a halt, it is because it has continued to feed on the discourse of the masters."[15] All this raises the pertinent question: how to use and understand the "male" within female discourse and not rely on the masters (i.e., repeat a masculine discourse on femininity)? This study has attempted that understanding of the place of the "male" in several ways: employing the tools derived from the masculine culture, but then discarding them in the discovery of new ones; a bibliography indicating where masculine theory interacted with or confirmed what it was that was unfolding; inclusion within the study of the effect of male aspects within the female unconscious (Jungians would say considerations of animus; Lacanians the phallic mother). I also maintain a persistent view of female anatomy as its own ground for metaphor,[16] moving it "beyond" its equivalence with a metonymic base of biologistic essentialism (determinism of anatomy) or fetishism.

I would add that the ways "male" has been included in this female syntax of the female unconscious have prevented a certain fusion with mother, not in the sense of Father's Law as wedge (or castrating device) but because mother herself does not want (what does she want?) such a fusion, which obfuscates or denies analysis. This indicates the very possibility, once in the territory of the unconscious, to remain close to *its* language while still asking questions of meaning.

The language that has evolved out of the interpretation of chapters as dreams, therefore, is no longer one of discursive syntax, but a lyrical-analysis. Whereas analysis emerges from the domain of position, relation

---

[14]Showalter, "Feminist Criticism in the Wilderness," in *New Feminist Criticism*, p. 265.

[15]Makward, "To Be or Not to Be . . . A Feminist Speaker," in *Future of Difference*, p. 102; Showalter also discusses this quote in "Feminist Criticism in the Wilderness," (p. 247) in her discussion of how the feminist obsession with revising, modifying, and attacking male critical theory keeps us dependent upon it. In the same essay, Makward states that neofeminist thought in France is "dangerously close" to repeating traditional formulations of femininity and female creativity. Jardine states (*Gynesis*, p. 43): "To what extent has the attempt in France over the past twenty years to bypass the human subject and dialectics led to the return of traditional notions of the 'feminine'?"

[16]See editors' introduction discussing Derrida's and Irigaray's relation to this issue in *The (M)other Tongue*, particularly p. 24.

and meaning (of the images), lyrical writing comes from extended meditations and associations of body-experience (without reducing that to biologic-determinism) to the images. The challenge is not to supplement one mode with another; it is not a matter, for example, of supplementing an interpretative theory of the dominant discourse with a lyrical rendition which remains anterior to meaning. It is more a matter of allowing one to become the other in an oscillating fashion even as that necessitates the disturbance of the discursive.

Analysis loosens, takes apart "whole" into parts, in order to find the proportion (portion of parts, their comparative relation); it asks about the significance of the parts, to themselves, to one another, to the larger text. Breaking up, analysis lowers, decenters, and language must be changed if analysis succeeds: one has a choice at that point to write the language as it breaks down or to translate it to a more familiar language (discursive syntax). When I did not translate, I found that where the unconscious pushed logical aspects of conceptualization to their limit, the lyrical style emerged; the lyric then deepened the analysis further, eventually over-reaching its limit and becoming again the lyrical, etc. The style is at once lyrical and analytical: where the lyrical exceeds the analytical, the section is set off on the page; where the analytical exceeds the lyrical, the introduction and afterword sections emerged.

"And this involves neither avoiding theory nor embracing it, but playing it off against itself; placing a violent new thought where the old thought falters and creating new fictions."[17] I have explored a piece of fiction that I realized contains a theory of the female unconscious, and in arriving at that theory through analysis, I ended up with more fiction, other fiction from behind, beneath the text, subtext, not only within each chapter but in what became a necessary rewriting of the end of a piece of fiction.

The indistinctness of the lyrical style (its nondiscursive, polyvalent nature) moves beyond subject–object distinctions, throwing the "Big Dichotomies" which Alice Jardine discusses so cogently, into question.[18] This requires an analysis not reliant on previous theories of the unconscious

---

[17]Jardine, *Gynesis*, p. 46.
[18]Ibid., p. 71, her discussion of Meaghan Morris's term "Big Dichotomies." Also her statement (p. 76): "To think this indistinctness in the twentieth century has been to think a crisis of indescribable proportions, to throw all of the Big Dichotomies into question: for if the exterior is interior, then the interior is also exterior; Man's soul is outside of him-self; history is but the exterior of his own no longer interior imagination." Though far from her intention, her sense here is remarkably aligned with Jung's theory of soul.

based on those dichotomies, but one that, like the lyric itself, emerges from the gaps and silences within the text, within the Big Dichotomies which are no longer fundamental.

Jardine discusses "tropological exploration" of rhetorical and thematic spaces, their movement and transformations, which she contrasts with a "topical list of definitions and identities."[19] In this study, such a tropological exploration in itself "produces" an analysis that precludes and even contests topical classification.

Metaphysics and the Authority of Legitimization

Through a lyrical-analysis, therefore, I have written the unconscious of another woman's text. My unconscious interpenetrating hers, the implication of each upon the other. As such, this project bears upon that place where contemporary French theory meets Jungian (archetypal) theory as well as psychoanalytic feminist theory: where one tries to come to terms with the threatened collapse of the dialectic and its representations, as well as the *Cogito* subject, and where one asks about multiplicity/polycentricity of figures and landscapes, circulation in methodology. And, I would add, which pertains to the shift from the primacy of castration as the dominant theme informing the theory of the unconscious.

Critics in France call American feminism pre-Freudian and pre-Saussurian in the ways it espouses natural over psychological life in a refusal of the unconscious, in its insistence on social structures as primary with a self more important than a subject or a multiplicity of reference, and in its view of language as communicative function instead of the effect of a human subject's inscription in culture.[1] What does it mean that I am a female Italian-American depth-psychologist who has written a lyrical-analysis of the female unconscious which moves polycentrically in places where neither subject nor object can be definitively posited? Am I suggesting a new form to be included in American feminism, one based on the primacy of the unconscious? Or am I stating that the study of the uncon-

---

[19]Ibid., p. 47.
[1]On the differences between French feminism and American feminism, see the introduction to *New French Feminists*, pp. xi–xiii; Jardine, *Gynesis*, pp. 42–47, 57–58, 63–64, 146, 233–236; Donna C. Stanton, "Language and Revolution: The Franco-American Dis-Connection," in *The Future of Difference*; Jane Gallop and Carolyn G. Burke, "Psychoanalysis and Feminism in France," in *The Future of Difference*.

scious of a woman is also feminist in the way it disrupts (phallocratic) structures of language and (antinomous) thought?

This study questions the logic of the subject: questions a subject which determines a theory of language, questions a subject acquiring organic unity through cognition, questions a subject which is master of its discourse. The way I have not been master over my discourse is the way "I" let the effects of the unconscious, the language of the unconscious, speak through "me," resulting in a lyrical-analysis.

Who is the subject that is the effect of this? Is it, as it is for Jane Gallop[2] and Catherine Clément and Hélène Cixous,[3] a bisexual subject? Is it, in Irigaray's terms, a subject of self-affection?[4] It is a subject of many "centers," a bisexual subject who knows the conscious and unconscious now through difference not opposition and who finds the shift from one to the other a syntactical, semantic, and a sexual one. Primarily it must be acknowledged that the language emerging from this entry into another woman's unconscious is a language with *no subject* (or object). No subject is the effect of this study, yet a person with access to the difference of many heterogeneous others in an unconscious peopled and landscaped. The effect is a bisexuality and one affecting oneself as moving out to affect others through oscillation among the speakings of many male and female "unconscious" people.

Does this bisexual one of self-affection have no master? Jardine quoting Shulamith Firestone: "It would take a denial of all cultural tradition for women to produce even a true 'female' art."[5] I do not maintain a radically anticultural posture in this work, particularly in ways I have drawn from Freudian and Jungian traditions, and my "complicity"[6] with those traditions became the bibliography of each chapter, and yet that is not to say that those traditions became or allowed me to become the master of my discourse.

The dichotomies of metaphysics are not sexually neuter (Cixous):[7] the under, the inferior, the nothing, and therefore the castrated has been female, and if the erection model and its Big Dichotomy (presence/absence: what about the biologistic essentialism behind so much of the Western

[2]Jane Gallop, *The Daughter's Seduction: Feminism and Psychoanalysis* (Ithaca, N.Y.: Cornell University Press, 1982), p. 127, and particularly 149–150.
[3]Cixous and Clément, *Newly Born Woman*, pp. xiv, 55–57, 84–87, 146.
[4]Irigaray, *This Sex*, pp. 132–134.
[5]Jardine, *Gynesis*, p. 54.
[6]Ibid., pp. 63–64.
[7]See Cixous, "Sorties," in *Newly Born Woman*, pp. 63–132.

17

philosophical tradition?) collapses, what happens to our exploration of those "under/nothing" spaces and are they still inferior? This project is the result of what occurs when a woman explores the unconscious, that is, the improper, empty, dark, silent, mad spaces of another (the other) woman.

Jardine quoting Jean-François Lyotard:

> To the obsolescence of the master narrative device of legitimation corresponds notably the crises of metaphysical philosophy, and that of the institution of the university which depends upon it. The narrative function loses its foundations, the great hero, the great perils, the great quests, the great goal.[8]

To write the unconscious of a narrative in order to write the unconscious is to let the narrative break down: John Reed no longer villain, Rochester no longer hero, Miss Temple no longer unmoved mover. The end no longer the end. Many voices, characters speaking where before there was only implied speech in silences; emotion contrary to or unexpected from the emotion of the text. The narrative has broken down and the unconscious is *not* translated to a paternal structure of thought or legitimate authority, not reverted to Big Dichotomies of another transcendental metaphysics.

Great Hero Father falls. Brontë's text itself anticipated all that I write here in this "Introduction" and even anticipated the crises of metaphysics and the authority of legitimization. For she was exploring the "under/nothing" spaces of mother–daughter symbiosis, love between women, death between women, madness and rage of women, while sitting right there under her father's blindness. And finally Patrick Brontë has fallen — if he had not, this present work would not have been possible. Now with the detumescence of the Father (not his death per se, for that would keep us cavalierly within the erection/castration, presence/absence model upon which the Western patriarchal tradition is based), does an entire metaphysics fall limp?

What are the implications of the fact that I found so much pertinent material on the female unconscious in a woman's text written over a century ago? The fact that the figures of Brontë's imagination continue to inform now a post-modern culture is itself a statement that some sort of metaphysics is at work, or at least requires comment. Is the suggestion one that John Reed or Miss Temple are "archetypes," do they require a metaphysics of a neo-Platonic domain?

---

[8]Jardine, *Gynesis*, p. 65. See Jean-François Lyotard, *The Postmodern Condition: A Report on Knowledge*, trans. Geoff Bennington and Brian Massumi (Minneapolis: University of Minnesota Press, 1984).

We can deconstruct Platonic and neo-Platonic metaphysics, but we still have to negotiate the figures in our dreams at night, a "conscience" which often speaks outside our intentionality, a vision which does not always correspond to literal seeing. How can it be understood that Brontë's figures have implications for an "unconscious" which was not even found or named during the time she wrote, that the structure of the John Reed metaphor, for example, informs an understanding of the modern symptom bulimia? How do we account for the fact that the obsessive-compulsive syndrome (not delineated until after her death) is elaborated upon by the analysis of Brocklehurst, and that a particularly female form of it, previously unnamed yet which is corroborated by my work with patients, is described from the analysis of Rochester?

Does the ontological status of the figures of Brontë's imagination need to be placed in a metaphysical realm? My sense is that they are formal and not bound to a specific historical culture, yet their manifestation is affected by and even configured by the particular culture in which they both appear and are studied. Brontë's imagination infused and became implicated with that of Jean Rhys, and we have not so much a "modernist" version of that imagination but more a manner in which that imagination becomes manifested in modernist culture.[9] Likewise this work is another manner, another "style"[10] in which that imagination becomes manifest in post-modern culture.

The post-modern culture, in which I write the imagination which is implicated with Brontë's, requires putting the authority of my own discourse into question, there is no master here, and the only authority becomes that of the "unconscious" figures and their landscapes themselves, all of which have persisted longer than Brontë or Rhys (and will persist longer than I do). Is it that the figures have the last word? Is there a last word when narrative itself breaks down in this crisis of modernity? How do "I" understand the process of putting my own lyrical-analysis discourse into question, the dismantler dismantling herself? J. Hillis Miller speaks of oscillation as dismantling.[11] I would say that the oscillation not only between lyric and analysis, but the oscillation of the two figures at the "end" of this book became my own dismantling of myself and my discourse.

---

[9]Jean Rhys, *Wide Sargasso Sea* (New York: Norton, 1982).
[10]Shoshana Felman, *Writing and Madness*, trans. Martha Noel Evans (Ithaca, N.Y.: Cornell University Press, 1985), pp. 131–134.
[11]J. Hillis Miller, "The Critic as Host," in *Deconstruction and Criticism* (New York: Continuum, 1985). He amplifies "parasite/host" as a way to conceptualize intertextuality in ways that are interesting.

What is left after such dismantling? A language of the unconscious which is one of many "feminine discourses."[12] Heterogeneous figures who speak. Beyond the face of things are the figures differentiating, speaking, feeling through the gaps and silences of the text to claim once again their place in a culture. The moment the authority moves to the heterogeneous figures now speaking yet once unconscious is where deconstructive criticism and Lacanian psychoanalysis intersect with Jungian thought, which first posited the autonomous discourse of unconscious "others" distinct from an "ego" that must be relativized by them.

These figures remain as the authority, yet since they continue to speak the inferiority of "our" desire, can we claim them as authority, make them and their relations into a new "science"? My sense is not that the unconscious and its study must include or preclude science, but that it would require a "radical" science (more radical than phenomenology's human science),[13] not a methodology of qualitative structures but sequences of relations between figures, between figures and "ego," proportions between figures and degrees of their manifestation, symptom as their inability to interlocute, data base as symptom. But we are speaking here of a "new" Father, and we recall that explorers of the unconscious have always grasped for him (in neurology and physical science, alchemy, linguistics and mathematics). First we have to survive the passing of the old. Any talk of science or a broad schematic structure now is nostalgic. Or a frenetic grasping when no one is left in authority.

And what prevents chaos here? The Frenchman said the unconscious is structured as a language. He then immediately darted into modern linguistics.[14] The unconscious has its own language, its figures speak and their

---

[12]See the third section, "Exchange," in *Newly Born Woman.*

[13]Cf. Amedeo Giorgi, *Psychology as a Human Science* (New York: Harper and Row, 1970); *Duquesne Studies in Phenomenological Psychology*, vol. 1, eds. A. Georgi, William F. Fischer, Rolf Von Eckartsberg (Pittsburgh: Duquesne University Press, 1971).

[14]Lacan's statement is: "the unconscious is structured in the most radical way like language, that a material operates in it according to certain laws, which are the same laws as those discovered in the study of actual languages, languages that are or were actually spoken" (*Écrits: A Selection*, p. 234). I can work from the first phrase of this statement, yet disagree with the rest. For Lacan, the unconscious is "transindividual, that is not at the disposal of the subject in reestablishing the continuity of his conscious discourse" (p. 49). And what structures it are not archetypes (p. 234) yet structures which reside outside the experience of community and personal history "in which his place is already

integral relations persist, and when we find the meaning of their language (which is not to translate that language to the linguistics of the languages of our conscious daily speaking) that meaning precludes chaos or babel.[15] To let the images of the unconscious speak in their own tongue, and inform us

---

[14](*continued*)
inscribed at birth, if only by virtue of his proper name" and determined by "permutations authorized by language" (p. 148). In my view, Lacan's return to the language of the unconscious, in an attempt to recover the primacy of the unconscious for psychoanalysis, is an important one, yet the unconscious does not speak in the language of mathematics (if it did, we would have equations and formulas for dreams), which is not to say there is not a mathematical and logical base of the unconscious (which Pythagoras knew and from which music derives), but one must return to the language endemic to the unconscious to determine such a base.

I believe that the Lacanian application of contemporary linguistics and mathematics to the unconscious is not a determination of the language of the unconscious. For the unconscious speaks nightly, and that occurs in images, in the discourse of figures traversing specific landscapes of their own design. It also speaks in slips of words and behaviors which are linked associatively to memories and images in the reservoir of consciousness. My sense is that Lacan's use of linguistics as the language of the unconscious is related to his devaluation of the Imaginary. When image is no longer Imaginary in a prejorative sense, and also no longer relegated to "preoedipal" territory, when Oedipus and Father's Law are no longer the standard to which the base of the unconscious falls short, then we will be closer to the language of the unconscious. An approximation to which this project is one.

[15]I am referring to the plurivocal discourse of the unconscious which entails a search for internal relations between images of the text. The syntax of the unconscious would then consist of "archetypal" images. See Kugler (*The Alchemy of Discourse*) who discusses (using Wilden following Benveniste) how Saussurian arbitrariness does not lie between signifier and signified but between signifier and object of reference. I claim that what still is necessary is an exploration of the relation of signified to archetypal image. Kugler demonstrates how particular sound patterns (signifiers) are nonarbitrarily tied through phonetic parity to clusters of archetypally related meanings (and he refers here to Jung's *Symbols of Transformation*, extensive etymological analyses of archetypal themes). Kugler recovers Jung's sense of archetype as invariant relationships determined by form not content, the emphasis on formal relationships instead of substance, and discusses the similarity between that and Lévi-Strauss's and Lacan's later work. His main thesis is that symbolism in an archetypal sense does not reside in relations between signifier and signified but that there is a symbolic (archetypal) level in language that is nonarbitrary and pertains to sound-to-sound relationships. However, the approach scrutinizing sound components too easily could avoid not only issues of the signified but also positional, sensate and emotive qualities of the image as well as its discourse other than that of its "proper" name.

of their position, intention, desire, language and meaning, is to affect the way we think about metaphysics. It refers to a metaphysics which is not nostalgic for the father, a metaphysics which is not logocentric, univocal, phallocratic or oppositionalistic, and, above all, not transcendent. Images not barred from but which consist of meaning.

What are the meanings of Brontë's images, with what are we left after all this dismantling? In Afterword II, what is summarized, from each of the lyrical-analysis chapters, is a theory of, or actually within, the female unconscious that takes as its baseline mother–daughter symbiosis. Within various levels of this symbiosis, various male figures appear in different possessive and dialogical relation to the daughter. Also, each encounter of the daughter with the emerging male figure pertains to various require-ments and intentions, and refers to a female continually shifting conscious referent (Bessie, Miss Temple, Miss Fairfax), as well as a female uncon-scious referent (Helen, Bertha). We are left with the beginning of a tenta-tive theory of the alteration of the figures of the female unconscious, their differentiation, language, ability to interlocute with the ego, distance from and proximity to the ego (and the effect of that upon specific "symptoms"), their relation to various landscapes, and the relation of landscape to meta-phors of female anatomy, all this without even speculating on what may be *beyond* determining this movement. One cannot say, better not say. Father limps.

There are other ways in which Brontë anticipated the crisis of phallo-cratic models. The landscapes of her novel metaphorically follow female anatomy more than they inform any developmental fantasy of linear growth. That is, the territories which the "heroine" Jane Eyre traverses previously have been read according to her (and thereby a woman's) psy-chosocial development, enough so that the novel has been discussed as a female *Bildgunsromane*.[16] What emerges from my analysis is the way each "fictional" place — Gateshead, Lowood, Thornfield — becomes an index of a portion of female anatomy describing not only the dimensions and parame-ters of the space but also who we are when we live according to it, and how it manifests through whom others see ourselves to be. Also, each landscape refers to another relation of "ego" to "world": ego corresponds to world differently from the red-room of the womb place, from the corridors of temple regions, from the mad-laugh view of the third-story leads.

---

[16]For example: Karen E. Rowe, " 'Fairy-born and human-bred': Jane Eyre's Education in Romance," in *The Voyage In: Fictions of Female Development*, eds. Elizabeth Abel, Marianne Hirsh, and Elizabeth Langland (Hanover, N.H.: Dartmouth College, 1983).

Therefore, Brontë conceived of female "development" not in terms of linear progression but as an uncovering of the unconscious related to body in a passage (the eyre) circulating up and down that body. She was close enough to the unconscious to register what we only have been discovering this century: that the unconscious does not follow deterministic laws of the physical sciences, nor can it be translated into those laws; its movement is spiral, it repeats and echoes, its speech is ambiguous and fluid, its figures heterogeneous and very much interactive with the landscapes in which they appear. The "heroine" of Brontë's novel never would have reached Thornfield (or been hired by it) if that mansion did not have the crimson drawing room mirroring that from which she Gateshead started. Each landscape is included in the next which draws from it in further delineation of its properties; progression through regression is the movement of the passages here.

Brontë also anticipated Freud which would not have surprised him.[17] We see in the passage from Gateshead to Lowood to Thornfield various aspects of the psychoanalytic states — oral, anal, latent, and genital. However, all refer to the daughter's negotiation of the various male figures emerging from the symbiosis with mother. Also, we do not find any indication of the typical Oedipal patterning. The daughter's encounter with the paternal figure cannot be separated from the space of mother–daughter symbiosis within which she resides when that encounter occurs and which in fact is necessary for it to occur. That encounter is not based on an erotic drive as much as it is subtended by a desire to extricate from the more antipathetic levels of the symbiosis.

We also find that a "genital sexuality" is operative only when the daughter has become differentiated enough within the (now "sympathetic") symbiosis with mother in order to pass, through the erotic male figure, back to (and through) the mother–daughter shared madness. That a woman cannot entertain a genital sexuality without returning (as differentiated) to the mother's madness (which attracted her to the erotic male figure in the first place, he is "married" to what it looks like), is how Brontë "founded" a female psychology before either Freud or Jung were born.

---

[17]Freud, *S.E.* IX, p. 8: "But creative writers are valuable allies and their evidence is to be prized highly, for they are apt to know a whole host of things between heaven and earth of which our philosophy has not let us dream. In their knowledge of the mind they are far in advance of us everyday people, for they draw upon sources which we have not yet opened for science." Stanley Cavell refers to Freud's statement of being preceded in his insights by the creative writers of his tradition (yet does not cite the reference from Freud) in "Freud and Philosophy: A Fragment," *Critical Inquiry* 13 (1987), 386–393.

Brontë's placement of the unconscious in regard to the ego and its passages through the body also differs from much work in depth psychology that places the unconscious below or behind that which is conscious. She conceived of it around: on the edge of interior and exterior (Gateshead windowseat), below (red-room vault), above (red-room lightbeam), within (Miss Temple's chamber), and upstairs (Thornfield's third floor). This raises some interesting issues: if the unconscious is "around" us, what does that imply for our understanding of "capping" it, keeping it beneath, riding it, mastering it? What does it imply for our sense that we can rise above (the bar separating it from consciousness) through symbol or metonymic links of signifiers speaking Other's desire?

The use of the metaphor of female anatomy in delineating passages of the unconscious returns us to critiques of essentialism: that the inscription of the female body only ascribes to the reigning (phallocratic) binary system. My sense is that once we move out of the anal and phallic approaches (active/passive and presence/absence) of polar opposition, there are various ways to explore gender differences not according to such oppositionalism. In the viewing of difference as "essential" to a study of the unconscious, I have been very much encouraged by the French feminists with the respect they have for gender and its relation to the unconscious, genderized landscapes of the unconscious (Wittig),[18] and the possibility of female languages of the unconscious. Although I am an Italian-American working on a British novel, French contemporary theory often confirmed my intuitions on the necessity of what it was that I was attempting by supporting my methodological attempt not to place any grid of depth-psychological systems upon the literature or use the literature as data for theory and to enter the subtext with as much detachment as possible from masters of discourse.

The importance of such inscription of the female body, without limiting it by determinism or fetishism, is that it led to insights on the unconscious and its workings which would otherwise not have been available. For example, the "madness" of women is not that they are of earth/womb (and finally in 1950 have risen with Mary), cannot sublimate as much as men, or

---

[18]See particularly Monique Wittig, *Les Guéllières*, trans. David Le Vay, (New York: Avon, 1973); and *The Lesbian Body*, trans. David Le Vay (New York: Avon, 1976).

have deficient superegos,[19] but that they sublimate often too far and do not know their way down (through body)[20] and out (to world). This is why the French feminist question — how does female *jouissance* write itself — is so important.

Therefore, I am suggesting that the unconscious figures *themselves*, their intellectual, sensate, and emotive discourses are what prevents chaos in the exploration of domains other-than-conscious. Jardine states:

> New figures must be found beyond theocentric representation. The *technē* has been threatened from the interior and exterior by a language it may have produced but which, in any case, it cannot seem to control. Freud heard that language, as did Nietzsche; and they both could only, if in different ways, *represent* it as the unmediated violence of Mitra, the Great Mother.[21] (Italics hers.)

To that I would add, of course, that Jung heard that language,[22] and so did Charlotte Brontë, begun perhaps as "mad" third-story laughter.

Whereas Jardine sees modernity's task (to name this unnameable space formerly in the shadows) correlative to the ending of metaphysics and Judeo-Christianity,[23] I see it more as modernity's struggle to let the unnameable *name itself*, which is correlative to the ending of the exclusive metaphysics of Judeo-Christianity as it is a summoning of a metaphysics necessitating a radical reformulation of not only secular yet sacred dimensions and boundaries.

---

[19]On Jung's discussion of the relation of women to earth and body, and the relevance of the papal declaration of the Assumption of Mary, see *CW* 9i, pp. 107–110. On deficient superego: Freud, *S.E.* XXII, p. 129; on incapacity to sublimate: Freud, *S.E.* XXII, p. 134.

[20]Due to a fear of the "desire" of their own wombs which includes hate and the articulation of that.

[21]Jardine, *Gynesis*, p. 81.

[22]See particularly C. G. Jung, *Memories, Dreams, Reflections*. Interestingly, in another context (*Gynesis*, pp. 141–142), Jardine discusses Freud's renunciation of mysticism ("For Freud, any conceptual system that valorizes that maternal space, the *Id*, is mystical.") and the resultant battles with colleagues valuing Mother more than Father, his "maternalistic Others," including Jung. She then states that the lesson of the late twentieth century pertains to the impossibility of living without an experience of the sacred. Yet she does not develop this idea and states that women theorists in France have not either.

[23]Jardine, *Gynesis*, p. 81.

Transference/Countertransference

Beyond the formalism of structuralism and semiotic narratology, Peter Brooks summons an "erotics of form" to return formalism to more human aspects of literature.[1] From the close analysis of the formal relations of the *dramatis personae* of *Jane Eyre*, a formal-erotic language has emerged in my work. My sense is that permeating my own lyrical-analysis are issues (issues which Brooks also discusses) of transference/countertransference that concern my relation to the text.

Lyrical-Analysis: The Unconscious Through Jane Eyre rests on the assumption that the constellation of figures in a work of literature and the dynamic organization of their movement over specific landscapes corresponds to the figures of the unconscious and their operational patterns. This premise directly relates to the theory of C. G. Jung that the unconscious is polycentric, heterogeneously peopled, and that its *dramatis personae* become the drama and narratives of literature. Although more psychoanalytically inclined, Brooks also works off such assumptions "that there ought to be, that there must be, some correspondence between literary and psychic process, that aesthetic structure and form, including literary tropes, must somehow coincide with the psychic structures and operations they both evoke and appeal to."[2]

Mary Watkins takes it a step further, a different step, presenting evidence from writers of literature on the intrinsic relation between the personifying that occurs spontaneously in the unconscious (issuing, she feels, from formative dispositions explored by Jung and his followers) and the personified characters of the literary text. In her view, depth and specificity of characterization, degrees of animation, and complexity of perspectives are indices of a psychologically advanced human as well as a "good" novel.[3]

The need to return the *dramatis personae* of either the unconscious or a literary text to a monocentric system, e.g., the Self, has been questioned and revised in post-Jungian thought, with its emphasis on polycentricity and circularity, as well as deconstructive/rhetorical criticism. The differ-

---

[1]Peter Brooks, "The Idea of a Psychoanalytic Literary Criticism," *Critical Inquiry* 13 (1987), 334–348; particularly p. 339.

[2]Ibid., p. 337. Brooks's statement of the assumptions underlying his study: "Freud works from the premise that all that appears is a sign, that all signs are subject to interpretation, and that they ultimately tell stories that contain the same dramatis personae and the same narrative functions for all of us" (p. 336).

[3]Mary Watkins, *Invisible Guests: The Development of Imaginal Dialogues* (Hillsdale, N.J.: The Analytic Press, 1986).

ence between the two relates to "bracketing the human realm from which psychoanalysis derives."[4] Brooks discusses how deconstructive/rhetorical criticism too often remains in the linguistic realm, bypassing the difficult and necessary issues in poetics that are pertinent for the passage from formalist to psychological interpretation.[5] Gallop would agree with him, and also states that our own unconscious (its desires and defenses) must be implicated in the investigation; she cites the work of Schor and Kahane for instances of critical self-implication.[6]

What does one want to claim, Brooks asks, in showing that the structure of a metaphor is equivalent to that of a symptom?[7] Perhaps one wants to claim that both are languages of the unconscious (certainly Jung knew that) which corresponds to the fact that symptom is also metaphor. The metaphor in a text, therefore, would be a different (healthier presumably) metaphor than that of the symptom for what the unconscious wants to be speaking. Brontë herself moved from symptom as metaphor to metaphor in narrative which became the beginning of her novels. Since *The Professor* is written more from the stance of Crimsworth, the "Heger figure," my sense is that *Jane Eyre* is the first self-analysis Brontë wrote. She put down the pen of her symptomatic letters to Heger and picked up the pen of a self-analysis, finding a narrative of the working of her unconscious, its *dramatis personae*, its conflicts no longer her "hysterical" grasping for the manipulating Belgian, yet now a revival of memory, Brontë her own analyst, her text an analysis, a recalling through metaphor of what had been repressed instead of repetition compulsion from that past in the present (Heger letters).

Most would agree that *Jane Eyre* as narrative discourse is a more adequate rendition of the unconscious past than were Brontë's symptoms. August 1846 in Manchester was the crossover from symptom to narrative discourse, Brontë the analyst of her unconscious. The result is the delineation of her creative imagination and the first thirteen chapters of *Jane Eyre*.[8]

---

[4]Brooks, "The Idea of a Psychoanalytic Literary Criticism," p. 337.
[5]Ibid.
[6]Jane Gallop's essay "Reading the Mother Tongue: Psychoanalytic Feminist Criticism," in *Critical Inquiry* 13 (1987), see p. 321.
[7]Brooks, "The Idea of a Psychoanalytic Literary Criticism," pp. 340–341.
[8]There are many intersections between the first thirteen chapters and Brontë's life: the similarity of the one brother and two sister constellation of the Reed, Brocklehurst, Ingram, and Rivers families with that of Brontë's siblings, and the characteristics of those sisters—Georgiana as a representation, in my view, of the "underside" of Anne, Eliza of Emily. That there was, in fact, an aunt, who

From chapter thirteen on, as Jane develops the erotic relationship through courtship with Rochester (something Brontë never passed through in life with Heger or any erotic male person), there is not an unconscious past corresponding to the novel's events which became more a rendition of what Brontë would have wanted to occur, in fact, a "subjective figment" or fancy. My own study of the female unconscious working through Brontë's inscription of that unconscious (as creatively imagined instead of fancied) leaves off at the thirteenth chapter and then ends itself.[9]

To this text through which Brontë was the analyst of her unconscious, inscribing a more adequate rendition of that unconscious, I have been both analyst and analysand. I intervened in the text by the act of reading and

---

[8]*(continued)*
was a stepmother of sorts, in the Brontë home, is a point unnoticed or uncommented upon by the biographers I read. Here was a rigid, Calvinist aunt who more than likely did not want the pressures and burdens brought on by these children placed under her care. We do know that this aunt did not like the climate of Haworth, that she did rule over the children strictly, and that her money was necessary for their future. Branwell was her favorite, and next came Anne. The aunt easily forgave Branwell's delinquency as John Reed similarly was pardoned.

Biographers often do note the point-by-point correspondence between Lowood and Cowan Bridge, Maria Brontë and Helen Burns, Reverend William Carus Wilson and Brocklehurst, and Mary Ann Evans and Margaret Wooler (with whom Charlotte did teach and spend evenings) together composing Miss Temple. Other nonarbitrary correspondence: Thornfield with Ellen Nussey's house; Heger with Rochester (Heger's letter to student Meta M. indicating his mentor-seducer role with younger women); also, the mad woman with the Leeds' story and Charlotte's anger at Mme. Heger. John Reed, Brocklehurst, and Rochester are elaborations and differentiations of the Zamorna and Northangerland characters of Angria.

The point here is not that Brontë's unconscious, and its manifestations in her narrative, is reduced to her literal life, but that when that unconscious manifested itself through configurations of her literal life as well as her narrative (for which her life was used as channel to the unconscious) that narrative has a relation to the unconscious which the narrative based more on subjective fantasy of a potential outcome either does not have or has differently.

[9]Edward Casey's discussion of the distinction Jung made between fantasy, " 'a subjective figment of the mind,' " and imagination, " 'an image-making, form-giving creative activity,' " is pertinent here [Edward S. Casey, *Imagining: A Phenomenological Study* (Bloomington, Ind.: Indiana University Press, 1976), p. 213]. Also see his discussion of Coleridge's distinction of fancy and creative imagination, pp. 184–185; as well as his article "Toward an Archetypal Imagination," *Spring* (1974). Also, I am indebted to Jane Gallop's use of "Interstory" and "Postory" in *Reading Lacan* for my usage of Restory in "ending" this book.

continually reexamining the text, particularly reading it through dream interpretation. My countertransferential desire to interpret (master?) the text resulted in the analysis, the latter term of lyrical-analysis.[10]

The lyrical result was the manifestation of myself as analysand, my transference to the text, as well as to Brontë. This transferential effect allowed me to explore landscapes and figures in the unconscious through a mode of submission otherwise unlikely, and relates to Cixous's sense of "inhabiting."[11] The bulimia in Chapter 1, the incest in Chapter 2, the girls' school in Chapter 5, the death between women in Chapter 9, the ward in Chapter 11, and the runaway in Chapter 14 are not part of the fabric of my literal history, yet as analysand and as a result of my transference to Brontë and her text, the unconscious of the text became revealed: her text became more my dream, and those aspects of the unconscious became more accessible to me experientially and theoretically than if I were exploring them "masterfully" instead of lyrically. My therapeutic work with patients of course contributed in these areas, as it did to every page of this work, but intimacy with the detailed image and feeling and meaning of the place came from the submission to Brontë's "authority" there.

The more I submitted to (became patient to, and therefore patient with) the text, associations were enhanced which then permitted more hidden signification of the text to emerge. The lyrical process therefore produced more text, more subtext, and from that place more significance of the main text opened, more analysis, that is, the analysis became more precise, made me master in the ways Cixous and Clément speak of (and relating to the mastering Jane learns in chapter seven), more masterful than if I had

[10]See Brooks, "The Idea of a Psychoanalytic Literary Criticism," p. 343. Also, I profited from Shoshana Felman's Lacanian perspective on transference and its relation between reader (Freud) and text (hysteric) in "Turning the screw of interpretation," in *Literature and Psychoanalysis: The Question of Reading: Otherwise*, ed. Shoshana Felman (Baltimore: John Hopkins University Press, 1980), see p. 118. Susan Rubin Suleiman discusses the relation and difference between Felman's and Brooks's perspectives of the transferential model of reading in her fine article "Nadja, Dora, Lol V. Stein: women, madness and narrative," in *Discourse in Psychoanalysis and Literature*, ed. Shlomith Rimmon-Kenan (New York: Methuen, 1987), see p. 127.

The foundational papers for my views on transference/countertransference include Freud, "The Dynamics of Transference," *S.E.* XII, p. 97–108, and Harold Searles, *Counter-transference and Related Subjects* (New York: International Universities Press, 1979).

[11]Cixous, *Newly Born Woman*, pp. 148–149, her "transference" to Dora, and Cixous's resultant interpretative and creative work from that is an example of the transferential effect which I am discussing here.

retained a master-relation to the text, if I had not yielded to the effects of its unconscious and the necessary alterations in syntax accordingly.[12]

Brooks describes Freud's view of "the relations of analyst and analysand in the transference as one of struggle — struggle for the mastery of resistances and the lifting of repressions," and Brooks likens that to the struggle between reader and text.[13] It is true that in the process of opening up my resistance (to the unconscious revealed through the text), Brontë's text often became my resistance which I had to work through in order to get to an unconscious which necessarily included my own.

Jardine discusses Philippe Sollers's "erotic merging at the interior of language." This is how I experienced the lyrical mode of approaching the text (being analysand to it); yet she continues that Sollers does this "through a radical dismemberment of the textual body, a female body."[14] I did not experience the struggle with the text as a struggle for mastery (as in master over it) affecting such a dismemberment. I felt instead that what I needed to know about the unconscious was in the text and what mattered was the perspective (oscillating between lyrical and analytical from which the final lyrical-analysis emerged) I took to it. I found a precise form emerging from the erotic merging, which left the text altered. Although the eroticism with Brontë and her figures was at times quite active and even aggressive, my sense is that her text was not dismembered.

At the beginning of the project, there was often a struggle, "dialogic struggle,"[15] between myself and the text, myself as analysand wanting to drop even more deeply into the unconscious of the text through the lyric mode (sentimentalism would push me out), and as analyst incisively wanting to pull out meaning from some aspect of the text (aridity would pull me back in). So the dialogic struggle Brooks describes became an oscillation resulting in a novel form of discourse.

Brooks's critic asks: "How can there be a transference where there is no means by which the reader's language may be rephrased in coherent and manageable form by the text-as-analyst?"[16] The rephrasing of my perceptions over the years of dialoguing with *Jane Eyre* is evident not only in the plethora of drafts and the perpetual breakdown of discursive syntax across

---

[12]Cixous and Clément, see the third section, "Exchange," in *Newly Born Woman*.

[13]Brooks, "The Idea of a Psychoanalytic Literary Criticism," p. 344.

[14]Jardine, *Gynesis*, p. 246. This entire section on Sollers, pp. 238–246, is illuminating.

[15]Brooks, "The Idea of a Psychoanalytic Literary Criticism," p. 345.

[16]Ibid., p. 346. The question was posed by Terence Cave in a review of Brooks's work.

drafts, but also in the way the form of lyrical-analysis slightly alters: some chapters opening themselves more to the analytical mode, others more to the lyrical, others holding the tension in a more reciprocal way, all depending on the content of each chapter. And the converse of the critic's statement holds as well: the text (as analysand) changed, rephrased its language, as I analyzed it; it changed to the extent that going beyond chapter thirteen was impossible, and a restory necessary, which then in its nascent form affected the rewriting of the lyrical-analysis of chapters 1–13, and this in turn altered, more than once, the Restory.

Chapter 1

Windowseat

There is no walk this day of wintry wind and slashing wetness. The child is relieved, she is not large enough to keep up with the cousins, John, Eliza and Georgiana. She hangs behind on the walk from which today she is grateful not to be returning with nipped fingers and a heart darted by chidings of the nursemaid returning to the mother, that Mrs. Reed, drawing up by the fire beside her three children. The sofa is not for this smaller cousin. Mrs. Reed has ordered her to keep a distance until she becomes more the natural child, the sofa welcoming only young ones contented. Jane, this mother says to her, you have not an attractive manner, not sociable, until you become of a lighter disposition, Jane, you are not of us.

The child wants to know what it is she has done, the aunt scolds the question demanding a distance. Jane withdraws into a room adjacent she is crawling into the windowseat, drawing the scarlet draperies on her right as there on the left the clouds bearing down their ceaseless rain. Protected by the windowpane yet not separated from those November elements, she opens the book of birds today drawn to the sea-fowl of a haunted terrain of the Arctic Zone.

From these pages: a lone rock upon billowing sea, broken boat on desolate coast, 'cold and ghastly moon glancing through bars of cloud at a wreck just sinking,' solitary churchyard with headstone (she sees as haunted), two ships becalmed (she sees as marine phantoms), there is a fiend and thief (she passes in terror), and then the 'black, horned thing seated aloof on a rock, surveying a distant crowd surrounding a gallows.'

In her own way she is happy with these images evoking stories vivid and mysterious as those of the nursemaid Bessie who while ironing and in pleasant mood would tell the ballads, the old fairy tales. She is happy until that occurs the most feared: the interruption, a voice — Madame Mope — the cousin John is calling. Weak in vision and conception, he cannot find her yet the sister Eliza points out the windowseat then leaves as the brother enters fully stout ordering subservience. He wears a dingy skin, thick lineaments and limbs, fourteen and only four years older yet so fully larger. 'He gorged himself habitually at table, which made him bilious, and gave him a dim and bleared eye and flabby cheeks.' Heavy limbs not holding much affection for the mother who indulges him or sisters, yet Jane he hates. His physical blows to her arrive many times a day, these attacks for which there is no appeal. The servants do not stand up to this young master and as for the mother: even when they occur in front of her, she never sees his blows.

'Habitually obedient' Jane follows his command to stand before him whereupon repetitiously his tongue thrusts in and out. Terrified of the blow forthcoming, her body withering yet not avoiding a look upon him of disgust. (He sneers) This is for your impudence with mama (he strikes her) for hiding behind the curtain, for the look in your eye like that of a rat. As she totters, he is demanding to know her exercise behind scarlet drapery. A book, he wants to see the book and as he grabs it he calls her dependent, how dare she rummage in his bookshelves for they are his as it will be his home soon; stand by the door, he is telling her to stand out of the way of any glass. She is clearsighted but she cannot see his intent. The book hurled through the air hits her and with a cry she falls, her head striking against the door cuts. The blood bursts forth with its sharp pain.

She calls him slave-driver, Roman emperor. 'I really saw in him a tyrant: a murderer.' He lunges at her, grasping what is a desperate thing now, a frantic flailing one—bellowing he says rat! rat! Cousins running to the brother's aid, calling mother. Girl child flying in a fury at a young master. Mother orders this ' "picture of passion" ' locked up in the red-room.

Raw coldness and bleakness desolation of a motherless child sees the mothering of other children; sofa-maternal warmth available only to others. She is not the natural child. Inferior, awkward, she cannot keep up, lags behind, the hands get nipped, frost-bitten fingers clutched. She is chided, she retreats; this the "depressed" child, isolated, cut-off, out in the cold, on the windowedge of outer and inner, in-between, marginal, forlorn child.

Sombre, solemn and tender, she crawls into the imagination. Sharp edge of rock surrounded by billowing waves, nothing holds her here; the vessels are broken and sinking; she goes into the depths of the dead at the churchyard finding then a fiend and thief and gallows witnessed by an aloof 'black, horned thing.' Promontory and dangerous descents with no containment: this landscape is cragged, icy, desolate, what life there is appears black, phantomlike, demonic.

Here is the rejected child; residing within reflections of isolation offer the solace. It is a frozen landscape. Lapland. Iceland. Arctic. Vast black space of whiteness; isolation absolute of no sound, without color, touch nothing. The silence abrasive, jagged rock edge sprouting only the dead twig broken descent. No voice, no help, no comfort: there is no mother here.

There is no mother but a rejecting (step) mother when the child is unnatural, preternatural, not sociable, does not fit into the society yet is marginal, of inferior other worlds, from worlds of otherness, heterogeneous. How the child lags behind, is not the natural child, is that attempt at an alterity the mother rejects.

Stepmother demands a distance from (rejects) child's desire to be unnatural, to be of what is not of nature, and also not sociable, not of society, not of the natural daily social world, yet child of inferior, lagging, recessed place; mother rejects child's desire to manifest more from what is other-worldly, unconscious, her unconscious desire. Stepmother's rejection sends child away, out of the drawing-room, out of sight, into an alcove, repressed.

It is the "schizoid" child on the windowseat, recessed into a sanctum of arctic elements. The stepmother has turned; the space between mother and child a vastness becoming demon and phantom. Child rejected to the demand of a mother's recess; the mother turns from this child to escape the windowseat forces herself. The gallows, fiend and thief, sinking and phantom vessels are as responsible for the stepmother's distance and scolding as does that distance send the child to those gallows. Mrs. Reed fears the place of this windowseat child as this place reflects her own petrification.

Windowseat child sits between scarlet drapery and winter storm. The elements bear down upon her, she is on the edge between exterior and interior worlds. The child sits where exterior becomes interior, that is the windowseat understanding where she is not separate from any elements, no difference, no difference between herself and any beating element, undifferentiated within (step) mother's recess. Symbiosis.

Undifferentiated from stepmother is not that the child is identical with her or identifies yet stands within and thereby for stepmother's unconscious, which makes child appear alien, non-adaptive to what is conscious and therefore revolting. This alterity into which stepmother pushes child back binding to the realms rejected.

Child retreats when stepmother orders it. Stepmother's demand for distance becomes child's frozen retreat behind some scarlet covering. Rejected, the child sits in stepmother's order which is an Iceland recess covered by scarlet. Symbiosis: within stepmother's demand is child's desire for the unnatural placing her in a recess undifferentiated from the death forces mother rejects yet holds child within.

This rejection binds child to mother's unconscious, is a failed attempt at separation, keeps the child recessed/repressed in the very (unnatural/ nonsocial) place mother shuns. The Ice Realm is not displacement of a desire for a sofa-mother yet is unconscious desire of mother to be thrown back to the origins, re-jecting child, throwing back child to the sources of other consciousness, unconscious desire. The Ice Realm is also child's desire to reside in the unconscious of mother which is the windowseat recess of the sofa-mother.

"Cold rejection" of the stepmother, what looks like space between mother and child, is actually child's retreat into the recess of mother's most feared, unnatural desire, frozen, becoming criminal. Antipathetic symbiosis: the

35

child's retreat into the recess of mother's criminal desire keeps that child upon some undifferentiated edge of no movement between interior and exterior, still windowseat with no parent of a human comfort or guide buffering, instead a stepmother's face now ghastly moon and wreck.

Elements slashing outside also the scolding inside. The child sits protected yet not separate from both in the windowseat containing the forces of a turning mother as ghosts in realms of death, no pulse here of feeling, the child sits suspended, breath held, unmoved. Undifferentiated space of a windowseat without movement: nothing moves the child here, psyche in a vacuum. When the child is most undifferentiated, not separate, she is protected by a vacuum, schizoid protection when nondifferentiated becomes vacuum suspension.

The schizoid retreat, windowseat moment, when inner is all one wants of the outer, out of relationship, out of touch, all devitalized where churchyard of grave, the sea its phantom, the black one is aloof and horned.

Out of a windowseat comes a text, images and verbal accounts of those marginal regions and her place within stepmother's rejection is to examine their delineation, configuration.

The universe of the windowseat, its 'death-white realms,' is demarcated by the child yet never solidified through signification, nor does the child ever herself become solidified while demarcating that universe. What could have been mother has reverted to threshold of a death realm whose objects are non-objects, cracked, aloof, sinking, fading, decomposing, and they do not require, even preclude positing Jane as an initiating human being, more deject, with no object, desire for non-object, longing for permanent residence in a place of no object and no subject, no being.

"Pre-narcissistic" place of windowseat threatening the eradication of any human, happy in the place of demons.

For Jane is happy in her windowseat. The temptation here is complacency in a place of demons. We have been humanly alienated to a degree where suspended between interior and exterior we are secure with the demons keeping us in the mother's circle without touch. Frozen place of intimacy: it comes with a complacency in haunted retreat, this is the windowseat temptation.

We avoid this Jane, child inferior and rejected, we despise this face reflecting gallow and granite edge. We run from Jane at her windowseat, we run to be more the natural child on mama's sofa, we are shunning the other cousin. She is not to know fireside chatter beside a mothering protective, more this awkward one lagging behind becomes content in her Iceland retreat.

'I was then happy: happy at least in my way.' She wants no interruption and this is when she is called by the bilious son of the stepmother. With the demons she has dropped to the depths isolation on the windowseat and here she becomes addressed by John Reed. He has been looking all over for her. He is not discerning, he gets the overview, but he is tenacious in his searching. He wants to find her.

His voice comes to us joking and with malicious sneer: Madame Mope. It comes to us snide and cruel. It comes to us, catches us in its hate for all we are. It is a voice without, a call, Jane is called. John Reed's interruption is part of her calling. Madame Mope. John Reed mocking her retreat which draws her out.

John Reed comes out of her landscape with its fiend and horned thing himself as tyrant-murderer. She is sitting in a psychic vacuum, inner as outer undifferentiated from mother, recess attracting fiend and thief. In the vacuum of the windowseat is also the beating rain from which she is protected yet not separate. Vacuum and invasion mutually attract. Within the order by the stepmother to vacuum recess is the drop to the ice edge rock bottom completely alone as she is assaulted by the demonic son.

What Mrs. Reed had punished was Jane's question back later termed impudence: what did I do? Jane's question posits her as a differentiated person in Mrs. Reed's presence requiring interlocution. Her question is her presumption that she is separate enough to be Mrs. Reed's interlocutor even as she resides within that woman's rejection and inferiority. It presumes that the child can dialogue from another viewpoint with whom has alterity and the stepmother returns she cannot, the push back (in) by the stepmother is the stepmother's turn away binding them.

Asking Mrs. Reed the question about what she has done indicates that when snapped at Jane does not easily capitulate, returns instead some spark. And it is this spark the stepmother would extinguish, cannot meet, wants away, removed not entirely yet on windowseat periphery, scarlet curtain, and it is to this that her explosive son attaches.

Mrs. Reed's punishment of Jane's "impudence" is also how the stepmother is blind to John's attack. John attaches to a scarlet curtain side of which Jane already is a part. Jane has her own red but it has been humanly alienated and become demonic, attached the demon Reed, in the face of the stepmother who cannot face it.

The scarlet curtain side of Jane to which the son attaches, through which he sees with his sister Eliza's sharp sight, is Jane's extension out from the recessed, marginal, inferior place. The curtain which implicates her with the natural world, is to what John Reed attaches.

The tyrant who greedily gobbles mother's baked pies takes us back to the world. He is the other side of the window retreat. Here is the red "burst" always threatening to break through the secret citadel, that explosion every schizoid lies over, closing eyes to, holding off, locking up. John Reed is the manifestation of the rupture from which Madame Mope continually defends. When John Reed bursts, Jane moves out of the schizoid place more to the borders of a lived world, now of the borderlines.

He wants her to show him the book, the text of the windowseat terrains, and it is her calling to bring that out. When John Reed bursts through the antipathetic symbiosis within mother's unconscious, Jane is compelled to carry out the text of that unconscious.

When there are not yet the words, we do not yet know a language to delineate these unconscious figures and their landscape into which we have been unconsciously placed by the stepmother, the unconscious expression becomes bodily possession: the John Reed seizure. Repetitive thrusting tongue and sudden blow.

He is our tantrum. He bursts out from a tremendous appetite, a gorging. He is inflated, the skin everywhere bloated the heavy limb; he is the grandiose exhibitionist. When there is the tantrum also here is the arctic retreat, schizoid child beneath. Arctic retreat covered by scarlet attaches a grandiose, craving son which draws us out to the breakfast-room.

When it comes, the burst seems to come from outside ourselves from someone despising us. Yet it extends from our isolation which leaves itself through outburst, outing, exit, sortie. John Reed claims that Jane's book on the Ice Realm is really his own, that she is not alone in it and even must emerge from her recess to return it to his world. Arctic ghosts desire a breakfast-room delineation through the John Reed possession.

Arctic ghosts first make their appearance in the breakfast-room: before we have learned the language of their expression, or how to mediate their entry, they emerge through appetite. John gorges at the table habitually and at school his mother sends him what in his schoolmaster's opinion is an overabundance of cakes and sweetmeats. Jane and John do not dialogue from the place in which she has been, not interlocution yet onslaught, cruder appetite, primary need, possession.

It is his book. The rhythm of his language a rage and greed a grasp of what is world. In the tantrum here is seizing, incorporating, taking back; a lashing out in order to feed, take in, absorb, become and have it all. His is a demand for an appetite to be satiated and more to a bloating, craving. His text is absorbed, consumed by appetite. John Reed's relation to the borderline regions is the demand for incorporation as possession, not delineation; the text which would configure and delineate becomes used as weapon, unmediated contact precluding inscription, covered with blood.

Since the ice region in which we sit is undifferentiated from John Reed and his cruelty — it is his book and we sit in daily fear of him — his demand moves us. His energy crude of a dingy skin, heavy limb, bleared eye, flabby cheek, his lineaments are thick: his flab and inflation are our lack of differentiation.

He orders her to approach and stand before him and she does 'habitually obedient.' The John Reed force perpetually recurs: 'He bullied and punished me: not two or three times in the week, nor once or twice in the day, but continually: every nerve I had feared him, and every morsel of flesh on my bones shrank when he came near.' Insult followed by blows, he strikes. When this force comes, we are taken in by it: 'Accustomed to John Reed's abuse, I never had an idea of replying to it; my care was how to endure the blow which would certainly follow the insult.'

Repetitiously we do what John Reed says because of his sheer brute force which arrives when we have sat happily too long in the Ice Realm. Our acquiescence to him pertains to being surrounded by Iceland demons alienated from all human relation and too complacent in that. What then erupts is a tremendous need cutting across all human proportion and natural boundary, forcing us along. And that need is our own as it is also that of Mrs. Reed.

> ◆§ Perpetual recurrence of the same thing: repetition compulsion. We have done what she has said to do, we live in her rule, we have left the room in her order and this has placed us in the realm of demons and we are happy there since it is the only way she holds us. She sends us to the place of her utmost desolation and then it is we must face the continual ravenous and bilious form of her hunger, her need, her unmet, unfed, now greed, after us, wanting our life, wanting all that we have touched. Daily attacks of us as she is blind to it is her windowseat, it is her son, we are desperately isolated and when he calls we obey 'habitually obedient,' it is his grandiose force that demands it and also we obey to get closer to her only life unconscious, we obey. §◆

Child recessed in mother's unconscious, when the desire of the unconscious is too recessed the child is assaulted by a tremendous craving, an appetite for an instant satiation, gorging, bilious, passing through mother and possessing the child. What removes her from the windowseat is John Reed's call to possession—his house, his book, his servant. The unnatural desire (too unconscious) hers as that of the stepmother, erupts to world as his gorging need, attacking, possessing her.

When our desire is to remain in the unconscious 'death-white realms,' when our desire to live out of the underside has been too long unconscious, what arrives is the craving. Need and craving emerge as the enactment of unconscious (unnatural) desire. Gateshead is where the first manifestation of unconscious realms is of impulse reaction, blood text permeated, and his flesh overwhelms us.

It is his book. Cruel master of Ice Realm he draws her out through the scarlet curtain, reminding her of the human scarlet side of the winter storm. There is no mother here yet a mother who has turned and that mother's son who interrupts within the mother's turn, bringing the child into the world with a smash, thud, blood trickling the pain of a severed head.

When we cannot yet speak the text of the recess to which mother sends us, cannot delineate the hate, stealing, death-dealing aggressivity and vacancy of that place, we become it in reaction to her son and her son's only language is curse from eruption at us. The ice-bottom engenders its own enflamed devil humanly manifested by John Reed who screams: you are dependent, you are not enough, you do not belong, you are a rat.

When he comes he beats in our heads all day, we hear his curse over and over, gradually bowing under in an inferiority we turn on ourselves to a burst. We find it difficult or impossible to hold any ground when he arrives. On the borderline, we have not a demarcated room, balancing on the windowseat and we totter when he hits.

John Reed comes through a stepmother's recessed windowseat where we do not have a differentiated place, have lost all balance, no sense of what is ours, dependent. John Reed comes when we have lost all sense of what is our substance, without any solidifying substance the John Reed attacks are merely repetitious shatterings. Primarily the movement of rejection, we sink back into windowseat recess, flesh on bones shrunk, only to be called out daily, mocked, struck.

Only motion of rejection and scission of the unconscious itself manifested daily in a John Reed scene without anything solidifying until the head open cracks and this day we strike back. When we have never replied to his abuse the day we do it is in the same manner we have been accustomed to receiving him, we lunge consumptively, becoming of his substance perhaps we think that solidifying.

The book hits, gash, and we lunge a tremendous gorging, we grasp. Flailing we seize for a consumption back. John Reed's possession of our text of arctic death images has become our possession by John Reed. We distend in appetite. Our habitual obedience to John Reed turns finally into lunge and the appetite now is ours: addiction.

We lunge back and our head breaks open, repetition compulsion becoming addiction. What could be scarlet force generated within mother's (unconscious) desire to become delineated now addiction.

    ◄§ Slave-driver. Roman conqueror. He inflates our need we want we have stepped out of some place sitting frozen vastness to take in order to burst sever he fills to crack open. Filling, no hold totter swirl what is this tunnel plunge to fill in turn she turns and our gorge expels, incorporate for expulsion we vomit him out oral burst, for others his inflation that moment to absorb for shattering recurrent release, anal burst. And those who yet the very act on his demand only to be filled, have stepped off the windowseat to fill the infinite space before it happily smacks let it crack bleeding genital burst as he whispers all through this night of the many lovers he is whispering of our dependency. For the slave driver, Roman conqueror, out of which on us her turn, expulsion within incorporation, bulimia. ও

We destroy ourselves on his command as we despise our need. It is his book, his assault is an embodiment of arctic demons. His attack and possession of us through his possession of the text on them indicates his relation to the arctic forces as that attack carries us off the windowseat of their realm. They will possess us bodily if yet not to be spoken through speaking with us.

These demons do not want to keep us windowseat recessed, we are called to carry them to daily life. Mrs. Reed's alterity made manifest. Yet as we cannot be Mrs. Reed's interlocutor (undifferentiated from her), we cannot through language carry out the windowseat unconscious within which we are bound to her.

Our lack of differentiation from her is the impossibility of speaking them, carrying out their text. As we cannot dialogue with Mrs. Reed, we cannot dialogue with the figures of the Iceland recess, only subjected as complacent object to their nature until he screams at us that torture, non-dialogically which is possession.

When John Reed calls we begin emerging out of recess more to breakfast-room, and his mode is of literal seizure, scission and compulsion. Broken boat, sinking wreck, broken cemetery wall, marine phantoms, fiend pinning thief's pack, gallows become his crack, seizure and our lunge back. His cruelty and mockery draw Iceland demon out of what was suspended now embodied through our lunge within his possession.

Tyrannizing as excessive, when John Reed calls we become addicted to thrust back. This bondage has been invisible, no one has responded to its tyranny over us. The servants see the blows yet do not speak and Mrs. Reed does not notice, is completely blind to the extent of his perpetual violence in attack which only emerges through her turned back, unconsciousness.

John Reed is part of Mrs. Reed's unconscious that attempts to sever the child out of itself, by having her embody the scission and mortification of its forces into what is breakfast world.

A false sense of self-sufficiency subtends the John Reed bondage. We say no one will believe us, no one knows the windowseat place. Inflated as he strikes we say we will retaliate. His presence necessitates the isolation out of which we repetitiously attempt to burst through his presence. Jane is alone with him and she cannot summon a human assistance.

Part of the John Reed inflation, and the general force of the Ice Realm demons, is that we think ourselves powerful enough somewhere to go it alone with him. A grandiose part has taken over without containment for we have yet no way to signify in mediated forms the possessing forms. Grandiose with no one with whom to bond, and we find ourselves in bondage to a cruel master of our worse appetite.

The book is hurled and when it hits the child is possessed. She flails. Servants say: picture of passion. John Reed is our passion in a possessed state. John Reed is our passion as we break the unconscious arctic forces out of a scarlet curtain side and we are possessed. He even possesses the book and there is no articulation of where we have been, only bloody incorporation of those violent and marginal forces. This is to have no perspective outside his will we obey habitually lost to his sheer force.

The book is coming toward her hurled by its demon. Demon fiend of her secret citadel now fully embodied in the room here attack. She is hit, going under, the blood sticky crimson stream of a neck as she lunges back. The tantrum attack: sometimes with the servants, we fail to see that she is hitting back.

John Reed emerges as fully bodied from the death realms of non-objects, required by mother's blindness, requiring to manifest the fissure and deathdealing seizure within the unconscious of mother's breakfast-room. And in his severance, splitting, scission, split head scission no longer of ghosts alone he binds her to life, life's blood, focus on another while bleeding, his possession requires her arrival to some sticky crimson current, undercurrent of mother's desire which crashes, explodes, cracks open.

The annihilating force rises after being shunned on the margin placed where no interior or exterior, neither subject nor object, threshold of unnatural force complacency, shadow of a rejecting mother holding in isolation the inferior desire breeding greed. Undifferentiated sitting in a windowseat recess of demons becoming our most primal hunger exhibitionistically flaunted.

A one-sidedness is the "evil" of John Reed, he comes where there are no other voices, no dialogue possible at all. Allowing the book to be possessed by John Reed is to forego language. The head cracked open cannot express design. Possession of the windowseat retreat: her passion consumptive in its lunge becomes the possession where she signifies only through thrashing, bodily seizures, herself now the (out)burst.

Bibliography

Freud, Sigmund. "Beyond the Pleasure Principle." *The Complete Psychological Works of Sigmund Freud.* Vol. 18. Trans. James Strachey. London: Hogarth, 1955.

Guntrip, Harry. *Schizoid Phenomena, Object Relations and the Self.* New York: International Universities Press, 1969.

Jung, C. G. "Anima and Animus." *The Collected Works of C. G. Jung.* Vol. 7. Trans. R. F. C. Hull. Princeton, N.J.: Princeton University Press, 1966. (Hereafter referred to as CW.)

_____. "The Syzygy: Anima and Animus." *CW* 9ii.

Kohut, Heinz. *The Analysis of Self.* New York: International Universities Press, 1971.

Kristeva, Julia. *Revolution in Poetic Language.* Trans. Margaret Waller. New York: Columbia University Press, 1984.

von Franz, M. L. *Shadow and Evil in Fairytales.* Dallas: Spring Publications, 1980.

Winnicott, D. W. *Playing and Reality.* London: Tavistock, 1982.

Chapter 2
Mirrored Phantom

Thrusting her on the stool in the crimson chamber these maids threaten to use a garter to secure but she stills, no longer completely in the thrashing as that ' "mad cat," ' never has she been so out of herself. Their voices, a singsong also din: she is dependent on Mrs. Reed, she is not equal to the cousins, so be useful, pleasant, be humble, then she would have a home, they say, Jane, if you are passionate and rude, there will be no home for you here, and what if God himself in the middle of one of your tantrums strikes you dead, and so if you don't repent, something bad, very bad, coming down this very chimney, it will come Jane and fetch you away.

The door locks behind them. The room is awesome and dreadful. Entirely of mahogany and crimson except white pillows and mattresses of the 'tabernacle' bed, white chair that 'pale throne' by the bed's head. Mr. Reed's last breath in this room a death spell precluding intrusion. Solemn, lonely chamber of grandeur. She is returning to her stool after trying the door, indeed locked, crossing now the looking glass with a fascinated glance she involuntarily explores. Facing her the white arms and a face with its glittering fearful eyes, here is the effect of a real spirit, half fairy, half imp of the dells of Bessie's evening story.

Superstitions with her as she returns to the stool. Rush of hot blood in her head beating the charged thought: why was she singled out in suffering, the accused condemned child? Headstrong Eliza respected; the golden, spoiled Georgiana indulged; and John never accused with his fiercest tyrannies: twisting pigeon necks, killing pea-chicks, breaking the buds of the earth's fruit, reviling his mother's flesh as he spoils her silk dress. To that mother he is still the darling, indeed, no reproach for John striking her. Unjust! Escape: run away or else it must be not to eat and not to drink. To that tumultuous stool child, it is the Older Jane, with distance of years, saying she suffered at Gateshead because she was a discord, heterogeneous, alien, also contemptuous of them in her own way.

Daylight is leaving the room chillier now. 'My habitual mood of humiliation, self-doubt, forlorn depression, fell damp on the embers of my decaying ire.' Wicked, she had just thought of starving herself, now she sees the death vault, is it not the uncle placed there, that uncle who took her a parentless infant and when dying required a promise of care from his wife for that infant, to rear as one of her own children this one, the alien one also noxious, the one that wife could not love.

She sits still watching the bed, a fascinated eye to the mirror occasionally, would not this spirit of an uncle rise to avenge the oppression of his sister's child? Ah, this grief may 'waken a preternatural voice' to pity, she stifles the desire, sits boldly upon the stool. Yet then a light gleams on the ceiling; adult Jane later conjectures lantern yet child sees 'herald of some coming vision from another world.' Heart beating a rush of wings, head on fever, presence there oppressing, bearing down a suffocation; she is letting out the wildest scream and now she is shaking that lock of the only door.

 The maids rush in at first they believe the child must be ill. Mrs. Reed, cap flying, marching down the hall smells trickery. The child begs she cannot endure it, let her be punished some other way, she will be killed in there. In the aunt's eye there is only a 'precocious actress' of 'virulent passions, mean spirit, and dangerous duplicity.' Abrupt thrust back in the room by the impatient aunt, the locked door closes as does a fit upon the child settling in unconsciousness.

We flail, dart, spit, never have resisted so entirely. Resisting we are taken. To resist John Reed is to be taken by him. Our possession by the force of him becomes our resistance to its (driven) eruption. When our only possibility of delivering the arctic elements off the borderline becomes unconscious blatant action in the breakfast-room, we are out of ourselves.

 Projection of hate, incorporated expulsion is to be that son, possessed by what appears objective psychic violence. No one sees or speaks when sees.

 No one sees or speaks when sees, the articulation of it will not come from outside ourselves and we are beside ourselves, out of ourselves, outside our selves. Entangled in him we give ourselves, what self for which a book aimed yet gashed, over to him, and left to himself he expands.

 The rush as she is most out of herself she is himself as he is that violent gush literalized for which there is not yet word or limit. Resisting all limiting, all the way resisting the maids' confinement, she is heel scraping floor, twisting back arched, she hisses.

 Placed in the room, forced on stool, the maids are saying her imprisonment has to do with something she is supposed to learn. Standing over her, they bark, it has to do with learning humility, something of repentance. She does not understand for she is the mad cat, she thrashes.

 The maids are called forth by what her lunge resistance at John Reed was attempting. She tried to resist his violent enactment of emerging unconscious force. The maids arrive to sever her from that incorporation: thrusting tongue hurled book blows now her lunge at him from which they separate.

 The maids come to tell us, in the possessed state, that we are mad. They hold our constitution as we are most out of ourselves. They feed us voices from more human, ordinary aspects; they carry our person in mind. These maids have never entered the Ice Realm nor seen our place within that death terrain, instead their view of us pertains to human affairs, garters, daily life requirement.

As John Reed has been the failed attempt at delivering out in articulate form the unconscious forces, this failed attempt evokes the maids. They will not have us reactively acting out forces once unconscious. They prohibit the (non-human) form in which we have been provoked to exhibit them, no home if mad cat.

Failure at the delineation which would constitute child as agent, narrator mediating psychic forces, becomes the maids' collective morality. For the morality of the maids' barking is collective: you will go to hell for your tantrum.

Our culture's handmaids do not guide us through the possessing forces of mother's recess, instead they moralize, and their collective morality wants to break the possession, sees an indulgence within the tantrum. Their human speaking is forthright, definite, collectively understood: they present God's proscription as a replacement for our failed inscription of unconscious force.

God's design of the otherworldly, collectively understood, arrives in order to break the John Reed possession. The maids of a collective standing drag us away from the territory caught enflamed madness through a speaking of God's retribution, some Father omnipotence. The maids' comprehension of God relates to the contiguity inherent within the John Reed possession itself, immediate reaction in either case.

Some Father's regimen an attempt to lock up the child a lesson of limiting the incorporated unconscious force. Retributive move to lock the burst (outing itself) away (back in); no one speaks to the child inside the possession, the maids locking her up do not see they lock John up with (in) her: isolation temptation of the John Reed possession.

As we resist externally imposed limit in the process of resisting his seizure which defies limit, our animal is maddened, and what comes are maids with binding garters speaking of God's punishment. Their response to the possession is not to educate us about John, or to instruct us about forms of his expression, or where we are going; working for Mrs. Reed, with a vengeance they fear the fit, any eruption of unconscious force to be locked away.

Maids use God's name to extricate us from bodily lunge. God is who is high to insure the unconscious not delivered nonhumanly as human blind incorporation Father prohibits. Sit still stool punishment in God's name justice done, let there resume an evenness and conformity.

In God's name the maids' barking comes from a vital fear of the nonhumanity of this mad cat resistance. Not approving of the form of our delivery of otherworldly realms, preferring us in conformity, they draw upon otherworld God-Father to urge adaptation to this world.

When we are in a John Reed possession, maids appear urging adaptation to a conforming stance through a God-Father proscription (' "you should try to be useful and pleasant" '), and this results in our being forced to a further recess in the room most remote. To forcibly attempt to even out the eruption of unconscious force drags us further into what is unconscious.

John Reed ruptures all boundaries, asks for severe limiting, the most isolated room in the house, large and solid, to hold the blast. The red-room has its stately qualities. Mahogany and damask, massive and shrouded, the uncle died here. A room of passage to beyond seldom visited by human, room of a passing to the more unseen forces not behind scarlet curtain yet through what permeates scarlet.

Child returned further recessed into the room never trespassed. A room so red.

A room so red, heavily textured crimson damask curtains hanging the bed and large windows of drawn blind, the carpet as scarlet as the cloth of the table at the bed's foot, the walls of pink blush. The father died here, a red-room in which the father is extinguished. What could be the structures of a father cannot survive in this room and the God-Father's strictures of the maids' bark do not limit the possession here which instead increases.

Here is a room not of the human, passage beyond the human, enhancing the child's preternatural faculties. She passes the looking glass, her glance is fascinated, half fairy, half imp attached to and peering out of her. Now her blood sucked out, given over to the Reed force, skin cast white, glittering frightened eyes, dazed as piercing, each in its own direction, her form a phantom air-suspended.

Mirrored phantom: she cannot recognize herself as identical in the mirror, no person to identify in mirror, no signifying human when dependent on the mother's recess within which the phantom she is. The red-room is where the other who reflects her is non-being, no longer is she excluded child, she is no child, no mirroring possible of her as human being, instead fairy, preternatural in possession of human body this the mirror reflects, this mirror reflection of the not-I, beyond-I, before-I.

The maid Bessie who locked Jane up also returns through a mirrored memory in the red-room as the storying of imp and fairy. Bessie has told the narrative for that which Jane cannot narrate yet instead has become. When the one who tells the narrative locks up the child, when the narrative told is locked up, then the person becomes imp.

No longer child listening to the story, while locked she only can recognize herself as the object the story attempted to impart, yet the story referent remembers once she was a listening child.

We have engaged with a thrusting son arising from the Iceland place, as he attempted to pull us out of the realm we have given ourselves over to it, a projection on that devil, and now we are infected, we touch a place first of animal and then of imp and phantom, and the room which reflects our preternatural counterpart is red, large, stately, its glamour scintillates.

John Reed's possession returns Jane to the phantom realm out of which that possession arose: the imp facing her mirrored brings to her mind the Bessie evening story as did the windowseat figures. Their mutual association indicates the homology of the mirrored red-room and windowseat phantoms. Now in this further recessed room, Jane is what she on the windowseat had only perceived.

Far from removing her from the windowseat phantom realm, John Reed's driving lunge and maid retribution pushed her further (back) into fusion with those preternatural forces.

She is charmed, held by the inspiring terror. Through a demonic son possession, Jane has entered realms of spirits seen through herself and she is fascinated by the mirroring glance. She has tried to overcome John Reed and now she is enticed by the nonhuman extent of the grandiosity.

After the mirrored glance, Jane sits down and an envy of her cousins turns in on herself. Mind beginning gyration: how is it others have the advantage, she is caught and condemned; they commit error and crime and are rewarded, she has not the fault and is attacked. She feels the unjustness of things, becomes argumentative and convoluted in thinking.

When who could be initiating agent is threatened—in a mirror we have seen phantom appearing through us—no person, nonhuman-being, and an envy calls us back to some human dimension: why do they get and we not presupposes person. The envy, as Jane pities herself, is an attempt to locate a human in the (red-room) place of preternatural.

Yet envy's resentment places us only closer to the evil spirits, animosity, evil spirits now in our heads convolute, cacophony. Here is "complex" talk: the brain in tumult, in the finest detail it accuses as it complains, but it does not suffer.

Her brain in tumult, snarled, her bad temper feeding on itself, still feeding John Reed's incorporation yet now in her head. Animosity of the head snarled. Animus of head. John Reed inside her head. Repetitiously attacked and even bleeding yet there is not present any human feeling for pain. No capacity of suffering, instead she whines.

Whining as the (unfelt) pain of a nonhuman attempting humanity. Suffering more requires the human touched. Out in the cold, on the windowseat edge of non-being, mad cat to phantom now a red-room of fascination, ghosts are herself, without a mediating human or touched humanly enough to suffer.

We are sitting in the Red Room. Seized by a grandiose, thrusting force, and the tyrant is beating, hurling and cursing, tongue as whip repetitious lashing. He is bloating us, we see our body inflating, we feel grotesque and about to burst. The blood breaks out, we lose our blood, we pale, and the stepmother orders us to a terrifying red-room locked.

Mother orders us to a locked red chamber which bears death, locked womb shattering into its blood flow saturating every textured tissue. Locked womb not bearing life yet life's decease.

Fit possession taking us through this red-room begins our initiation into bloody caverns of mother's dank, insidious, and morbid nature. Further within mother's recess now bloody cavern. Puberty ritual at the breaking of our blood. Hermetic vessel holding the rupture nightmare. Red-room return to our rupturing within locked womb of mother's body. Red-room as modern menstrual hut.

He enters us inflating, we incorporate him driven need, bloated attempt to express criminal and death force, what are the voices, articulated images of that other world, we incorporate him, bloated to burst them forth spilling of the blood returning to interior red chamber asking who are the spirits of our fate/face mirrored.

The red-room question where we face in detail his demonic aspects: he is tearing apart the bird and poultry, breaking earthly fruit, reviling his mother's flesh.

Severing, crushing, bursting, returning to a memory of that pure demonic aspect of nature pulverizing all nature: the landslide, avalanche, flood, hurricane, wildfire turning nature over to its underside, underworlds, otherworlds. When we sit in a blood cavern following his burst he is our question of that inflated demonic force pulverizing all nature, of nature, how is he of our nature for we have been blamed as he has acted up.

 John Reed. As we have witnessed his action, picked him up walking in this world on its edge of annihilation we have claimed he is not of the female; this rape on every street, not discerning he has an overview, daycare repetitious raping and children playing on plastic clown now bullets in chests, curbed glass car crash, thief of a capsule poisoned. But we know he comes in our dreams, configured by men the tyrant-conqueror lighting the furnaces of concentration camps, incinerating Hiroshima, napalming Vietnam, and the deploying of ballistic missile; pulverization of animation, we have found him in our dreams as men how is he in our nature yet in the blood chamber perhaps in the bleeding monthly his action our regard. Bloated we hold him PMS, addiction and internal family violence, we are blamed for his cruel action.

The red-room has its temptations which would attach us to a continual incorporation of this John Reed force. The first we have seen as fascination; we are charmed suspended by the grandiose effort of overcoming him and its result in phantom mirroring. Another is anorexia. We have attached to Mrs. Reed through the one reviling her, her tyrant, yet then she locks us further recess.

We sit alone, the rapacious attack has gone on in the main part of the house, and in this solemn, remote room he is beating inside our head. We realize we cannot overcome John Reed and she still loves him better.

He still her darling as the anorexic moment of his tyranny where we sit on red-room stool, constricted further recess, becoming a turn of killing force upon ourselves as the ultimate prohibition of him which is to be most constricted no outburst possible as possessed by him we will starve ourselves to death. He demands so in her love for him.

The anorexic movement to literalize deathworld is the desire within the John Reed possession to live from defilement, loathing, the tyrannizing and revolting while locked up by the (step) mother's order. The John Reed incorporation takes its second form in this more remote room.

Pre-signifying, when we cannot yet delineate the figures of her recess, John Reed manifests in breakfast-room as expulsion lunge and in red-room as skeleton, the corpse within the tyranny. Grandiose form of escape from the John Reed oppression is to be most possessed by him in the red-room place where the outbursts are no longer, only the petrification of literal death, yearning skeletal manifestation.

Anorexia requires a metaphor of death world. The anorexic brain is 'in tumult,' hyperactive: 'revolted slave,' 'bitter vigour,' 'rapid rush of retrospective thought.' Head aching blood from the blow still brain in tumult when we will to literal death starve. What cools, what arrives in what cools, is the narrator.

Older Jane speaking from the distance of many years: 'now, at the distance of—I will not say how many years, I see it clearly.' The one who narrates the story can speak to the child of her marginal aspect. When there is no human within the possession, fit too closely with what drives demonic, best to go to the human we will become, the one who sees apart, narrates the drama of the heterogeneous forces once unconscious.

The narrator posits the possibility of a differentiated signifying body: 'I was a discord in Gateshead Hall . . . a heterogeneous thing, opposed to them in temperament, in capacity, in propensities.' The narrator perceives our relation to what opposes, to whom we are noxious, describes the drama of our cast, the effect of our indignation, our contempt for who are the other characters.

Narrator's distance cools to stone the anorexic place goes to vault, sees through, sees below, distance of the narrator moving anorexia to see through itself to the Father's vault at its base in the red-room locked in by mother.

Jane cools, embers of ire dampened by the familiar depression this time holding a vault. Dead ancestor rising while she is sitting still in the room of Mrs. Reed's punitive rule, father spirit entrusting her to good care, now in all his wisdom would avenge.

We call on the larger ghosts to break the hold of malevolent others. The John Reed explosions have within them the death of a father.

As we sit in the solemn red-room following the breakfast-room outburst, we remember that John Reed comes from a place of deep loss, and that death has to be arrived at, layers peeled, compulsions to tumultuous brain to starvings to sitting still, cooling ember, find the vault.

The father is dead, and in the room of his dying we are asked by our mothers to sit and know some devastating blood powers scintillate, preternatural forces through body. The mother has not known these forces herself. We are sent by her into the majestic cavern of blood-depths to know the forces when the father is dead.

But we cannot sit here unguided and alone any more than could she, we cannot sit within Mrs. Reed's loss, her forces unheeded and only projected she thwarts us. As we have not been able to know her in our distinction, we cannot suffer the loss.

The father is dead but we cannot face it, for we will see him as that light above, we will look up to him instead and we will say bless me father, give me your power. Power of the dead, idealized father to make her love us in our place inferior. When we have not been able to differentiate enough for delineation of where we reside unnatural, preternatural, as a last resort from the assault of demonic sons, we call upon the larger ghosts.

> ◄§ And we have looked up and said give us your word,
> father, power avenge. Looking up to him when that mother
> shunned us to her windowseat where we are met by her son
> bilious and thrusting, and she put us in a room of grandeur
> isolated to learn the constriction, the father died there, she
> honors him, it is now the only way to make her love us
> because he is on our side, where is he, he is above in a light
> crack the room is dark but the light cracks a door opened he
> enters. This is wrong but we do not know another way of
> getting to her but to look up at the one she has admired our
> father who art in heaven he is descending it constricts our
> throat, he will not let it be known, our mouths are silenced
> as we scream we are penetrated. And the fathers continue to

take the advantage, our call for their word becoming immediate entry, entering from above they put their hand on our
mouth and they say it is all a part of it and not to tell and we
give one first scream in a throat choking we tried to tell her,
we begged her, please please Mrs. Reed I cannot endure it —
' "Forgive me! I cannot endure it — let me be punished some
other way!" ' — but she did not believe us and she pushed us
back in, refusing to see the years also her silencing. And we
thought we had doors, that our openings could be closed that
we knew those hinges existed but now there are no doors for
he broke through them all, splinters everywhere. Blood secular initiation of mockery now crude violation. How does this
blood relate to the other monthly of where are our mothers in
these horrifying seizures of dilation of constriction. ঌ

Father is of the word. The father we look up to, in order to escape the
red-room and also the son's recurrent attacks, is the father whose word to
care for the child makes the stepmother promise. The father is of the word
expected to hold our fate from a distance. He leaves his word as Law and
departs. His word is mediation of our care, of the passage of our history,
word as symbolic mediation.

In the red-room, his word, we look up to it for distance from these ways
of oppression, collapses, his word broken, collapsed his symbolic function
in the red-room of Gateshead Hall where we are infiltrated inside crimson
chamber.

Father's refusal to remain above, to hold the distance through promise
word, his word does not separate us from the damask secret chamber when
we want to use that word to escape his son, the urge of hate of hunger; also
when his word is not mother's desire.

Father not to be an escape from son, father relates to son. Nondifferentiated from mother on windowseat, in red-room, her men of no appeal,
John Reed comes from the rage ordeals, Mr. Reed more the pure terror
ordeals.

Related forces, father and son: the red-room has its white mattresses, a
white throne by the bed's head and in this place Jane passes from John's red
raging to his father's white ghost seizure. Entering the stream of blood,
forced by the stepmother to enter the stream of blood recessed between
them, here the God is white winged power of savior, we had incorporated
John Reed until submerged in blood-depths we face our white God first
thinking ourselves immune.

Dilation. John Reed, human mimetic of nonhuman forces, his grandiosity becomes our red heat, arms flailing, eruption at every cavity. He infil-

trates until we burst out/open with his driving pressure. He enters every vein and is exploding out of us, inflated sonorous thrusts. This mode of being possessed pertains to swelling and dilation: our muscles inflate, the blood vessels dilate, all is of turgor, reddening, seething — our mouths open as the hunger becomes roar we demand to be fed.

Constriction. In the wake of John Reed arrives his father's spirit, terrifying. First there is an awe of this father we apprehend as spirit, 'herald of some coming vision from another world.' Sunken vault to overarching light we reach beyond ourselves to extremes eliminating any human negotiation. We would like his help in the form of avenging, but we will not address him directly in fear of his preternatural properties. He takes us beyond the human, his word a promise of power to separate us from the oppression of son's drive, to remove us from within her recessed desire, yet we cannot speak, we give ourselves under him, borne down by him, held in place.

He bears down upon us no longer seething as we are depressed beneath him, he comes closer, looming over, we try to shrink, hold back, turn in on ourselves, implode. This mode of being possessed pertains to deflation and constriction: our muscles contract, blood vessels constrict, all is of pallor, coldness, we petrify. Winged almighty, descending, pressing down upon us to infiltrate. If we speak any of it we are a liar. Overwhelmed, mouth open as silent screams our mind given over to him we fall under.

      ◄§ Mr. Reed mentoring. His door always of the many locks. Books shelved floor to ceiling. He sits concentrating, head's spark caught by the only skylight. He opens the door if we bow our heads, this entry takes a shyness, it takes some terror. We are crouched in the corner with his image. Through our ears we receive him first the voice booming. Head bowed, we must not look at him yet draw him in our every sinew snapping with his circuit. We use our mind for him. Wanting to ask for guidance yet terrified instead we produce that outpour quenching somewhat the thirst of his only son the one from whom we run toward the beam of our reflection eye of the father. He holds us still. He is opening our skull to investigate the spark of synapse, his instruments sound their metal in our head. We know the cry of pain would betray him; we sit boldly on our stool. Drilling the tools to their finest point then he moves a nerve we forget our name. He has found the dendrite of mystery; gleaming, he reaches for its source. Stitching later with the black thread he undoes the last row, cutting back the thread and stitching again this time a row more perfectly aligned. The terror has inspired, we are

charmed, our head is bowed, he is standing over us, hand on
our head a heralding. We tremble to a quaking, we fall
under a fit. ❧

At first we are inspired, we think we can escape his son and the red-room
through him, yet he bears down too heavily, depresses. 'My habitual mood
of humiliation, self-doubt, forlorn depression, fell damp on the embers of
my decaying ire.' He comes out of the "depression" following the John Reed
exhibitionistic and "manic" bursts. Omnipotent pressing down a sadistic
aggressivity which at times we prefer to the thrusts of his son.

Stepmother's rejection propelled us to realms unnameable requiring
delineation from a windowseat ledge. Hierarchies of psychic forces arrived
in various sizes requiring different modes of relation once called mysteries
of initiation.

Different forms of seizure. John Reed is grandiose yet his base is human,
Jane could attempt to lunge at him, project her hate onto him she was
possessed. The terror she felt as he approached turned to disgust and a rage
as she tried to overcome this one who began more on her level, attacked her
horizontally. He starts out as stepbrother.

John Reed as that enraged deathdealing force which emerges from and
pulls us out of the Ice Realm, off the windowseat edge back into breakfast-
room; through him we return to the daily room, screaming and flailing. We
begin to hear our voice and at last others hear us. This attempt to separate
from Ice Realm through enacting its cruelty richochets: the literal contiguous
action of criminal force not a delineation mediating dialogically a return to
daily world, yet we plunge further now into the unconscious, locked inside
what is mother's body, locked womb of mother's interior body.

The uncle-spirit is distant, her idealization of him is how he comes from
quite a distance. 'Tabernacle bed.' 'Pale throne.' He resides outside of Jane's
personal history, outside her age and size, beyond human dimension.
Emerging from earth bowel as well as the illuminated height of a stately
chamber, vertical axis impersonal level. He descends constricting with a
rush of wings, he is not of the human or a human base, appears to her as
preternatural the almighty spirit these generations has been of Father.

He descends as she remembers he had stood by her as an infant. His
arrival a possible red-room delivery; she would like him to carry her back to
a better daily world, severed from the oppression by Mrs. Reed's John. She
requests the distance of his word through the mode is power.

Temptation of power-manipulation, he involves us in deals, in plotting,
manipulation by power when most fused within the womb also of mother's
body here the maneuver. Plots for power when new vision herald from the
unnameable may move us out of the red-room, sever from any of her

recess, lift us father, use your word to keep this red chamber unnameable, forbidden object.

When through manipulations by power we try to bypass or objectify the hold of Mrs. Reed and her son, the plot suppresses, further fall into recess. Descending Mr. Reed is no longer of the human, so abstract that to address him requires complete loss of consciousness when we want to escape that most unconscious (secret forbidden) place of her red depths.

The maids' manipulation of power, working in the service of Mrs. Reed, to constrain the John Reed possession with God's strictures, did not serve to sever Jane from the possession yet deepened it further recess. Likewise, uncle's word of promise does not deliver yet descends.

Again we become seizure, Reed seizure: he sweeps down as a large-winged presence, she collapses in convulsion, limbs of lightning. Overriding each convulsion here an omnipotent Father pressing down. We are caught beneath, circuits firing as invaded from above to a constriction further into non-being: the other side of the John Reed possession.

Father's refusal to stay above, his word of promise that we be cared for does not stay above and sever us from the damask chamber when we implore it as escape, displace us father, and also when his word is not the mother's desire.

For Mr. Reed has 'required a promise' that the child be mothered as that mother's own child. His word was to guarantee cozy sofa embrace excluding windowseat excluding red-room to guarantee against alien, preternatural forces of rejection, the criminal, deathdealing of scission, explosion.

Yet mother's desire has been not to care for yet hate this child, has been that the child reside in the realm of revulsion and rupture, which has been the place this child has met even been possessed by mother's (unconscious) desire. From that domain child has beckoned word to separate her out instead it lowered touching.

Care for one cannot be required by another, and Mr. Reed never consulted that mother of her desire. He did not consult Mrs. Reed, instead he faded away. And in dying out he said to the mother: look after this little one, care for her, she is special to me, keep the word, make the promise. And fathers have left the mothers even as they demand care for favored daughter, attached to a daughter while leaving the mother then must shun that daughter.

Father's attachment to daughter returns his word to mother's (unconscious) desire, to those blood death-depths where she desires daughter reside. When our position in the red-room calls on Mr. Reed who descends, no longer is language symbolic function constituting itself at the repression of (severance from) blood relation to mother. Instead incest with father becomes predicated by that with mother from which daughter attempts (unsuccessfully) to be lifted above.

The moment father's word touches mother's secret chamber (in which he once extinguished) becomes our shattering. Too close, immediate contact without mediation, word not delineation of the damask chamber yet familial incest, incest with father while inside the blood womb where he died, faded away, returning for our delivery, too close and nothing gets delivered, nothing even spoken, throat choked constricted we fall under.

Gateshead as that place of contiguity where word touches the blood depths to which we have recessed: the text became covered by blood in the breakfast-room; omniscient, omnipotent Father lowered in the red-room and his word became silenced, no word, all word covered by further recess fit of depth. Gateshead is the place of unmediated presence, presignifying, familial incest, the literalization of his word entering her womb through our channel choking us, in a word — hysteria.

Hysteria as that moment when father's word will not be separate from the desires of mother's blood yet has not been able to delineate that red chamber. Not hysteria as the search for maternal fusion, yet as that place already fused within what is also mother's body into which father descends.

Hysteria as the attempt to let the father's word appropriate to itself the maternal chamber. The hysterical moment is when the word refuses to be any longer mere sign above warranting mother as severed object, and becomes the passage of father's word into the desire of mother's blood through daughter when there is not yet a way to delineate and as a way to attempt to delineate this familial incest.

What subtends the red-room scene of hysteria is the requirement that word descend into mother's blood and that become specified to serve what has too long been mother's secrets forbidden.

We cannot use father to escape mother and mother's son, the hysterical moment demands it. For at Gateshead, father and son revert into one another. Father's symbolic function, word holding promise, word as release of non-being death force through signification, or even the paternal metaphor of need's eruption, does not occur when father's word we try to keep separate from mother's desire, no delivery of unconscious image to a daily world in fact lightning crack.

His visit overwhelms us, too weighted, we have held all we can of him, to crash. We have come from the threshold of the unconscious, through the John Reed force laden with a rage not knowing its limit or constriction; we face the challenge of the larger ghosts and we begin to sense a human limit. Gateshead as that place of contiguity, infiltration, no mediation where the crash shatters the red-room's fascination, numinous archetypal breakdown.

Father and son Reed revert to one another. At the base of the John Reed bursting inflation is the death vault of father (anorexia: dilation to constriction). Then the father's prohibitive word's requirement becomes our flailing as of his son: again we are in seizure as the promise father becomes our violent thrashing (hysteria: constriction to dilation).

We become possessed, they infiltrate, inflating and deflating us at their will, and this form of attachment to them is our bond with the rejecting mother, an effort to signify forces of preternatural desire to and of that mother. Possession by each Reed a failed attempt to delineate unconscious realms to her for instead of signification, there is blatant act, seizure, deed, fit.

The violent, omniscient and avenging aspects of yet unnameable realms articulate themselves through us in possession, becoming bodily seizure when we cannot mediate them through language delineating their images. Signification of the contradictions within unconscious: the tension and interplay there, dilation and constriction of its forces require articulation, the specification of their differentiation.

Stepmother's rejection sent Jane to the preternatural realms unconscious yet that symbiotic rejection also precluded expression of those unnamed regions which became the child's possession. The child incorporates what has possessed, infiltrated, as expulsion when there has been no mother holding at all, no human mediation provision from impingement.

At Gateshead there is no language at all, no Reed asks our speaking but instead maids' sing-song monologue on our dependency, God's retribution, and we do not speak of or to that which grips.

Only contiguous there, presences immediate contact we project, act-out, possessed in fit. Swept away and the red-room stay is locked. She has been locking us in with the violent infiltration of these forces. Our menstruation is a part of it.

At the first blood we are no longer daughter to a father. We know we have a violent pulsation within our pelvis and that if we worked off this power it might debilitate him, that he is weakening, the father is deceasing, decreasing, and we have this tremendous force stirring in our veins, womb, and pelvis.

Our mother does not want to know it, as she has not wanted to sense her forces only unconsciously remaining subservient to them. Our mother does not want to see it, once the blood stirs in a vagina, we are no longer her extension, she curses us for having our own womb, the impudence of the singular way we encounter dilation/constriction forces beyond conscious life she can only call false (our experience in the red-room is a lie) and we blame her for delivering us such a body (that she forced us into the red-room).

With the coming of the blood arrives the question whether we give this force over to him (repressing it by escaping through his word) as she has her entire life, or do we recognize through it that he is deceasing, we are stirring with a vital force, he is deceasing and our mother will not see it.

With the coming of the blood, we are left with no father and the curse of a mother. Mother is abandoned, she has no love; she is tortured herself, strained, resourceless, continually worn down, crippled, harried, and mean. She has tried to cover it with the promise of Father's word, but instead curse. We are left with deceased, descending father and the curse of a mother through which we begin death passage to regions yet unnamed.

It is not like the ones of which we have heard: males entry to monster's belly, threats of vagina dentata, a swallowing and rebirth. In our perilous initiatory journey through death regions there is a hurled book, pointed attack, swooping visitation, a rising from a death vault to then lower, the threat not of being swallowed but of infiltration and invasion.

He gets in our veins in various ways firing out a death in a fit. Each male force another initiatory ordeal at Gateshead taking the form of possession. John and Mr. Reed ordeals to differentiate the psychic depths of her rule: can we cross through to the side of otherness (male forces) to signify the broken boat stranded on desolate coast, fiend, churchyard, gallows, as well as the son's thrusting tongue and revilement of mother's flesh; that phantom mirrored and the dead father vaulted rise to a descent what is the language of the specific death images of these recesses, what is their desire.

Mrs. Reed orders Jane to a locked red chamber bearing death. The child is thrashing when she enters, sits still long enough to find herself as phantom and is invaded by unseen preternatural force. Mrs. Reed does not believe Jane, thinks the child is faking, that here is an 'artifice' of a 'precocious actress.'

The mother indulging son's greed while unconscious to his cruelty, mother living out her hungers blindly in the gorging bilious and raging son, cannot see the fit of the possessed child as anything but false. Child as actress, child a figure in the drama of unconscious forces; child has itinerary, configurations of *dramatis personae*, drama of the heterogeneous psychic forces, repetitious plots. Child passes through the itinerary of her psychological drama, daimonic fate history. Child as actress in the red-room scene of *dramatis personae*.

It is this 'artifice' statement of the mother which accompanies the fit itself. An aspect of Jane's reality cannot place her stepmother's ghost husband, thinks it superstition. The child and Mrs. Reed have not been able to let metaphorically configure through their nature these voices calling from beyond that which is adaptive conscious stance. Father-spirit of the word is descending. The mother does not know how to delineate the differentiation of death forces and their interplay in the blood. Deceased Father descends, mother does not know. Before we can know we have to go through some ordeals.

◄§ 'The room was chill, because it seldom had a fire; it was silent, because remote from the nursery and kitchens; solemn, because it was known to be so seldom entered. The housemaid alone came here on Saturday's, to wipe from the mirrors and the furniture a week's quiet dust; and Mrs. Reed herself, at far intervals, visited it to review the contents of a certain secret drawer in the wardrobe, where were stored divers parchments, her jewel-casket, and a miniature of her deceased husband; and in those last words lies the secret of the red-room: the spell which kept it so lonely in spite of its grandeur.'

Mrs. Reed. Over again she strokes. Hands to those parchments, thumbs rubbing frame, miniature in a frame. Her silk dress has been torn by her son and it is sinking in some water. Chin squared skin aged thirty-six years old she manages the household. Her hands are lean, long-fingered, large knuckled, aging stroke of his picture. Blood pushed through his heart then aorta pulse portrait perfect she knows him better this day, turning she looks upon the red tabernacle bed she hears his requirement makes his promise she wants him to leave. Never was he with her in this grandeur crimson chambered before the sickness and he never felt her contractions, the mirror's phantom through her contractions the way her blood pulled back, pale cheek he never saw her pale cheek. He dies afterall leaving her a waif. And the girl knocks on the door yet the woman screams only one of us can be in here at once never will I wait with you child in layers of scarlet damask for you would seek in its every fold the oily dust of cracks no housemaid's hand could reach. The screeches of my children pull me out with no interest to enter this jewel-casket but when my long finger taps the parchments here also the child Jane knocking Jane it is inevitable now knocking.

Miniature husband, I stroke your miniature, you remain wisp even reappearing within this frame, I cannot find you concrete evidence. My body constricts around your memory. My womb cramps always menstruating and yet when I sit in this room with you husband the scent of my discharge creases your framed visage until all blood stops. It is the moment

you cease breathing no oxygen and I harden more than you
always were the softer. In this room, some optic nerve urges
atrophy. My iris by you never seen. The arm with which I
do not write numbs. My ankles are crossed and the gap
between my knees still frightens me. Sturdy black shoes want
to tap to some love music instead I shun you husband were
more interested in my eyelash on the pillow, make a wish,
yours that I remain with waif, what is red crusted, this lid is
granular, the curtain crimson folds I do not notice, I have
not stopped spotting since you left. ⧔

Bibliography

Elaide, Mircea. *Rites and Symbols of Initiation.* Trans. by Willard R. Trask. New York: Harper and Row, 1958.

Gallop, Jane. *The Daughter's Seduction: Feminism and Psychoanalysis.* Ithaca, N.Y.: Cornell University Press, 1982.

Guntrip, Harry. *Schizoid Phenomena, Object Relations and the Self.* New York: International Universities Press, 1969.

Hannah, Barbara. *The Problem of Women's Plots in "The Evil Vineyard."* London: Guild of Pastoral Psychology. Pamphlet No. 51, 1948.

_____. *Religious Function of the Animus in the Book of Tobit.* London: Guild of Pastoral Psychology. Pamphlet No. 114, 1961.

Honey, Margaret, and Broughton, John. "Feminine Sexuality: An Interview with Janine Chasseguet-Smirgel." *The Psychoanalytic Review* 72 (1985): 527.

Irigaray, Luce. "The 'Mechanics' of Fluids." In *This Sex Which Is Not One.* Trans. by Catherine Porter. Ithaca, N.Y.: Cornell University Press, 1985.

_____. "Is Her End in Her Beginning?" *Speculum of the Other Woman.* Trans. by Gillian C. Gill. Ithaca, N.Y.: Cornell University Press, 1985.

Kohut, Heinz. *The Analysis of Self.* New York: International Universities Press, 1971.

Kristeva, Julia. "From One Identity to an Other." In Leon S. Roudiez, ed., *Desire in Language.* New York: Columbia University Press, 1980.

Lacan, Jacques. "The Mirror Stage as Formative of the Function of the I." *Écrits: A Selection.* Trans. by Alan Sheridan. New York: W. W. Norton and Company, 1977.

_____. "On a Question Preliminary to any Possible Treatment of Psychosis." *Écrits: A Selection.* Trans. by Alan Sheridan. New York: W. W. Norton and Company, 1977.

Lange, Carl George, and James, William. *The Emotions.* New York: Hafner Publishing, 1967.

Miller, Alice. *The Drama of the Gifted Child.* Trans. by Ruth Ward. New York: Basic Books, 1981.

Oesterreich, T. K. *Possession.* Trans. by D. Ibberson. Seacaucus, N.J.: University Books, 1966.

Rapaport, David. *Emotions and Memory.* New York: International Universities Press, 1971.

Rush, Florence. *The Best Kept Secret.* New York: McGraw-Hill, 1980.

Schwartz-Salant, Nathan. *Narcissism and Character Transformation: The Psychology of Narcissistic Character Disorders.* Toronto: Inner City Books, 1982.

Todorov, Tzvetan. *The Fantastic.* Trans. by Richard Howard. Ithaca, N.Y.: Cornell University Press, 1975.

von Franz, M. L. *Shadow and Evil in Fairytales.* Dallas: Spring Publications, 1980.

Chapter 3

Apothecary

Is this a nightmare from which she is emerging? Here red glare crossed with thick black bars. The voices swirling are muffled. Slowly she is being lifted, it is an arm behind her, tenderly supporting her to a sitting. Resting safely against it, red glare now nursery fire. The nursemaid Bessie with a basin in hand at the foot of the bed and the gentleman behind her, he is not related to Mrs. Reed. She is immensely relieved that he is a stranger. It is Mr. Lloyd, not the physician whom Mrs. Reed calls for herself and the children, but the apothecary, called when the servants are ill.

This man is asking her does she know him. She pronounces his name giving him her hand which he takes smiling. They will get on well he is saying and he is instructing the nursemaid that there are no disturbances for the child that night, and now he is leaving with a suggestion of a return the next day. Yet the shelter departs with him and a great grief falls upon her as the door shuts behind him. Bessie is afraid of this sickness of the child, she is asking the other maid to sleep with her in the nursery, and so it is that Jane hears them discussing her ' "fit" ' with its passing white figure and trailing black dog, the tappings on the door, the light over the uncle's grave, all in the child's screams, now that child lies in dread.

The narrator Jane notes that to the day she feels the shock of the red-room, yet addressing Mrs. Reed she says she ought to forgive the woman: 'while rending my heart-strings, you thought you were only up-rooting my bad propensities.'

Now the child is wrapped in a shawl by the hearth and the tears on her cheek they are those silent tears and even with the cousins being out with their mama, even with Bessie beginning a kindness, now without reprimand or flagging, still the nerves are racked, nothing soothes.

Bessie's attempt: here is the tart on the painted china plate with its rose-buds nestling that bird of paradise Jane always admired could never touch and here now too late. Bessie suggests book. Jane asks for the favorite it is *Gulliver's Travels* more of interest even than the fairy tales whose elves she could not find though she looked beneath leaf and mushroom, yet Gulliver's diminuitive and tower realms she is sure they are located on her earth and so today she turns to the favorite book. Yet no charm instead the giants and pigmies turn malevolent and this Gulliver resembles 'a most desolate wanderer in most dread and dangerous regions.' The book is placed beside the untasted tart.

Bessie begins to sing a ballad of an orphan child, Jane begins to cry. And so it is when Mr. Lloyd returns in the course of the morning, he asks whether she has been with tears, whether she is in pain. Bessie claims the child cries because she could not go out in the carriage that day with the Reeds. The man responds she is too old for that pettiness. And Jane wounded by the false charge is saying the tears have nothing to do with the carriage, she hates the carriage, she cries because she is miserable.

The eyes of this man attend her. Steadily while upon her she sees that they are small, gray, not very bright but now she would say shrewd and looking at her he asks what it was yesterday made her ill. Bessie replies, the child had a fall. Fall! The man is exclaiming this one is no baby she can walk easily enough. With mortified pride the child's words: I was knocked down but that did not make me ill. The dinner bell rings, the apothecary sends Bessie down.

Ensuing dialogue she says she saw the ghost of her uncle while shut up without a candle in a room no one else would enter at night; and also she is unhappy for other things.

Gently he inquires whether she would tell him the other things.

She is moved by the request yet she pauses in the first moment she has been asked to speak. After nervous hesitation, she is telling him she has no father or mother, brother or sister.

He suggests she has a kind aunt and cousins.

But the cousin knocked her down and the aunt shut her in the red-room.

The house is beautiful, it is a fine place to live.

The maids remind her that she has less right to be there than a servant, and she would be glad to leave it.

What about any other relatives?

Possibly there are low relations, with the name Eyre.

Would she like to go to them?

The child reflects, sees the ragged clothes, fireless grates, the manners that are rude. She declines saying that poverty is analogous with degradation and crudeness, she is 'not heroic enough to purchase liberty at the price of caste.'

Would she like to go to school?

Images from Bessie's stories of the back-boards, the discipline, and John Reed's hate of it but then more of Bessie's story: young ladies and their paint- ing, songs, French books. It would be a separation from Gateshead. Yes, she would like to go to school.

At night she overhears the nursemaids' talk and learns that Mr. Lloyd's recommendation of school was accepted by Mrs. Reed. And then the maids are talking about her parents and for the first time she learns that her mother married a poor clergyman, the match being beneath her, she was cut off by her father. While visiting the poor, the husband contracted typhus fever, mother caught it and they died a month apart. The nursemaids are agreeing the child deserves a pity, yet her suffering would be easier to take if she weren't such a ' "little toad," ' were more a beauty like the blue-eyed long- curled cousin Georgiana—the image of whom whets their appetite for dinner, they fancy a Welsh rabbit with roast onion.

Red barred by black the hollow sounds, rushing wind, whirlwind. The nightmare ends, our senses still devoted to it, we awake to its shades. Glaring red we sweat and the black bars jar us.

Leaving the possession on the same path she entered, Jane emerges from an unconsciousness through the red glare of the nightmare carrying her to the fit.

Nightmare's red scorching until shielded nursery hearth, the arm holding her is neither terrifying nor winged, instead very tender. Black bars a grate for a fire now hearthed. The upperside of the red textured horror is nursery fire barred. Red-room reverts to nursery as the arm uplifting is of a stranger. She wakes to the strange apothecary, gentle stranger, unfamiliar and therefore welcome.

He lifts her and supports her in a sitting position, stranger support. He raises her, all the stranger that one should lift her tenderly out of what is not yet conscious, glaring recess of secrets crimson chambered. The guardian supports her rise to a sitting position, no longer flattened as shattering seizure beneath a lowering deceased Father, yet sitting, facing servant with basin figuring the ground of nursery fire, resuscitation to daily chamber.

Strange apothecary, human arm her rise, gentle other unfamiliar, heterogeneous thereby protective, not a Reed, what lifts her out of unconscious glare, the glare of the silence, the blindness within the Reed family, gap in the family as glare she went under when asked to face his word in her blood seared to glare; the return is through this one not of the family.

And what is at her feet a servant of basin, the maid who locked the red-room door now nurse wiping out her fit in return to nursery bed: we leave the possession on the same path we entered, unconscious and conscious realms transpose.

Here the nurse is maid and he is the lower physician. Lower than physician, not of a high class, called for the servants, closer to the base, of base minerals he knows the combination and he soothes what ails, his hands in the oils of roots, herbs, gums, his hands of the oils touch our baseness, inferiority, where we ache he touches, soothing ointment.

Physician of the lower regions where lie our shame, humiliation, our unnatural desire, physician of servants, he touches what is inferior, kept down, below, behind (the dead ancestors, our shadows, what is revolting, ugly, freakish in quality) he sees through our symptom to its lower interior wound.

He tends to servant, he tends to who handles daily care physicality, domestic chore, the simple human requirement, here a human base. The apothecary is outside the Reeds and their forces, distance through human base his arm is able to ease her out of the charred hollow of what was seizure. How he is heterogeneous to Reed is how he touches and heals the inferior; he meets her where she has carried for the family the heterogeneity and gives it a human lift.

Within the Reed possession, sojourn to unconscious forces, gone to death margins where our throat clutched, swallowing breath as we smashed against a human limit, unspeakable rupture. For that place of holding the tension between the inherent contradictions of the blood (inflation/constriction) and his symbolic word has shattered.

We extended ourselves through a grandiosity to limits of a crash returning us to someone human. For that mirror had reflected phantom as well as fascination, we may have stayed in the remote room of death as preference or lowered ourselves to the literal death of its vault until the seizure.

Stepmother locked us in until deceased Father descended until we know now his word could not survive his death yet requires this embrace in her red chamber. Through mother's order we realize that father's word will not remain disembodied, requires human base to which we awake.

The father lowered and who raises us is who touches inferior confirmation of where we have gone under the father's descent, Mr. Lloyd, lower physician.

We have extended ourselves through a grandiosity to limits of a crash returning us finally to someone human only now ready for what can be human arm supporting it is not a Reed we had gone through the Reed to death demons now we only want to be here with who has his hands in the earth elements, apothecary.

For a long while we have been complacent with those phantoms, happy in cragged terrain we became of the demon and gallows, not privileged in any human relation with who is mother we were of her ice realms fragmented as comforted there until the son burst us to rise to a father of a word power numinous seizure we convulsed in a writhing fit. We tried to run and we were shaking that locked door, shuddering.

Lying in the memory of the seizure, we shudder again while waking in some human encasement. Quivering of this skin, sudden quivering to the skin of who is human, quivering skin as first definition here a human. Sent to the limits of some unconscious realm and this shuddering dread begins a sense we are human even as we return from what has been preternatural. We are ready to have an human arm backing yet not before we begin to shudder.

Within Mrs. Reed's turn, spirits of the psyche take us away from everything profane but not without offering a way back. At first it may seem unrelated to that which seized us. He is not the physician of the family. Mr. Lloyd is that moment of human shuddering relief after possession by the more unconscious disturbing forces.

He first asks, ' "Well, who am I?" ' He is who locates his name, has a stake in her identification of him, will not be fused with the glare place. He slices through the possession not through reprimand or a further isolation yet through identifying his human substance and asking her relation to that. Simultaneously, he preserves her humanity against encroachment, provides the space in which she can locate herself without infiltration, injury.

> ◄§ Mr. Lloyd. Consistent tweed. Writhing body's blood
> sparks may have been chasing him we thought we saw it yet
> instead he sits still and the red scorching now ribbons encir-
> cling some magic protective circle encloses screams subsiding
> we are not within her sight or embodying what is her blind-
> ness. Spices, myrrh and aloes, boiled lemons and he also
> recommends a soup of garlic; thickly skinned hands smelling
> of leather have caressed the oils do not enter instead the arm
> backs, clock's chime he leaves on schedule protective guard-
> ian his instructions say no disturbance, shielding us from
> further invasion his tweed consistent. In his carriage he car-
> ries a shelter. §►

When he leaves for the night, shelter departs, and the emergence to human after a residence in regions of the dead, depresses. We return naked, exposed, empty, no longer at one with demon-son and his Father-God, after the stunning shock of otherworlds, our humanity is inadequate, cowering in dread as Mr. Lloyd departs.

The emotions accompanying the descent have been a disgust, rage and terror. Those rising with us in the return are shuddering dread and despair. The child lies in dread sensing the ways she has been visited by a white figured relative of the dead, the maids are whispering it was accompanied by a black dog.

We are enough apart from the red-room that we can dread, there is a quivering skin which separates ourselves from phantom though an ambiva-lence pervades this dread, will we return afterall, or has the seizure taken? Bessie is afraid to be alone with the child in the echoes of realms not of this life, the child may die she says, asking for another maid's presence along-side, extra dosages of human in room of death-child.

'Ghastly wakefulness' when the spirits of the dead are too close and our skin is young, we had been seized, and the only shield for the night has departed. In asking our relation to his human identity (named), he posited our humanity (named) not possible in the windowseat/red-room posses-sions and still tenuous becoming ghastly dread; if we stay awake, we are.

She is marked. The visits of figures from the unconscious through who is mother mark. There is no physical sign of it yet reverberation of the nerves to this day shocked. This violent agitation of nerves: the deceased Father's word can no longer cover the repressed desire for union with her unconscious body; the impact of the stepmother's unconsciousness making Jane consubstantial with the death Father jarred the nerves to this day, further shattered. Some say "nervous break," it has been a shock.

From within the night dread of the child, the narrator speaks to Mrs. Reed of the shock. 'But I ought to forgive you, for you knew not what you did: while rending my heart-strings, you thought you were only up-rooting my bad propensities.' Heart-string rent, stepmother wrenched, she did not want this heart a unity she ripped its string, violently torn, cleaved to the heterogeneous heart.

A heart which now knows the contradictions: the expulsion within incorporation, the pull blood penetration of up-lifting word of promise; heart of the hysteric who knows that the Father she addresses is dead and descended; our bad propensity to want a homogeneous heart without contradiction, she cleaved our heart our mark.

'You knew not what you did.' Cruxificion when one has humanized the numinous Father. A human is speaking what once was unseen Father's word unspeakable. Our mother as Pilate's ruler desires to keep the Father invisible, omniscient his word not to speak blood contradiction.

Narrator Jane addresses Mrs. Reed, stepping outside the text. Outside text the first person addressed by the narrator is Mrs. Reed, the teleology of text is an interlocution with Mrs. Reed: to become narrator, to see the heterogeneous figures and their plot is to find a differentiation within what was unconscious and thereby have a perspective to Mrs. Reed, address her without possession.

Emerging human from unconscious glare anticipates the narrator who speaks a time when the possessions have been negotiated, the "masters" mediated, when we may emerge as dialogic narrator, meeting the unconscious desire of the text, arising from the rupture within the first chapter of the impossibility of interlocution with that stepmother, reprimand sending child to unconscious.

(This address of the narrator also suggests an homology between Mrs. Reed and the reader who, perhaps like the stepmother, may have turned from the unconscious in which Jane resided, read the surface only, dismissing this narrative as pubescent fantasy; reader too may need to read the text of the unconscious which from the perspective of the narrator is now the text [Jane Eyre] herself.)

The shock tore Jane out of the red-room fascination, but the senses still are not hers. The sweets do not soothe; after residing in realms uncon-

scious, of otherworlds, the earthly world looks and tastes even reads differently. Blandness and a desolation, insipid world now in comparison.

Her appetite has been altered upon return. Where she once knew its
drive, now it is alternative, the sweets do not soothe: visits from dead and
deathdealing figures affecting her "instinctual drives."

Everything around appears faded, ugly, dreadful. There are objects
which once held a delight, they would catch her eye: now they are plain and
they recede, she has not a taste for anything, only a faint pounding in a
head which does not want to collect anymore, no flavor, no nuance, nothing in the world beckoning, all sits gray and there is no animation.

Here is what appears as "despair." It is not that she is absent in life or that
she is in despair, as much as she is entirely present to death while attempting to return to life. *Gulliver's Travels* had been a favorite tale because she
expected she could find its lands of Lilliput and Brobdignag on her earth.
But after the red-room seizure, some (childhood) belief in the worldly
translation of otherworldly forces is no longer possible, there is not to be
merely literal (re)placement. Her survival of the red-room posits her necessity as mediator between, a speaking of the figurative translation of unconscious to world.

Our calling has been to bring out the text of the unconscious, windowseat possession by John Reed has said that incorporation and blatant action
is not the text emergence yet further recess. Red-room possession by Mr.
Reed has said text may be symbolic function but cannot be severed out
from (sever us from) mother's desire.

We have met the Father's word as descending figure in the mother's
unconscious, asking what is the figuration of the unconscious, we know
now it cannot be located in a point for point correspondence on earth, and
we have a choice to die to it incorporating and possessed by it, or impart it,
carry its metaphor out. This child has been to a place precluding literal
translation to natural world and she lies suspended between death realm
and lived world, not yet able to speak figurative mediation.

Unlike the threshold place of the windowseat, she is not happy here.
Collision with numinous (archetypal) Parent shatters complacent collusion
with mother's unconscious: the naive hope that we can both resume knowledge of that omniscient, universal Parent through that unconscious place as
well as be delivered from it by him.

Orphan is where we relinquish fusion with the unconscious forces, no
longer windowseat complacency, we find ourselves desolate only slowly
learning to reside in a human sense. Recognition of ourself as orphan
requires human orientation. We mourn for the passing of archetypal Parent in this discovery of a mortal human body, we cry as orphan for we have

been alone through hell, felt the pulse of the dead, returning hollowed the desolate wanderer.

> ◆§ Despair. Burnt umber and an olive green also chrome green deep alongside a burnt sienna coagulating chest. The world out of these eyes gray to all affect. No Reach. They need company to guard against us. Looking at us in a side glance they whisper of a black dog trailing. We see only a lone tree as we pass and even this glance we cannot hold. Having been shocked we are disinterested. Hands offering to us only mirage of some longing in a chest clogged sienna burnt. §◆

Hollow after the fit, after the fit we are hollow, lightning shot through limbs and this jolt cannot be sweetened away. The tart no longer appeals; too late for the china bird of paradise; Gulliver a desolate wanderer in regions of dread; the child sits under shawl by hearth crying for the orphan.

Bessie singing an orphan child ballad. Of lonely moor and gray rock the orphan saying ' "Ev'n should I fall, o'er the broken bridge passing,/ Or stray in the marshes, by the false lights beguiled,/ Still will my Father, with promise and blessing,/ Take to His bosom the poor orphan child." '

Yet no Father Heavenly full dove bosom, word of promise that blessed one descended, we looked up, red-room child beseeching an aid, Bless me Father, instead of bosom reception uplifting he penetrated to a seizure suffocating more isolated only return we cry too late is this maid's tale.

Orphan despair is where we can no longer find the protection for our unconscious experience through whom was Omniscient Parent. Orphan is when we mourn the loss of uplifting through word of Father which was to deliver us. Nothing can express where we have been, the old ballads and tales no longer recount it, and we do not know the form or meaning of unconscious realm desired.

The call of John Reed has carried her on a perilous trip through a red-room hell and now more than ever at Gateshead she is alone, not even ghosts for company. As we approach a humanity after the fit, Bessie is kinder, she has held the basin, offers treat, sings a song, yet this caretaker still sings of Father with promise and blessing, there is no mother's voice speaking more accurately our passage and the room swirls without such mother now here a motherless bland swirl: long-waved echoes of unheard sound pulling us in their tide.

After the shock, shuddering we know ourself fully as orphan and for the first time we suffer it; interpenetration of unconscious with conscious becomes our orphan suffering, for when we are identified only exclusively in either extreme we whine. Beginning to offer a recognition of our humanity and loss of Savior Father as we return rent (by her) is the return of Mr. Lloyd.

Mr. Lloyd stands in the interstices of unconscious and conscious realms while clarifying his human identity. Child's shuddering skin as first definition of a person non-fused accompanies Mr. Lloyd's return the next day. Child was broken apart in fit; the fit an essential dismemberment resulting from the inflating fusion with the bursting son and with the potentially uplifting word of Omniscient Parent. This mourning loosens, dismemberment becoming suffering, allowing the child to move the possessions through her, return to a humanity, the arm she awakens to is humanly tender and when he returns the next day, he inquires upon her crying.

Each possession requires something of us; as we pass each through us we relinquish some of our preter-human size which requires assuming more a human size speak in language those forces, human condensation, configuration.

With Mr. Lloyd's return, Bessie tries to make surface excuses for the orphan pain. The Bessie input at this juncture is a denial of the realms from which we are being lifted. Bessie is who will not accept our residence in realms beyond the natural yet instead reduces our state to the infantile. Even as we summon Mr. Lloyd, a Bessie part does not want the revelation of the landscape lying at the core of the child's misery, instead packages it in daily occurrence, thereby negating the essential horror of the death journey as well of the necessity of signifying that.

Bessie is that moment when a return of consciousness occurs only through repression of unconscious seizure in naive honor of the Father's continual omnipotence/omniscience, that all word stay distant from red-room secrets.

And Bessie's surface accounts (the child cries because she could not go out in carriage, had a fall) are precisely what provoke Jane to a 'mortified pride,' 'self-esteem being wounded by the false charge,' allowing the child to begin to express what subtends the suffering of where she had been.

Bessie's is the position against which we push off when our pride and self-esteem want to be located in the unconscious where we have resided, not wanting merely to translate it contiguously to natural occurrence, reduce it to infantile state, and let it be forgotten. There begins a self speaking in the contradiction to the Bessie repression.

After the red-room, we are larger than Bessie's account and it becomes a matter of self-esteem to speak from the depths of where we have been is the base of who we are, esteem for that rent, heterogeneous heart.

Bessie is who would have us rise out of the red-room too fast without negotiating that death chamber back with us. 'But how could she divine the morbid suffering to which I was a prey? In the course of the morning Mr. Lloyd came again.'

His eye shrewd, Mr. Lloyd peers, he sees through Bessie's contrived surface account of Jane's distress. The lower physician assisting to carry the vision of the dead back to life does not fall for the simplistic Bessie cover. His arrival statement is ' "What, already up!" ' – that we cannot quickly rise above it, covering over where we had been. His arrival signals the articulation of the messages within the sickness, the direction within the fit, the word of her 'morbid suffering.'

Apothecary seeing through the earth's minerals, her materials, peers through them to their transposition to healing quality, death property; an alchemist, does not treat literally yet extracts from the material its figurative significance to cure. He refuses a literal reductive interpretation of the child's symptom, instead, physician of inferiority, he meets the wound behind, beneath, where in the lower regions we have been wounded he shrewdly sees through to that profundity, does not infantilize Jane yet tells the maid the child is too old to cry for not going out in a carriage, too old to fall down.

Child says: I was knocked down but that did not make me ill. Mr. Lloyd sends Bessie down to dinner. Carrier back to humanity, to carry us back he knows of otherworlds they have seized. His mediation is what lowers Bessie so the child can speak from the base of things, dismissing silly childish mishap to hear outcast child cast out to preternatural realms marking.

If the maid had stayed fixed in her position, had not gone down to dinner, there would have been another sort of possession. Bessie's requirement for consciousness through red-room repression implies another seizure: if no one had lowered to listen to the underlying meaning of the red-room, Jane would have had to reside in a hysteria, flailing a continual pleading for the recognition of the reality of those phantom forces attempting delineation.

At Bessie's descent: ' "I was shut up in a room where there is a ghost, till after dark." ' The beginning of acknowledging that the forces another calls unconscious are real is the beginning of a differentiation from Mrs. Reed and the Gateshead perspective that the forces of our seizures are not real therefore must remain unconscious.

Mr. Lloyd begins mirroring her through language: she says she is unhappy for other things, what are the other things? Reflecting and following, he gives her stance and voice a space, a sounding. He asks for elaboration. His concern is with the human, her human pain, holding her through language mirroring. Mirrored human.

The one who lifts us up asking to impart unconsciousness to consciousness, mirrors. Extension of the red-room mirror, he was hired by Mrs. Reed. The stepmother does not require a literal death, she called the lower physician who mirrors the child out, mirroring through language provides a space for the delineation of the secrets of the blood chamber. Mr. Lloyd is an extension of the place where Father lowered, humanized to (unconscious) desire. Mr. Lloyd humanly wants Jane to speak her desire and his human base is what Mrs. Reed hired.

An extension of the mother's unconscious blood desire is that the unnatural child begin to speak from the depths of that blood, finding its meaning, its translation not to be provided through a son incorporation or a repression through the Father design, speak from the depths of that blood, womb of blood find the figures of its desire of unconscious speaking when the father is dead. She hired Mr. Lloyd who asks what makes the child so unhappy, when Bessie goes down.

Phantoms of that mirror operate even as a human is here mirrored: the red-room pull back urges a silence. Jane pauses, a 'disturbed pause,' critical moment.

Whispers of red-room fascination lingering call us back, desiring only in itself we remain of phantoms, silenced human. To speak of them humanly would preclude the return eternal return remaining undifferentiated, condemning any otherness, not in relationship.

Denial of all depths is the Gateshead human consciousness, therefore to speak of unseen force there requires a non-human-being. Split now it is a choice, to speak humanly relate we fear loss of damask mystery.

She begins to locate herself through his mirroring, which precludes her fusion with him. His continual mirroring return to her allows a differentiation between them becoming the emergence of language which places her places.

The windowseat and red-room possessions occur repetitiously when we have never been asked to speak them or when we have refused to speak when asked. Blood ordeals not signified incorporate. What is language when word is not severed from or identified with the unconscious realms, yet speaks through them, is language of the unconscious, possession is placed humanly differentiated through such figurative language and this attempt is Mr. Lloyd's mirroring.

We often remain silent after the red-room experience in fear of breaking our bond with eternal powers, for we were one with that winged descending Father afterall; if we word it humanly we will lose its unnatural terror and beauty and our immortal fusion with that. If we speak to this mortal man we sacrifice the eternal forms of no dying and if we remain silent of those recesses we never will die.

The discrepancy between the grandiosity of those forces and our human (inferior, servant) selves accounts for the contradiction we first experience between the red-room and Mr. Lloyd.

She is saying to Mr. Lloyd that she is unhappy for other things. ' "What other things? Can you tell me some of them?" ' Mirroring through language, reflecting recessed figures — ghost, cousin knocking down, aunt shutting in — by interlocution. Figures of what previously was unspeakable when we face whose presence is asking to receive them.

'Children can feel, but they cannot analyze their feelings; and if the analysis is partially effected in thought, they know not how to express the result of the process in words.' No words in the red-room or through that mirroring, post-red-room through his human lift to consciousness mirroring she knows relief is through impartation.

By his mirroring she reflects on her unhappiness, its meaning, 'the analysis is partially effected in thought,' now its speaking the meaning in analysis of what underlied her seizures is that she has no family. To speak from the unhappiness is to differentiate the depths from which she had been knocked down and locked up. Her location takes shape in this mirror through analyzing the fragmentation not through illusory, childlike (Bessie) unity.

Speaking the analysis of unhappiness provides definitive ground, no longer windowseat edge of another's unconscious realm but some room upon demarcated ground, here her property, here her definition, analysis of unhappiness, she does not have a family, she was hit and locked up, she is treated as a servant of the house.

Speaking to Mr. Lloyd of who was the human in the red-room, who was the human in the red-room and what is the meaning of this Gateshead life for her and eventually she is not only what occurred in the red-room. She is no longer blood ordeals yet does not abandon them altogether through simplification in a Bessie fashion.

The ordeals of Gateshead now analysis having impact on his human sensibility. The red-room scene is what carried Jane out to Mr. Lloyd and he is the natural extension of it as he opens himself to engage with its effect.

The advantage of the uncle's shock descent is the residue caution of travelling through death regions uneducated. Some of the grandiosity has been negotiated. She speaks to the apothecary.

First she says she has no family. Analyzing the meaning of the red-room arrives at the death of family. At the break of the hold of archetypal Parent, there is no family. No family is her property. Instead of returning to the windowseat, she speaks from the windowseat. At the base of possession by unconscious forces (Reeds knock us down, shut us up, ever exposed as penetrated), there is a profound separation, scission, fragmentation, dislocation, no family, presupposing the undifferentiated bond with a stepmother.

What results from Mr. Lloyd's mirroring is the speaking of her fragmentation which is the analysis of the meaning of the windowseat and redroom, that they are the landscapes prior to a mirror human image, properties for a rent self.

She says she has no immediate family yet she could not live within the poverty of her Eyre relatives. Less than a servant in Gateshead's wealth, yet the Gateshead value still holds her: she claims the poverty of her relations and from her Gateshead stance that appears only degradation.

She claims the poverty of her relations. 'Fireless grates, rude manners and debasing vices,' human relations of her name debasing, kin too lowly. Low relations called Eyre, to relate humanly lowly beneath Gateshead, beneath red-room grandeur, is to err. Errare: to wander from the truth, to be mistaken; errer: manner of progressing, or to make an error, err. To relate humanly is lowly, is to err, to be of errant, deviant, wandering, stray to astray, to be erroneous in conclusion, 'synonymous with degradation.' She would prefer the Gateshead tyranny over the poverty of her father's family.

To know herself as eyre is also to have itineration and find the justice of that. Eyre: circuit rode by itinerant justices appointed to it. Justices in eyre. What is justice, how to proceed. She may have to wander to find her circuit to learn the justice, where there is justice, what is the correct way to proceed. The right of passage. She prefers Gateshead tyranny possessing.

The Gateshead (material) wealth holds the worth so demon/divine arrive as seizure there. Jane is held within the same view necessitating Mrs. Reed's perception of the falsity of the uncle's visitation, that is, that which exists and matters is grossly material, exclusively.

Gateshead tyranny preferred. Here she is held in place by being prohibited a place, there she would wander. She would not be a beggar to know her family which is the Gateshead perspective ushering in the outraged and inflated John Reed in the first place.

Either a grandiosity or poverty in relations, she cannot imagine a worthy relatedness outside Gateshead. Some of the deathworld horrified fascination still appeals more than what is human relation, to relate humanly is to eyre, within this first interlocution of relating humanly to eyre is lowly, degradation.

To relate humanly is also to learn to hear, through eyre, let another in, interlocution, which is to relate not in seizure, she is humanly located by who is the first to hear her and who she first (likes what she) hears.

When Mr. Lloyd hears she is not ready to know human relation, finding her suspended relative to unconscious, he inquires of school. John Reed hated his school, wants no part of the figurative translation of explosive force to what is society.

> ✒ John Reed at school. Their smile for the teacher, pet of teacher, they smile I will rip it off until the blood underneath. They prance. At recess they prance holding careful beneath arms the milk jar squeaking clean so they could put in the precious seeds. Their teacher's lesson on seeds and those green plants. Milk jars prancing with the sand and the seeds. I am hiding behind the tree until I see them and then I charge. I charge and aim for the jar. It explodes under my foot I love the sound of the seed cracking. I grind my foot into the ground so it can eat up every bit of seed. Then they are crying so I pull their braids and I take the ribbon and throw it to the ground to make a grave for their dear earth. The girls with their perfect smiles, perfect frocks, perfect arithmetic and here am I in the corner of the dunce. My grin is wet, my shirt is hanging, the skin on my knee is torn apart and I watch the mud in the ripped skin, mud and blood and the blood is getting hard to a crust, crust on my bread the best. And I am sitting in the corner they call it the discipline. I pick the scab. ✒

Mr. Lloyd is an extension of the red-room fit, he sees the forces with which we have been struggling and suggests a discipline, not Reedian, more a Bessie story, we imagine learning French, we imagine the art class, hand's craft the minded hold of that force, school. Our way back is similar to that of our entry: Bessie's story inscribing otherworlds draws us.

In the dialogue with Mr. Lloyd, he follows her, they each have a say, he does not talk at her, speak more or louder. He begins with another viewpoint, of another, not a Reed, but gradually he yields his viewpoint (it is a beautiful place to live) to her singular discourse with a level of empathy. He is that aspect which is the potential for her developing empathy, through which she would begin to enter the perspective of another placing her outside Gateshead offsetting John Reed's inflation and rage.

Mr. Lloyd does not exercise by authority, interpretation, or any sort of seduction. Neither grandoise or patronizing he does not attempt to supply an education or take care of her himself. He does not reappropriate Jane's red-room experience into his own design, his structure of (masculine) consciousness or another paternal law.

For that Father's word lowered, law of omnipotent/omniscient Father sunk to mother's blood which became a Mr. Lloyd assistance of Jane to articulation: can you tell me some of the other things making you unhappy? Mr. Lloyd is not an extension or replication of the Father's Law overriding mother's desire, yet that moment Father's law descended through daughter into mother's blood desiring impartation.

Mr. Lloyd is that moment of condensation into language of the contradiction within realms once unconscious. His mode precludes phallocentric authority; he is not master, the red-room descent, heart now rent heterogeneous heart requires that the one arriving be non-authoritative. Yet Mr. Lloyd also is clear: he provides precise questions, firm in his identity, never losing his definition of self or his position towards her throughout he knows himself solidifying substance, cohesive identity. Clear and non-authoritative, he does not operate an univocity (that there is only one way for her to proceed now which he knows before she does), yet explores the plurality of possibilities.

Mr. Lloyd is where our clarity is not also univocity (for in the Father's Law of past they were contingent) which is the effect of the red-room seizure, Father's crash. His resiliency and openness to the effects of Jane's unconscious is the beginning of her differentiation of the heterogeneous figures of that unconscious which is the start of her desiring to know the selves, her properties, go to school.

His focus on the specificity of her discourse (heterogeneous to his own, his own perspective) involves the risk of loss of his position, identity, loss of himself, death. He does not attempt to adapt her to his viewpoint or order and thereby he risks unsettling his own position, risks his own unconscious plunge. The ability to meet another's psychological heterogeneity risks one's own death; Mr. Lloyd is inferior enough for such risk, already knowing the inferior, underside.

He does not insist on her education in a masculine mode, in the dialogue with him what gets imagined is a Bessie school. Not a Reed school where one beats up, where the eruption of John Reed even beats up master, but Bessie school where what is mastered is a plurality of crafts.

Mr. Lloyd sends us to the place where girls learn to read, write, speak, sing, draw, impart the story. Woman not of materia, passive, inert commerce exchange between men as in the Gateshead possession by son exchanged for possession by father. The masterful possession of Gateshead implied the right to exchange the female yet Lloyd assisting her passage through Gateshead, arranges to send her to school not as commerce exchange, he gets nothing from it.

Through the interlocution with Mr. Lloyd, the meaning beneath the Gateshead possessions becomes delineated as the lack of family and denigration of human relation; the articulation of specific figures as ghost, cousin, father's poor family; and what then emerges is the (unconscious) desire to go to school.

He is that mediating passage for us to go to a girls' school to learn what is the language of the locked crimson chamber. School of languages toward which we begin a movement yet only when he gets Mrs. Reed's permission. What to be learned is the function of Mrs. Reed's desire, post-red-room school of language and craft is based on/by her desire.

Not the authority, inferior physician he mediates horizontal crossings of temporal, spatial, class dimensions. He mediates her movement through preter-human realms to the human to a particular caste and then out of Gateshead, spatial movement, change of place in what will be now is directed toward a future, temporal horizons broaden. Enlarging her dimensions of time, place, class, he stands outside/beside the Gateshead manor/manner of continguity/contiguity, immediacy.

Empathy is the transmission of his mediation. He takes on her unique perspective, and he mirrors her location, her property. His empathic level does not pertain to the acquisition of what was her experience; he has never had similar red-room experience yet he peers into, approximates who she is in what was seized there. His mirroring her location (temporal, spacial, societal) is a recognition of her heterogeneity to the place, that she belongs in a different place to learn a new vocabulary.

He has not had our experience. Introject to project accurate mirroring of location and property all the intimacy we can (with)stand after residence in Gateshead's corners.

Archetypal forces strike and we hit bottom and inquire on our family. Where lies the wealth? What is caste? How to avoid the ancestral traps? His mediation passes through temporal dimensions, she finds a past. The tart and plate no longer please, Gulliver not any longer the favorite book, and overhearing the maids are speaking who were her parents. The parents of a past, some family was tangential now is in our overhearing, we hear overall a parental death.

After the Mr. Lloyd interlocution we learn of parental limit. When we are no longer of the gods or phantoms, yet in relation, we hear our parents die, our parents' limit, our parents abandoned us also to a meagre human mortality. Parent not Father's law or Mother's magestic chamber, inflating/deflating, yet parent is human and dies and is dead not even ghost and we will die.

Sacrifice of the immortality of the gods who were parent, sacrifice of their godly, omnipotent quality is Mr. Lloyd's entry and speaking to him of our unhappiness our human property. When we speak our unhappiness to who mirrors, we identify our human requirement of human parent, hear for the first time our parents' story, which is to begin to sense the plot of the drama in which we are one figure, locate ourselves in a storyline reaching beyond our personal history, one figure in the drama of many, *dramatis personae*, our property.

Overhearing the maids: it was a marriage of poverty which estranged her mother from the Reed family. Mother left the wealthy family of gentry for a poor minister. Her mother knew the poverty of Gateshead but substituted for that a literal poverty with one who saw the wealth only in a divine unseen, and it killed her.

Jane has seen that the divine unseen has body: it suffocates, it arrives with a black dog and stirs the wind with the rustle of its large wings penetrating to a fit body seizure. From her mother's history she knows that the way to leave Gateshead is not a literal move separating from the Gateshead site of seizures to a word of spirit, severance from reactive impulse becoming debilitating poverty. Yet here this Lloyd is mediating a move from Gateshead through a Reed permission and how may that include body?

Hysterical, choking fit, the hysteric recognizes that Father's law (which had been bodiless, its impartial philosophies and mathematics relieving us from corporal matter of density and desire) has body; recognizes that beneath Father's law, word of his spirit, has been a desire for body, blood of womb body. Through Gateshead she has known body only through alternating unmediated seizures precluding interlocution; what is the father's word of this body and its mother's blood chamber, and how to find her speaking the desire of unseen forces within a protection more embodied?

    ❖ She left us to die with him, die from her body of us. She left to leave her body this Gateshead mansion all she knew of body for his ministry. She severed from her mansion to find a spirit in him pulling as it did toward the house of death. We do not want to understand her choices, we want her breast, we want to pull at its warm milk even sour spurting we do not want to hear of her choices of a ministry word of spirit she followed the paltry father to parishioners on fever, none can take that heat with no body, leaving her mansion only the fever returned to her not enough body to take the heat of spirit, she left us. And the other-mother abandoned remains only kept in mansion body her spirits they are demons becoming ours as we sit on her edge shunned. She left us not to die with him. ❖

Learning the ancestor's drama, plot of drama of which we are extension, takes us to school. Mediating her configuration of plot residing beyond the

Gateshead contiguity, he orients her to her fate, the call from the dead, enraged/enlightened male forces of a mother abandoned.

Many are possessed repetitively by John and Mr. Reed yet few go to school to learn the vocabulary and figurative value of their seizures, carry those seizures to signification.

Marginal child has been possessed by the more malevolent forces. It is not that we have to learn to become less marginal or avoid the emerging unconscious forces and voices, for they come as our design from all mothers, coming through (antipathetic) symbiosis with mother in various ways marking us, even leaving messages requiring translation to a human symbolic.

We can hear the voices from the unconscious and engage with them, learn to hear them without possession. The possession is our ignorance of a mediated relation to them, how we can speak them in a language, speak through them in a language, speak a language through them, which is not the possession by them which is madness.

The dialogue with Mr. Lloyd is prototype for an interlocution with the possessing forces themselves: it suggests that she has to go to school to learn to identify herself clearly and open an ear to what is their message, listening to the call of those voices surrounding mother's rule, listening to their promise, their curse, their requirement, mirroring that while asking what makes them unhappy, what do they want?

For these "evil" voices arrive with message: madame mope, you are dependent, nothing. They arrive to tell us we are stuck on her windowseat where interior is all we know of exterior, too complacent in the ice realm, somewhere only frozen. If we do not let some of the "evil" come before us and know it as our own, we stay forever on the windowseat, floating then frozen, as always situated in a mother's fearful rule, never attaching to the earth, never can hold forth on this earth.

To learn how some of the "evil" coming before us is also our own desiring articulation of what was unconscious is to begin a differentiation not to be absorbed by mother's rule.

They arrive as evil and dreadful voices concomitant with our attempt to be wrenched out of her recesses. Yet we find that John Reed, though he removes us from the windowseat, sends us through a crash to a more remote chamber; and Mr. Reed, though he promised red-room delivery, sends us through a fit to further recess unconscious.

These forces ultimately pull us further into her recess, we are not to sever from the unconscious into which she has unconsciously ordered us. Their messages of severance do not imply extrication from her depths yet differentiation within those depths which is to speak them out analyzing their aspects: it is John Reed's book, bring out the text of the ice realm delineating its specific properties, its drives; it is Mr. Reed's word, speak the contradictory forces within the red-room, fervid to dampening ember to vault, is delivery.

Differentiation within recess is what is required in the translation of unconscious regions to the human, which implies separating from Mrs. Reed's immediate rule, which constitutes school.

Learning to let configure the contradictory forces — dilation and constriction — (the expulsion of incorporation, the incorporation of disembodied word's fit) — without being possessed by extremes of inflation and deflation is the lesson of marginal forces.

For we had been clutching desperately to mother through her recesses, preferring possession since she alienated us, outcast child extension of her dread as desire requesting interlocution (what did I do?). Fused, we were floating in her realms unconscious eternal images as she alienated us. They arrive as "evil" voices when we too long have been humanly undifferentiated in a symbiotic alienation.

They offer a promise of delivery from her hold yet ultimately return us further clutched as we go under, for they have told us we are nothing, we are dependent, we are a rat, they swoop down in seizure to show us that using their possession is not the way out of her realms searing and shrivelling us, only pushing us further in, nothing her most cragged cavity.

They arrive as father and son possessing us first as we sit antipathetic symbiotic within recesses of the alienating mother. For generations we have been alienated from these mothers so remaining secretly bound with the unconscious of she who values more father and son.

And she has pushed us away, no cozy sofa merged mother bliss instead her arctic thief, learn to steal for her love. We clasped beneath and her demons came to rupture us within her every recess. Heart rent. They were severing, tearing, delivery and we were seized under in extrication attempt from her eternal most horrorific depth.

Mother's unconscious requirement is that we let son and father pass through us as we take their forces, expansion and constriction, life forces, blood forces of her recess, carry them out differentially translated which is to become humanly differentiated recess not possessed.

Differentiation within her depths: to ask who are the forces, what do they desire and how do they configure in our ancestral plot is the meaning of our analysis. Can we reside within realms of which she situated us, can we reside there differentiated human and carry them back, imparting.

We need an education in differentiation to translate their messages of severance to an analysis within the eternal images with which for long we have sat. We are talking now to a person with eyes shrewd and kind not violent. We need an education in a differentiation through discourse which is not abandonment to incorporation, symbiotic alienation.

> ~§ Apothecary-condensation-alchemist; 4 a.m. vigil, diplopia, paresis, contractures, paraphasia we will not speak it and there is not your question 'who am I' the room is empty empties. Devils in head exhort silence at father's constriction we have no word only foreign language and not even that prayer works for the devil's head is on fingernail as father expires until we choke and a Breuer man receives the emission talking cure. Talking cure for thirsts and repulsion to thirst, skeleton frights, desire to dance to that music playing through the dying man's wall. Glare to hearth a bar subtends chimney sweeping with him fit converts to word condensation to an indecent charge until some school social works. §~

Chapter's ending open-ending. Chapter's end not a definite event, this conclusion does not finish as did the others of a passion lunge, of a convulsive fit, remains open, the suggestion of school accepted but not yet implemented, the maids' appetite expressed yet not yet satiated. Not a chapter pushing forward a momentum to definite closure, more an unfolding, opening to what desires who she is and the appetite is delineated yet not demanding a consumption.

This unfolding is Mr. Lloyd's mediation. Appetite is mediated, named, imaged as blond curled cousin desire, not seized, and such mediation identifies Jane: crying beneath shawl, once favoring book and treat and plate (her past aesthetic, her taste), her unhappiness, her parents, that she is a toad.

Mr. Lloyd's methodology of mirroring identifies her heterogeneous to the family, her contradictory sides (she wants to leave Gateshead but not go to her father's family) and her desire to go to school. His mediation of the Gateshead mode of immediacy and closure of what is appetite allows unfolding desire, perhaps desire the needs of Gateshead cover.

Compared to blue-eyed Georgiana summoning the desire of Welsh rabbit, Jane is the unnatural, freakish child. The servants say toad. Her mother's death taught her that severance from Gateshead body for love in a poverty ministry means literal death. Taken from the natural mother's arms unnaturally early, Jane was thrown to the land of the dead, region of ghosts, imps, a desolate wanderer, a horned black bird, a demon son of greed and an uncle savoir who seized her in a fit. In carrying her back to this world to educate herself, Mr. Lloyd asks about her family, she faces the poverty of her family. She wants to go to school.

Bibliography

Breuer, Josef and Freud, Sigmund. "Studies on Hysteria." *The Complete Psychological Works of Sigmund Freud*. Vol. 2. Trans. James Strachey. London: Hogarth, 1955.

Edinger, Edward F. *Anatomy of the Psyche*. LaSalle, Ill.: Open Court Publications, 1985; Chapter 7, "Separatio."

Eliade, Mircea. *The Sacred and the Profane*. Trans. by Willard R. Trask. New York: Harcourt, Brace and World, 1959.

Freud, Sigmund. "The Dynamics of the Transference." *The Complete Psychological Works of Sigmund Freud*. Vol. 12. Trans. James Strachey. London: Hogarth, 1958.

Gallop, Jane. *The Daughter's Seduction: Feminism and Psychoanalysis*. Ithaca, N.Y.: Cornell University Press, 1982.

Herzog, Edgar. *Psyche and Death*. New York: G. Putnam and Sons, 1967.

Hillman, James. *Healing Fiction*. Barrytown N.Y.: Station Hill, 1983.

Irigaray, Luce. The "Mechanics of Fluids." In *This Sex Which Is Not One*. Trans. by Catherine Porter. Ithaca, N.Y.: Cornell University Press, 1985.

Jung, C.G. "The Development of Personality." *The Collected Works of C. G. Jung*. Vol. 17. Trans. R. F. C. Hull. Princeton, N.J.: Princeton University Press, 1954.

Kohut, Heinz. *How Does Analysis Cure*. Chicago: University of Chicago Press, 1984.

Perera, Sylvia. *Descent to the Goddess: A Way of Initiation for Women*. Toronto: Inner City Books, 1981.

von Franz, M. L. *The Feminine in Fairytales*. Dallas: Spring Publications, 1979.

_____. *Shadow and Evil in Fairytales*. Dallas: Spring Publications, 1980.

Winnicott, D. W. *The Maturational Processes and the Facilitating Environment*. New York: International Universities Press, 1965.

_____. *Playing and Reality*. London: Tavistock, 1982.

Chapter 4

Black Pillar

Daily waiting, no word of school, more marked is the separation between her and the family, she sleeps alone small closet, meals alone all time in nursery. Aversion so rooted in Mrs. Reed's eye the aunt will not endure for long this child yet no allusion to the school. Cousins avoid her, once John attempts a chastising, Jane is leveling on his nose a blow, he runs to the mama now ordering her children never to associate with the smaller cousin.

' "They are not fit to associate with me." ' It bursts from the bannister. Though a stout woman, Mrs. Reed nimbly she is rushing up those stairs a whirlwind flinging the child into the nursery, crushing her on the crib's edge, daring her to rise, to speak. A voice speaks through the child uncontrollably: what would Mr. Reed say? The aunt's look a fearful wonder is it child or fiend who continues saying: uncle Reed and papa and mama know, they see you shut me up in the nursery, you wish me dead. The response a boxing of ears.

For an hour Bessie does the homily: I am the wicked and abandoned child. November and December and now half of January passed, Christmas and New Years were the usual festivity, excluded, I witnessed Georgiana and Eliza in muslin and ringlet descending to the music below, the glasses clinking the good cheer, I would sit on the stairhead the hum of conversation beneath, doors opening and closing. I did not want to be in that company, would have preferred Bessie in a kindness in the nursery, yet she is in the livelier kitchen, I remain alone; there is my doll. Sitting doll on knee, fire lowering, tugging at strings of the clothing undressing to the bed with doll nightgown folded, 'cherishing a faded graven image,' I fancy it with sensation as we lie in bed and listen to the company departing, occasionally Bessie would come with a bit of dinner, twice a kiss.

15th January. Eliza and Georgiana not yet summoned down. Eliza preparing to feed that poultry of which the eggs she sells to the housekeeper, then hoarding the money received also from the gardener for the flower-roots, she ties up that money, she would sell her own hair for it, for its security she entrusts it to her mother's keeping with a high interest recorded accurately.

Georgiana on her high stool, artificial flowers and feathers adorning her curls, she commands me as I assist in the cleaning as Bessie's under-nursery-maid not to touch the furniture of those dolls. I was straightening them at the window, now I sit breathing on the frost flowers dissolving to a carriage arriving, it is more the hungry robin who catches my 'vacant attention,' and I am tugging on the window's sash to deliver the crumbs of my breakfast.

Now Bessie is pulling me out of pinafore, scrubbing my face with the coarse towel, for it is I who am being summoned below. I am standing before the breakfast door, so unused to any territory outside the nursery, fearful, who would want me, I tremble. 'What a miserable little poltroon had fear, engendered of unjust punishment, made of me in those days!' Ten minutes of 'agitated hesitation,' neither able to return to nursery or proceed to breakfast room until a bell from the latter clanging now I must enter. Who is it beside Mrs. Reed here I look up at a black pillar appearing to me 'the straight, narrow, sable-clad shape standing erect on the rug.'

Mrs. Reed signals approach; he is asking my age and name and then whether it is I am a good child. Impossible now the affirmative, I am silent. The aunt replies for me the less said on that the better. We shall have some talk then, he sits in a chair drawing me up to him the face of the great nose and mouth, the teeth so prominent! He wants to make sure I know that the wicked go to hell and burn, that I know I must repent ever being the discomfort to a benefactress. Benefactress! Now the Bible, he is wanting to know my fondness for this book. I reply my pleasure is in the Revelations, book of Daniel, and Genesis, and Samuel, bit of Exodus, Kings, and Chronicles, and Job and Jonah. He hopes I like the psalms. No, Sir. Shocking to him. I say they are not interesting.

Proof of a wicked heart! I must pray to God to transform that heart from stone to its flesh. I am wondering on such operation when Mrs. Reed orders me to sit and carries on the conversation herself. She tells this Mr. Brocklehurst she wants my admittance to his Lowood school, but those teachers upon me must keep a strictest eye because I have a tendency to deceit and she wants me in this hearing. Cruel wound for I had always strove to obey, please her strenuously and now heart cut by the accusation in front of a stranger. She can only spoil this 'new phase of existence which she destined me to enter . . . sowing aversion and unkindness along my future path.' Transformed now only to the noxious child.

All liars are in the lake burning with fire and brimstone, yes, the teachers shall watch her. He is assuring: plainness prevails to the point of poverty, habits are hardy, ' "humility is a christian grace" ' as is consistency above all desired by Mrs. Reed. The proof of success of the mortification of worldly pride his daughters remark on the plainness of the Lowood girls acting as though never before had they seen a dress of silk. He leaves but not before handing Jane the Child's Guide recounting the sudden awful death of a child addicted to falsehood and deceit.

Mrs. Reed and Jane are left alone. The silence in which the woman sews becomes the surveillance of her by the child seeing this woman possibly 36 or 37, square-shouldered, strong-limbed, stout not obese, the under-jaw is solid, low brow and eye 'devoid of ruth,' skin opaque with flaxen hair, she runs the household thoroughly, dresses well, is never ill, cleverly manages with an authority only derided at times by her own children, her attire is handsome.

Sting of her words to that mind becoming 'passion of resentment,' her eye on mine and she orders me out, to the nursery, back. I walk to the door, then back across to a window and then right up to her. I must speak a turn